INUBAKA

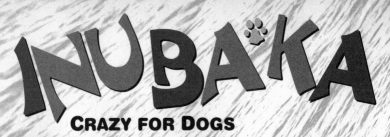

CRAZY FOR DOGS

15

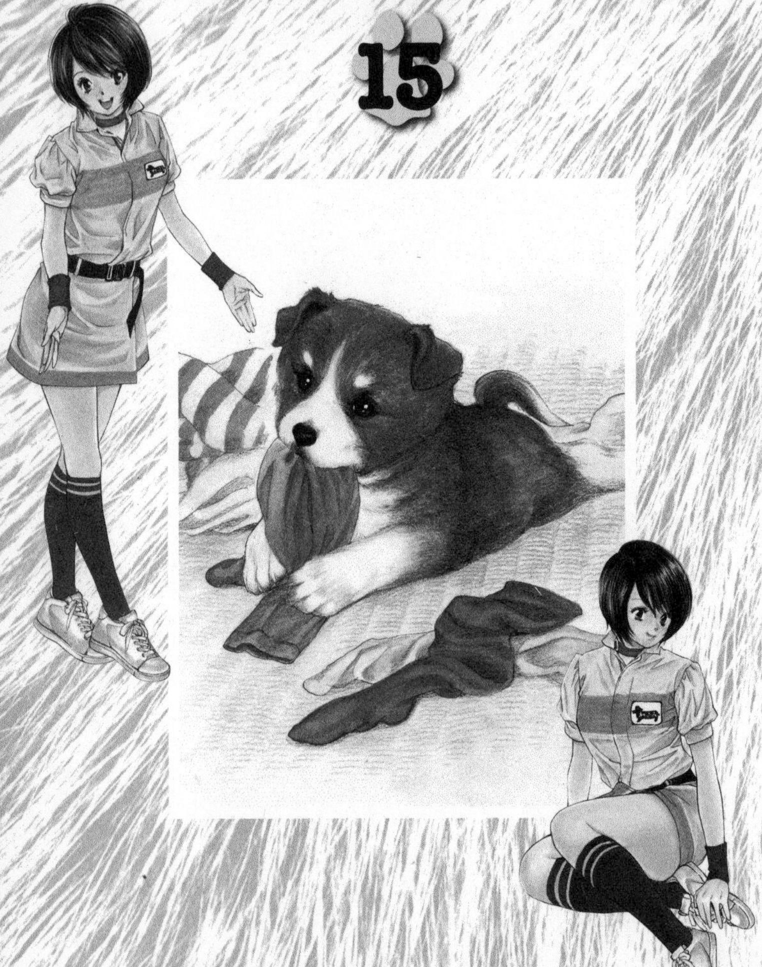

YUKIYA SAKURAGI

Contents

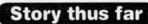

Story thus far

Teppei is the manager of the recently opened pet shop Woofles. He intended to breed his black Labrador Noa with a champion dog, but instead Noa was "taken advantage of" by an unknown and unfixed male dog!

The unknown dog's owner was Suguri Miyauchi, and her dog was a mutt named Lupin. Suguri is now working at Woofles to make up for her dog's actions.

Suguri's enthusiasm is more than a little unique. She has eaten dog food (and said it was tasty), caught dog poop with her bare hands and caused dogs to have "happy pee" in her presence. Teppei is starting to realize that Suguri is indeed a very special girl.

A year has passed, and Noa is finally mated with a champion dog and safely delivers adorable puppies. This gets Suguri yearning for Lupin to become a parent too. To get Suguri to realize the difficulties of bringing non-purebred puppies into the world, Teppei challenges her to find a home for Hinomaru, a mutt about the same size as Lupin. While Suguri is out looking for a home for Hinomaru, a man she meets at a park volunteers to take him. From the man's strange comments and behavior, however, Suguri soon realizes he is not the kind of person she thought he was and manages to avoid giving Hinomaru over to him.

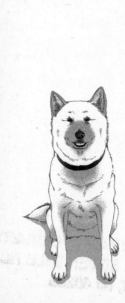

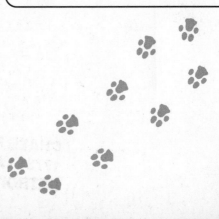

CHARACTERS

Lupin

♂ *Mutt (mongrel)*

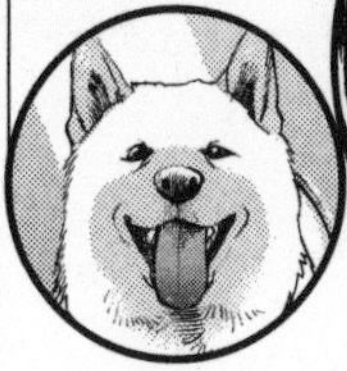

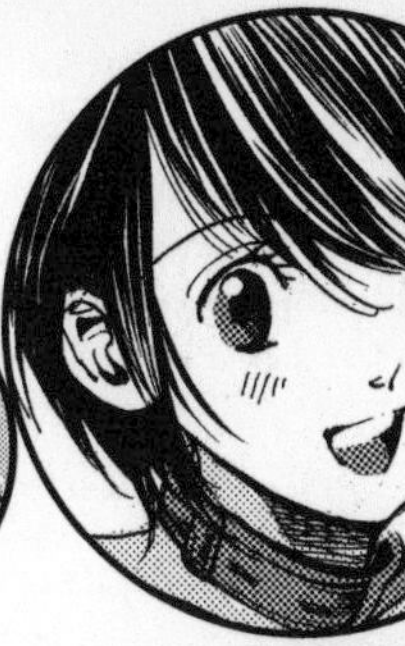

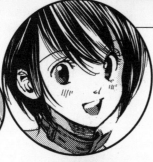

Suguri Miyauchi

Seems to possess an almost supernatural connection with dogs. When she approaches them they often urinate with great excitement! She is crazy for dogs and can catch their droppings with her bare hands. She is currently a trainee at the Woofles Pet Shop.

Noa

♀ *Labrador retriever*

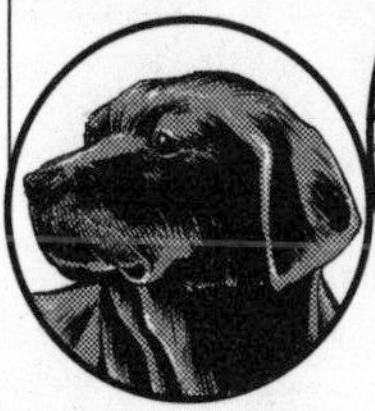

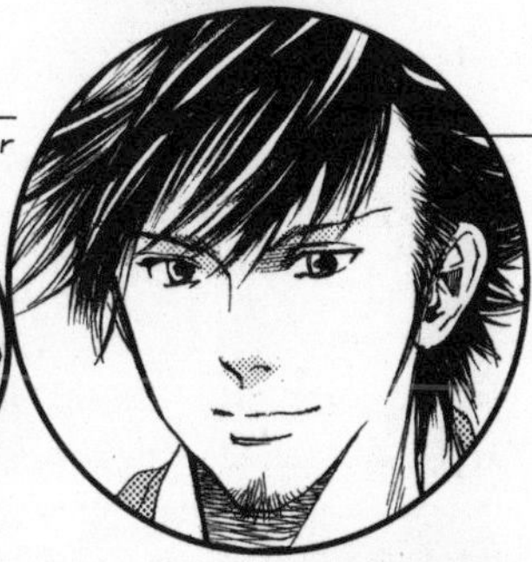

Teppei Iida

Manager of the recently opened pet shop Woofles. He is aware of Suguri's special ability and has hired her to work in his shop.

Momoko Takeuchi

The Woofles Pet Shop (second location) pet groomer. At first she had many problems and rarely smiled. But after meeting Suguri she's changed, and the two are now best friends.

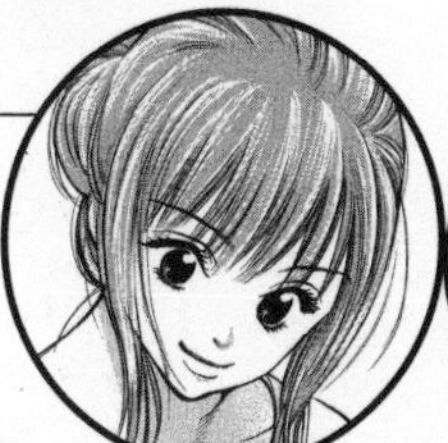

Mel

♀ *Toy poodle*

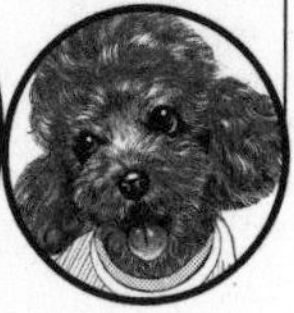

Kentaro Osada

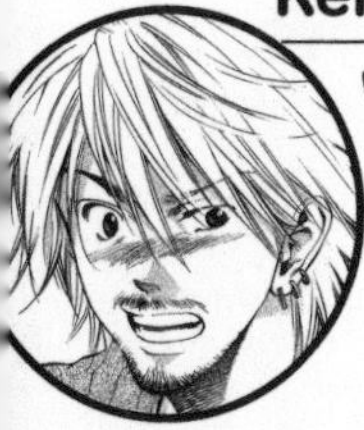

Wannabe musician and Teppei's buddy from their high school days. Teppei saved Kentaro when he was a down-and-out beggar. He has a crush on the piano instructor Kanako.

Show Kaneko

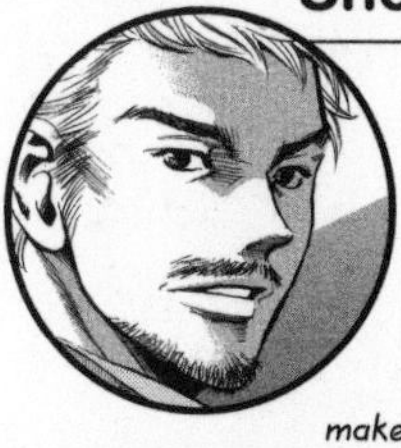

Manager of the main Woofles store and Teppei's boss. He is very passionate about the business and makes TV appearances from time to time.

Kashima

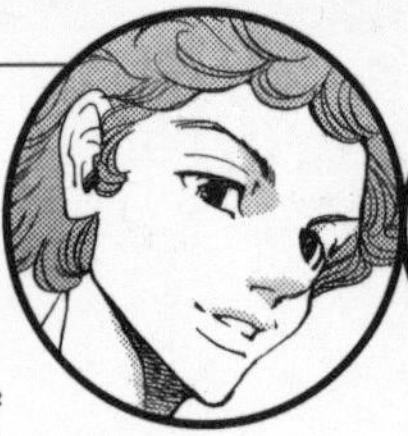

A good friend of Teppei's since they were in school together, he runs the Dog House Kashima dog shelter. He has passed on the task of finding a home for Hinomaru to Suguri.

Hinomaru

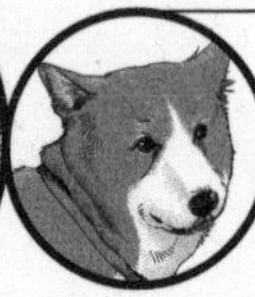

♂ Mutt

An abandoned dog that was taken in by Kashima. He has trauma from being abused by his former owner, making it hard for him to get used to new people.

Woofles Regular Customers

Chizuru Sawamura

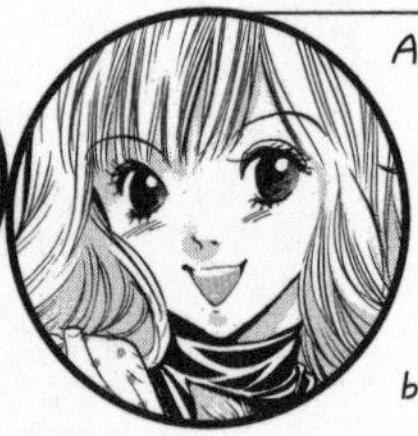

Adopted a Chihuahua, Melon, after her longtime pet golden retriever, Ricky, alerted her that Melon was ill. She works at a hostess bar to repay Melon's medical fees.

Melon

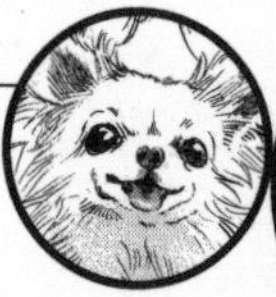

♂ Chihuahua

Hiroshi Akiba

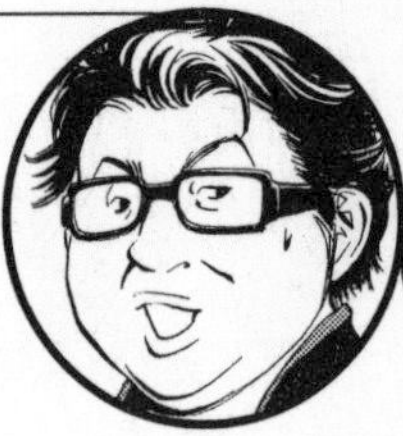

Pop-idol otaku turned dog otaku. His dream is to publish a photo collection of his dog, Zidane. He is a government employee.

Zidane

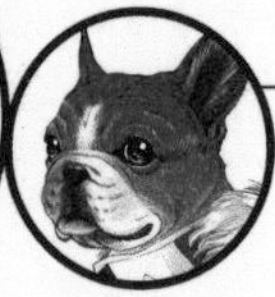

♂ French bulldog

Kim Hyeon-Jun

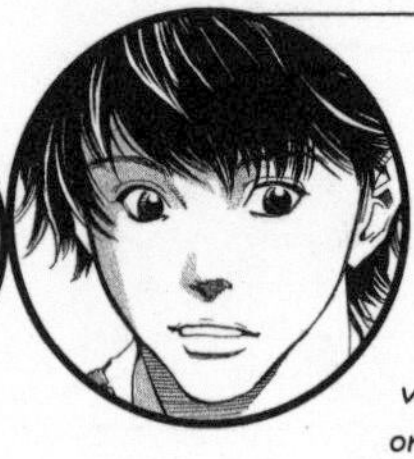

An international student who had a phobia of dogs. He has been working hard to get over it in order to get close to Suguri, whom he has a crush on. He bought a Shiba dog named Chanta and even sleeps with her!

Chanta

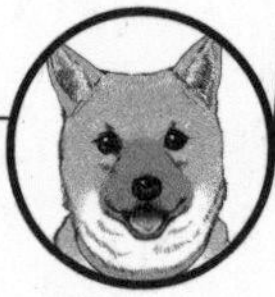

♀ Shiba

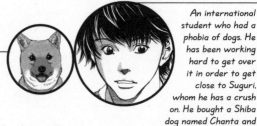

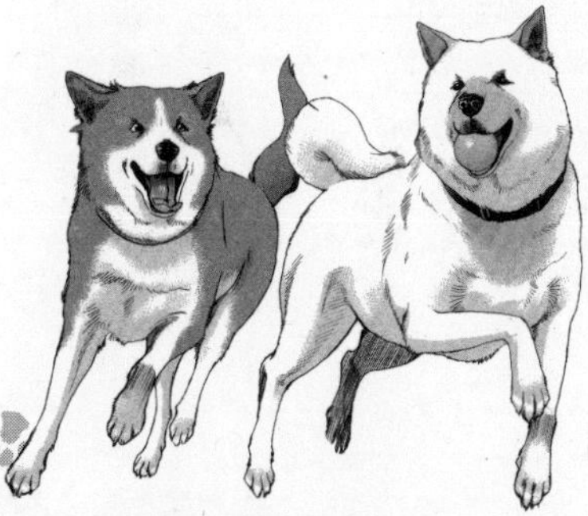

INUBAKA

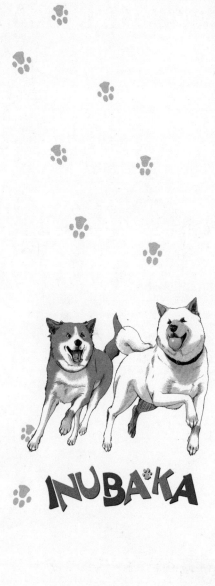

CHAPTER 152: HINOMARU'S DESTINY

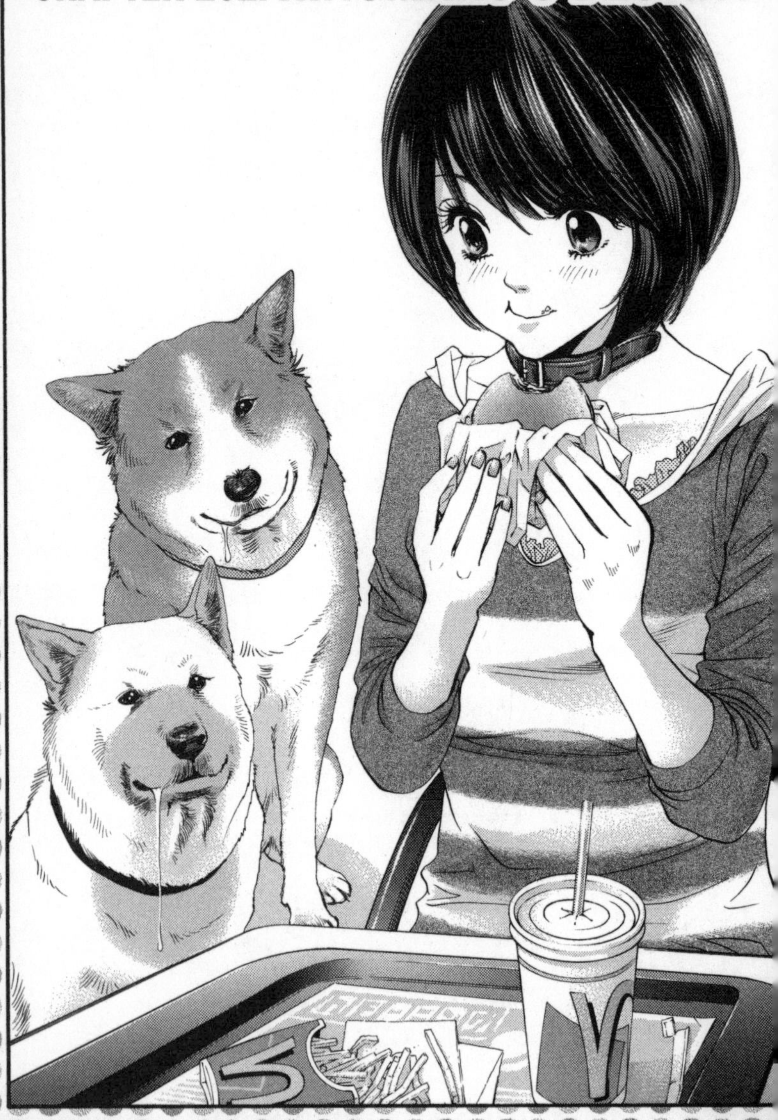

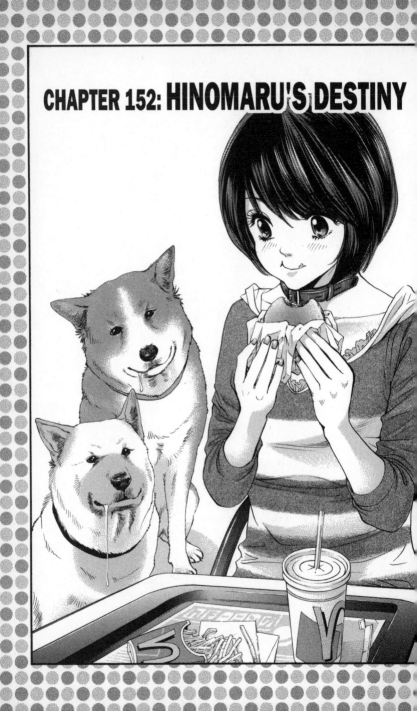

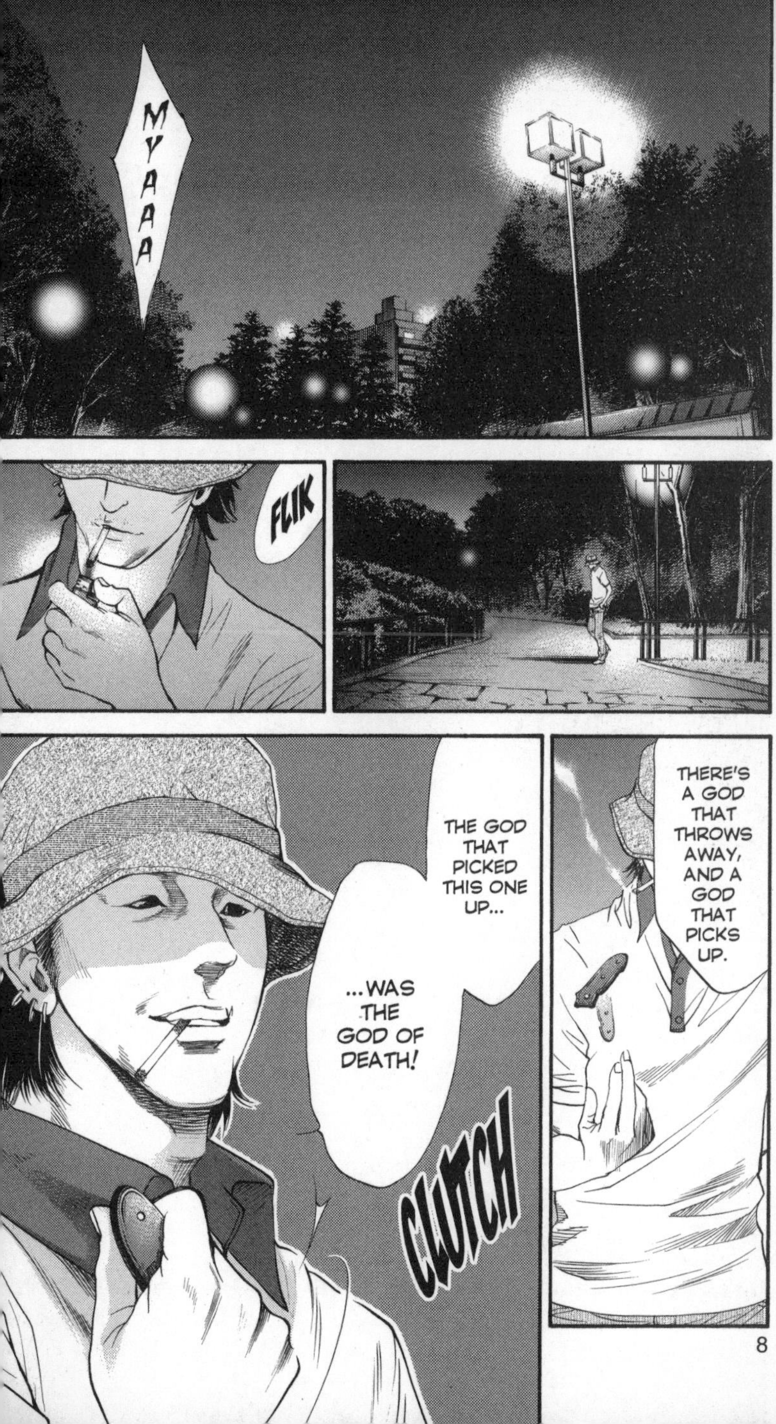
MYAAA
FLIK
THERE'S A GOD THAT THROWS AWAY, AND A GOD THAT PICKS UP.
THE GOD THAT PICKED THIS ONE UP...
...WAS THE GOD OF DEATH!
CLUTCH

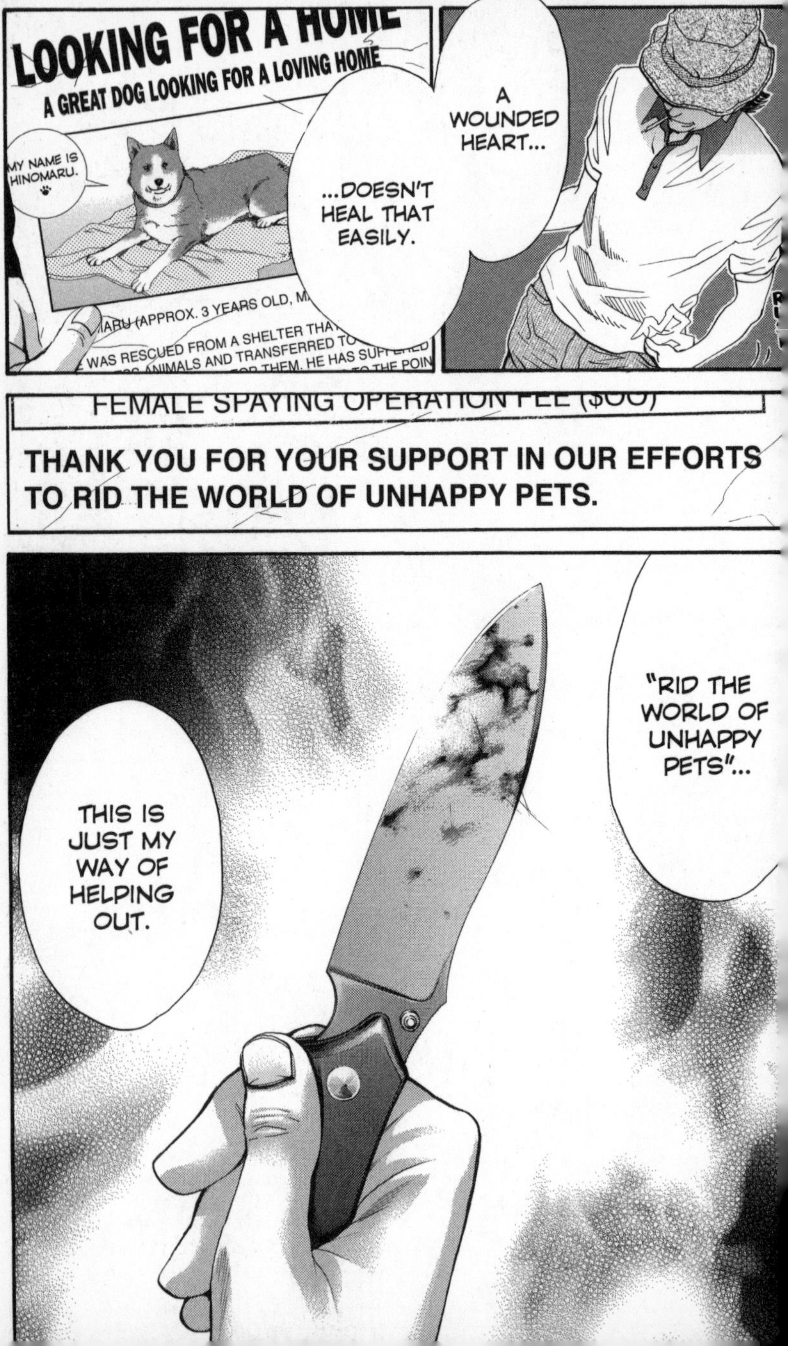
A WOUNDED HEART...
...DOESN'T HEAL THAT EASILY.
LOOKING FOR A HOME
A GREAT DOG LOOKING FOR A LOVING HOME
MY NAME IS HINOMARU.
(APPROX. 3 YEARS OLD,
WAS RESCUED FROM A SHELTER THA
ANIMALS AND TRANSFERRED TO
FEMALE SPAYING OPERATION FEE ($00)
THANK YOU FOR YOUR SUPPORT IN OUR EFFORTS TO RID THE WORLD OF UNHAPPY PETS.
"RID THE WORLD OF UNHAPPY PETS"...
THIS IS JUST MY WAY OF HELPING OUT.

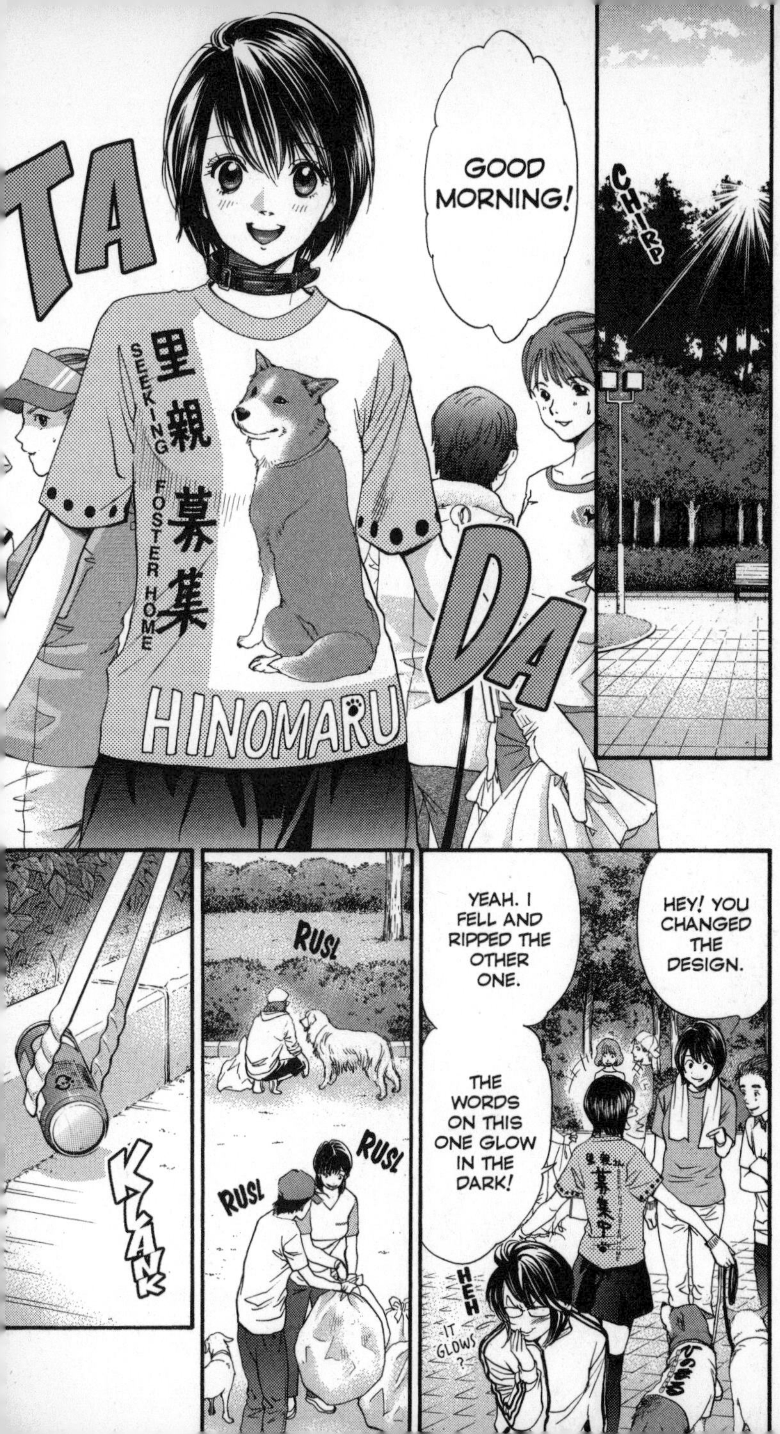
CHIRP
GOOD MORNING!
TA
DA
里親募集
SEEKING FOSTER HOME
HINOMARU
HEY! YOU CHANGED THE DESIGN.
YEAH. I FELL AND RIPPED THE OTHER ONE.
THE WORDS ON THIS ONE GLOW IN THE DARK!
HEH
IT GLOWS?
RUSL
RUSL
RUSL
KLANK

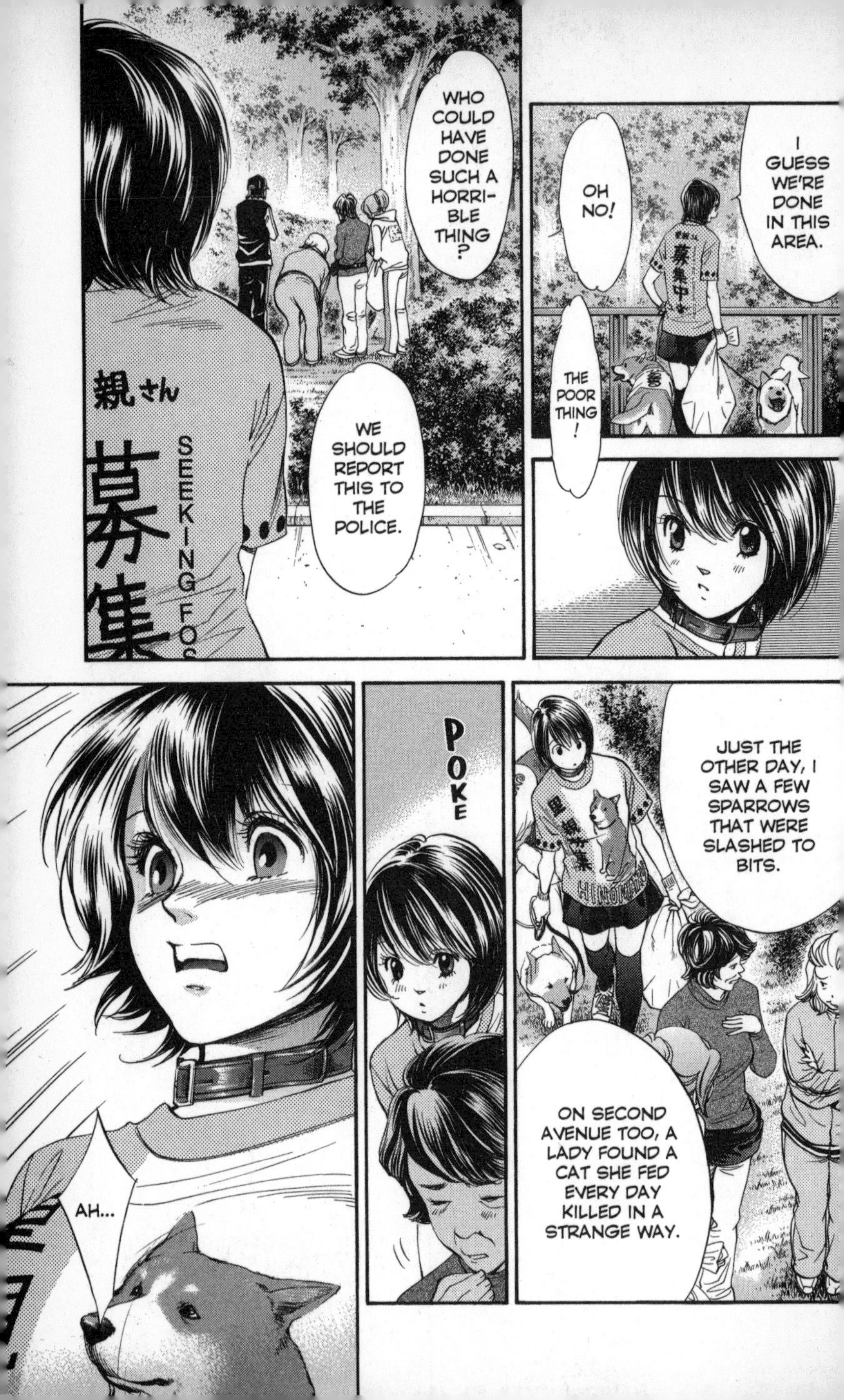
I GUESS WE'RE DONE IN THIS AREA.
OH NO!
THE POOR THING!
WHO COULD HAVE DONE SUCH A HORRIBLE THING?
WE SHOULD REPORT THIS TO THE POLICE.
親さん
募集
JUST THE OTHER DAY, I SAW A FEW SPARROWS THAT WERE SLASHED TO BITS.
ON SECOND AVENUE TOO, A LADY FOUND A CAT SHE FED EVERY DAY KILLED IN A STRANGE WAY.
POKE
AH...

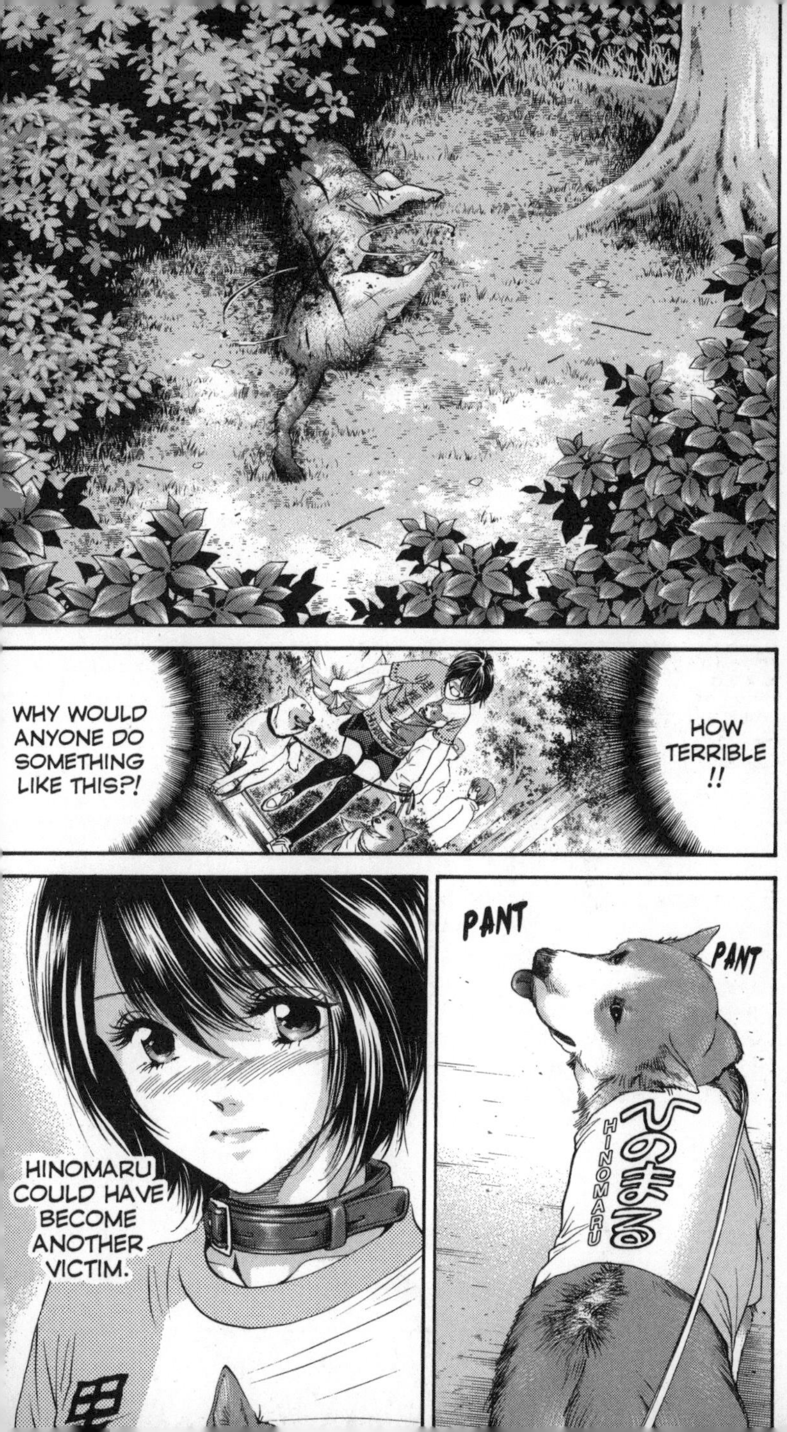
HOW TERRIBLE !!
WHY WOULD ANYONE DO SOMETHING LIKE THIS?!
PANT
PANT
ひのまる
HINOMARU
HINOMARU COULD HAVE BECOME ANOTHER VICTIM.

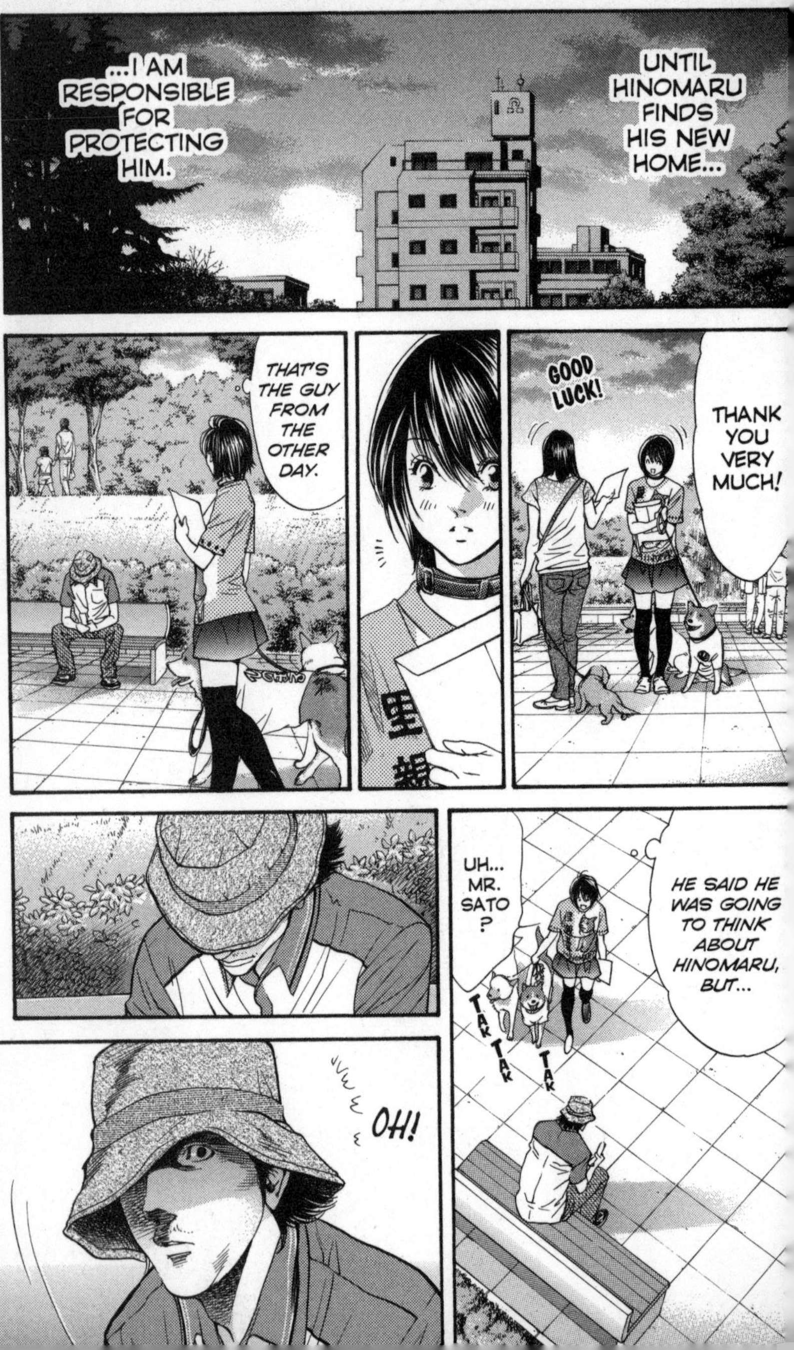
UNTIL HINOMARU FINDS HIS NEW HOME...
...I AM RESPONSIBLE FOR PROTECTING HIM.
THANK YOU VERY MUCH!
GOOD LUCK!
THAT'S THE GUY FROM THE OTHER DAY.
HE SAID HE WAS GOING TO THINK ABOUT HINOMARU, BUT...
UH... MR. SATO ?
TAK TAK TAK
OH!

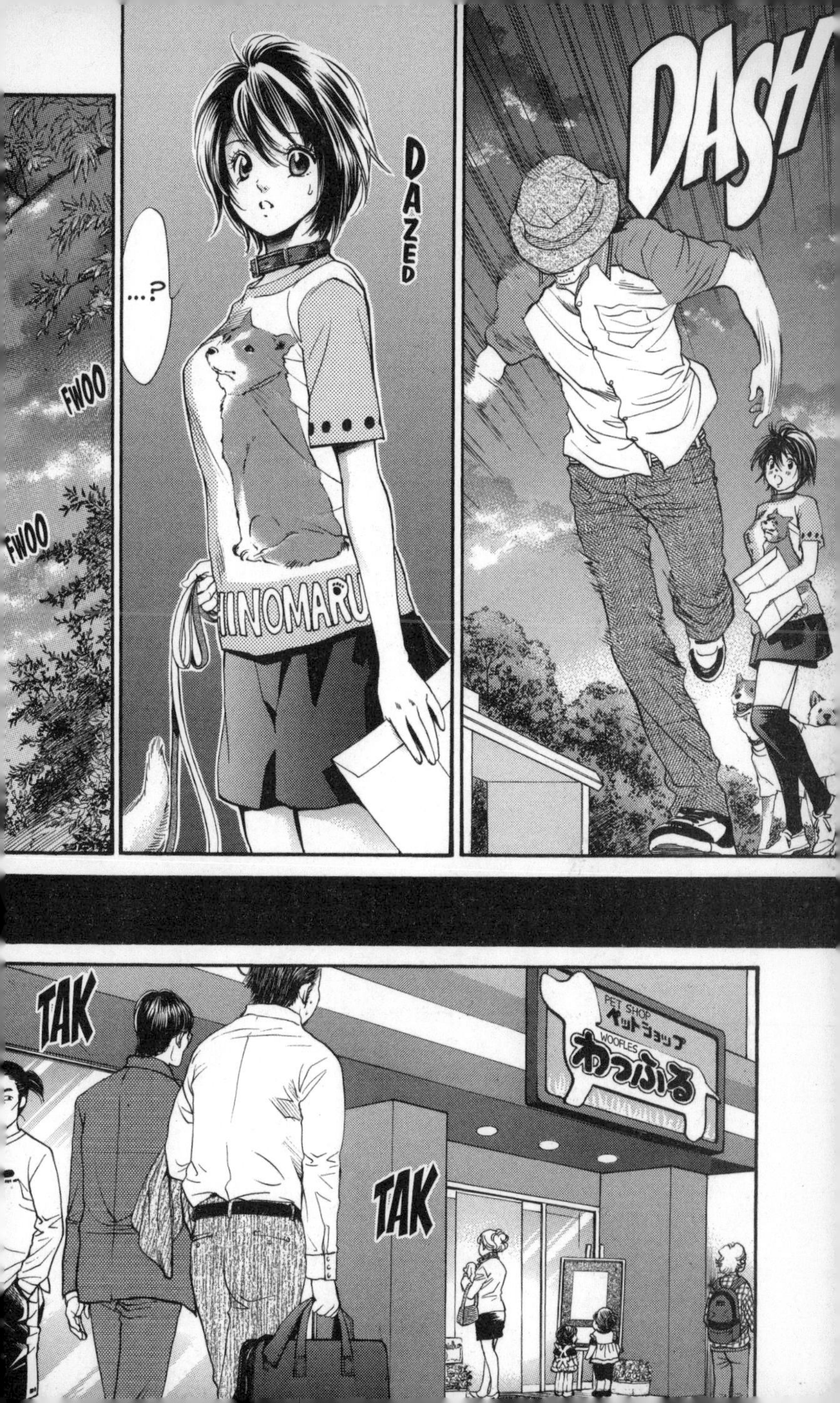
DASH
DAZED
...?
FWOO
FWOO
TAK
PET SHOP
ペットショップ
WOOFLES
わっふる
TAK

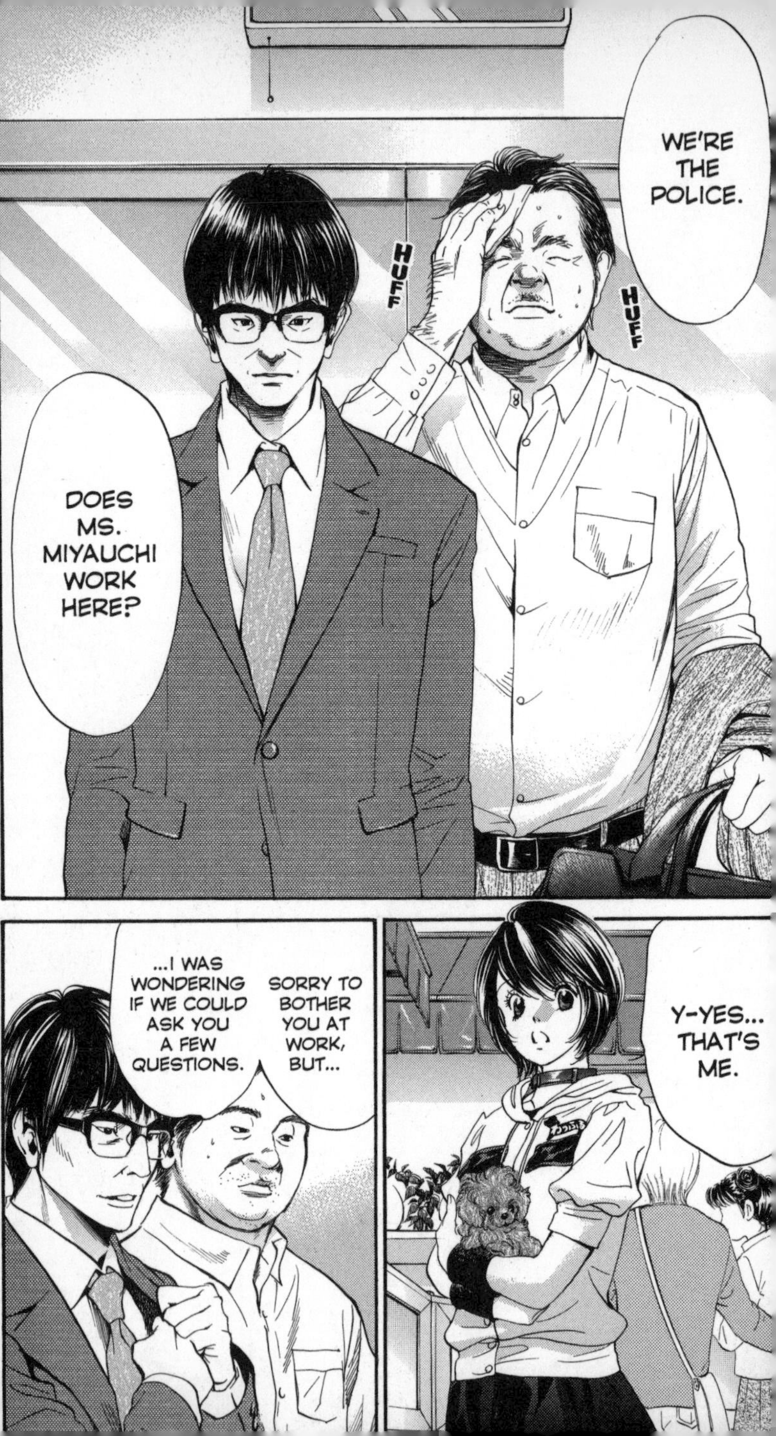
WE'RE THE POLICE.
HUFF
HUFF
DOES MS. MIYAUCHI WORK HERE?
Y-YES... THAT'S ME.
SORRY TO BOTHER YOU AT WORK, BUT...
...I WAS WONDERING IF WE COULD ASK YOU A FEW QUESTIONS.

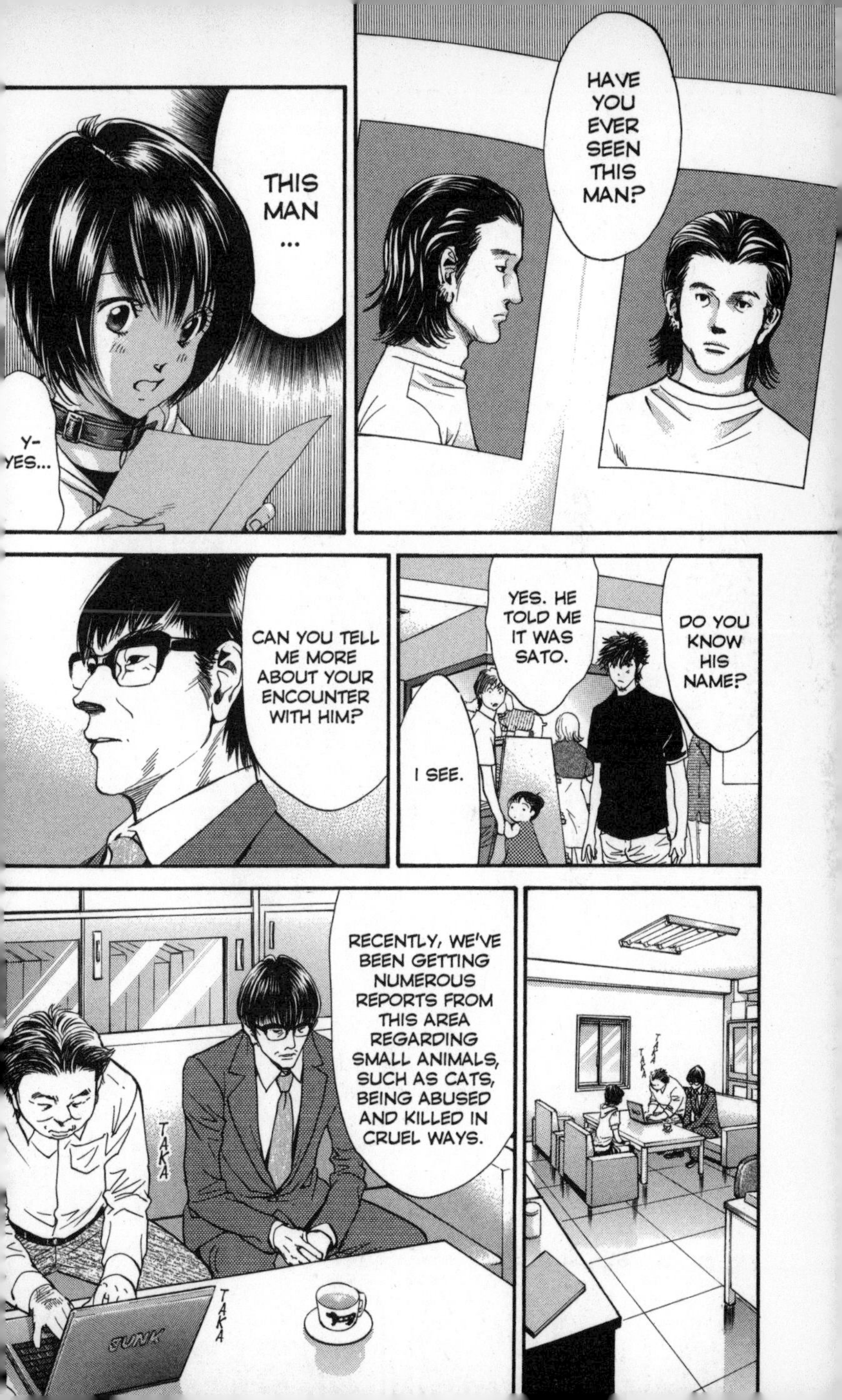
HAVE YOU EVER SEEN THIS MAN?
THIS MAN ...
Y- YES...
DO YOU KNOW HIS NAME?
YES. HE TOLD ME IT WAS SATO.
I SEE.
CAN YOU TELL ME MORE ABOUT YOUR ENCOUNTER WITH HIM?
TAKA TAKA
RECENTLY, WE'VE BEEN GETTING NUMEROUS REPORTS FROM THIS AREA REGARDING SMALL ANIMALS, SUCH AS CATS, BEING ABUSED AND KILLED IN CRUEL WAYS.
TAKA
TAKA
SUNK

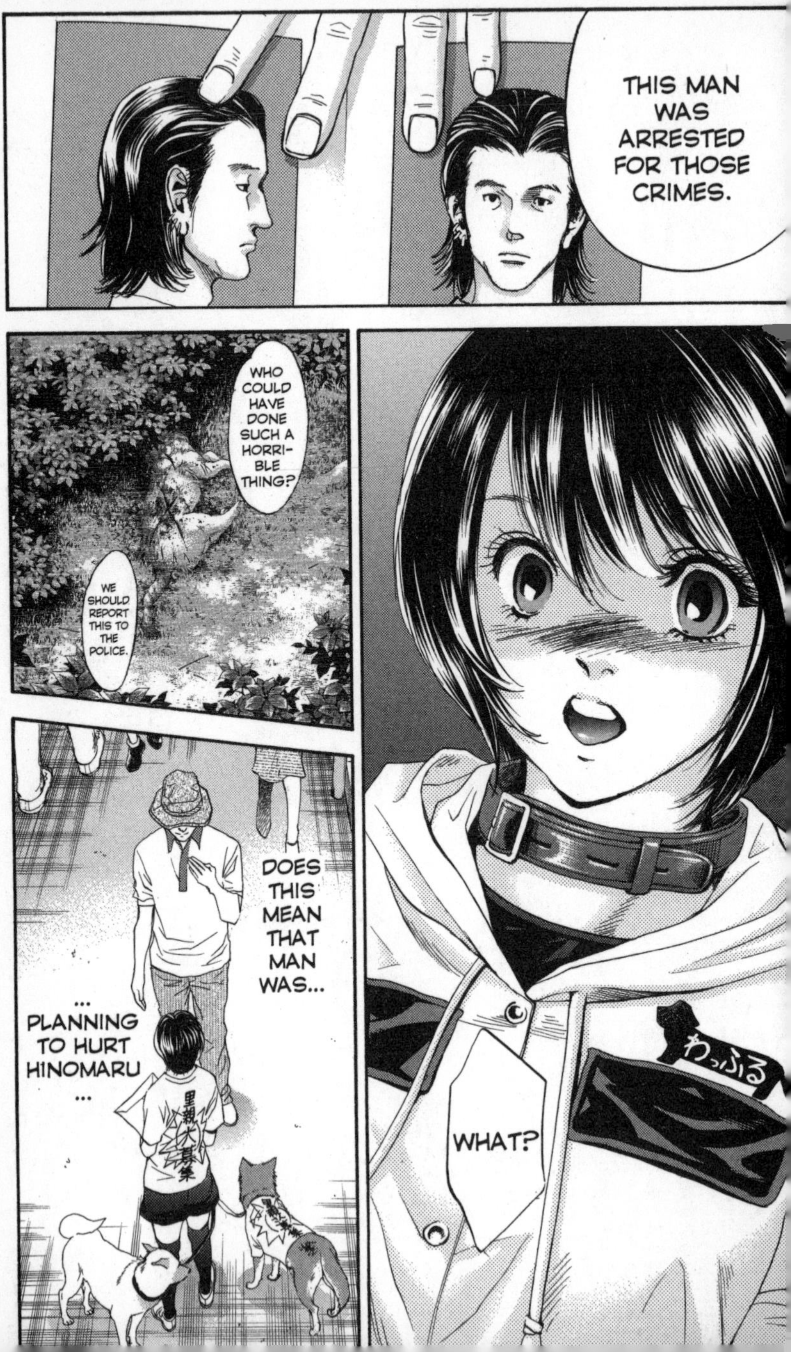
THIS MAN WAS ARRESTED FOR THOSE CRIMES.
わっふる
WHAT?
WHO COULD HAVE DONE SUCH A HORRIBLE THING?
WE SHOULD REPORT THIS TO THE POLICE.
DOES THIS MEAN THAT MAN WAS...
...PLANNING TO HURT HINOMARU...
里親犬募集

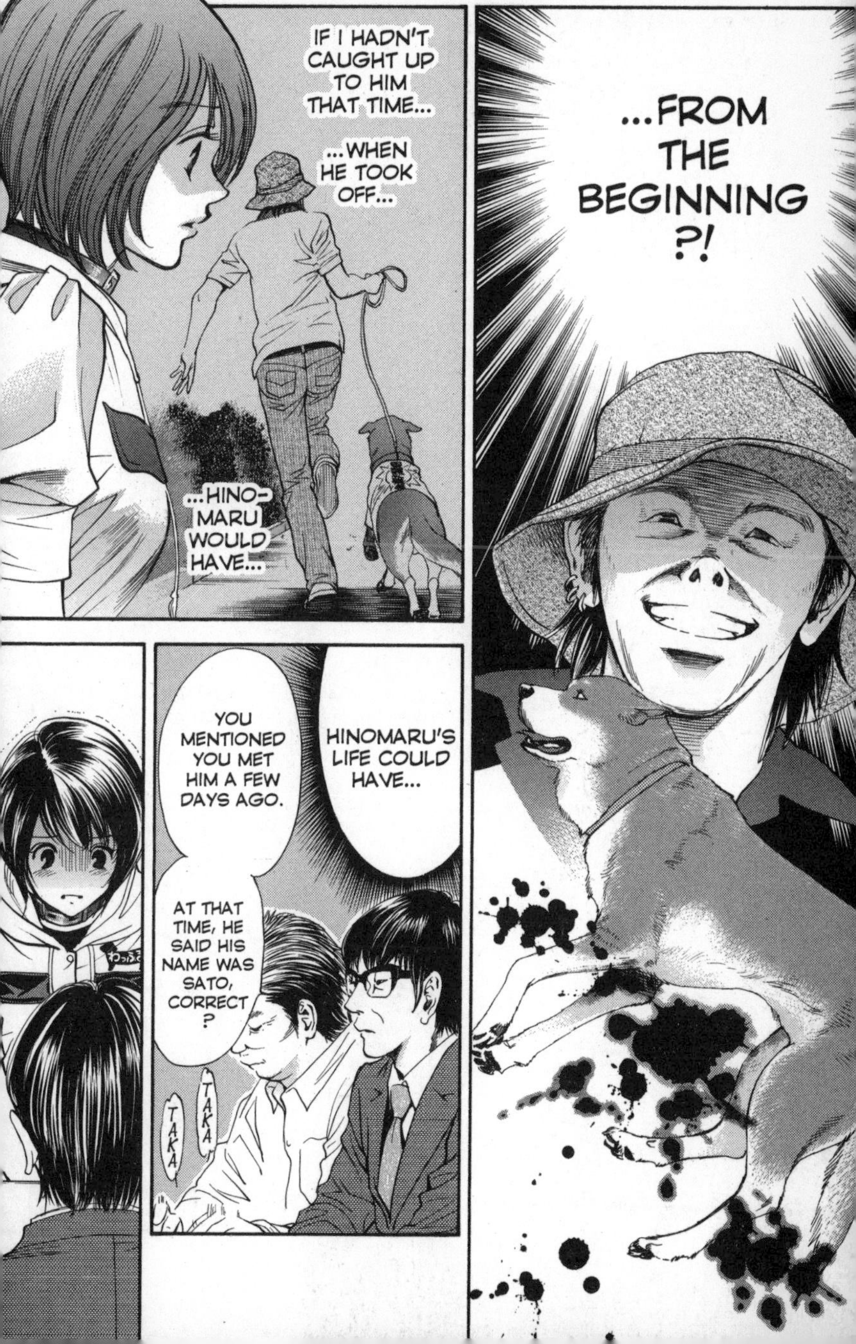
...FROM THE BEGINNING ?!
IF I HADN'T CAUGHT UP TO HIM THAT TIME...
...WHEN HE TOOK OFF...
...HINO-MARU WOULD HAVE...
HINOMARU'S LIFE COULD HAVE...
YOU MENTIONED YOU MET HIM A FEW DAYS AGO.
AT THAT TIME, HE SAID HIS NAME WAS SATO, CORRECT ?
TAKA
TAKA

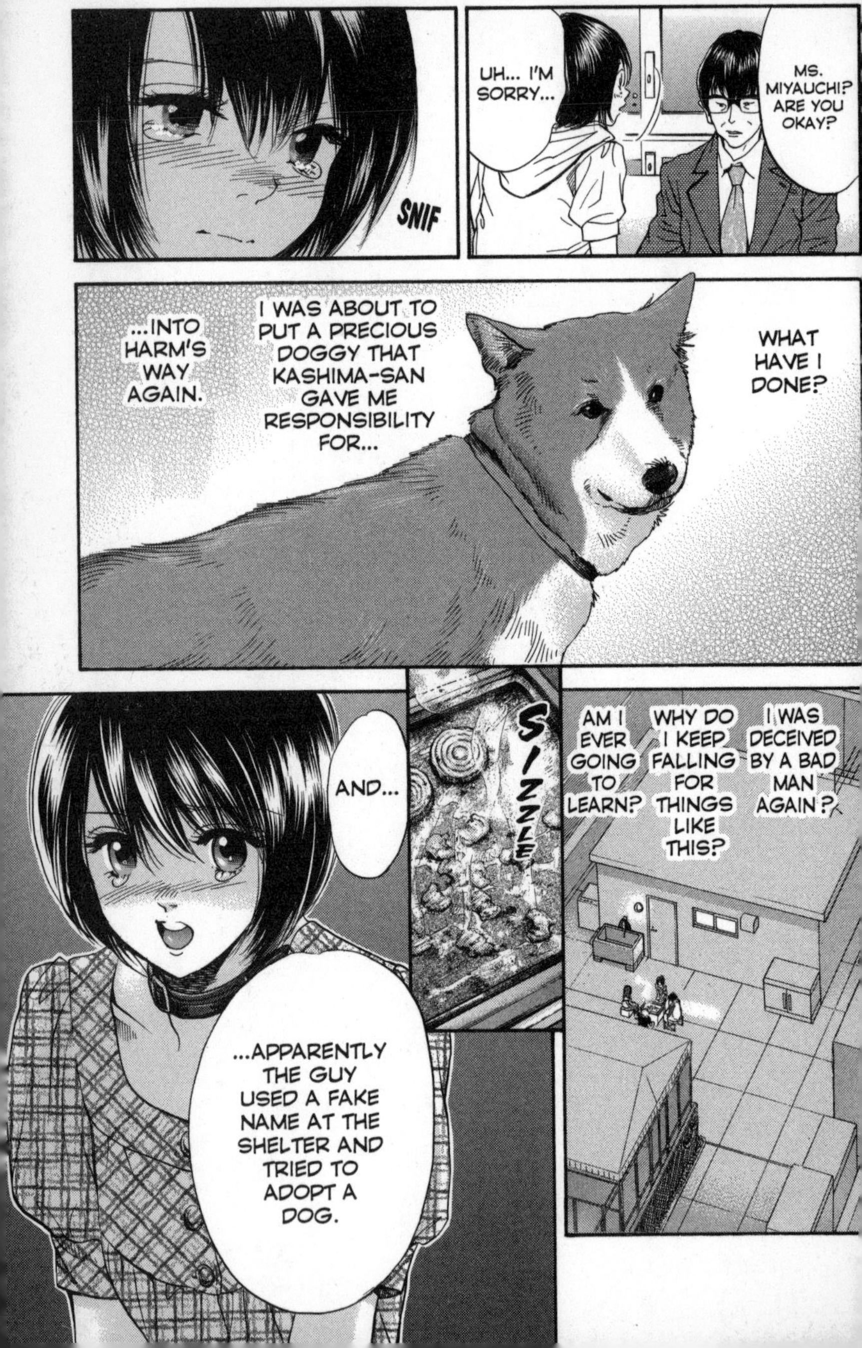
MS. MIYAUCHI? ARE YOU OKAY?
UH... I'M SORRY...
SNIF
WHAT HAVE I DONE?
I WAS ABOUT TO PUT A PRECIOUS DOGGY THAT KASHIMA-SAN GAVE ME RESPONSIBILITY FOR...
...INTO HARM'S WAY AGAIN.
I WAS DECEIVED BY A BAD MAN AGAIN?
WHY DO I KEEP FALLING FOR THINGS LIKE THIS?
AM I EVER GOING TO LEARN?
SIZZLE
AND...
...APPARENTLY THE GUY USED A FAKE NAME AT THE SHELTER AND TRIED TO ADOPT A DOG.

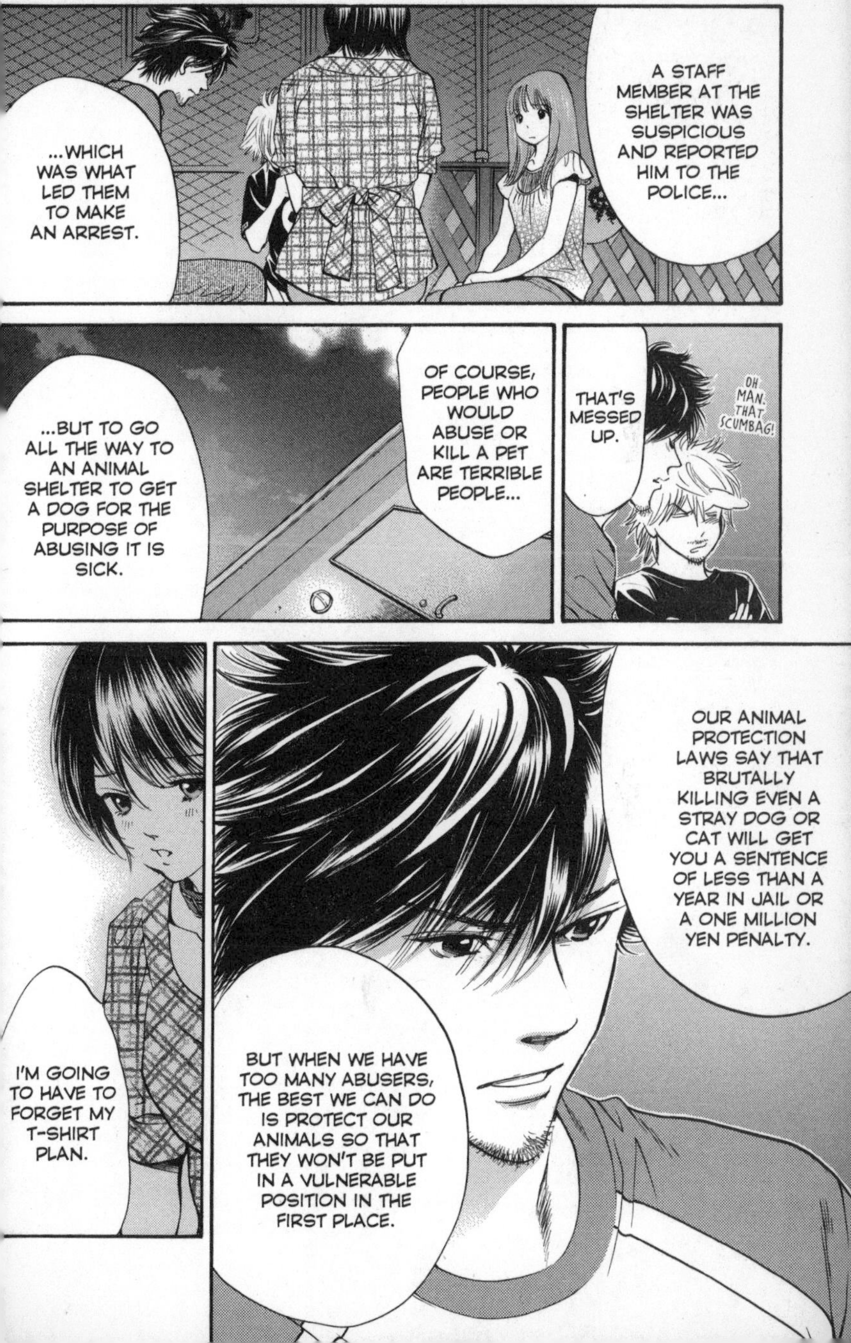
A STAFF MEMBER AT THE SHELTER WAS SUSPICIOUS AND REPORTED HIM TO THE POLICE...
...WHICH WAS WHAT LED THEM TO MAKE AN ARREST.
OH MAN. THAT SCUMBAG!
THAT'S MESSED UP.
OF COURSE, PEOPLE WHO WOULD ABUSE OR KILL A PET ARE TERRIBLE PEOPLE...
...BUT TO GO ALL THE WAY TO AN ANIMAL SHELTER TO GET A DOG FOR THE PURPOSE OF ABUSING IT IS SICK.
OUR ANIMAL PROTECTION LAWS SAY THAT BRUTALLY KILLING EVEN A STRAY DOG OR CAT WILL GET YOU A SENTENCE OF LESS THAN A YEAR IN JAIL OR A ONE MILLION YEN PENALTY.
BUT WHEN WE HAVE TOO MANY ABUSERS, THE BEST WE CAN DO IS PROTECT OUR ANIMALS SO THAT THEY WON'T BE PUT IN A VULNERABLE POSITION IN THE FIRST PLACE.
I'M GOING TO HAVE TO FORGET MY T-SHIRT PLAN.

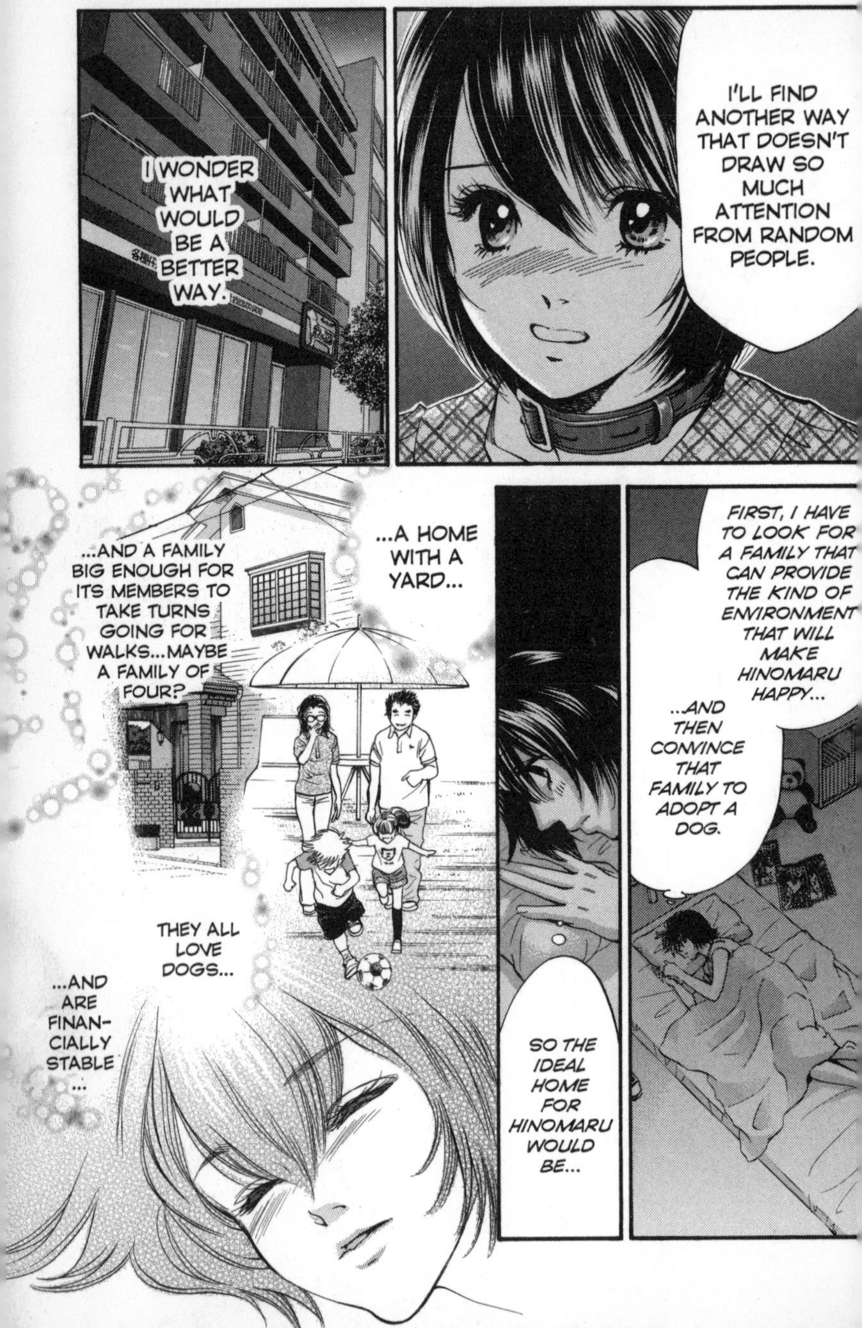

I'LL FIND ANOTHER WAY THAT DOESN'T DRAW SO MUCH ATTENTION FROM RANDOM PEOPLE.
I WONDER WHAT WOULD BE A BETTER WAY.
FIRST, I HAVE TO LOOK FOR A FAMILY THAT CAN PROVIDE THE KIND OF ENVIRONMENT THAT WILL MAKE HINOMARU HAPPY...
...AND THEN CONVINCE THAT FAMILY TO ADOPT A DOG.
SO THE IDEAL HOME FOR HINOMARU WOULD BE...
...A HOME WITH A YARD...
...AND A FAMILY BIG ENOUGH FOR ITS MEMBERS TO TAKE TURNS GOING FOR WALKS...MAYBE A FAMILY OF FOUR?
THEY ALL LOVE DOGS...
...AND ARE FINAN-CIALLY STABLE...

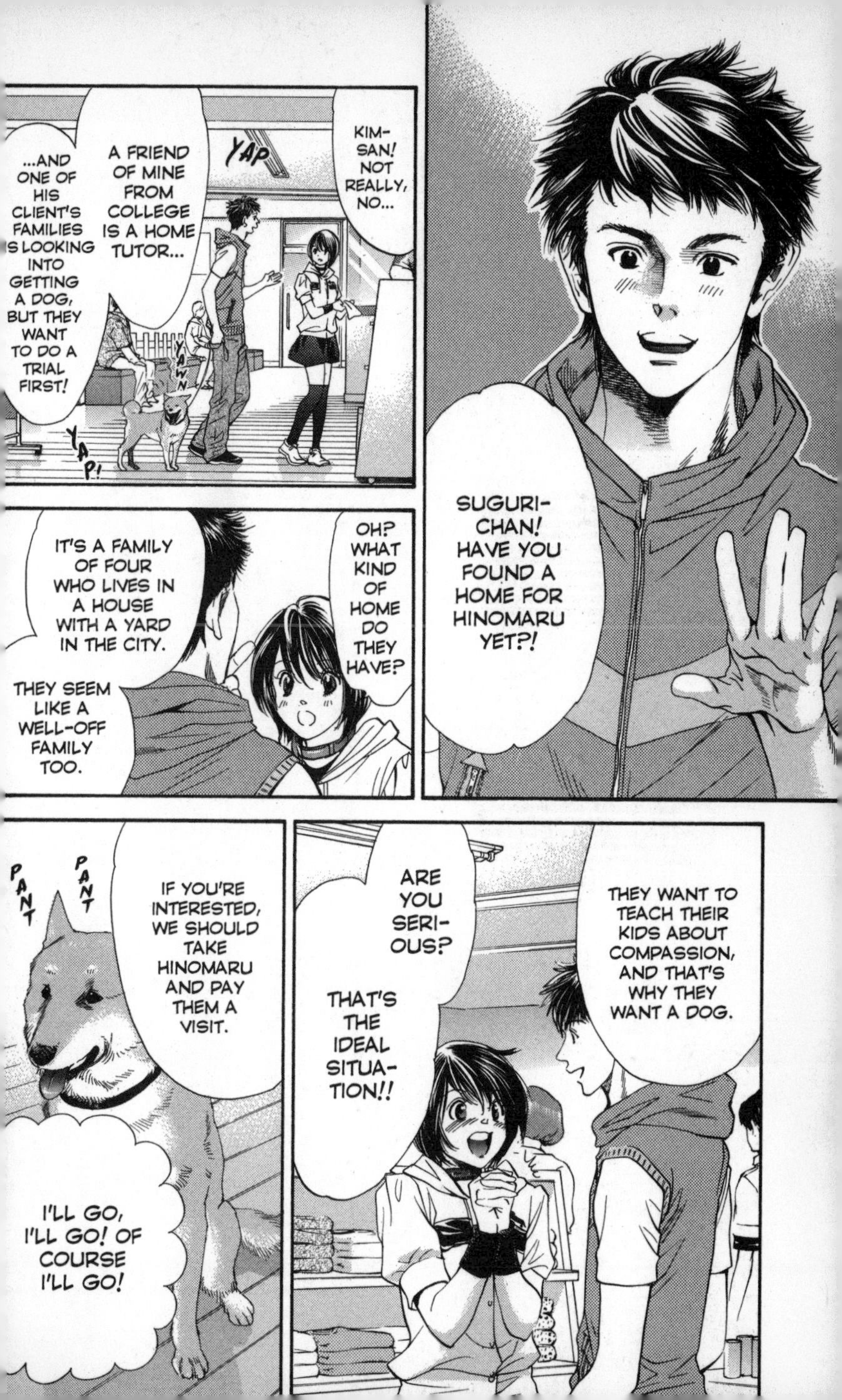
SUGURI-CHAN! HAVE YOU FOUND A HOME FOR HINOMARU YET?!
KIM-SAN! NOT REALLY, NO...
A FRIEND OF MINE FROM COLLEGE IS A HOME TUTOR...
...AND ONE OF HIS CLIENT'S FAMILIES IS LOOKING INTO GETTING A DOG, BUT THEY WANT TO DO A TRIAL FIRST!
YAP
YAWN
YAP!
OH? WHAT KIND OF HOME DO THEY HAVE?
IT'S A FAMILY OF FOUR WHO LIVES IN A HOUSE WITH A YARD IN THE CITY.
THEY SEEM LIKE A WELL-OFF FAMILY TOO.
THEY WANT TO TEACH THEIR KIDS ABOUT COMPASSION, AND THAT'S WHY THEY WANT A DOG.
ARE YOU SERI-OUS?
THAT'S THE IDEAL SITUA-TION!!
PANT
PANT
IF YOU'RE INTERESTED, WE SHOULD TAKE HINOMARU AND PAY THEM A VISIT.
I'LL GO, I'LL GO! OF COURSE I'LL GO!

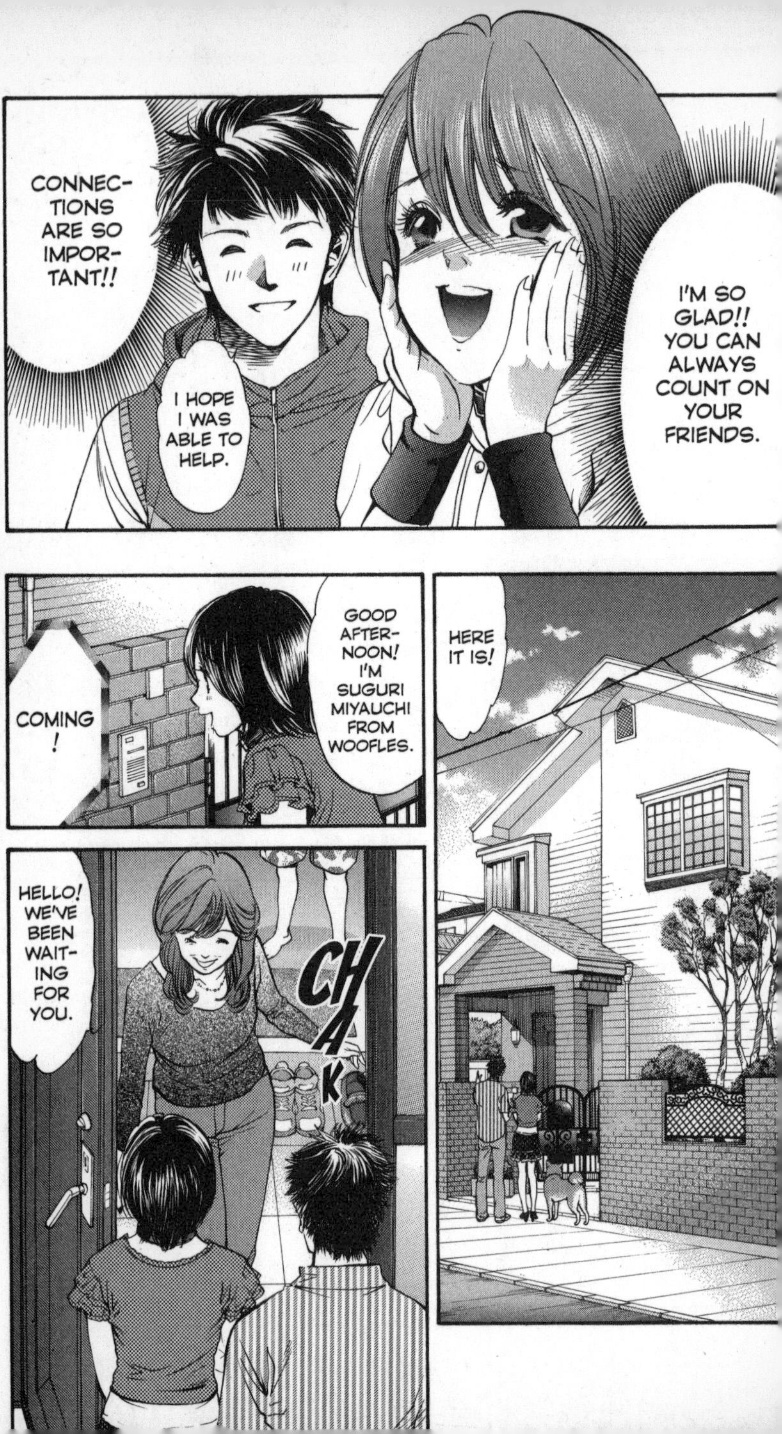
I'M SO GLAD!! YOU CAN ALWAYS COUNT ON YOUR FRIENDS.
CONNEC-TIONS ARE SO IMPOR-TANT!!
I HOPE I WAS ABLE TO HELP.
HERE IT IS!
GOOD AFTER-NOON! I'M SUGURI MIYAUCHI FROM WOOFLES.
COMING!
HELLO! WE'VE BEEN WAIT-ING FOR YOU.
CHAK

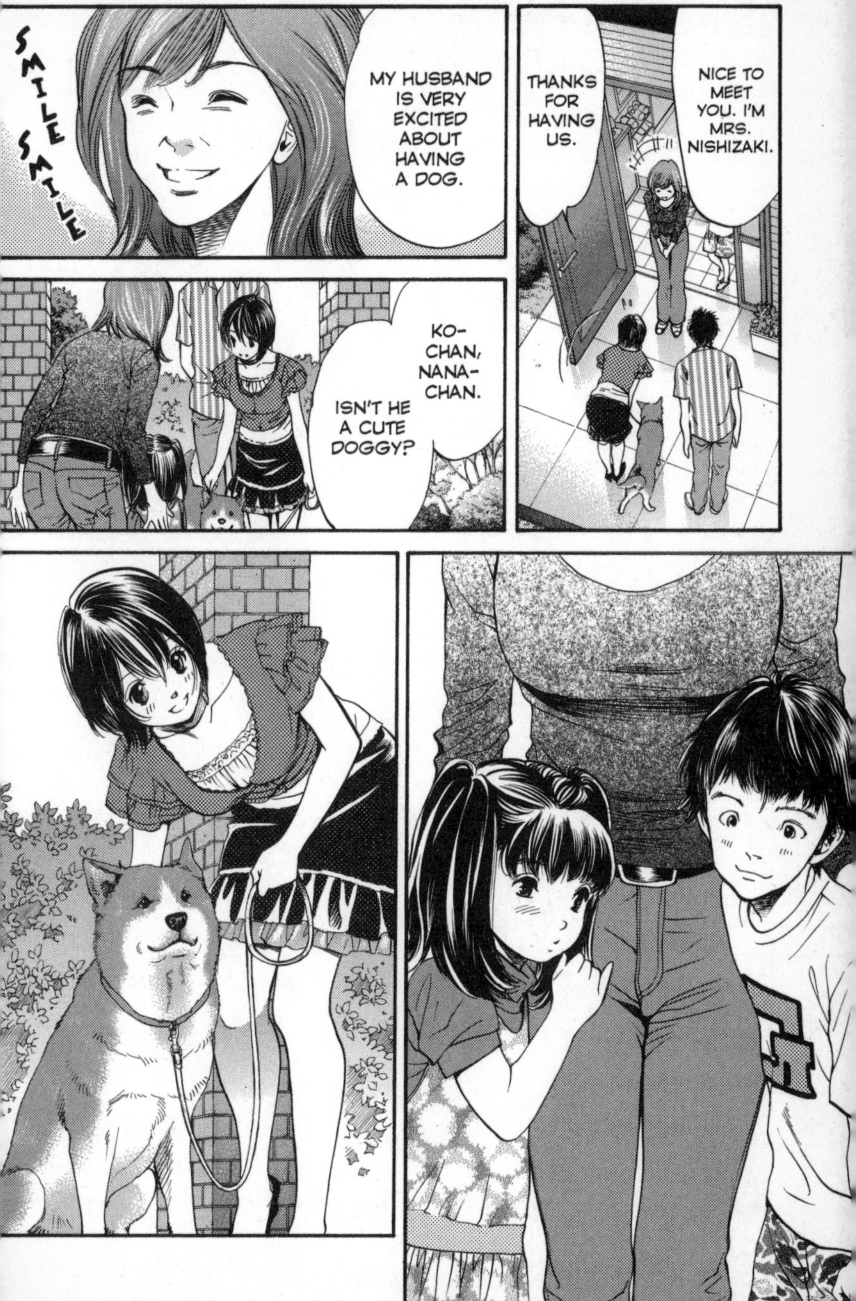
NICE TO MEET YOU. I'M MRS. NISHIZAKI.
THANKS FOR HAVING US.
MY HUSBAND IS VERY EXCITED ABOUT HAVING A DOG.
SMILE SMILE
KO-CHAN, NANA-CHAN.
ISN'T HE A CUTE DOGGY?

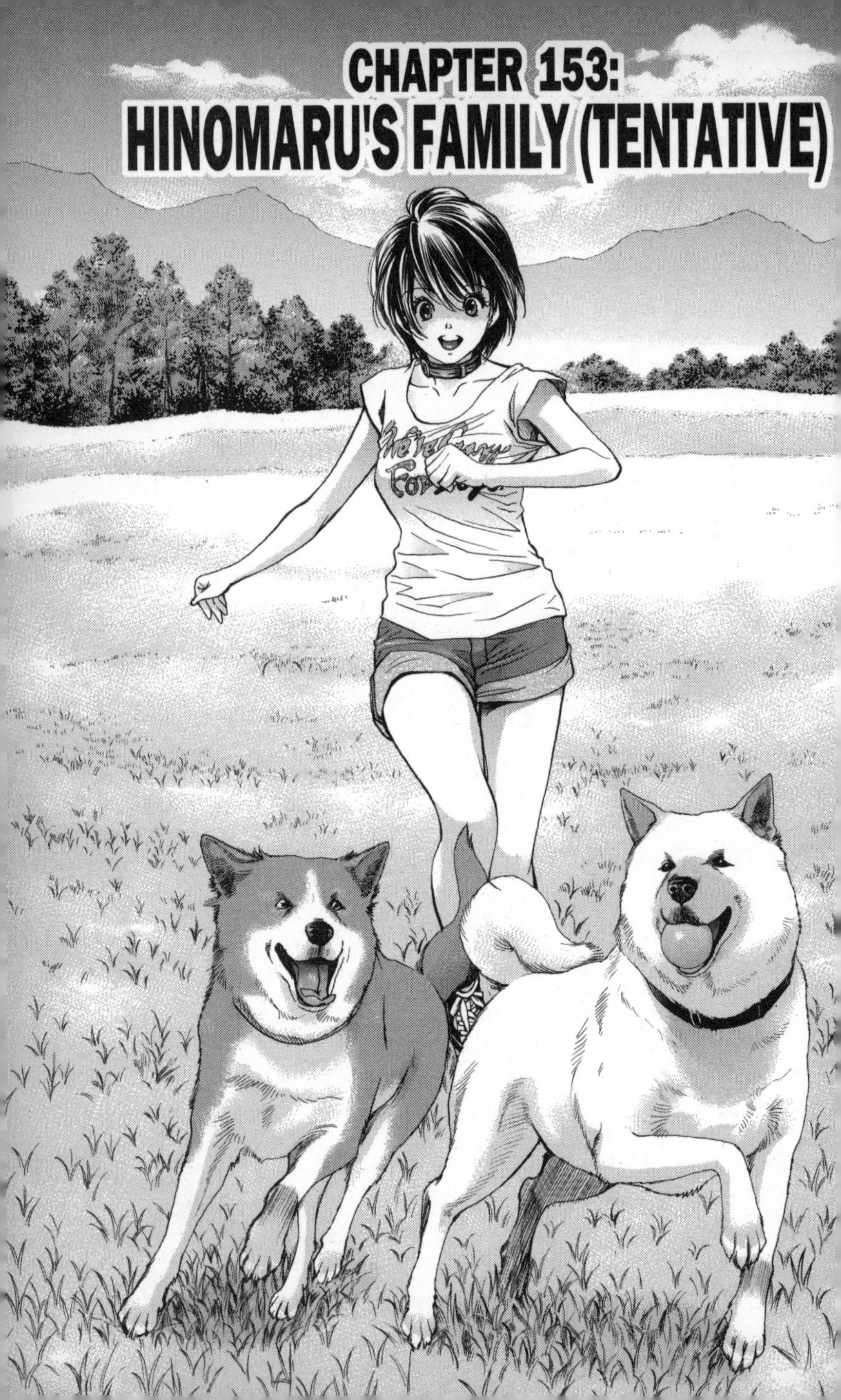
CHAPTER 153:
HINOMARU'S FAMILY (TENTATIVE)

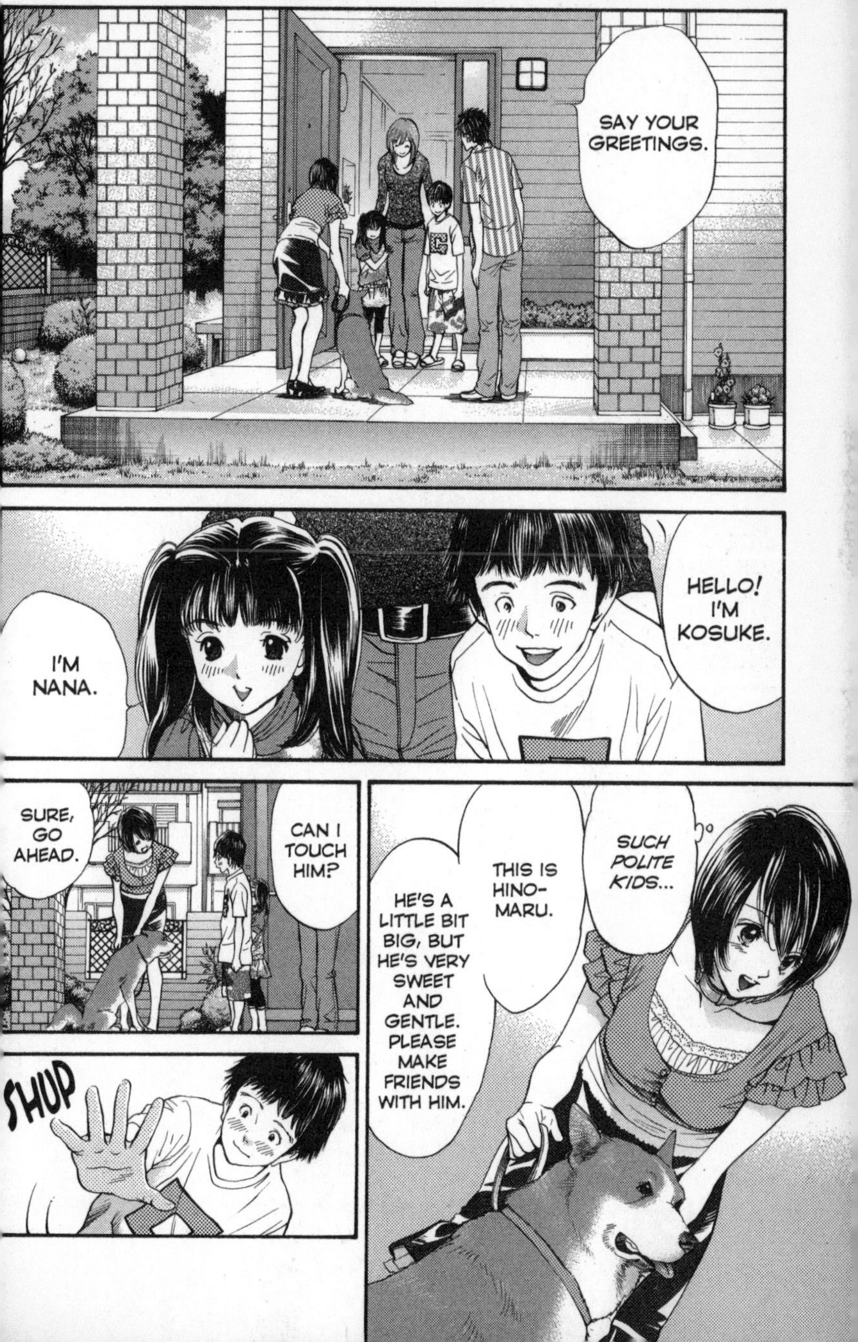
SAY YOUR GREETINGS.
HELLO! I'M KOSUKE.
I'M NANA.
SUCH POLITE KIDS...
THIS IS HINO-MARU.
HE'S A LITTLE BIT BIG, BUT HE'S VERY SWEET AND GENTLE. PLEASE MAKE FRIENDS WITH HIM.
CAN I TOUCH HIM?
SURE, GO AHEAD.
SHUP

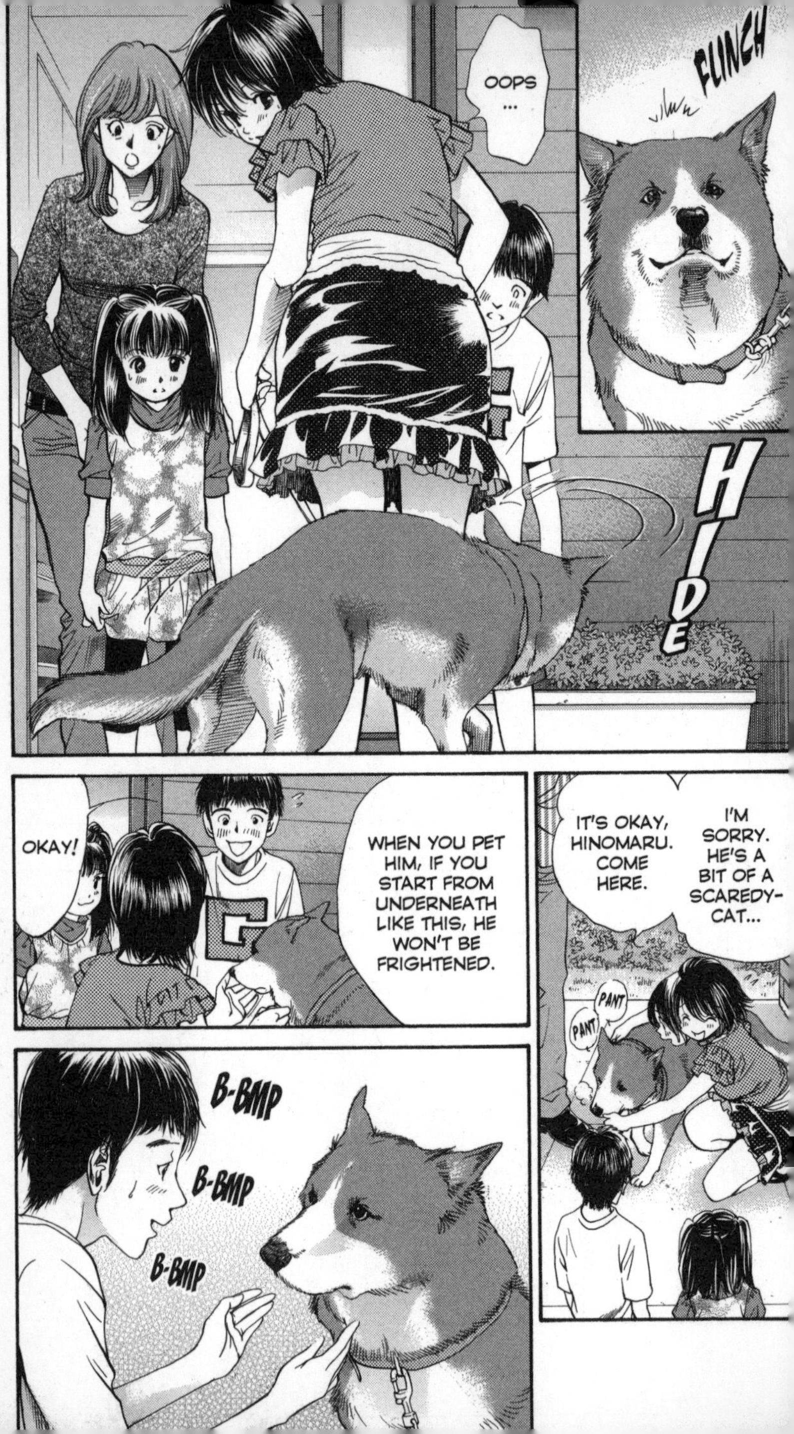
FLINCH
OOPS ...
HIDE
I'M SORRY. HE'S A BIT OF A SCAREDY-CAT...
IT'S OKAY, HINOMARU. COME HERE.
PANT
PANT
WHEN YOU PET HIM, IF YOU START FROM UNDERNEATH LIKE THIS, HE WON'T BE FRIGHTENED.
OKAY!
B-BMP
B-BMP
B-BMP

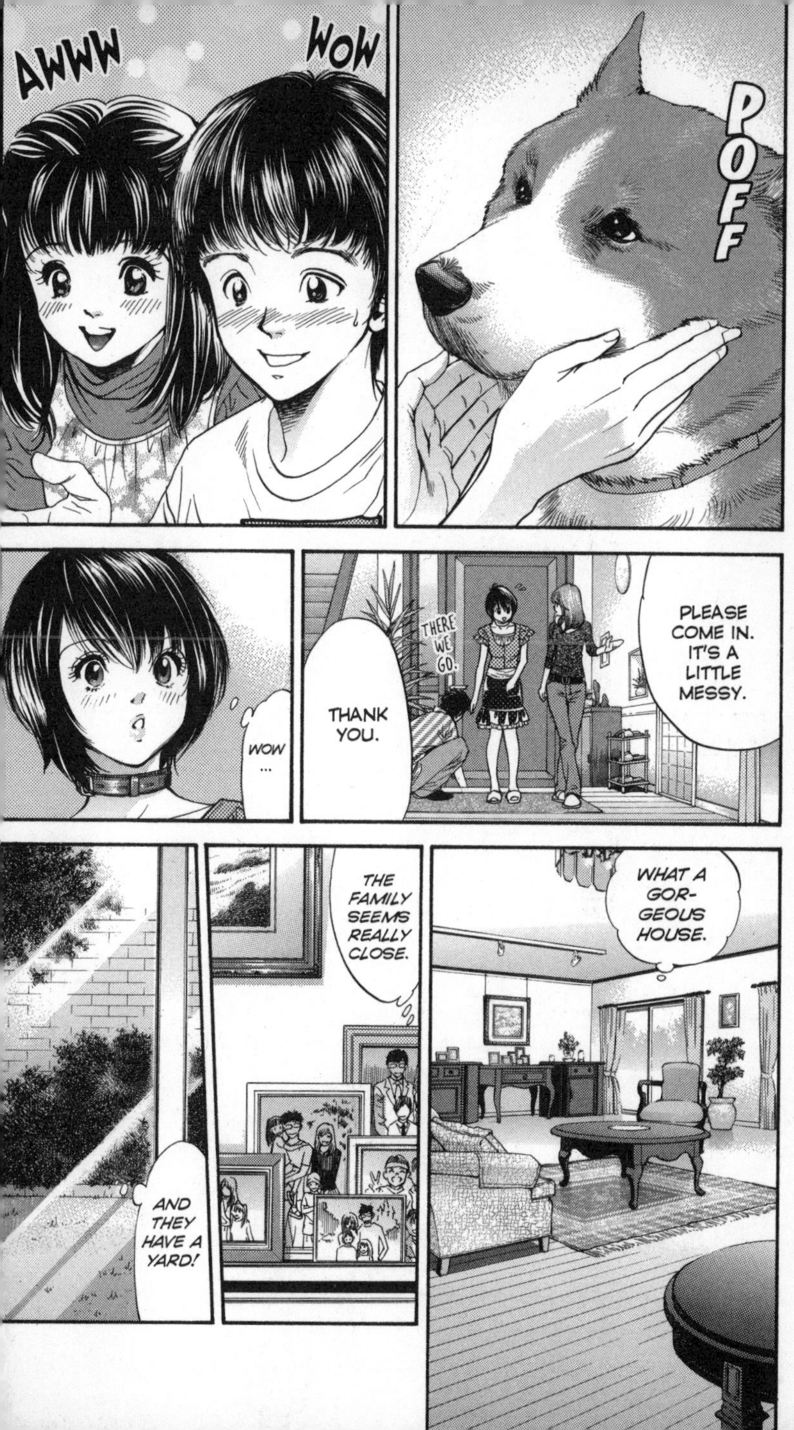
POFF
WOW
AWWW
PLEASE COME IN. IT'S A LITTLE MESSY.
THERE WE GO.
THANK YOU.
WOW ...
WHAT A GORGEOUS HOUSE.
THE FAMILY SEEMS REALLY CLOSE.
AND THEY HAVE A YARD!

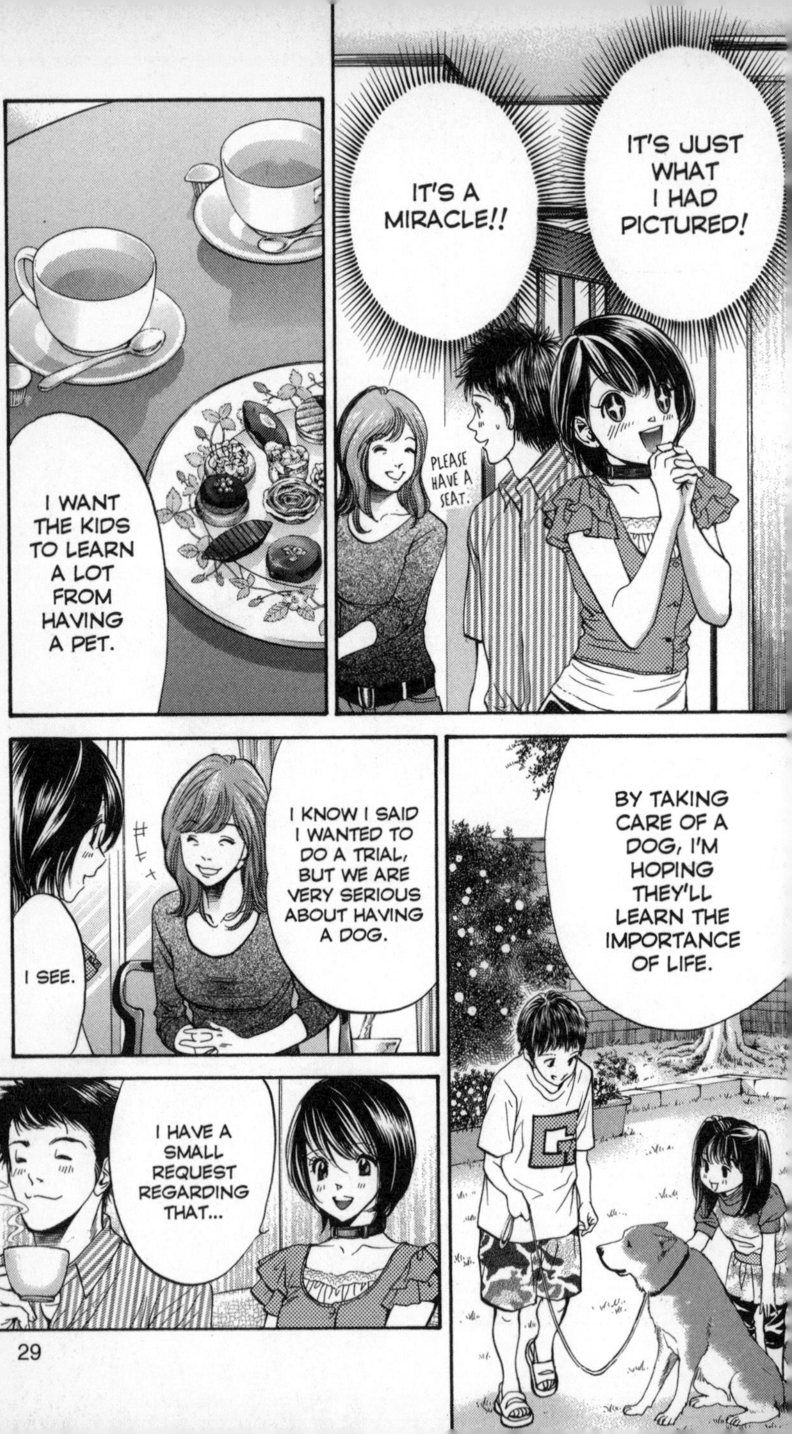
IT'S JUST WHAT I HAD PICTURED!
IT'S A MIRACLE!!
PLEASE HAVE A SEAT.
I WANT THE KIDS TO LEARN A LOT FROM HAVING A PET.
BY TAKING CARE OF A DOG, I'M HOPING THEY'LL LEARN THE IMPORTANCE OF LIFE.
I KNOW I SAID I WANTED TO DO A TRIAL, BUT WE ARE VERY SERIOUS ABOUT HAVING A DOG.
I SEE.
I HAVE A SMALL REQUEST REGARDING THAT...

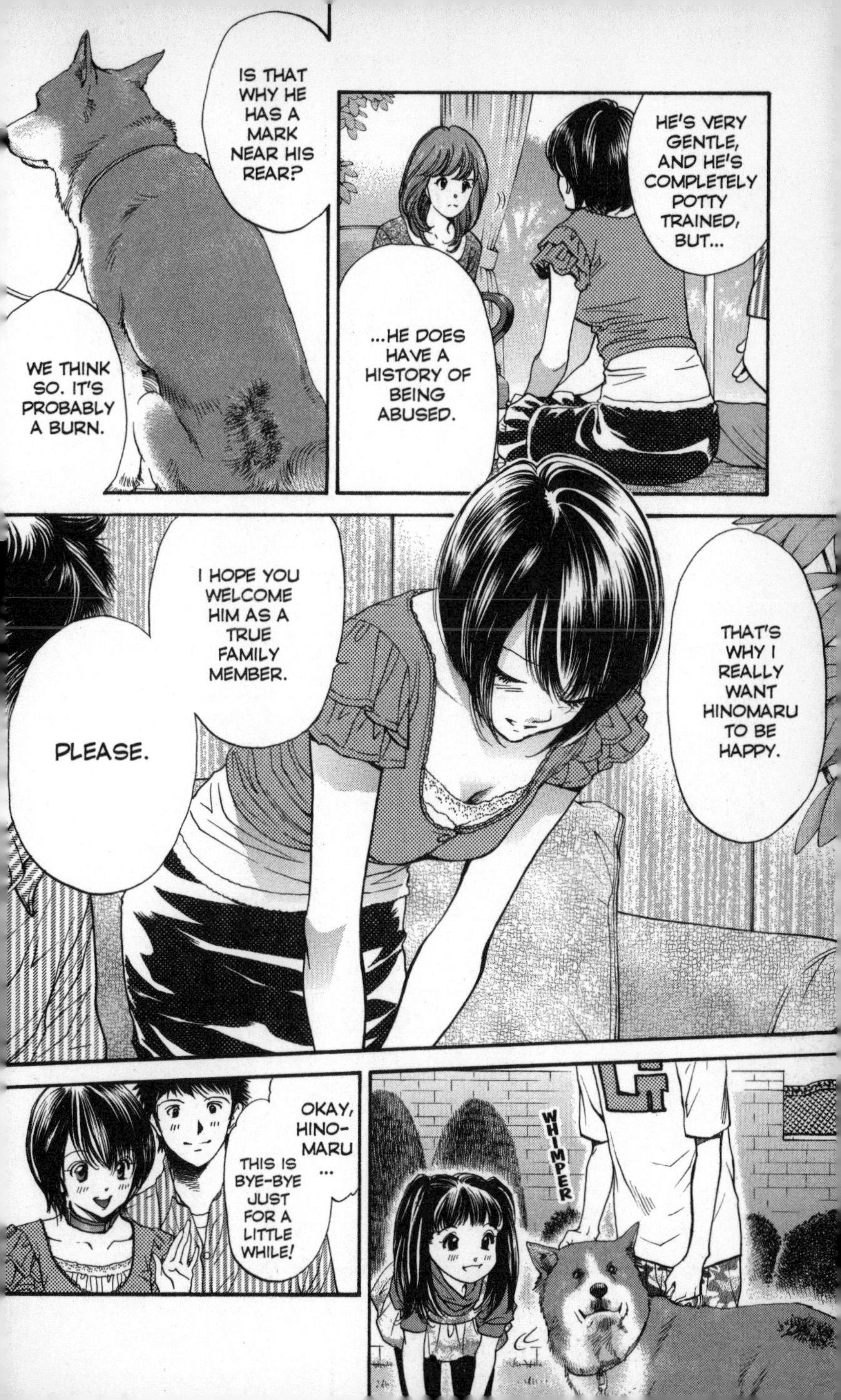
HE'S VERY GENTLE, AND HE'S COMPLETELY POTTY TRAINED, BUT...
...HE DOES HAVE A HISTORY OF BEING ABUSED.
IS THAT WHY HE HAS A MARK NEAR HIS REAR?
WE THINK SO. IT'S PROBABLY A BURN.
THAT'S WHY I REALLY WANT HINOMARU TO BE HAPPY.
I HOPE YOU WELCOME HIM AS A TRUE FAMILY MEMBER.
PLEASE.
WHIMPER
OKAY, HINO-MARU...
THIS IS BYE-BYE JUST FOR A LITTLE WHILE!

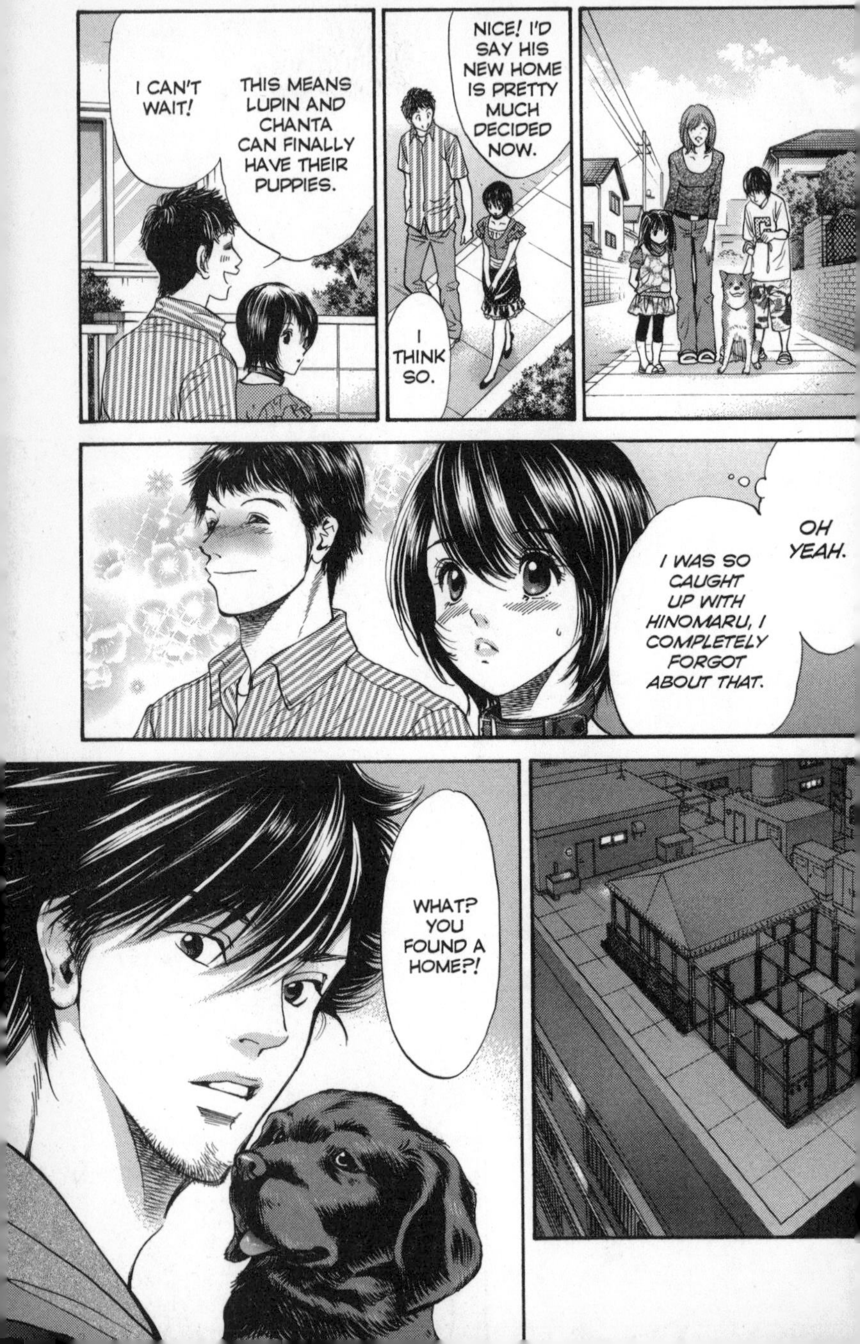
NICE! I'D SAY HIS NEW HOME IS PRETTY MUCH DECIDED NOW.
I THINK SO.
THIS MEANS LUPIN AND CHANTA CAN FINALLY HAVE THEIR PUPPIES.
I CAN'T WAIT!
OH YEAH.
I WAS SO CAUGHT UP WITH HINOMARU, I COMPLETELY FORGOT ABOUT THAT.
WHAT? YOU FOUND A HOME?!

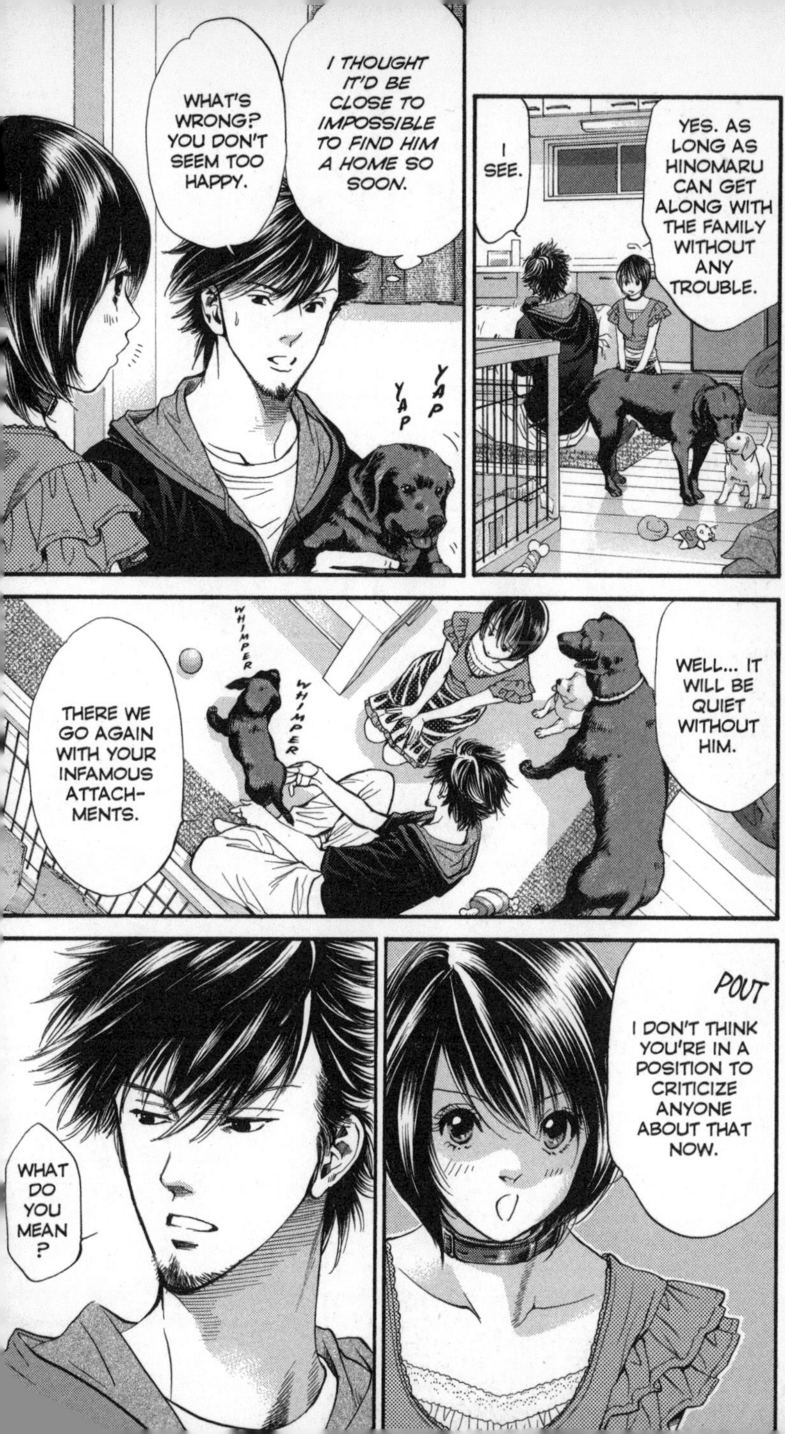

YES. AS LONG AS HINOMARU CAN GET ALONG WITH THE FAMILY WITHOUT ANY TROUBLE.
I SEE.
I THOUGHT IT'D BE CLOSE TO IMPOSSIBLE TO FIND HIM A HOME SO SOON.
WHAT'S WRONG? YOU DON'T SEEM TOO HAPPY.
YAP
YAP
WELL... IT WILL BE QUIET WITHOUT HIM.
WHIMPER
WHIMPER
THERE WE GO AGAIN WITH YOUR INFAMOUS ATTACH-MENTS.
POUT
I DON'T THINK YOU'RE IN A POSITION TO CRITICIZE ANYONE ABOUT THAT NOW.
WHAT DO YOU MEAN?

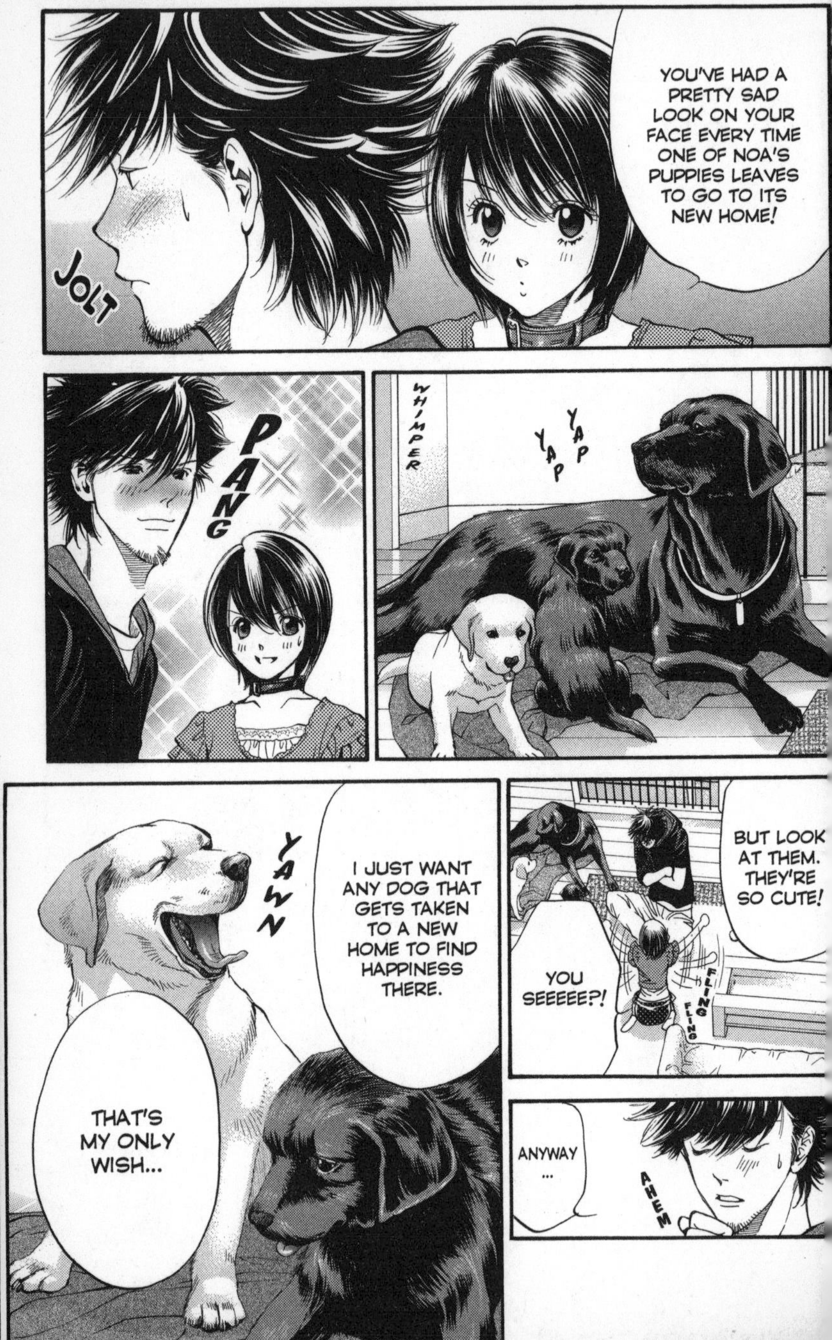
YOU'VE HAD A PRETTY SAD LOOK ON YOUR FACE EVERY TIME ONE OF NOA'S PUPPIES LEAVES TO GO TO ITS NEW HOME!
JOLT
YAP YAP
WHIMPER
PANG
BUT LOOK AT THEM. THEY'RE SO CUTE!
FLING FLING
YOU SEEEEE?!
ANYWAY ...
AHEM
I JUST WANT ANY DOG THAT GETS TAKEN TO A NEW HOME TO FIND HAPPINESS THERE.
YAWN
THAT'S MY ONLY WISH...

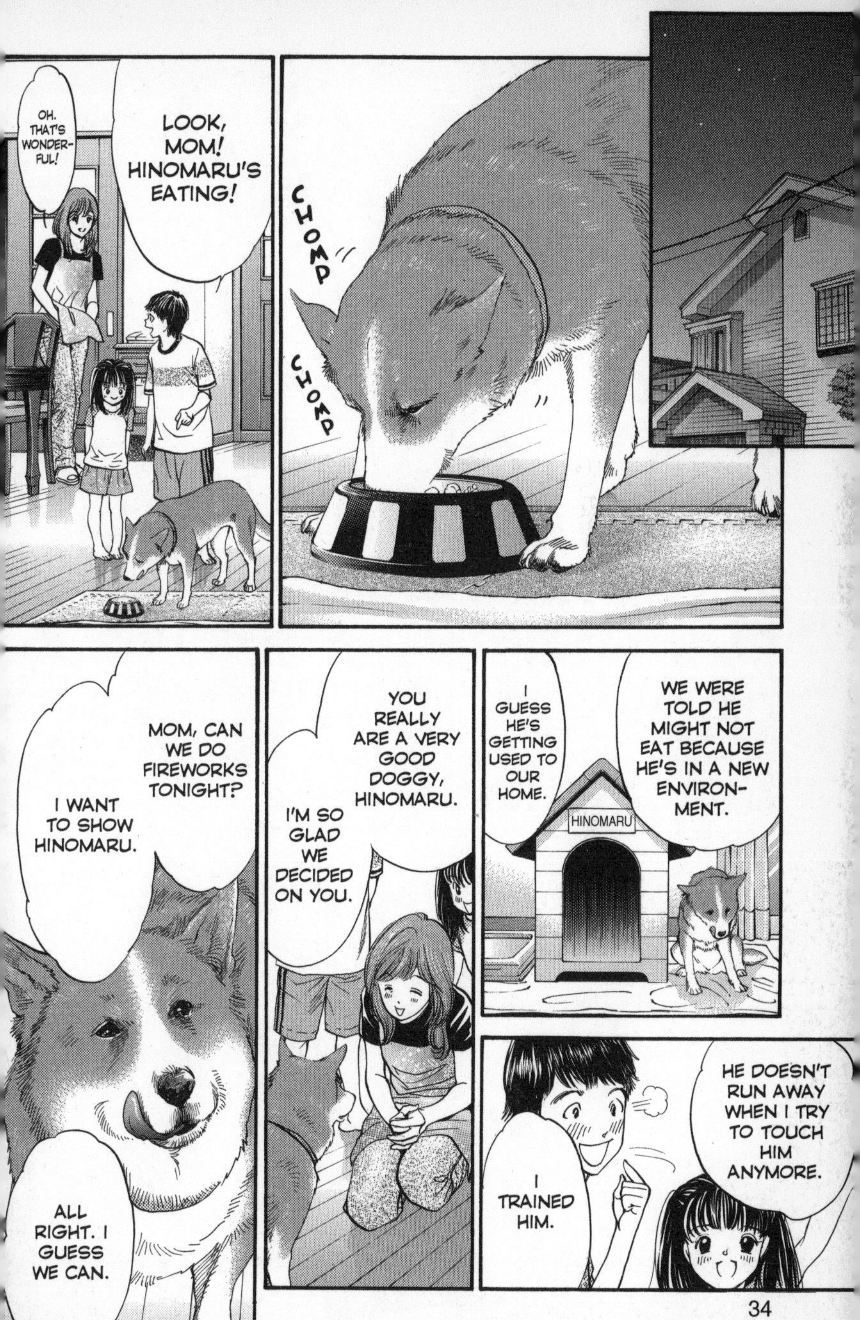
CHOMP
CHOMP
LOOK, MOM! HINOMARU'S EATING!
OH. THAT'S WONDER-FUL!
WE WERE TOLD HE MIGHT NOT EAT BECAUSE HE'S IN A NEW ENVIRON-MENT.
I GUESS HE'S GETTING USED TO OUR HOME.
HINOMARU
HE DOESN'T RUN AWAY WHEN I TRY TO TOUCH HIM ANYMORE.
I TRAINED HIM.
YOU REALLY ARE A VERY GOOD DOGGY, HINOMARU.
I'M SO GLAD WE DECIDED ON YOU.
MOM, CAN WE DO FIREWORKS TONIGHT?
I WANT TO SHOW HINOMARU.
ALL RIGHT. I GUESS WE CAN.

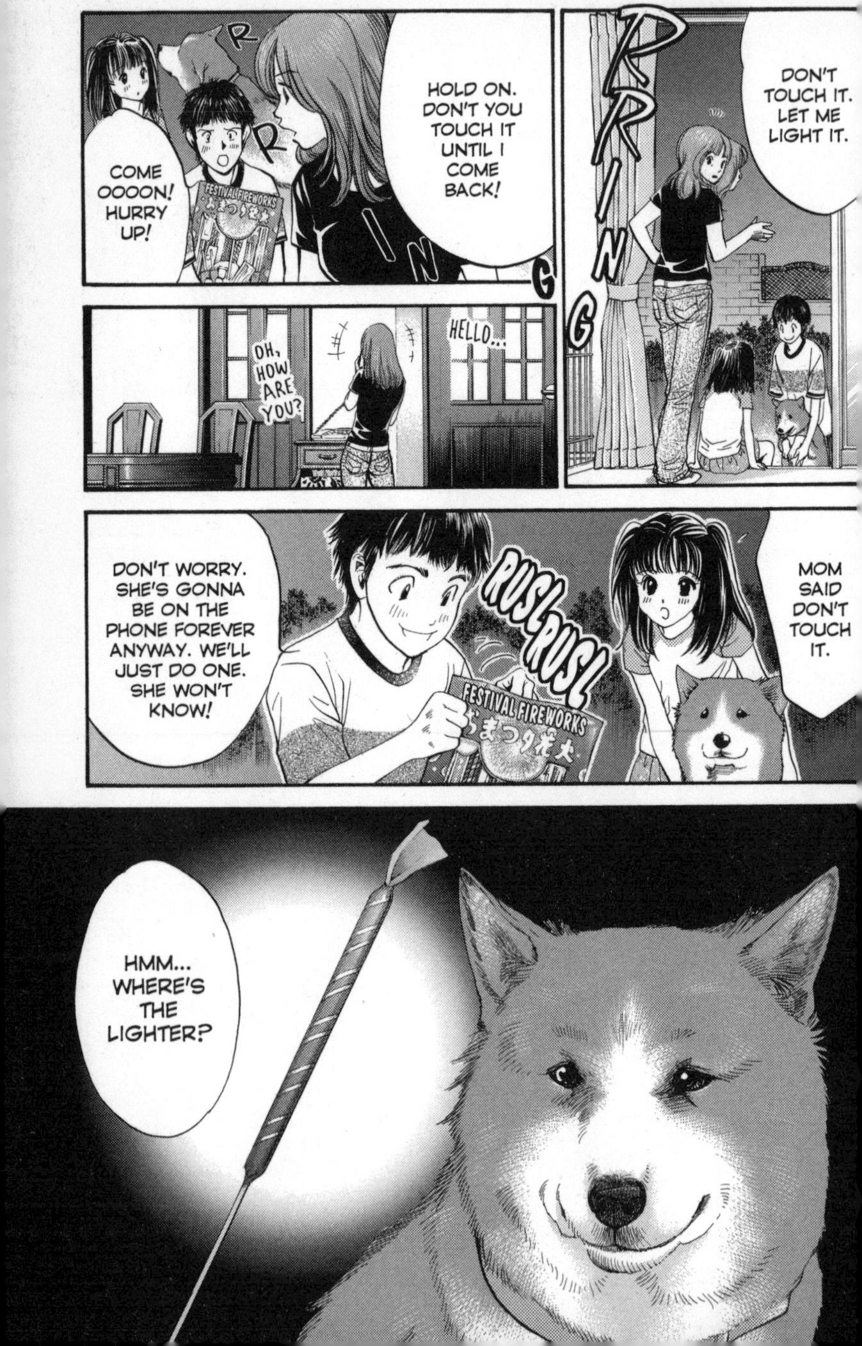
DON'T TOUCH IT. LET ME LIGHT IT.
RRRING
HOLD ON. DON'T YOU TOUCH IT UNTIL I COME BACK!
RRING
FESTIVAL FIREWORKS
COME OOOON! HURRY UP!
HELLO...
OH, HOW ARE YOU?
MOM SAID DON'T TOUCH IT.
RUSL RUSL
FESTIVAL FIREWORKS
DON'T WORRY. SHE'S GONNA BE ON THE PHONE FOREVER ANYWAY. WE'LL JUST DO ONE. SHE WON'T KNOW!
HMM... WHERE'S THE LIGHTER?

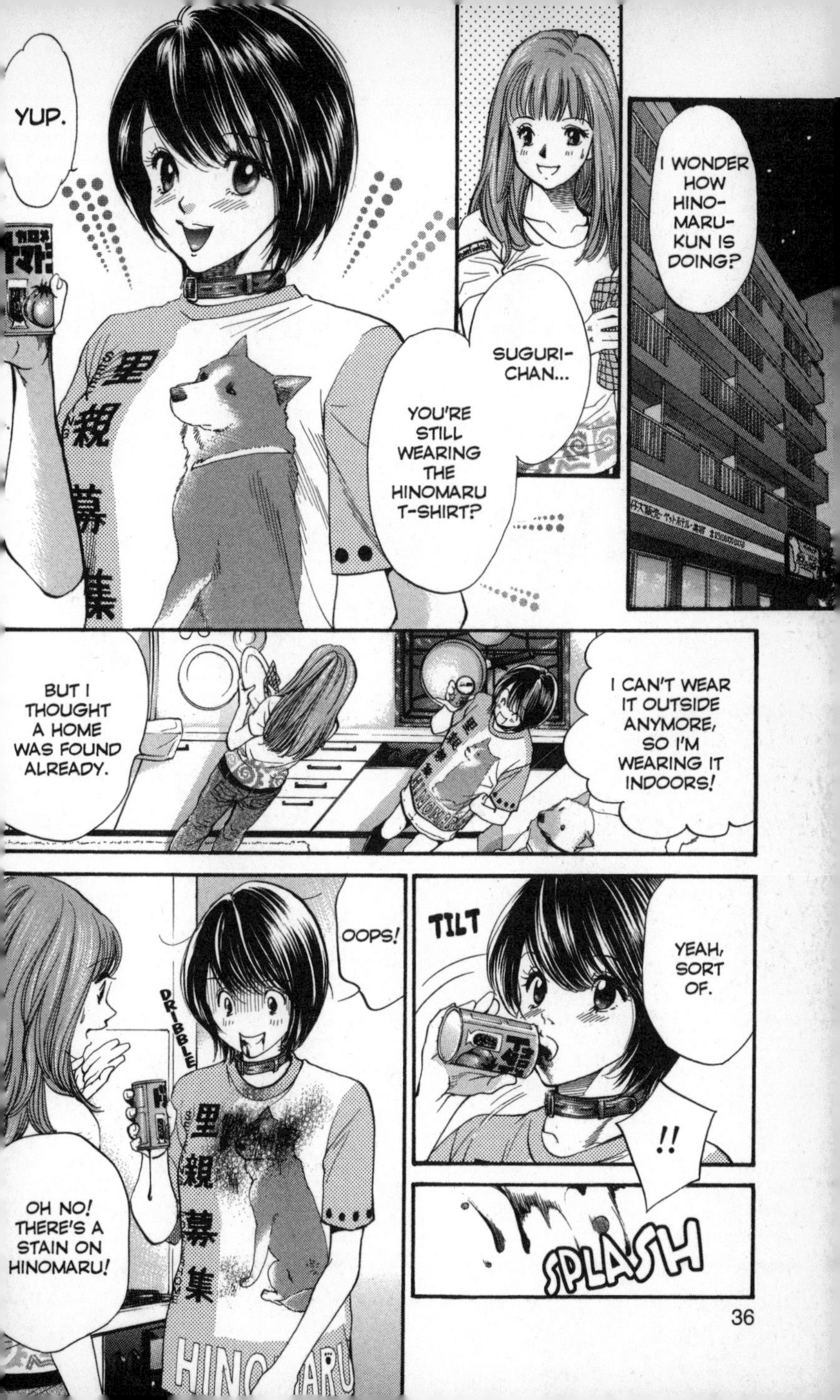
I WONDER HOW HINOMARU-KUN IS DOING?
SUGURI-CHAN...
YOU'RE STILL WEARING THE HINOMARU T-SHIRT?
YUP.
I CAN'T WEAR IT OUTSIDE ANYMORE, SO I'M WEARING IT INDOORS!
BUT I THOUGHT A HOME WAS FOUND ALREADY.
TILT
YEAH, SORT OF.
!!
SPLASH
OOPS!
DRIBBLE
OH NO! THERE'S A STAIN ON HINOMARU!

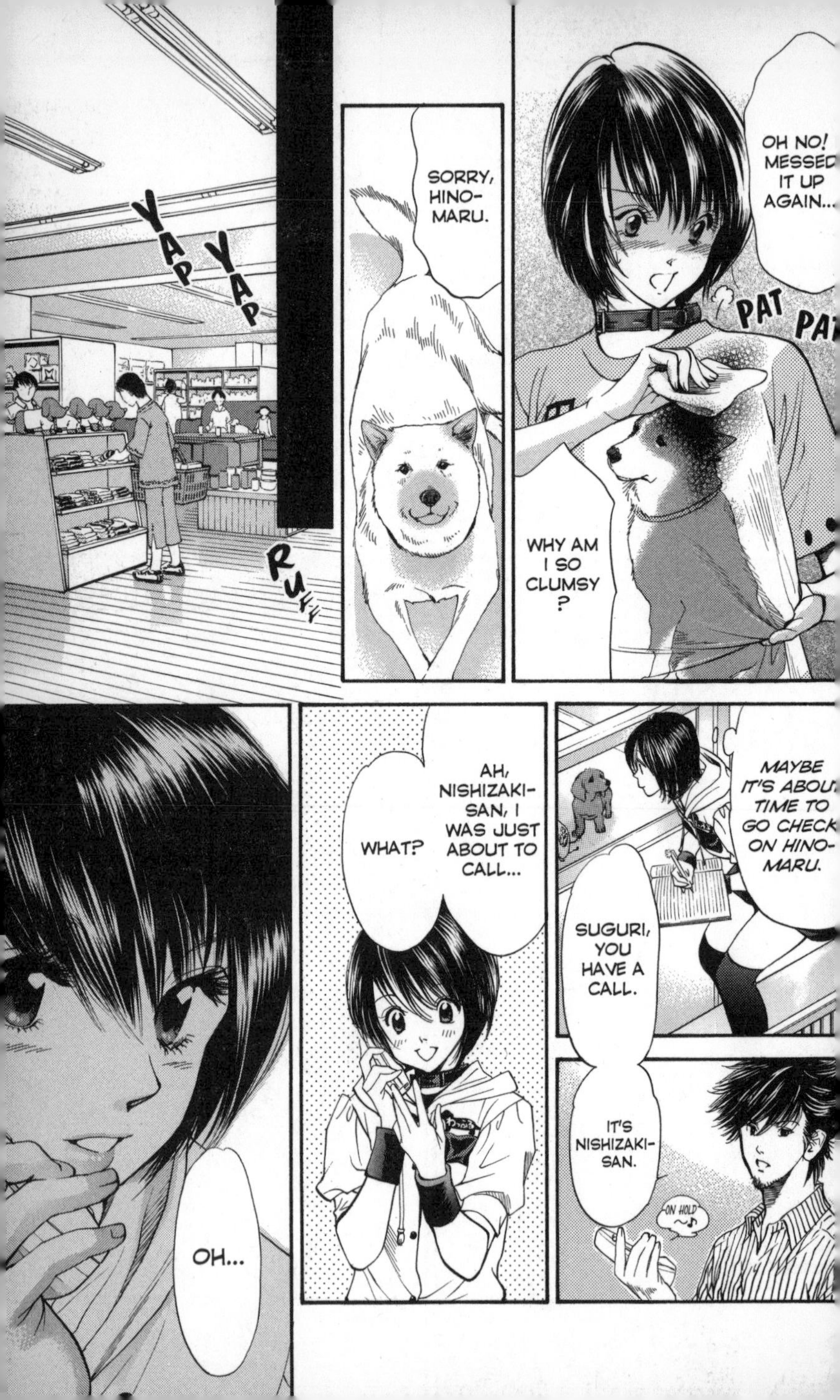
OH NO! MESSED IT UP AGAIN...
PAT PA
WHY AM I SO CLUMSY?
SORRY, HINO-MARU.
YAP YAP
RUFF
MAYBE IT'S ABOU TIME TO GO CHECK ON HINO-MARU.
SUGURI, YOU HAVE A CALL.
IT'S NISHIZAKI-SAN.
ON HOLD ~♪
AH, NISHIZAKI-SAN, I WAS JUST ABOUT TO CALL...
WHAT?
OH...

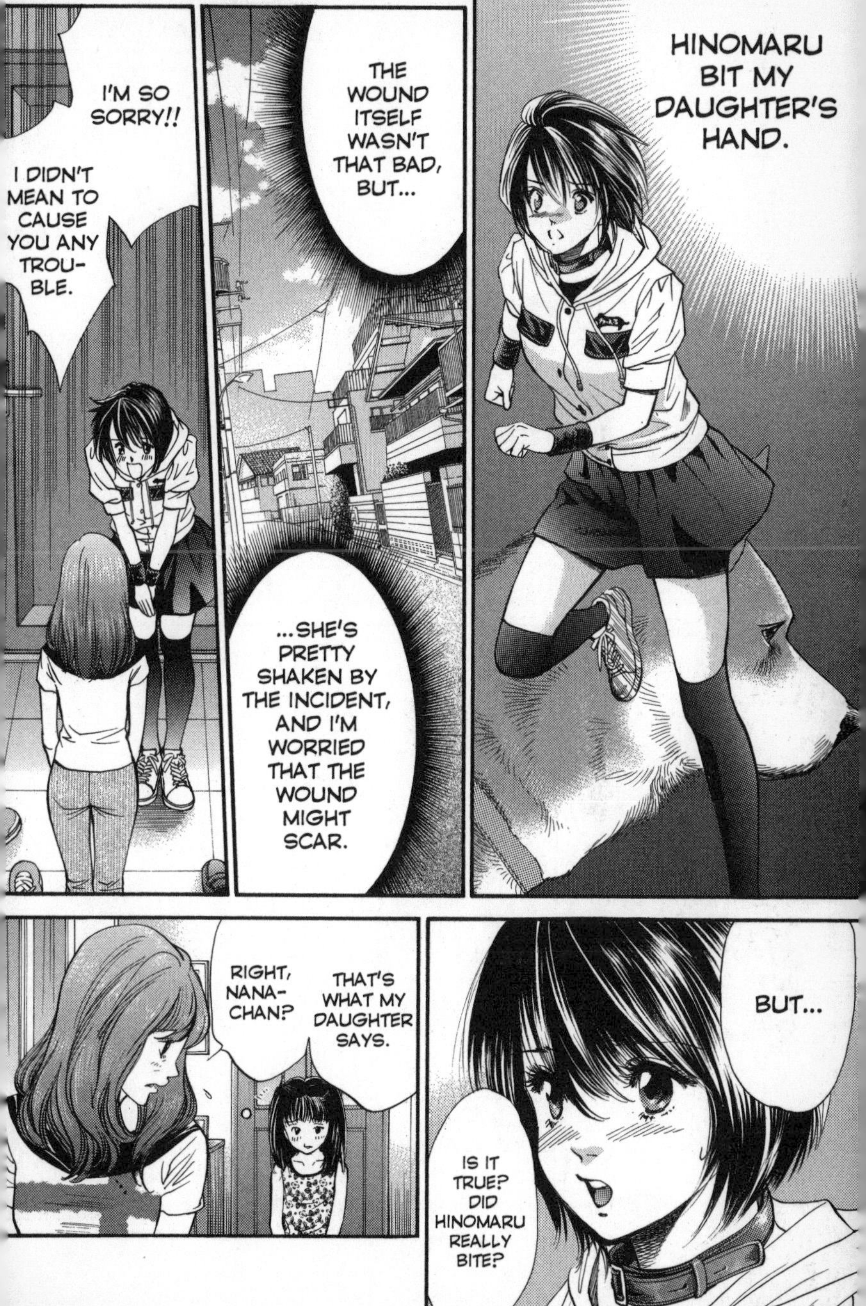
HINOMARU BIT MY DAUGHTER'S HAND.
THE WOUND ITSELF WASN'T THAT BAD, BUT...
...SHE'S PRETTY SHAKEN BY THE INCIDENT, AND I'M WORRIED THAT THE WOUND MIGHT SCAR.
I'M SO SORRY!!
I DIDN'T MEAN TO CAUSE YOU ANY TROU-BLE.
BUT...
IS IT TRUE? DID HINOMARU REALLY BITE?
THAT'S WHAT MY DAUGHTER SAYS.
RIGHT, NANA-CHAN?

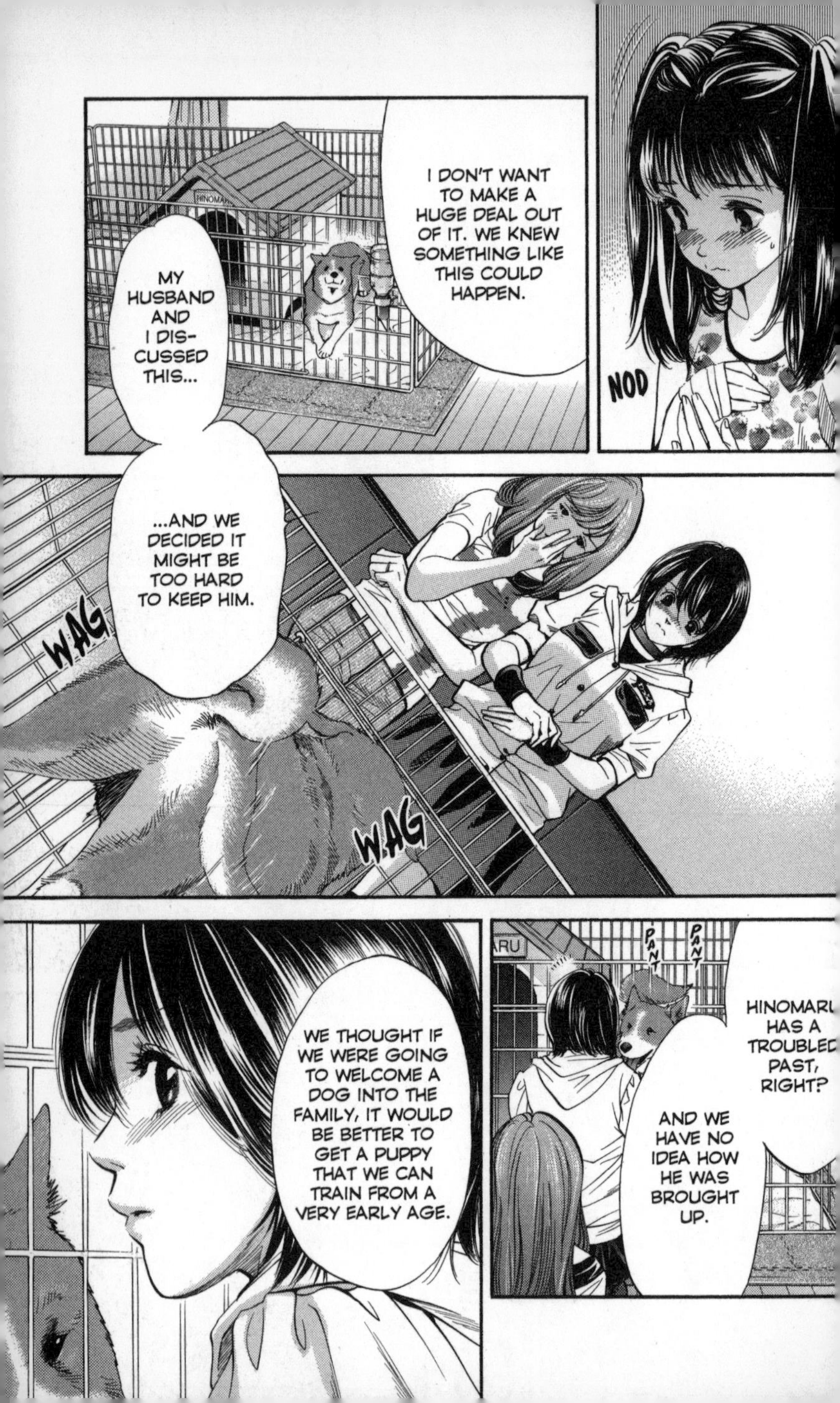
NOD
I DON'T WANT TO MAKE A HUGE DEAL OUT OF IT. WE KNEW SOMETHING LIKE THIS COULD HAPPEN.
MY HUSBAND AND I DIS-CUSSED THIS...
...AND WE DECIDED IT MIGHT BE TOO HARD TO KEEP HIM.
WAG
WAG
PANT
PANT
HINOMARU HAS A TROUBLED PAST, RIGHT?
AND WE HAVE NO IDEA HOW HE WAS BROUGHT UP.
WE THOUGHT IF WE WERE GOING TO WELCOME A DOG INTO THE FAMILY, IT WOULD BE BETTER TO GET A PUPPY THAT WE CAN TRAIN FROM A VERY EARLY AGE.

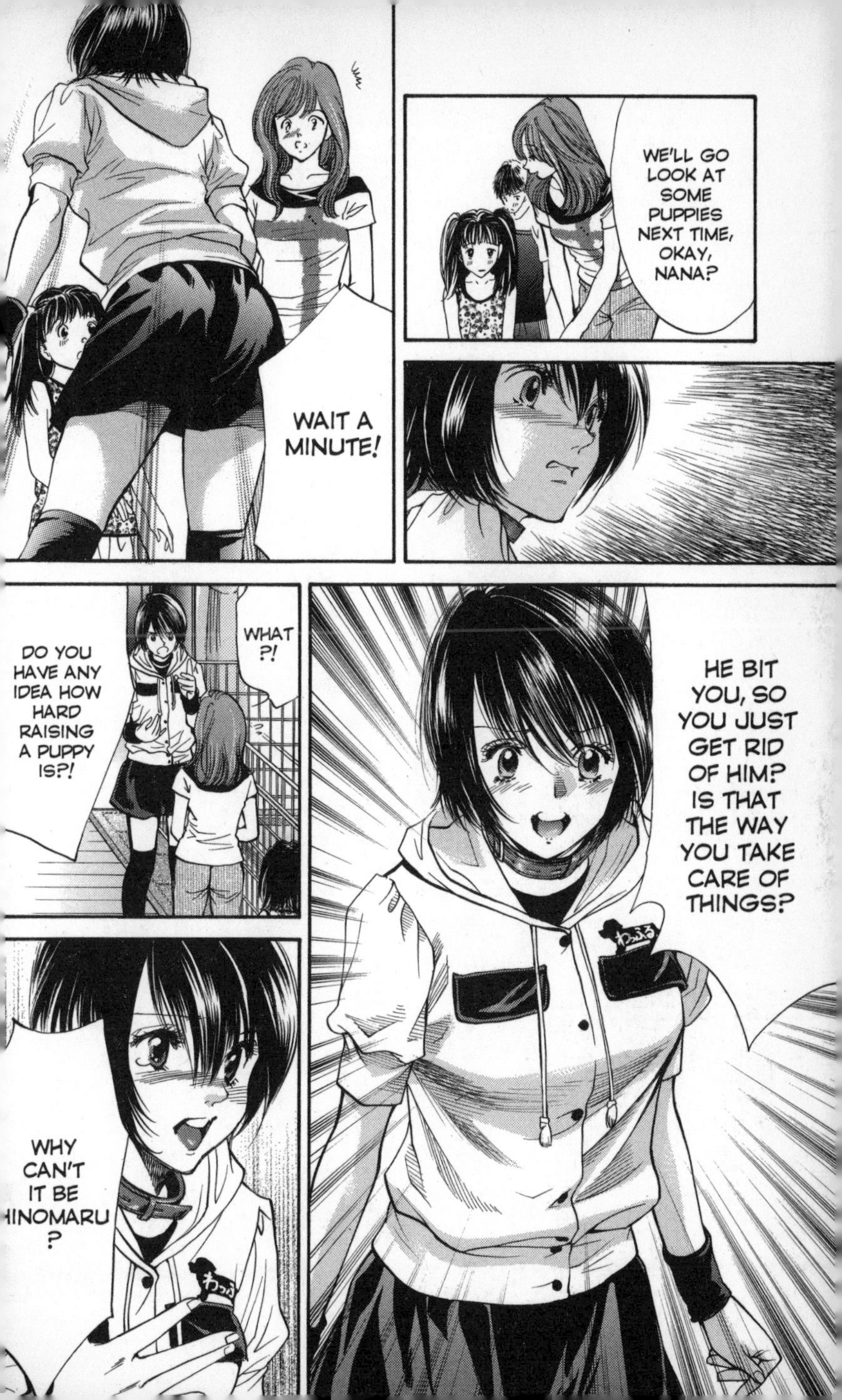
WE'LL GO LOOK AT SOME PUPPIES NEXT TIME, OKAY, NANA?
WAIT A MINUTE!
HE BIT YOU, SO YOU JUST GET RID OF HIM? IS THAT THE WAY YOU TAKE CARE OF THINGS?
WHAT?!
DO YOU HAVE ANY IDEA HOW HARD RAISING A PUPPY IS?!
WHY CAN'T IT BE INOMARU ?

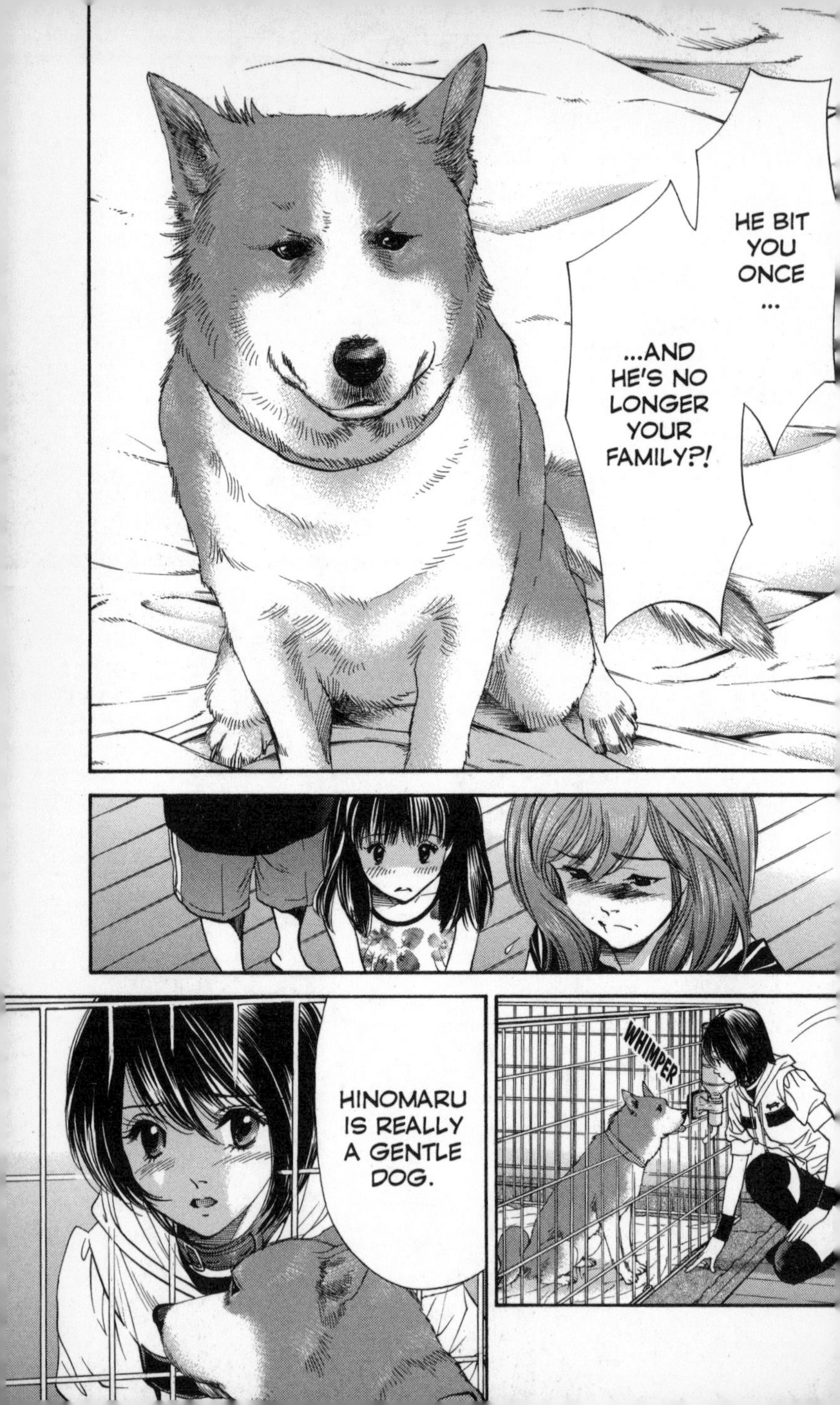
HE BIT YOU ONCE ...
...AND HE'S NO LONGER YOUR FAMILY?!
WHIMPER
HINOMARU IS REALLY A GENTLE DOG.

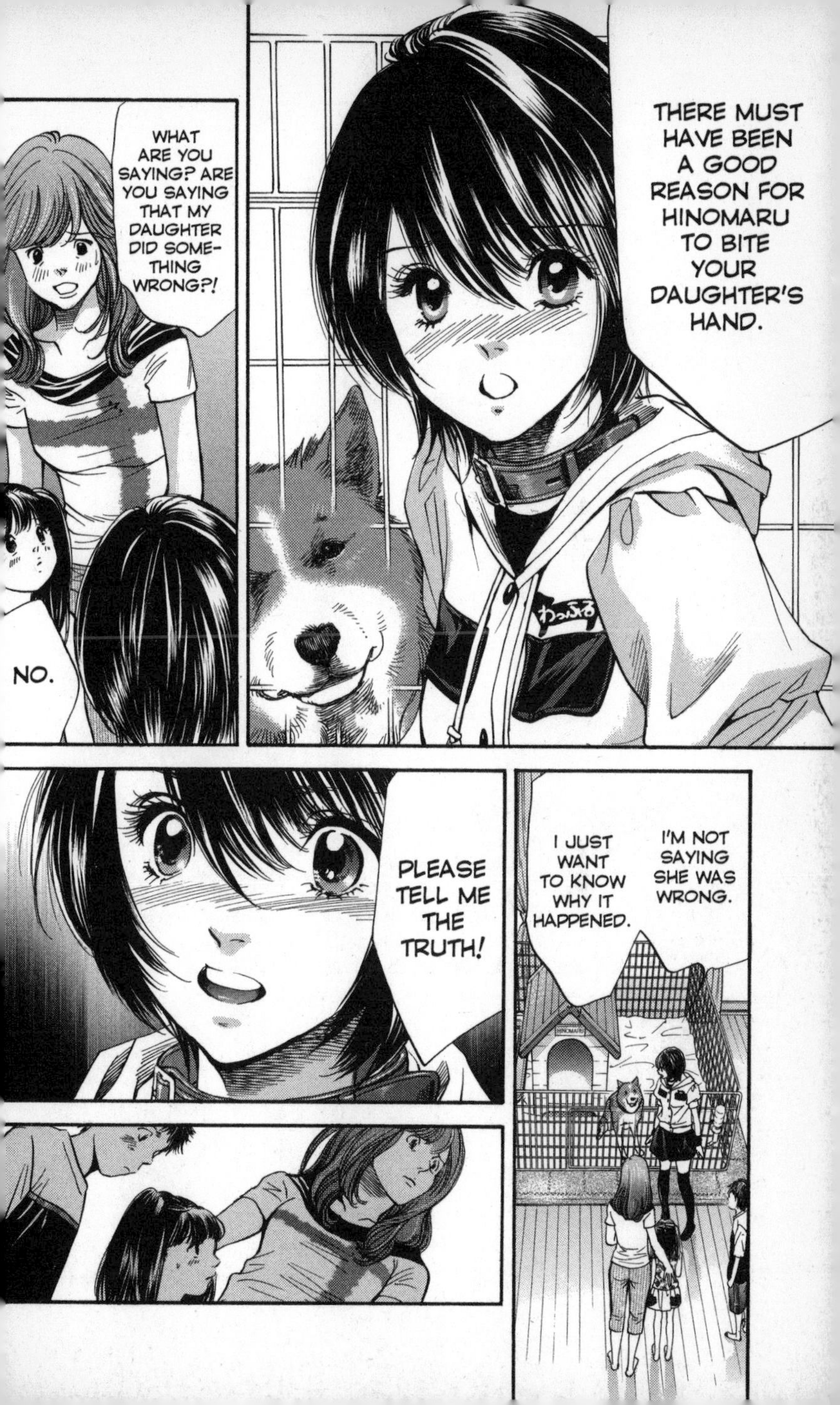
THERE MUST HAVE BEEN A GOOD REASON FOR HINOMARU TO BITE YOUR DAUGHTER'S HAND.
WHAT ARE YOU SAYING? ARE YOU SAYING THAT MY DAUGHTER DID SOMETHING WRONG?!
NO.
I'M NOT SAYING SHE WAS WRONG.
I JUST WANT TO KNOW WHY IT HAPPENED.
PLEASE TELL ME THE TRUTH!

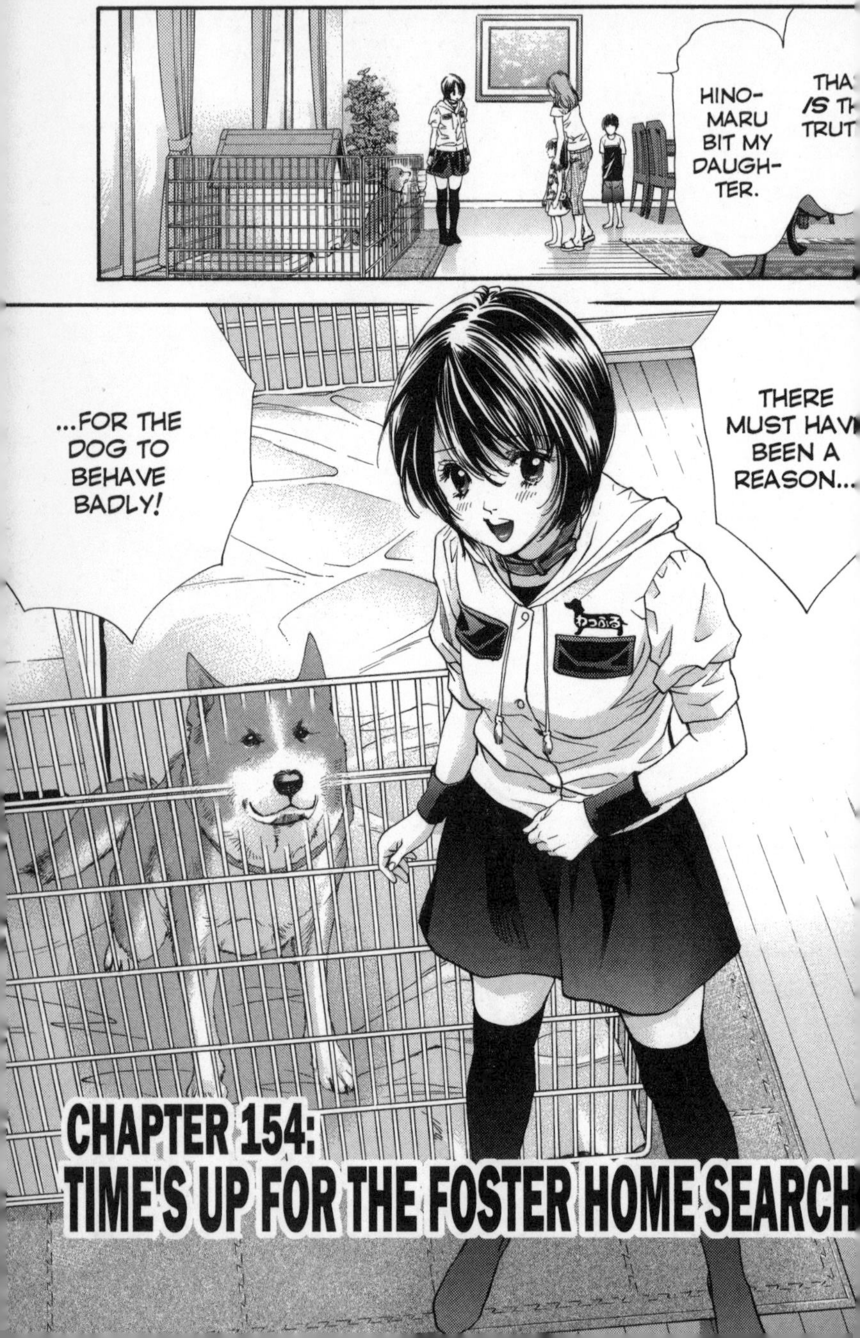
THA IS TH TRUT
HINO-MARU BIT MY DAUGH-TER.
THERE MUST HAV BEEN A REASON...
...FOR THE DOG TO BEHAVE BADLY!
CHAPTER 154: TIME'S UP FOR THE FOSTER HOME SEARCH

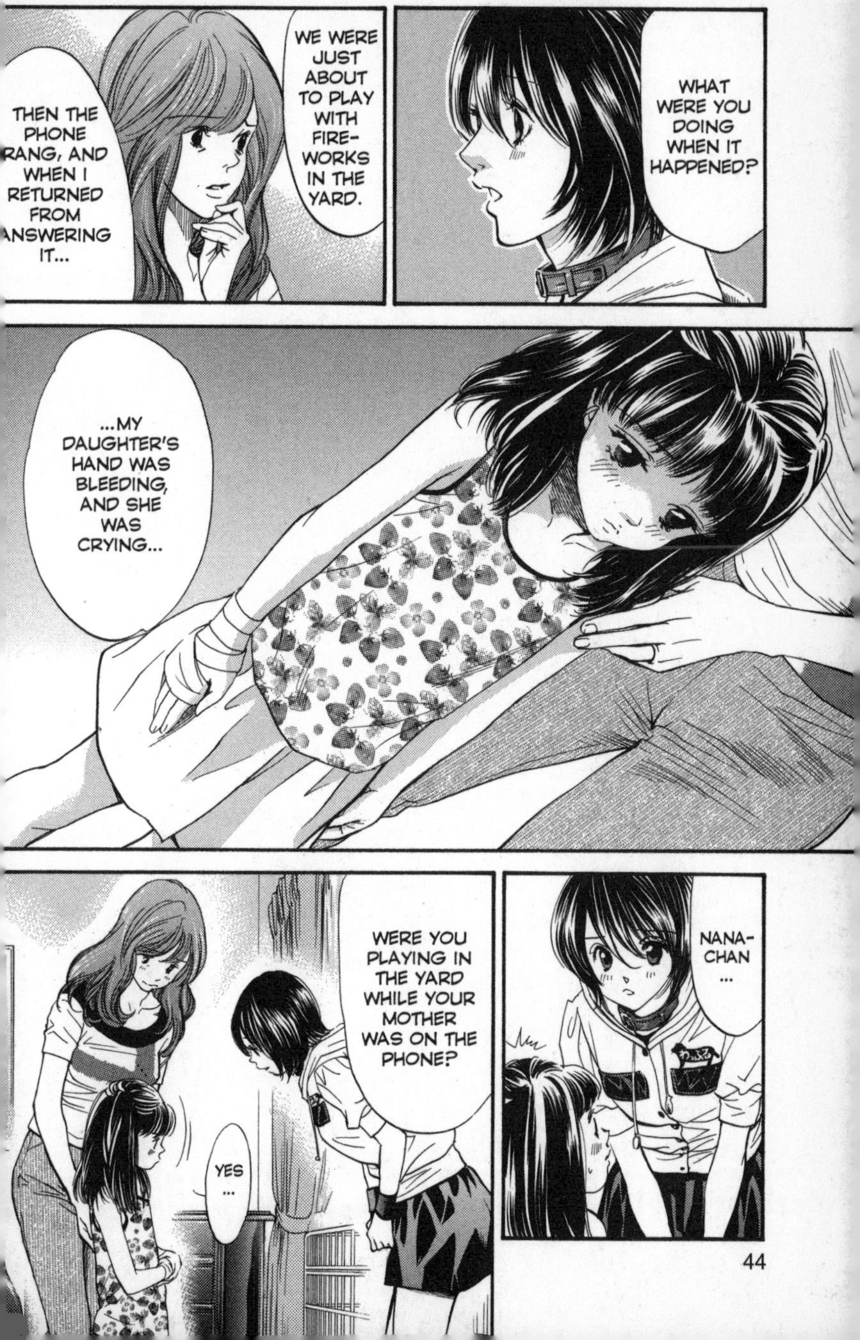
WHAT WERE YOU DOING WHEN IT HAPPENED?
WE WERE JUST ABOUT TO PLAY WITH FIRE-WORKS IN THE YARD.
THEN THE PHONE RANG, AND WHEN I RETURNED FROM ANSWERING IT...
...MY DAUGHTER'S HAND WAS BLEEDING, AND SHE WAS CRYING...
NANA-CHAN ...
WERE YOU PLAYING IN THE YARD WHILE YOUR MOTHER WAS ON THE PHONE?
YES ...

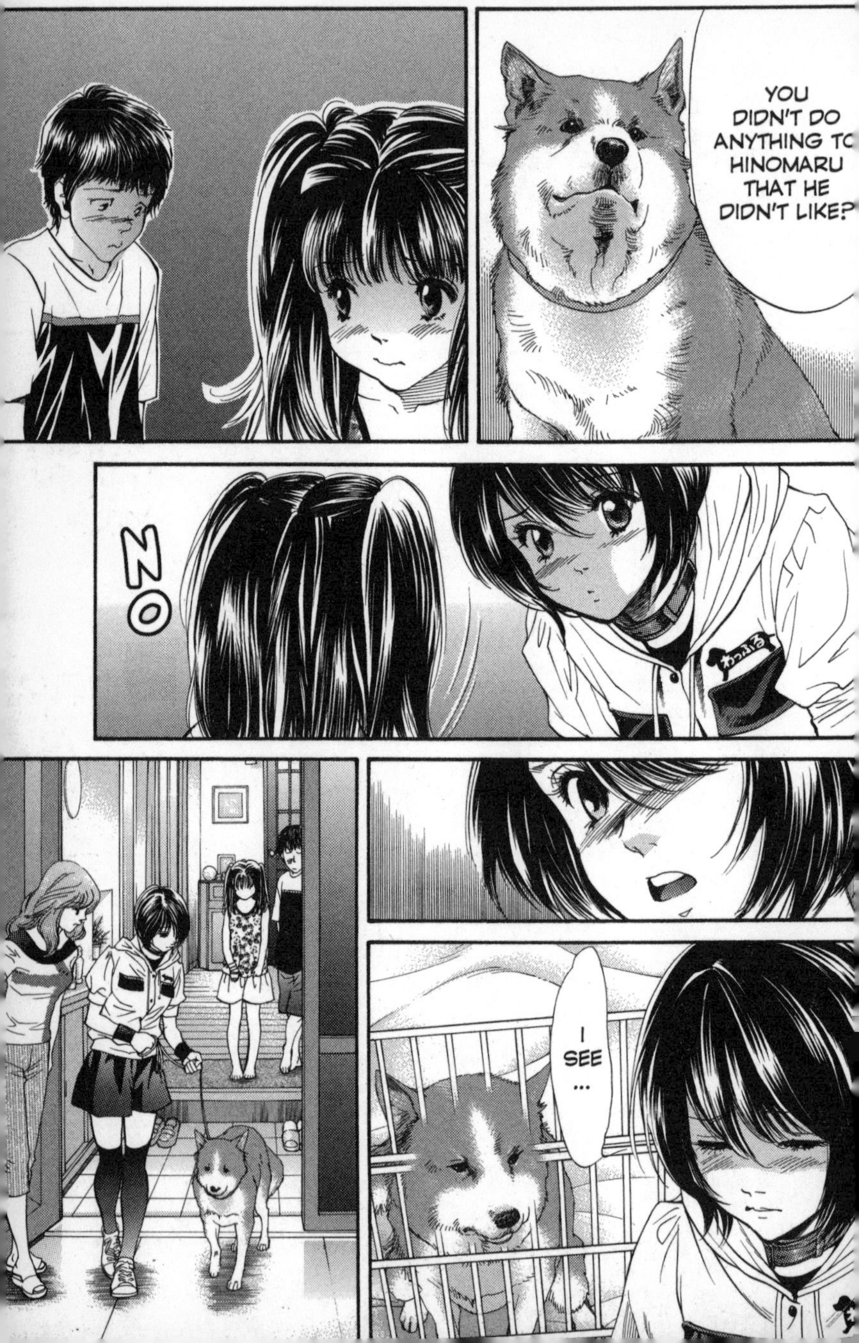
YOU DIDN'T DO ANYTHING TO HINOMARU THAT HE DIDN'T LIKE?
NO
I SEE ...

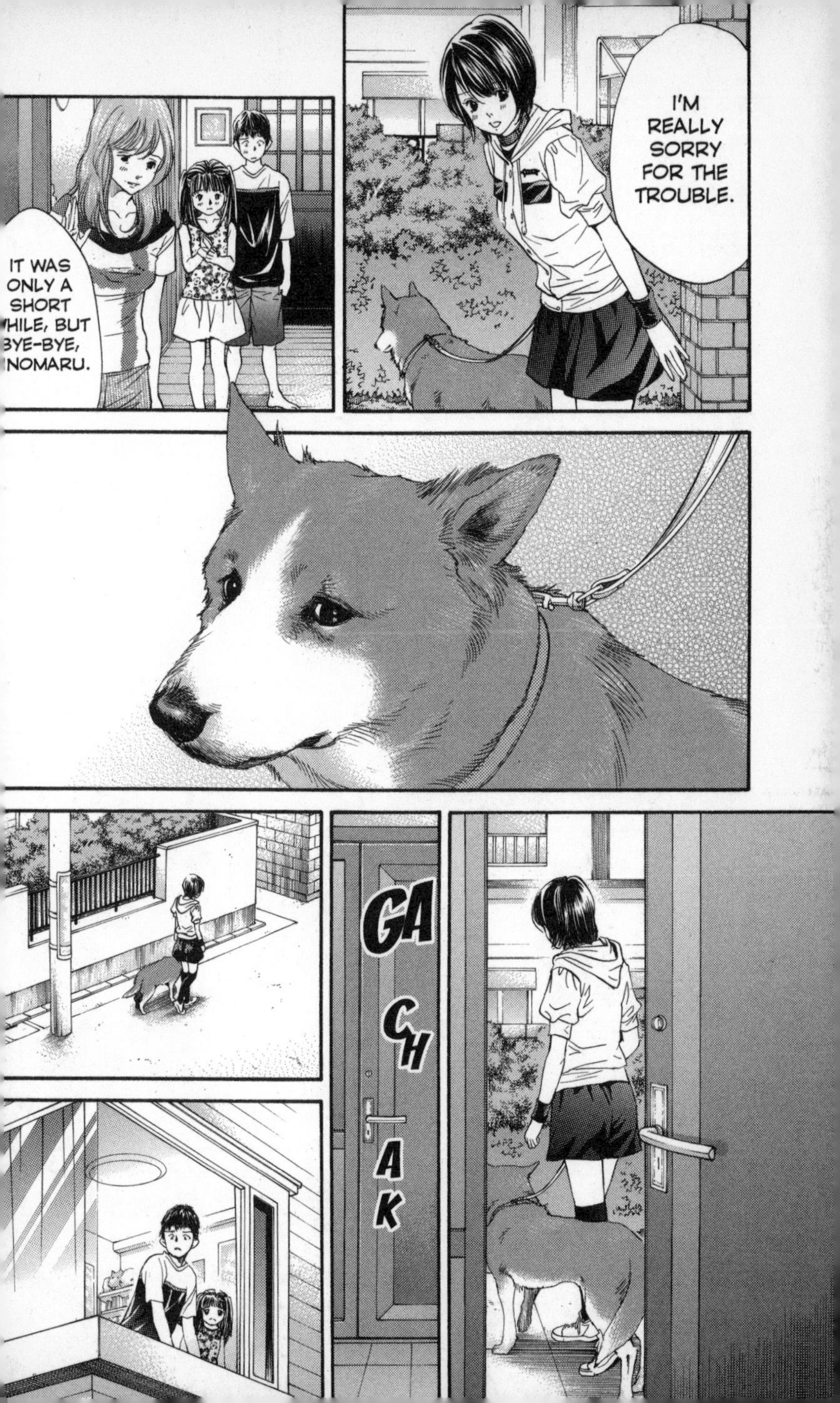
I'M REALLY SORRY FOR THE TROUBLE.
IT WAS ONLY A SHORT WHILE, BUT BYE-BYE, INOMARU.
GA CH AK

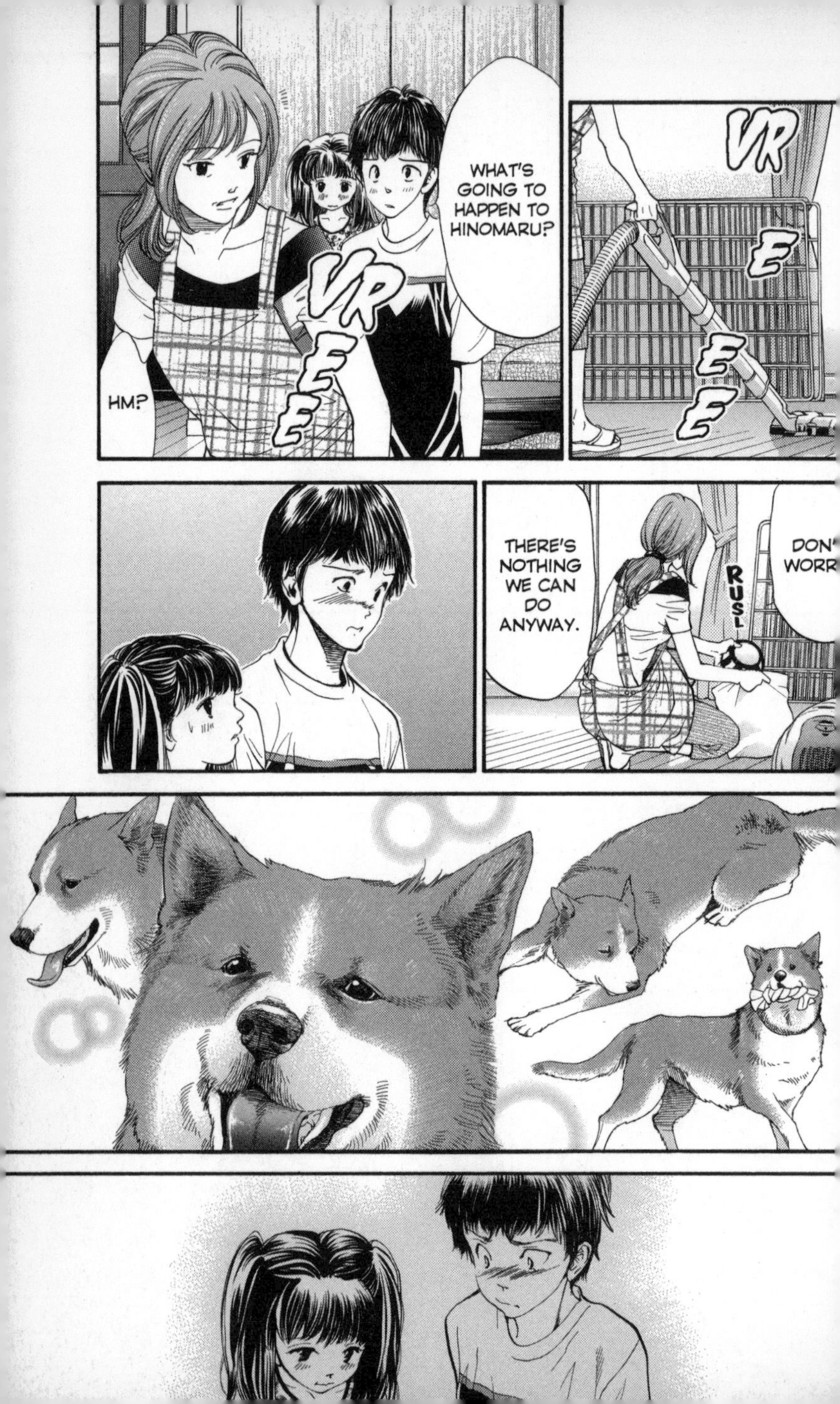
VREEE
WHAT'S GOING TO HAPPEN TO HINOMARU?
VREEE
HM?
DON' WORR
RUSL
THERE'S NOTHING WE CAN DO ANYWAY.

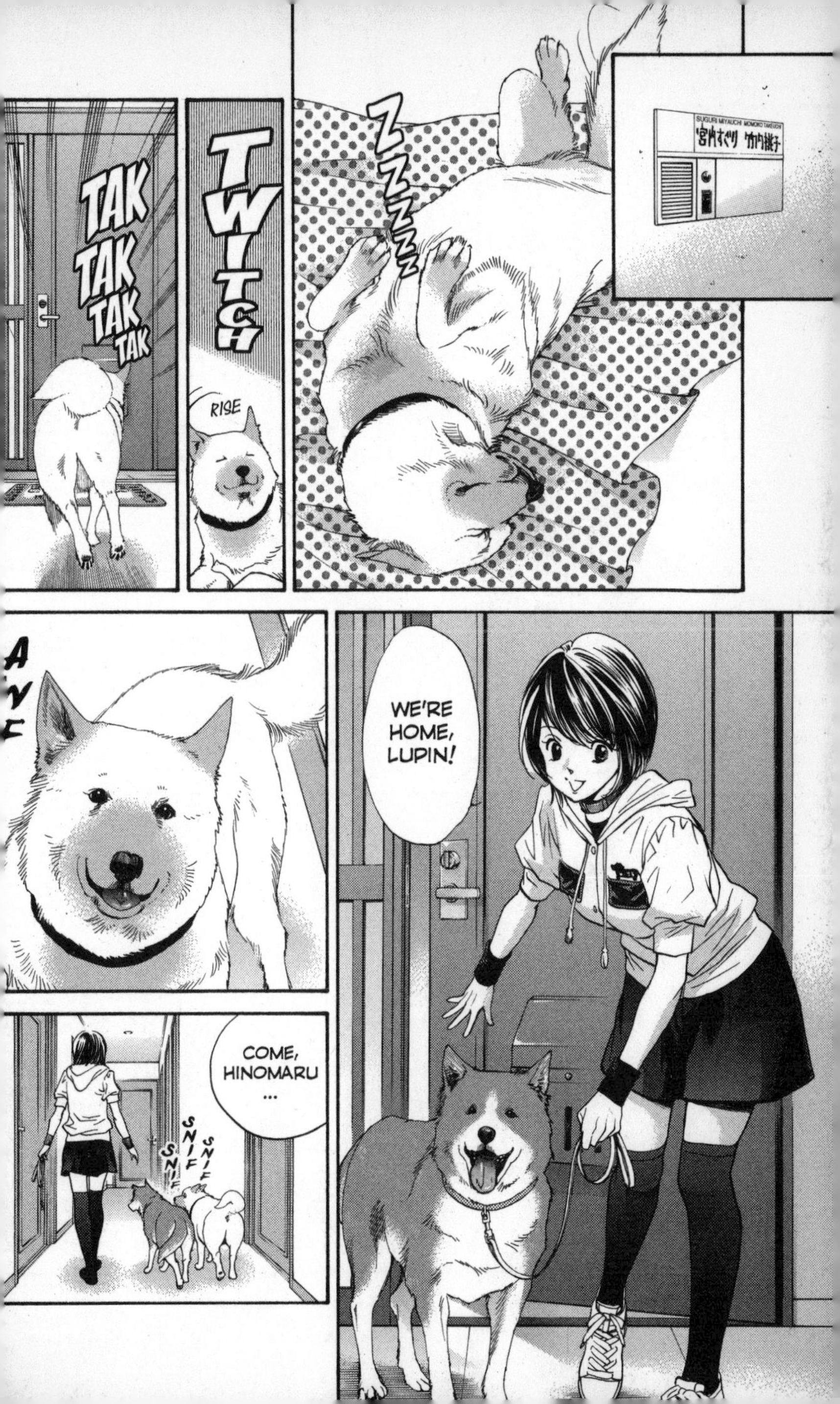

SUGURI MIYAUCHI MOMOKO TAKEUCHI
宮内すぐり 竹内桃子
ZZZZZ
TWITCH
RISE
TAK TAK TAK TAK
WE'RE HOME, LUPIN!
COME, HINOMARU ...
SNIF SNIF
SNIF SNIF

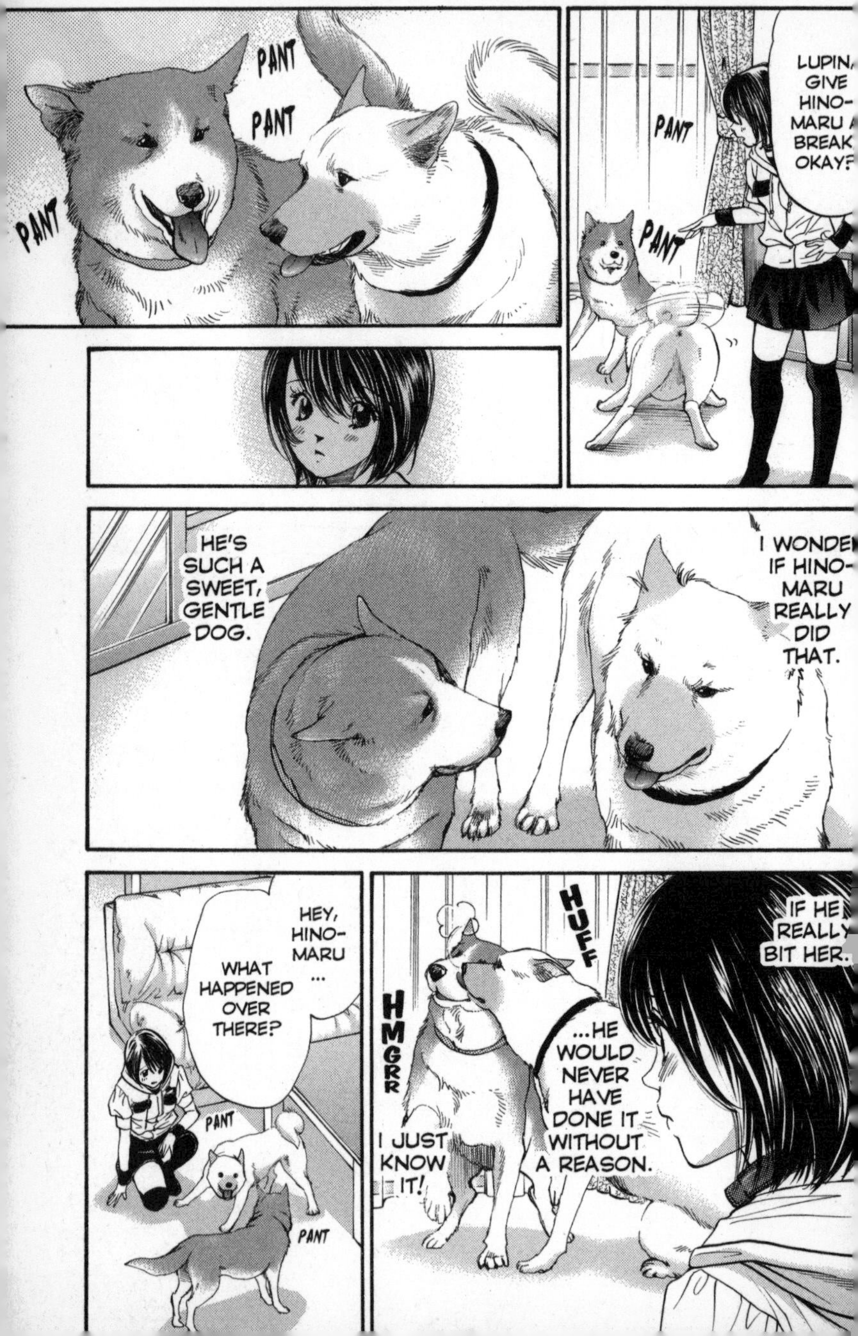
LUPIN, GIVE HINO-MARU A BREAK OKAY?
PANT
PANT
PANT
PANT
PANT
I WONDER IF HINO-MARU REALLY DID THAT.
HE'S SUCH A SWEET, GENTLE DOG.
IF HE REALLY BIT HER...
HUFF
...HE WOULD NEVER HAVE DONE IT WITHOUT A REASON.
HMGRR
I JUST KNOW IT!
HEY, HINO-MARU...
WHAT HAPPENED OVER THERE?
PANT
PANT

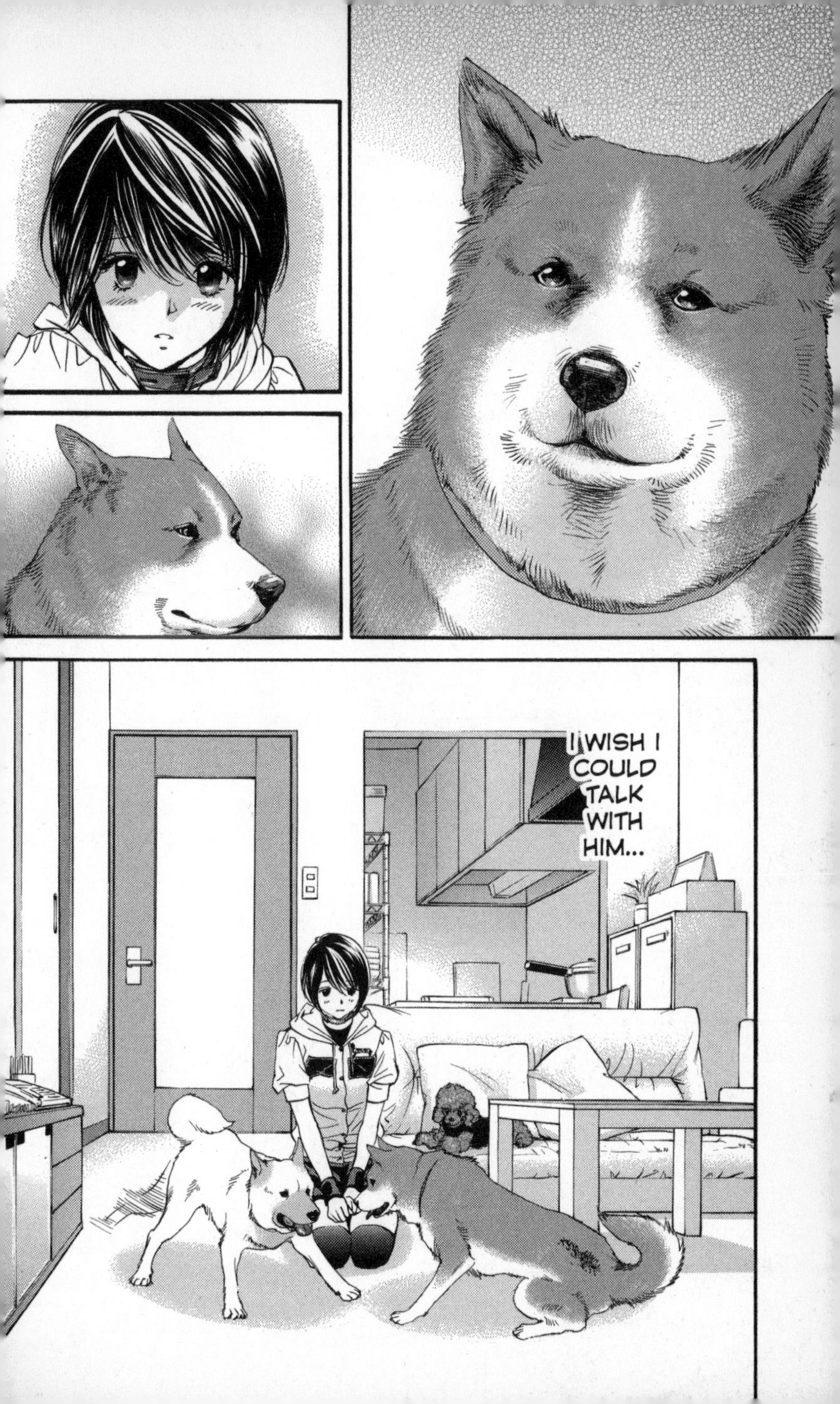
I WISH I COULD TALK WITH HIM...

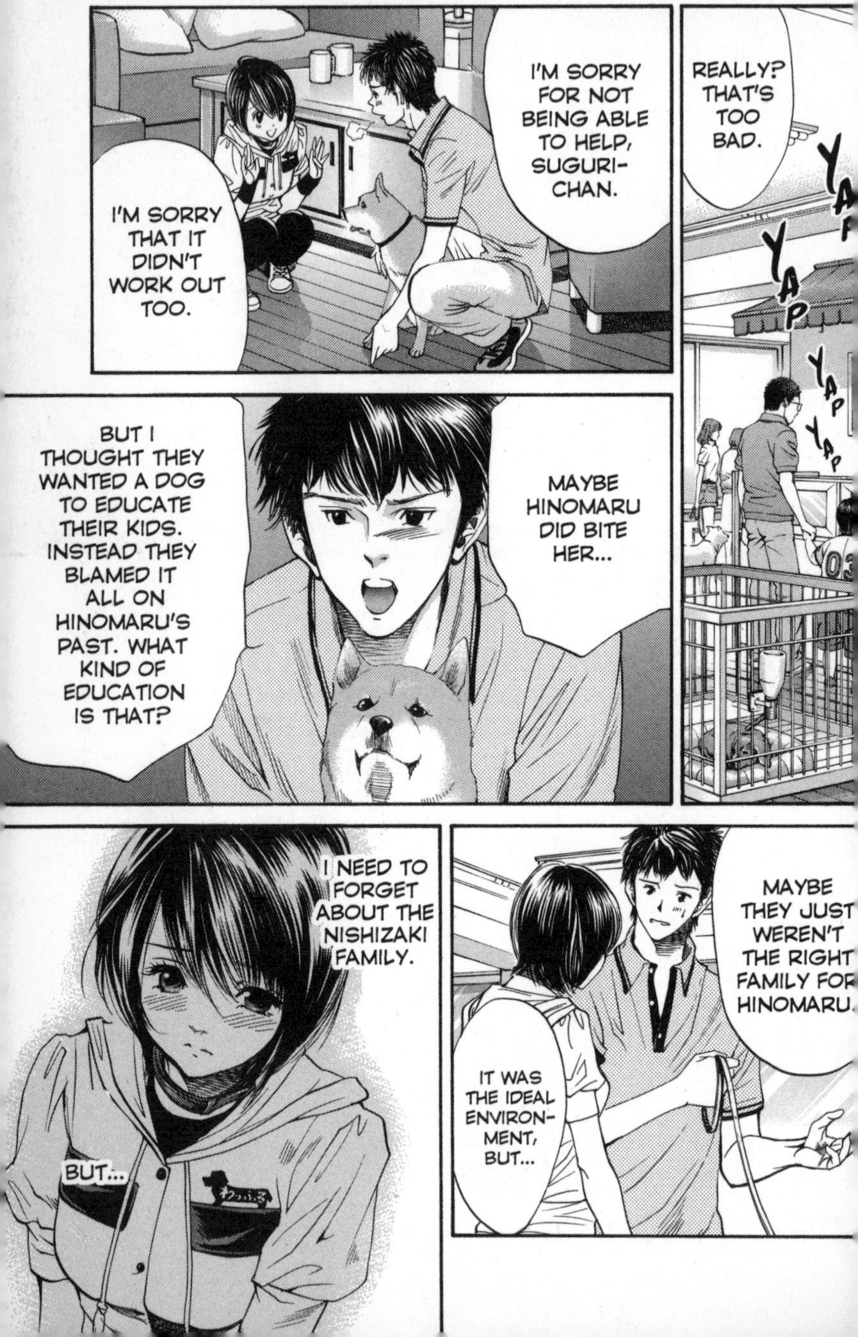
REALLY? THAT'S TOO BAD.
YAP
YAP
YAP
YAP
YAP
I'M SORRY FOR NOT BEING ABLE TO HELP, SUGURI-CHAN.
I'M SORRY THAT IT DIDN'T WORK OUT TOO.
MAYBE HINOMARU DID BITE HER...
BUT I THOUGHT THEY WANTED A DOG TO EDUCATE THEIR KIDS. INSTEAD THEY BLAMED IT ALL ON HINOMARU'S PAST. WHAT KIND OF EDUCATION IS THAT?
MAYBE THEY JUST WEREN'T THE RIGHT FAMILY FOR HINOMARU.
IT WAS THE IDEAL ENVIRON-MENT, BUT...
I NEED TO FORGET ABOUT THE NISHIZAKI FAMILY.
BUT...

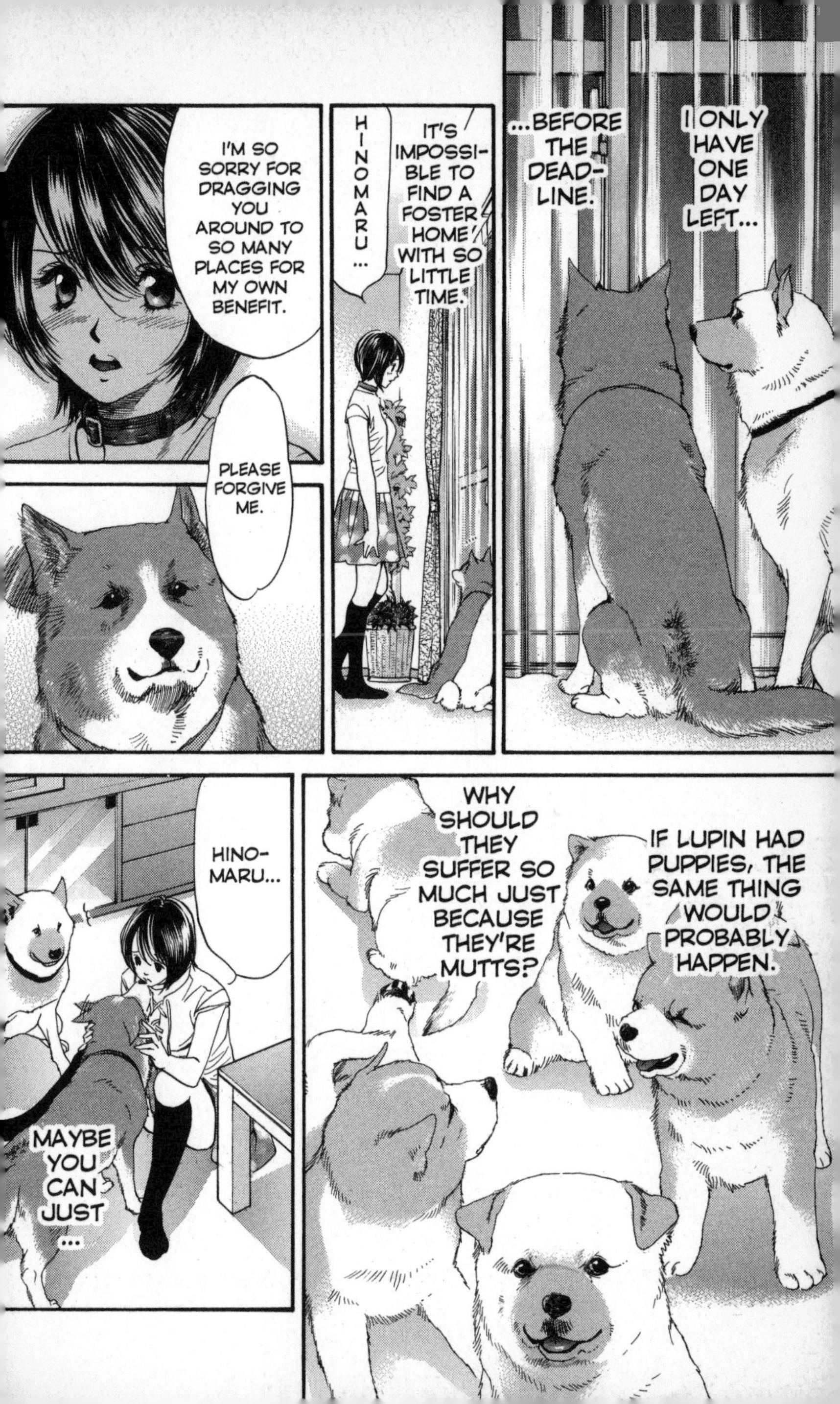
I ONLY HAVE ONE DAY LEFT...
...BEFORE THE DEAD-LINE.
IT'S IMPOSSI-BLE TO FIND A FOSTER HOME WITH SO LITTLE TIME.
HINOMARU...
I'M SO SORRY FOR DRAGGING YOU AROUND TO SO MANY PLACES FOR MY OWN BENEFIT.
PLEASE FORGIVE ME.
IF LUPIN HAD PUPPIES, THE SAME THING WOULD PROBABLY HAPPEN.
WHY SHOULD THEY SUFFER SO MUCH JUST BECAUSE THEY'RE MUTTS?
HINO-MARU...
MAYBE YOU CAN JUST ...

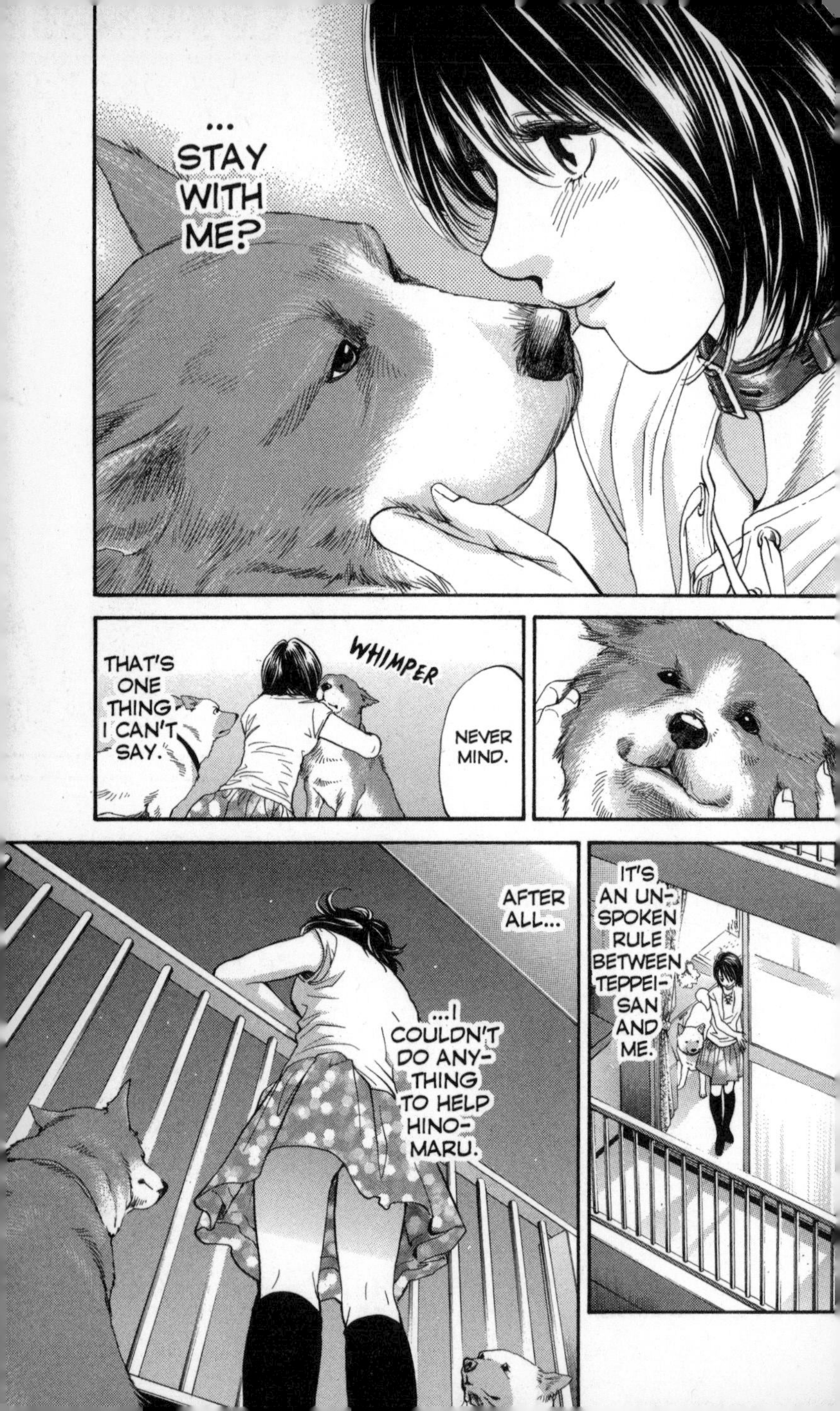

... STAY WITH ME?
NEVER MIND.
WHIMPER
THAT'S ONE THING I CAN'T SAY.
IT'S AN UN-SPOKEN RULE BETWEEN TEPPEI-SAN AND ME.
AFTER ALL...
...I COULDN'T DO ANY-THING TO HELP HINO-MARU.

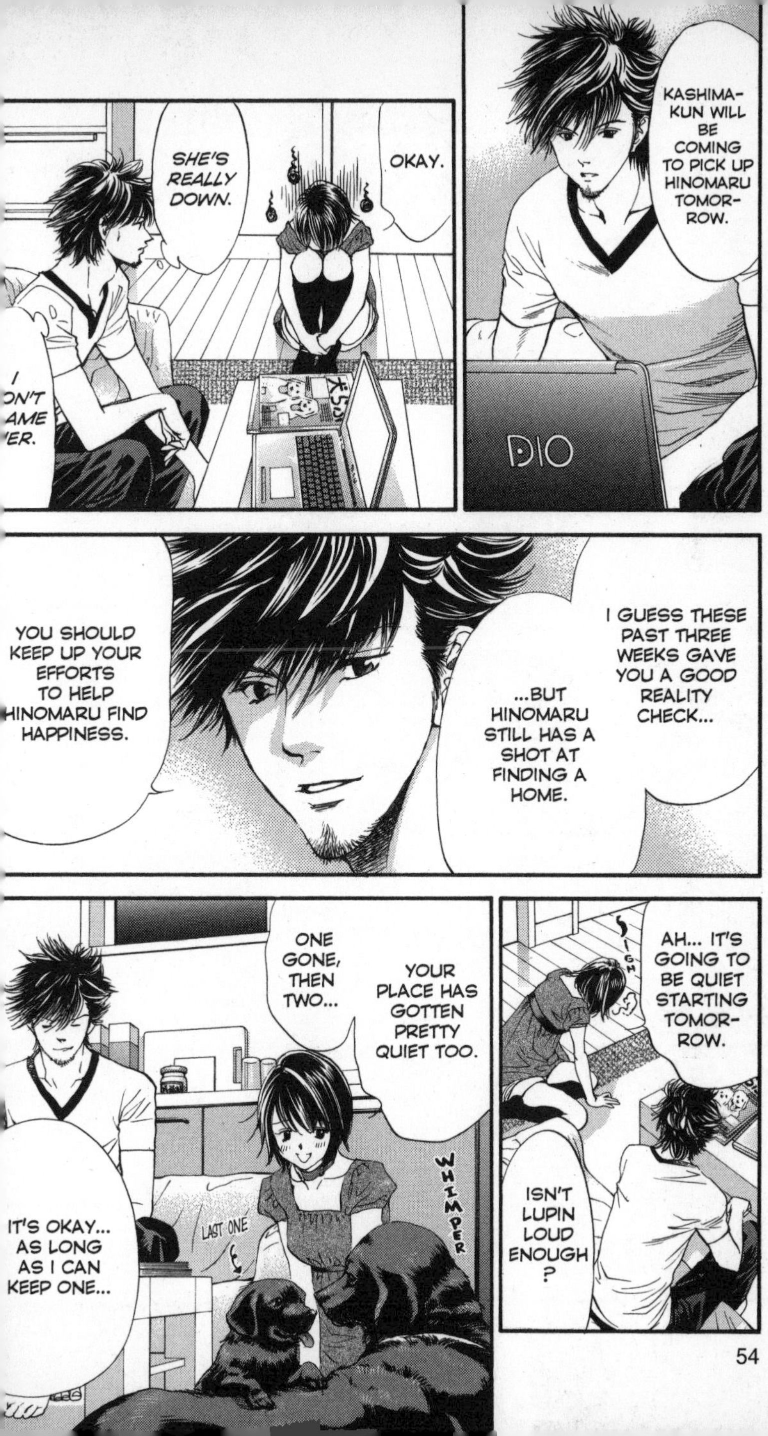
KASHIMA-KUN WILL BE COMING TO PICK UP HINOMARU TOMORROW.
OKAY.
SHE'S REALLY DOWN.
I GUESS THESE PAST THREE WEEKS GAVE YOU A GOOD REALITY CHECK...
...BUT HINOMARU STILL HAS A SHOT AT FINDING A HOME.
YOU SHOULD KEEP UP YOUR EFFORTS TO HELP HINOMARU FIND HAPPINESS.
AH... IT'S GOING TO BE QUIET STARTING TOMORROW.
SIGH
ISN'T LUPIN LOUD ENOUGH?
ONE GONE, THEN TWO...
YOUR PLACE HAS GOTTEN PRETTY QUIET TOO.
WHIMPER
LAST ONE
IT'S OKAY... AS LONG AS I CAN KEEP ONE...

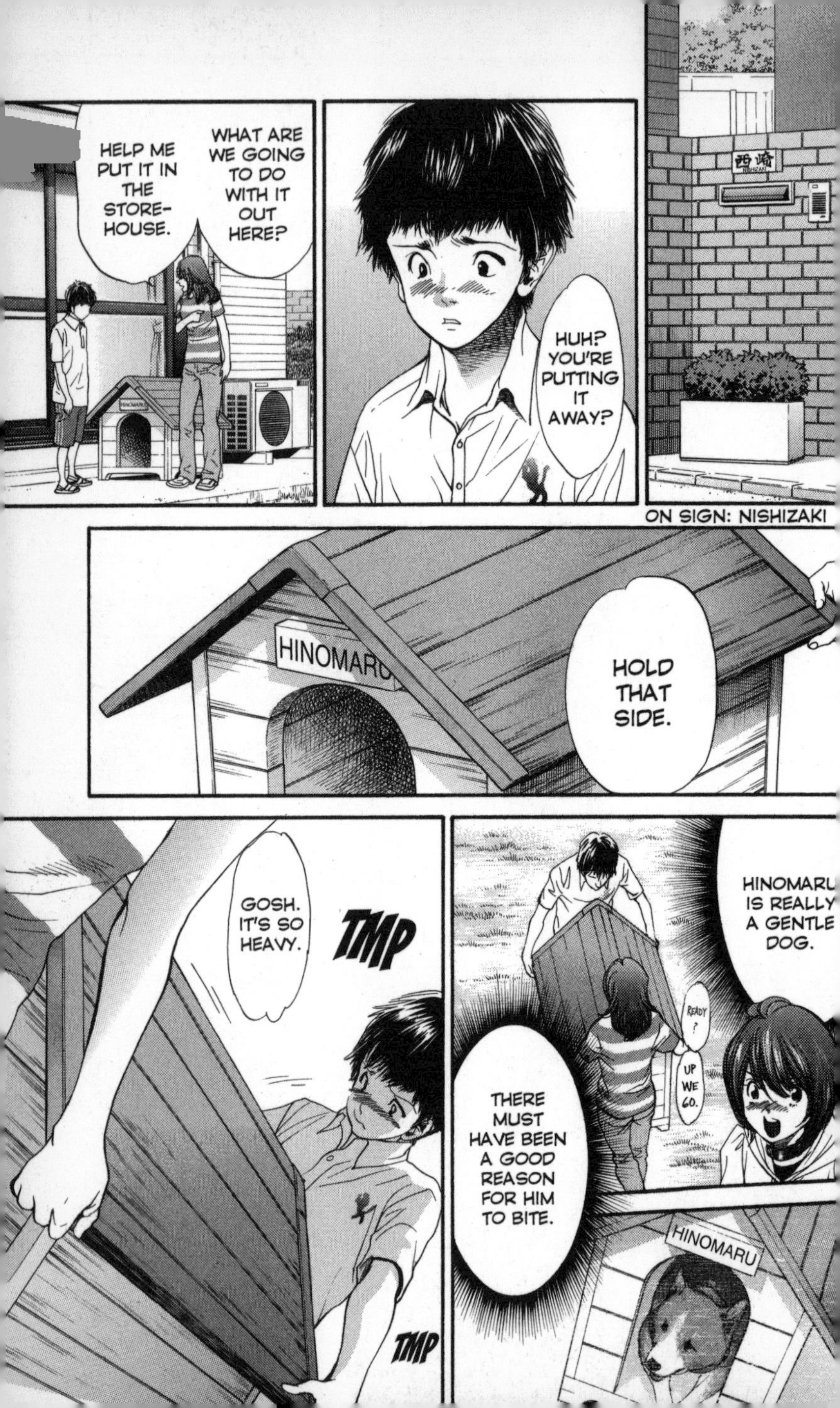

西崎
NISHIZAKI
ON SIGN: NISHIZAKI
HUH? YOU'RE PUTTING IT AWAY?
WHAT ARE WE GOING TO DO WITH IT OUT HERE?
HELP ME PUT IT IN THE STORE-HOUSE.
HINOMARU
HOLD THAT SIDE.
HINOMARU IS REALLY A GENTLE DOG.
READY?
UP WE GO.
THERE MUST HAVE BEEN A GOOD REASON FOR HIM TO BITE.
HINOMARU
TMP
GOSH. IT'S SO HEAVY.
TMP

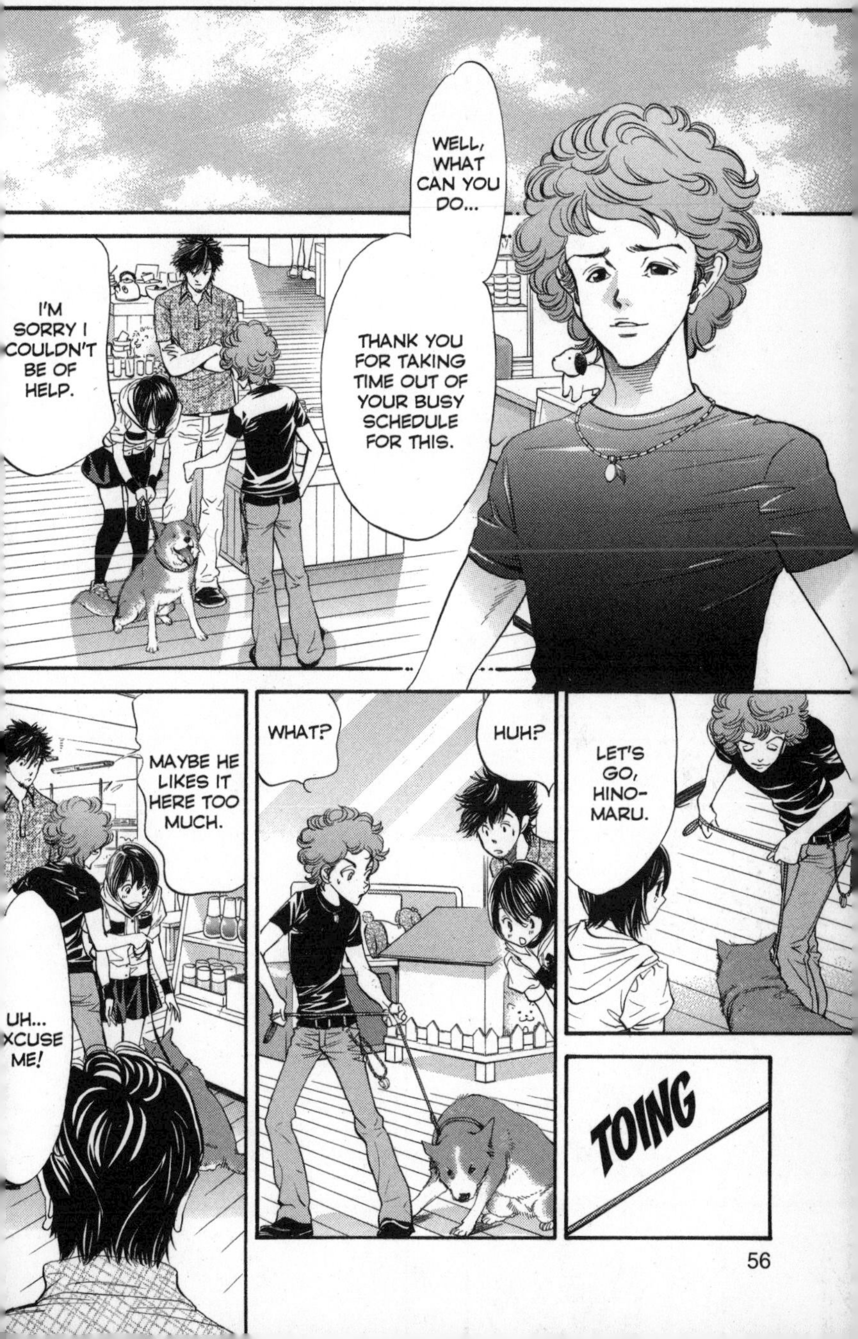
WELL, WHAT CAN YOU DO...
THANK YOU FOR TAKING TIME OUT OF YOUR BUSY SCHEDULE FOR THIS.
I'M SORRY I COULDN'T BE OF HELP.
LET'S GO, HINO-MARU.
TOING
HUH?
WHAT?
MAYBE HE LIKES IT HERE TOO MUCH.
UH... XCUSE ME!

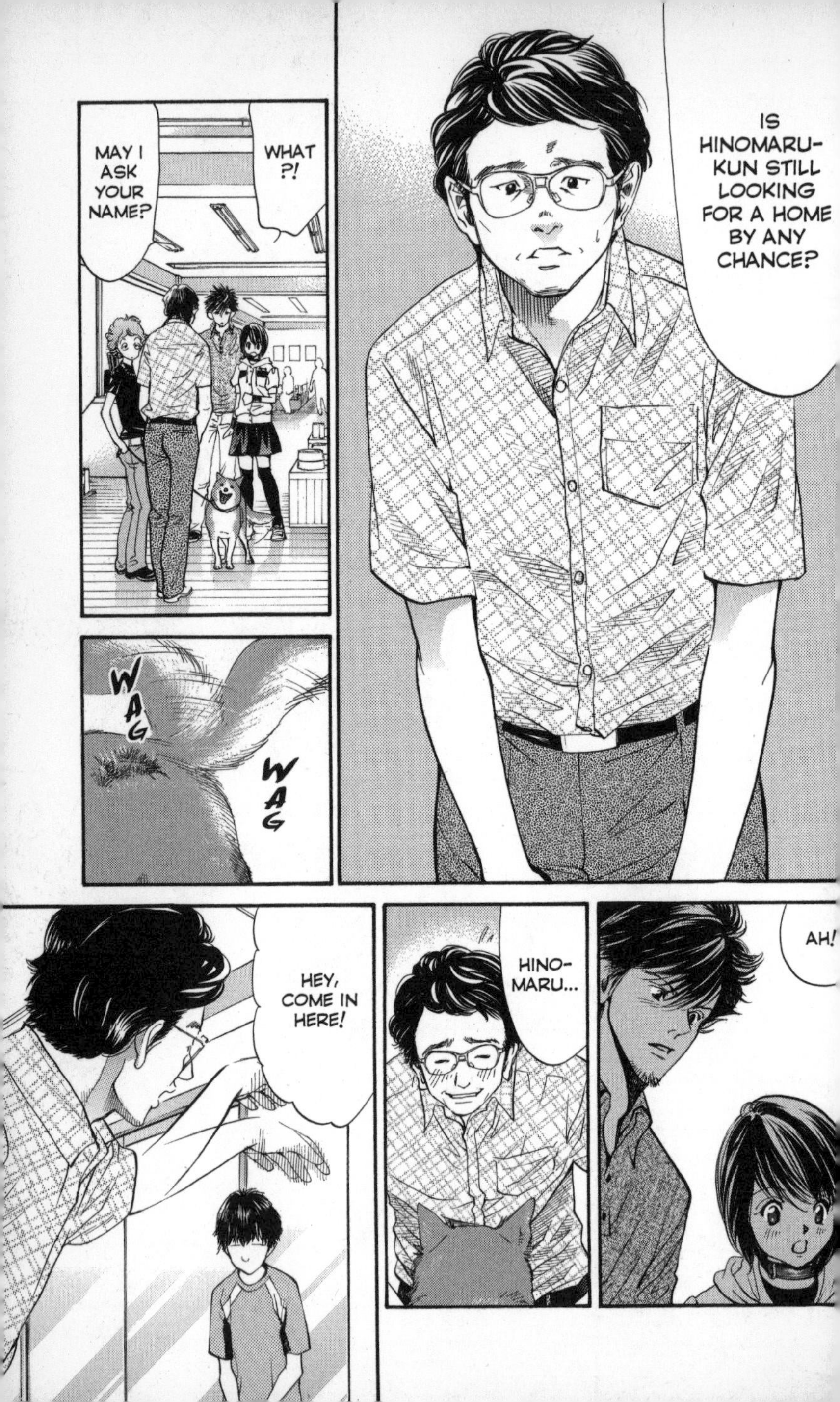
IS HINOMARU-KUN STILL LOOKING FOR A HOME BY ANY CHANCE?
WHAT ?!
MAY I ASK YOUR NAME?
WAG
WAG
AH!
HINO-MARU...
HEY, COME IN HERE!

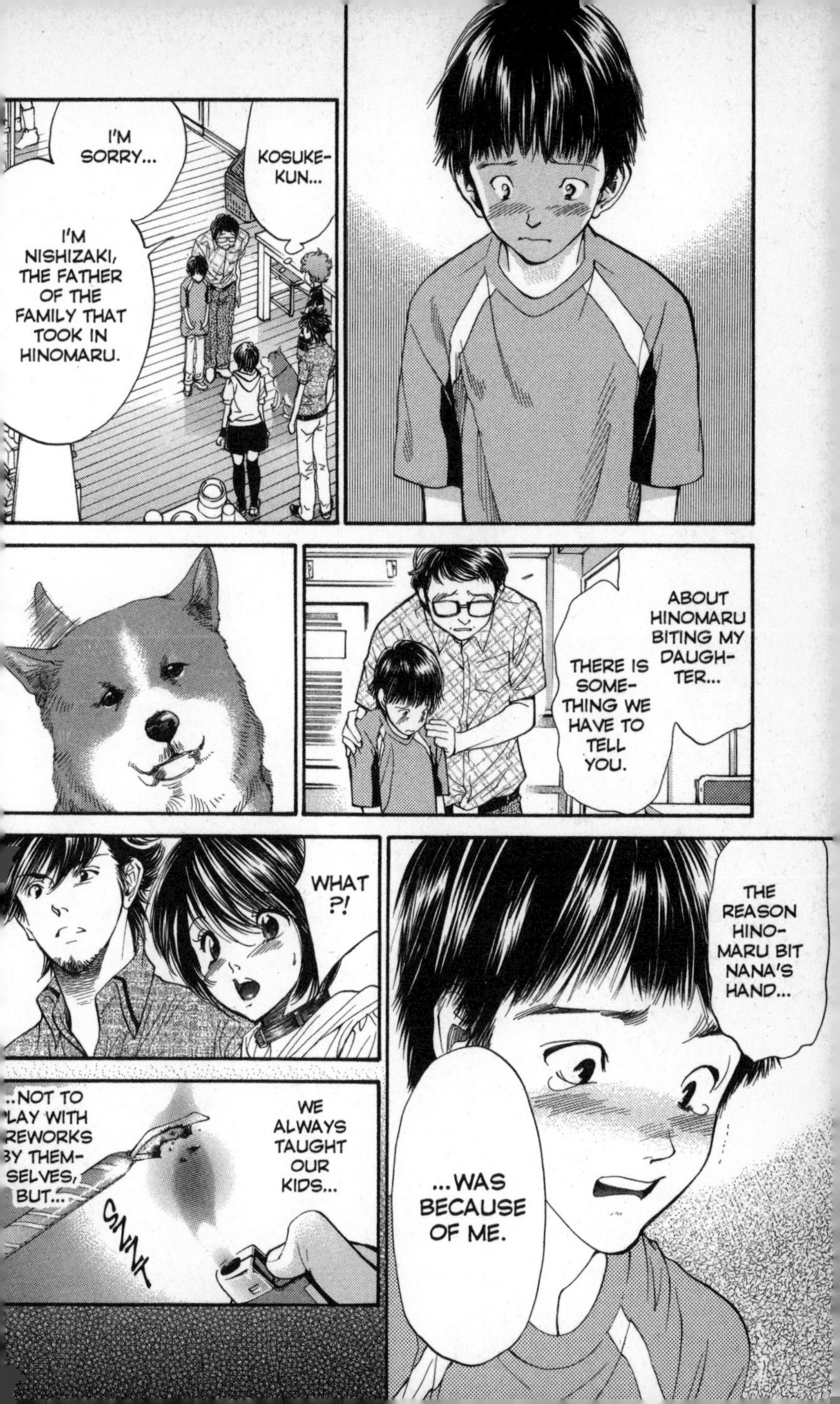
KOSUKE-KUN...
I'M SORRY...
I'M NISHIZAKI, THE FATHER OF THE FAMILY THAT TOOK IN HINOMARU.
ABOUT HINOMARU BITING MY DAUGHTER...
THERE IS SOMETHING WE HAVE TO TELL YOU.
THE REASON HINOMARU BIT NANA'S HAND...
...WAS BECAUSE OF ME.
WHAT?!
WE ALWAYS TAUGHT OUR KIDS...
...NOT TO LAY WITH REWORKS BY THEMSELVES, BUT...
SNNK

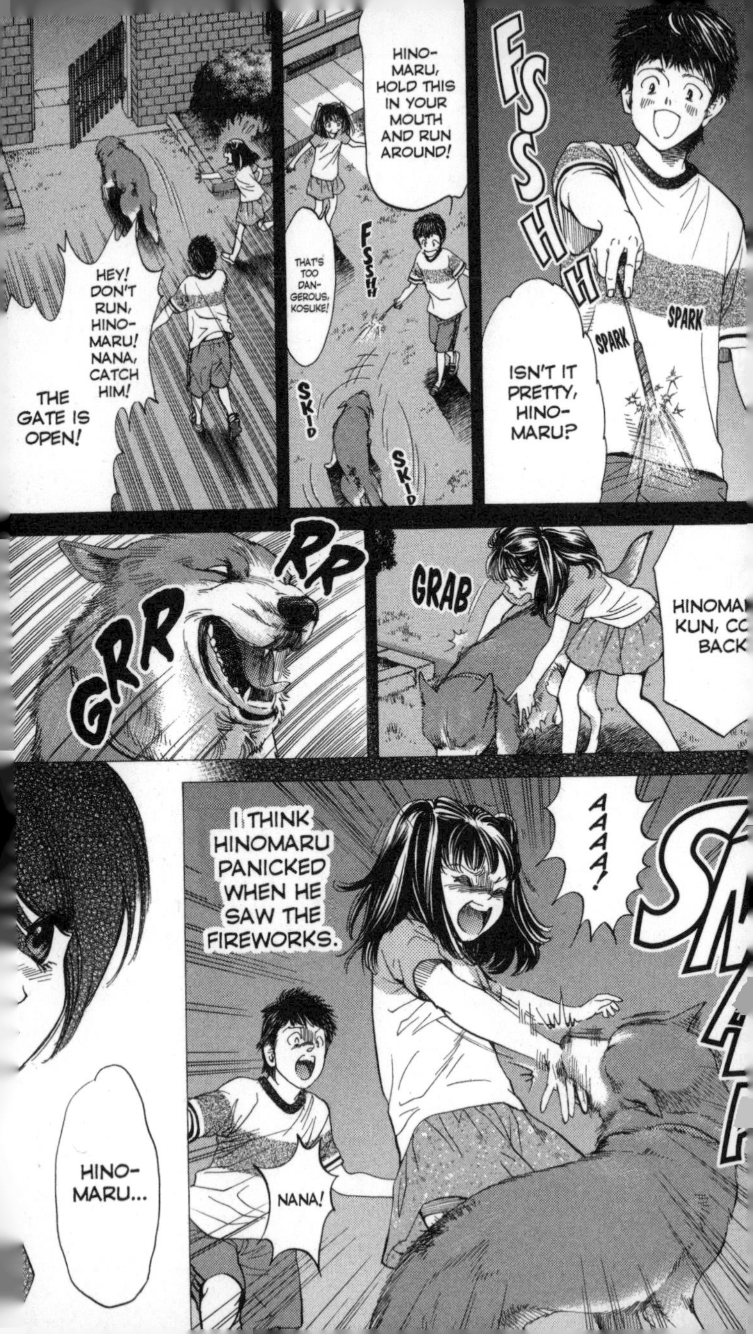
FSSHH
SPARK
SPARK
ISN'T IT PRETTY, HINO-MARU?
HINO-MARU, HOLD THIS IN YOUR MOUTH AND RUN AROUND!
FSSHH
THAT'S TOO DAN-GEROUS, KOSUKE!
SKID
SKID
HEY! DON'T RUN, HINO-MARU! NANA, CATCH HIM!
THE GATE IS OPEN!
HINOMA KUN, CO BACK
GRAB
RR
GRR
AAAA!
I THINK HINOMARU PANICKED WHEN HE SAW THE FIREWORKS.
NANA!
HINO-MARU...

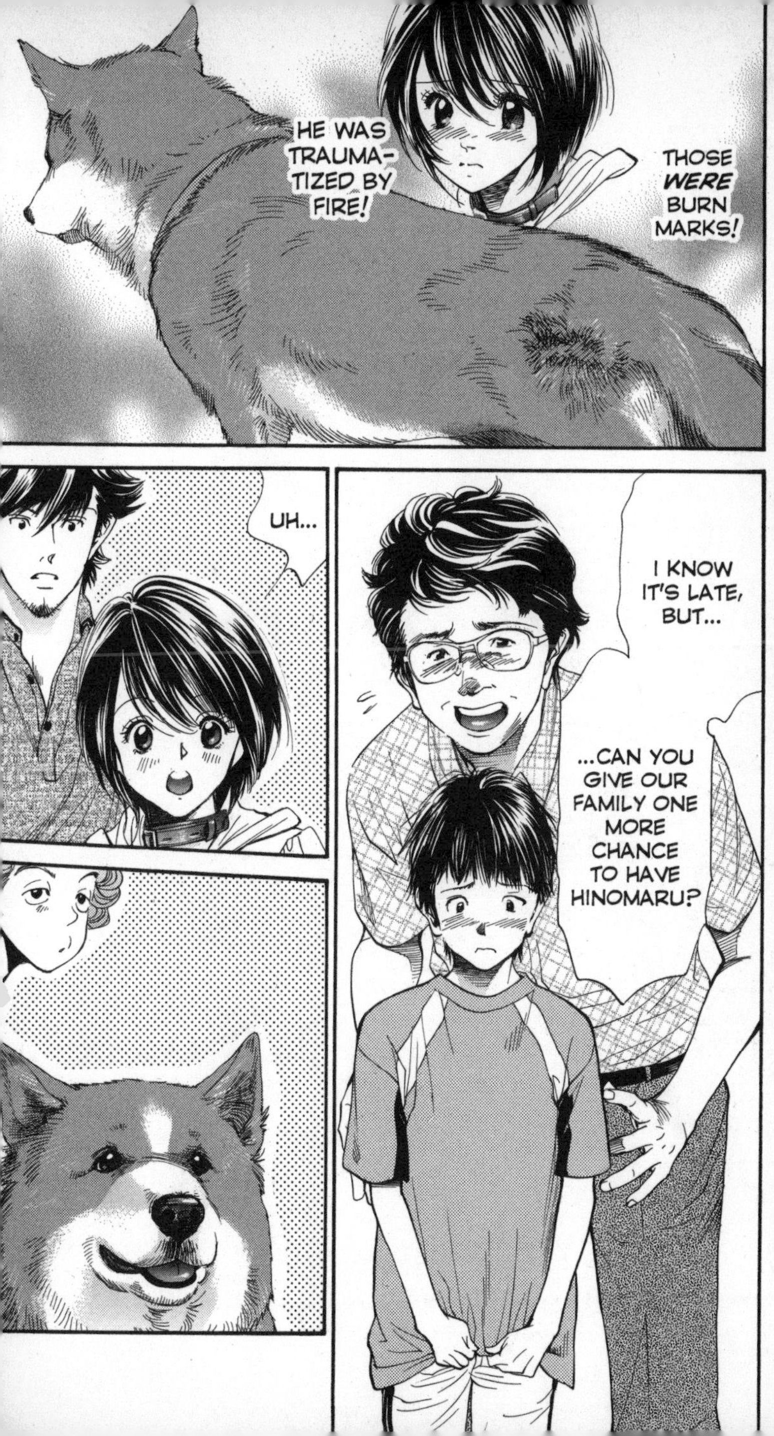
THOSE *WERE* BURN MARKS!
HE WAS TRAUMATIZED BY FIRE!
I KNOW IT'S LATE, BUT...
...CAN YOU GIVE OUR FAMILY ONE MORE CHANCE TO HAVE HINOMARU?
UH...

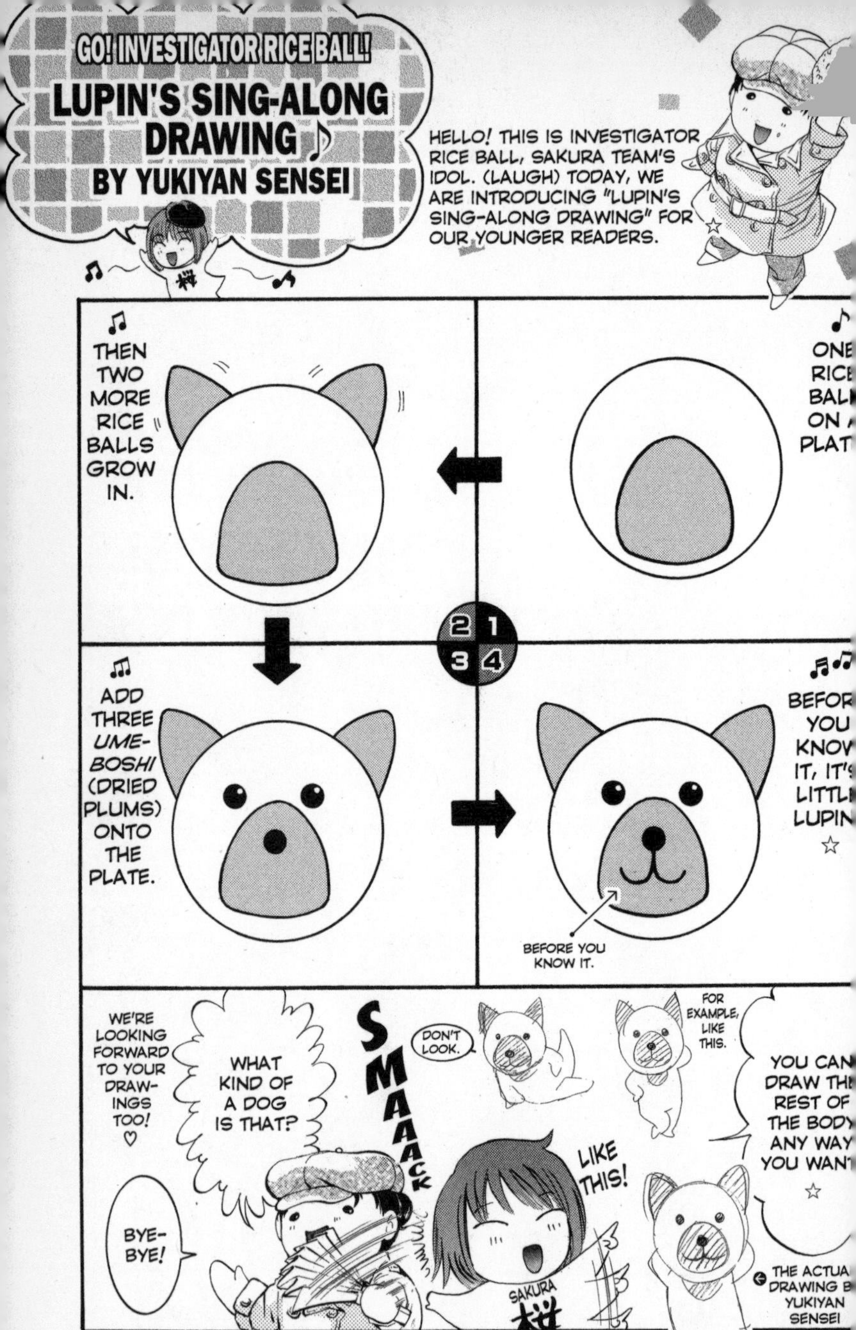
GO! INVESTIGATOR RICE BALL!
LUPIN'S SING-ALONG DRAWING ♪
BY YUKIYAN SENSEI
HELLO! THIS IS INVESTIGATOR RICE BALL, SAKURA TEAM'S IDOL. (LAUGH) TODAY, WE ARE INTRODUCING "LUPIN'S SING-ALONG DRAWING" FOR OUR YOUNGER READERS.
1 ONE RICE BAL ON PLAT
2 THEN TWO MORE RICE BALLS GROW IN.
3 ADD THREE UME-BOSHI (DRIED PLUMS) ONTO THE PLATE.
4 BEFOR YOU KNOW IT, IT'S LITTL LUPIN ☆
BEFORE YOU KNOW IT.
YOU CAN DRAW TH REST OF THE BOD ANY WA YOU WAN ☆
FOR EXAMPLE, LIKE THIS.
DON'T LOOK.
THE ACTUA DRAWING B YUKIYAN SENSEI
LIKE THIS!
SAKURA 桜
SMAAACK
WHAT KIND OF A DOG IS THAT?
WE'RE LOOKING FORWARD TO YOUR DRAW-INGS TOO! ♡
BYE-BYE!

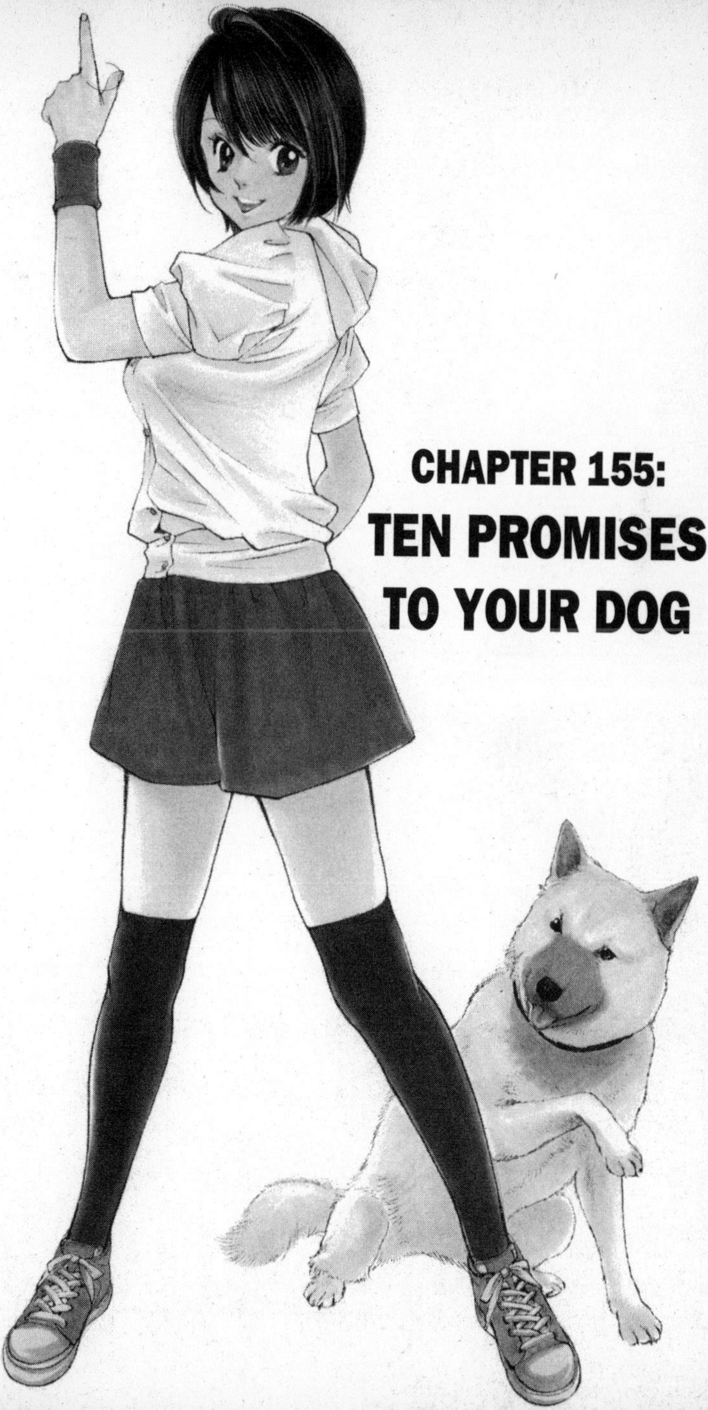

CHAPTER 155:
TEN PROMISES TO YOUR DOG

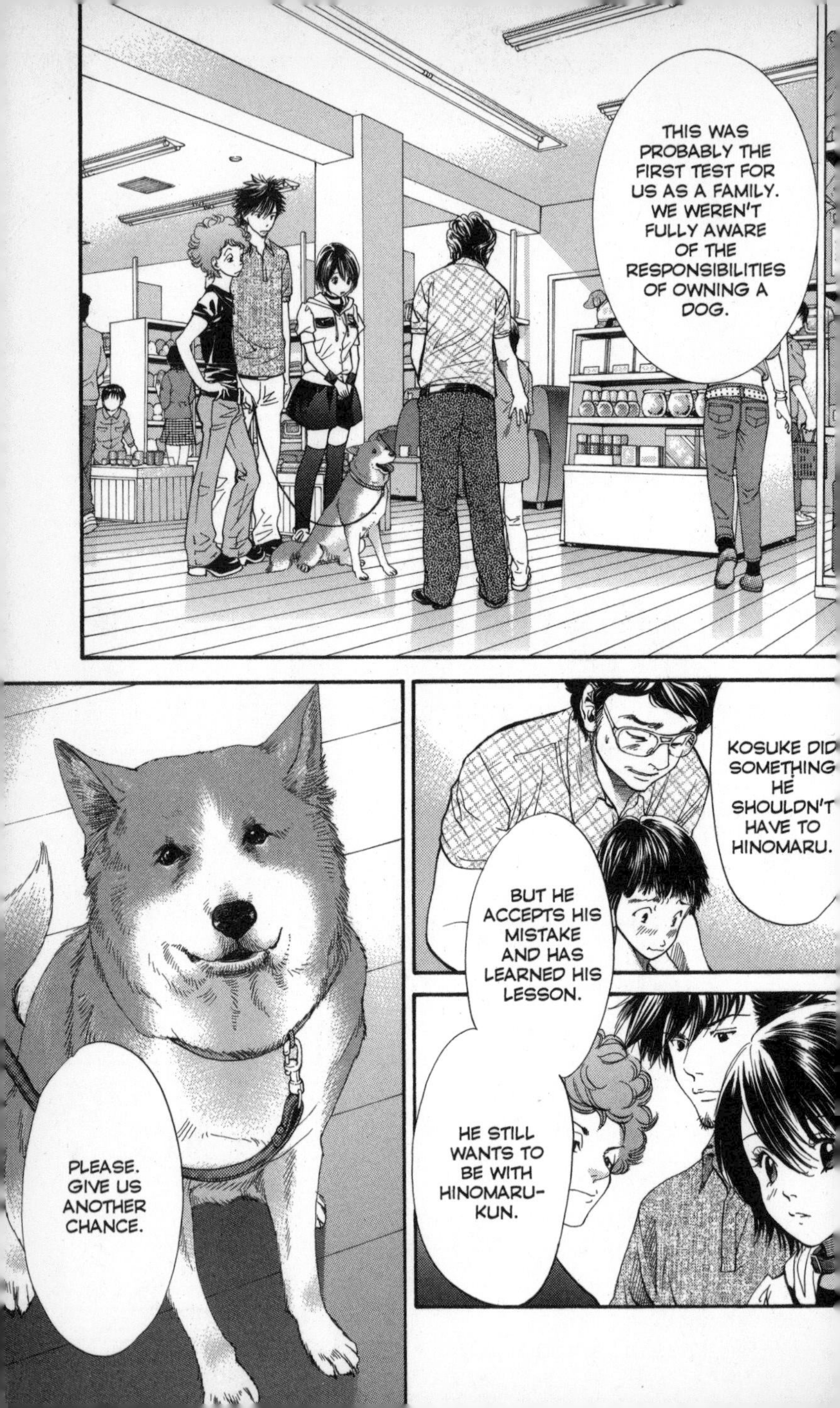
THIS WAS PROBABLY THE FIRST TEST FOR US AS A FAMILY. WE WEREN'T FULLY AWARE OF THE RESPONSIBILITIES OF OWNING A DOG.
KOSUKE DID SOMETHING HE SHOULDN'T HAVE TO HINOMARU.
BUT HE ACCEPTS HIS MISTAKE AND HAS LEARNED HIS LESSON.
HE STILL WANTS TO BE WITH HINOMARU-KUN.
PLEASE. GIVE US ANOTHER CHANCE.

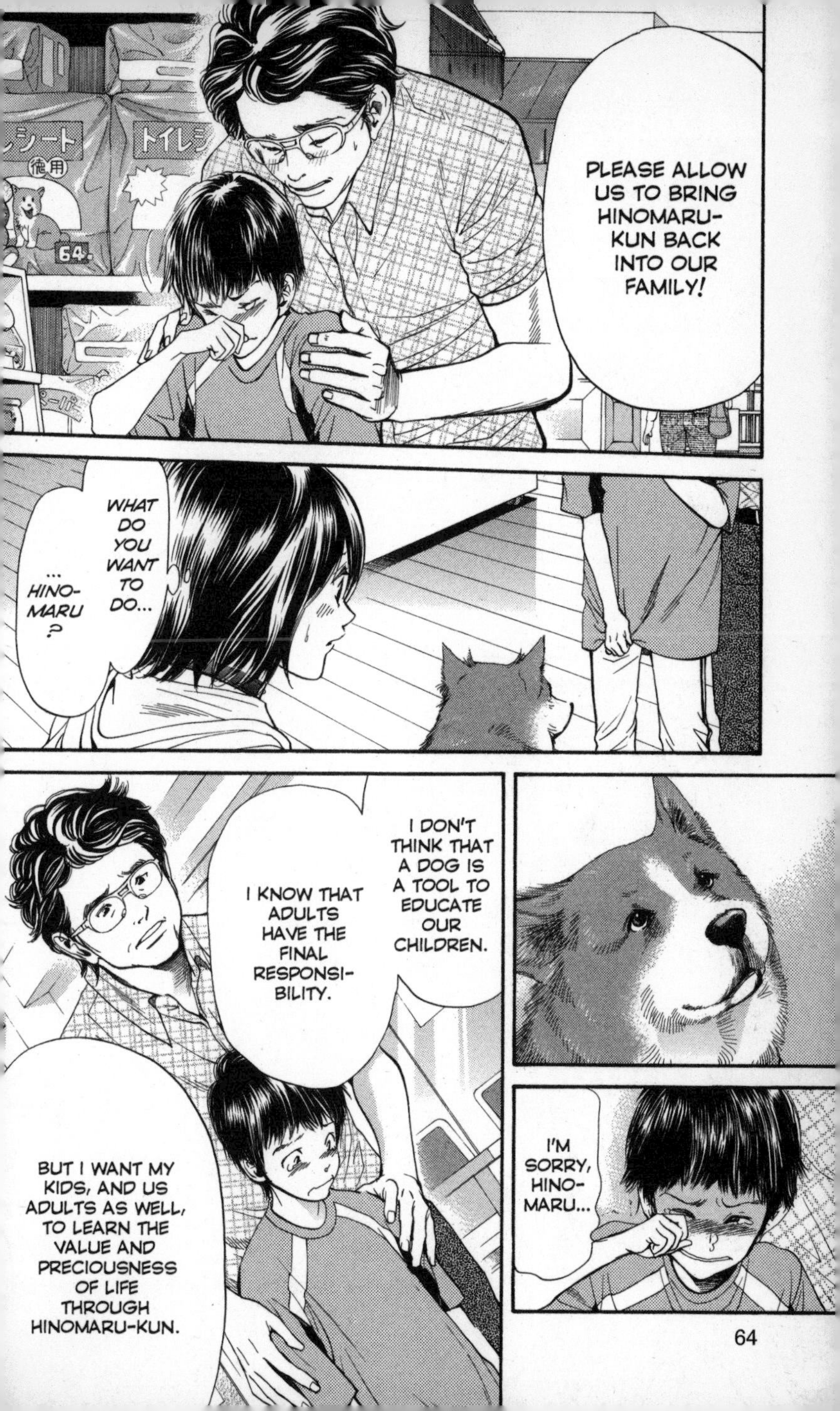
PLEASE ALLOW US TO BRING HINOMARU-KUN BACK INTO OUR FAMILY!
WHAT DO YOU WANT TO DO...
...HINOMARU?
I'M SORRY, HINOMARU...
I DON'T THINK THAT A DOG IS A TOOL TO EDUCATE OUR CHILDREN.
I KNOW THAT ADULTS HAVE THE FINAL RESPONSIBILITY.
BUT I WANT MY KIDS, AND US ADULTS AS WELL, TO LEARN THE VALUE AND PRECIOUSNESS OF LIFE THROUGH HINOMARU-KUN.

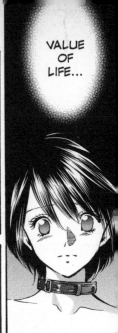

VALUE OF LIFE...

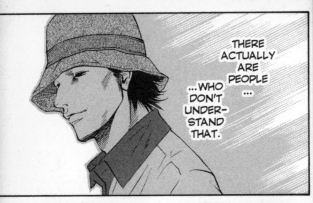

THERE ACTUALLY ARE PEOPLE ...

...WHO DON'T UNDER-STAND THAT.

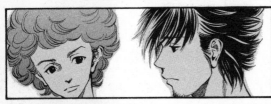

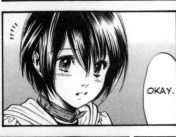

OKAY.

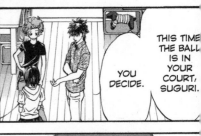

YOU DECIDE.

THIS TIME THE BALL IS IN YOUR COURT, SUGURI.

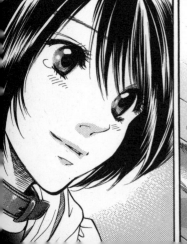

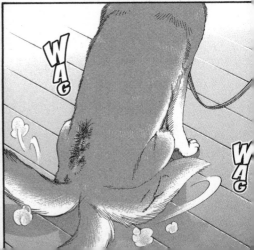

WAG

WAG

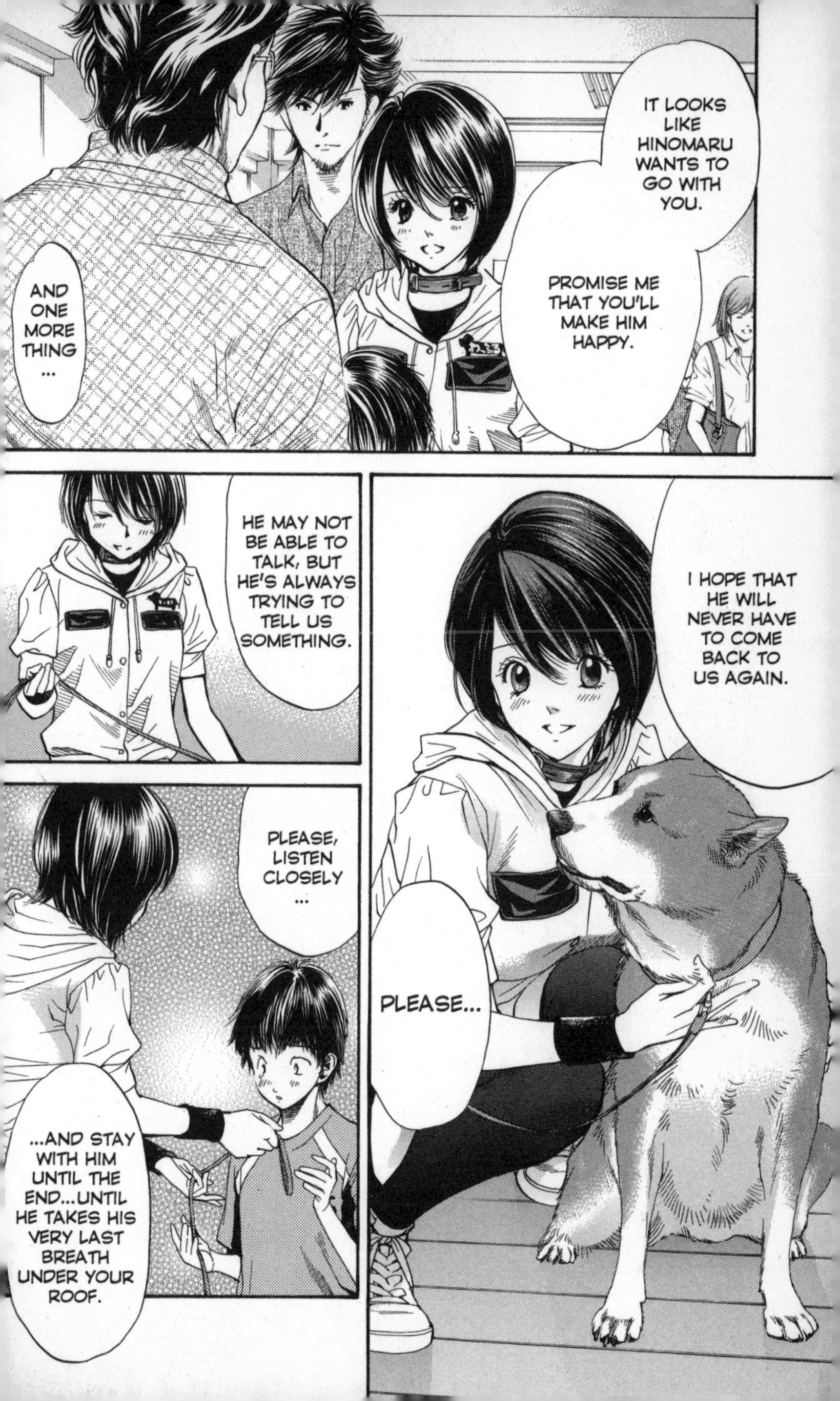
IT LOOKS LIKE HINOMARU WANTS TO GO WITH YOU.
PROMISE ME THAT YOU'LL MAKE HIM HAPPY.
AND ONE MORE THING ...
I HOPE THAT HE WILL NEVER HAVE TO COME BACK TO US AGAIN.
PLEASE...
HE MAY NOT BE ABLE TO TALK, BUT HE'S ALWAYS TRYING TO TELL US SOMETHING.
PLEASE, LISTEN CLOSELY ...
...AND STAY WITH HIM UNTIL THE END...UNTIL HE TAKES HIS VERY LAST BREATH UNDER YOUR ROOF.

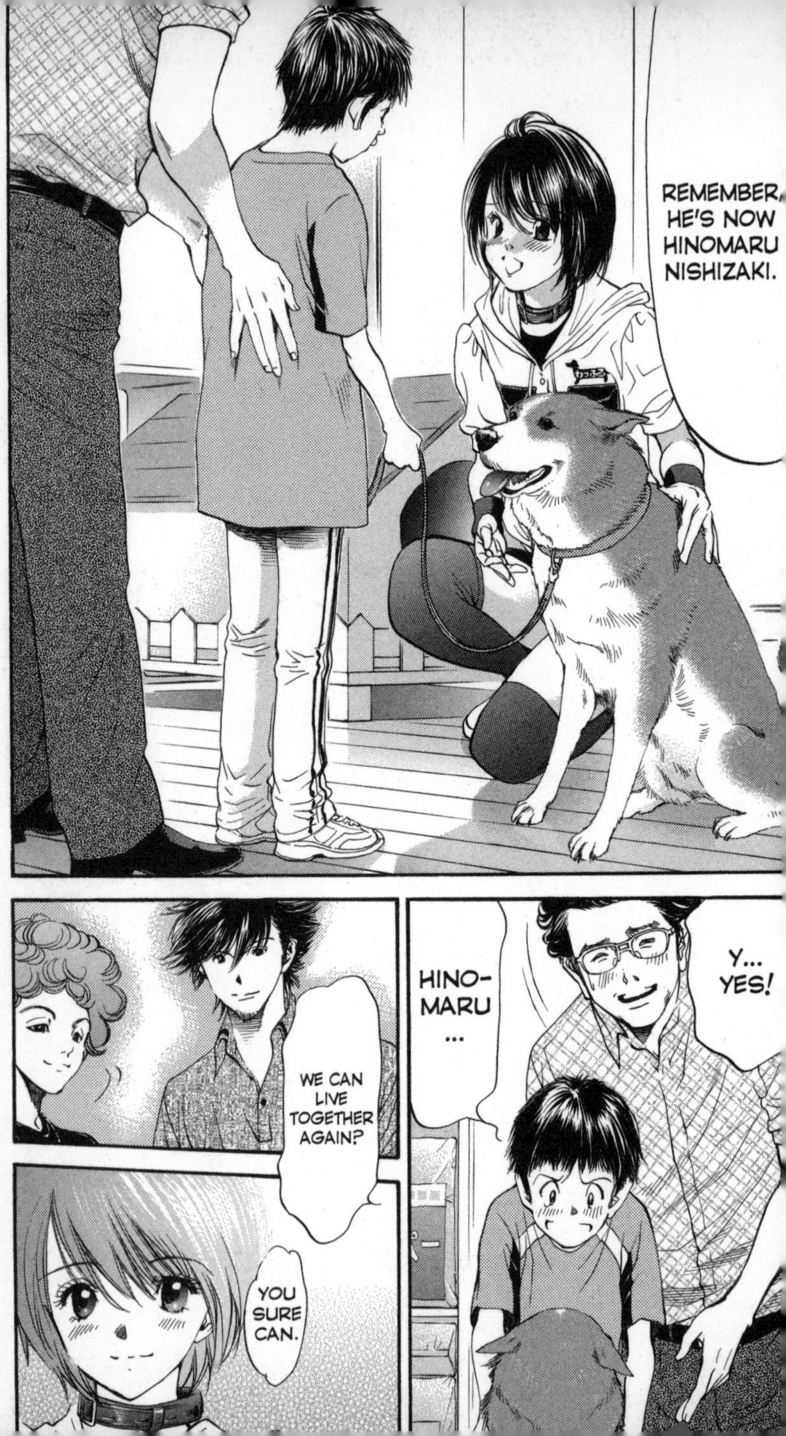
REMEMBER, HE'S NOW HINOMARU NISHIZAKI.
HINO-MARU ...
Y... YES!
WE CAN LIVE TOGETHER AGAIN?
YOU SURE CAN.

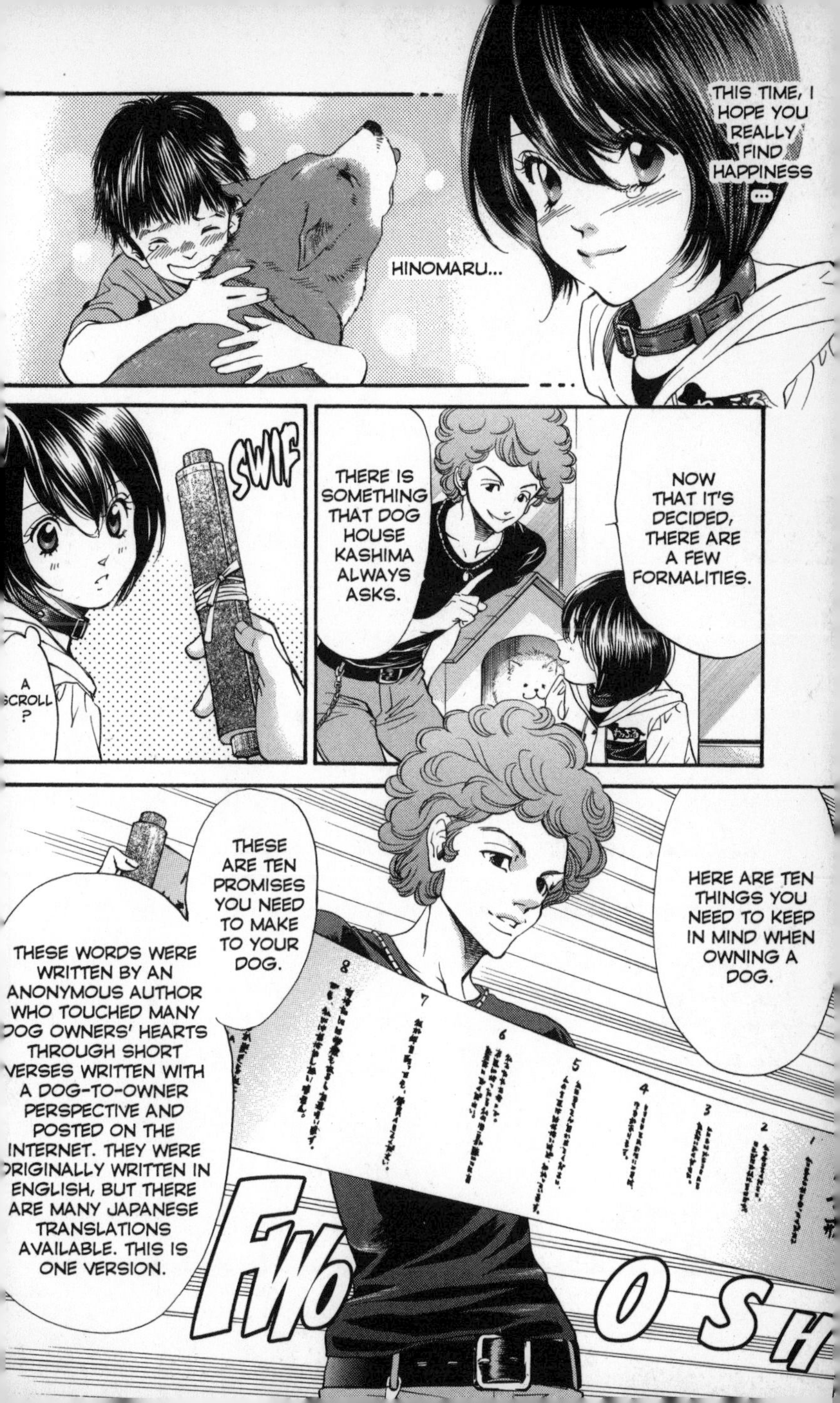
THIS TIME, I HOPE YOU REALLY FIND HAPPINESS...
HINOMARU...
NOW THAT IT'S DECIDED, THERE ARE A FEW FORMALITIES.
THERE IS SOMETHING THAT DOG HOUSE KASHIMA ALWAYS ASKS.
SWIF
A SCROLL?
HERE ARE TEN THINGS YOU NEED TO KEEP IN MIND WHEN OWNING A DOG.
THESE ARE TEN PROMISES YOU NEED TO MAKE TO YOUR DOG.
THESE WORDS WERE WRITTEN BY AN ANONYMOUS AUTHOR WHO TOUCHED MANY DOG OWNERS' HEARTS THROUGH SHORT VERSES WRITTEN WITH A DOG-TO-OWNER PERSPECTIVE AND POSTED ON THE INTERNET. THEY WERE ORIGINALLY WRITTEN IN ENGLISH, BUT THERE ARE MANY JAPANESE TRANSLATIONS AVAILABLE. THIS IS ONE VERSION.
FWOOSH

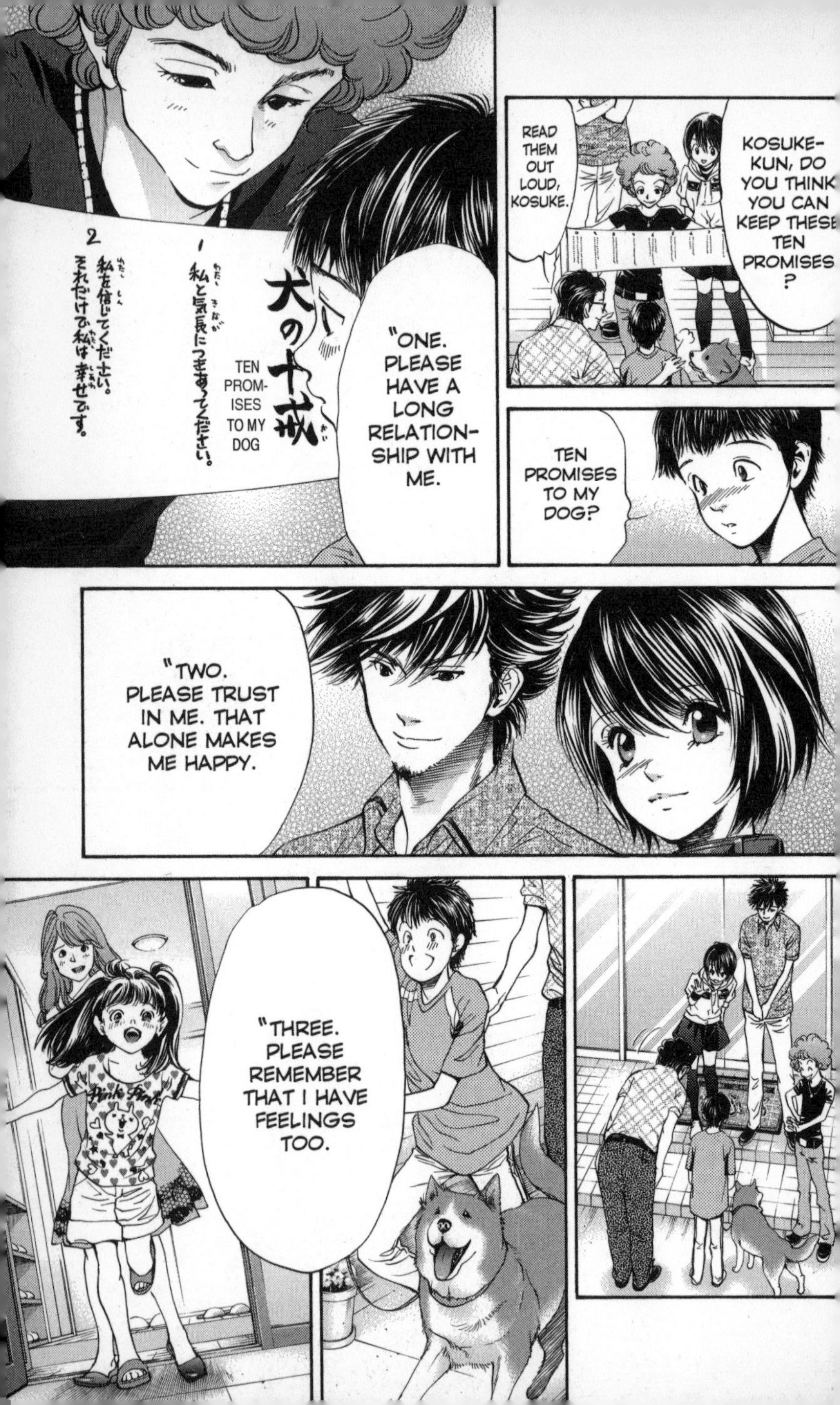
KOSUKE-KUN, DO YOU THINK YOU CAN KEEP THESE TEN PROMISES?
READ THEM OUT LOUD, KOSUKE.
TEN PROMISES TO MY DOG?
犬の十戒
TEN PROMISES TO MY DOG
1 私と気長につきあってください。
2 私を信じてください。それだけで私は幸せです。
"ONE. PLEASE HAVE A LONG RELATIONSHIP WITH ME.
"TWO. PLEASE TRUST IN ME. THAT ALONE MAKES ME HAPPY.
"THREE. PLEASE REMEMBER THAT I HAVE FEELINGS TOO.

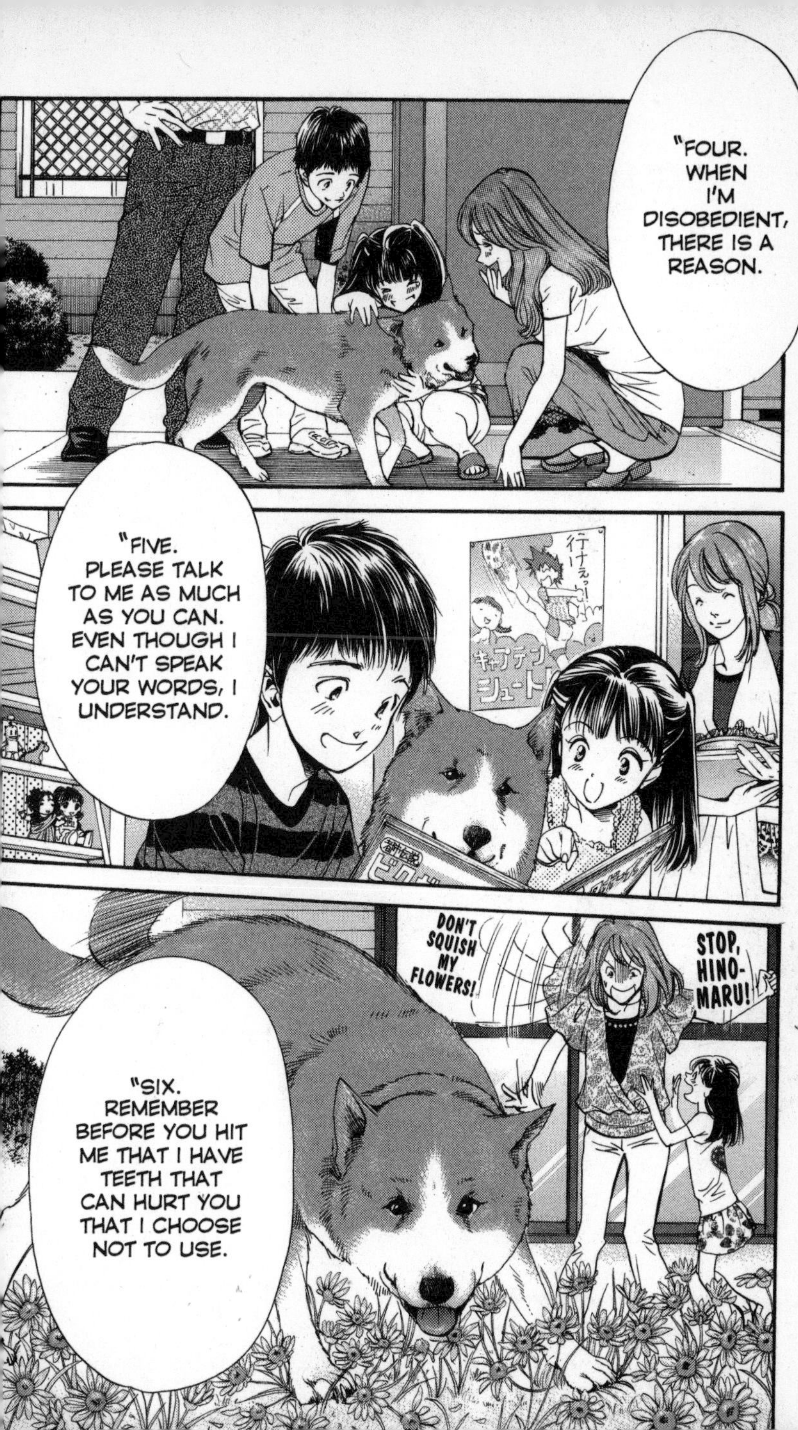
"FOUR. WHEN I'M DISOBEDIENT, THERE IS A REASON.
"FIVE. PLEASE TALK TO ME AS MUCH AS YOU CAN. EVEN THOUGH I CAN'T SPEAK YOUR WORDS, I UNDERSTAND.
STOP, HINO-MARU!
DON'T SQUISH MY FLOWERS!
"SIX. REMEMBER BEFORE YOU HIT ME THAT I HAVE TEETH THAT CAN HURT YOU THAT I CHOOSE NOT TO USE.

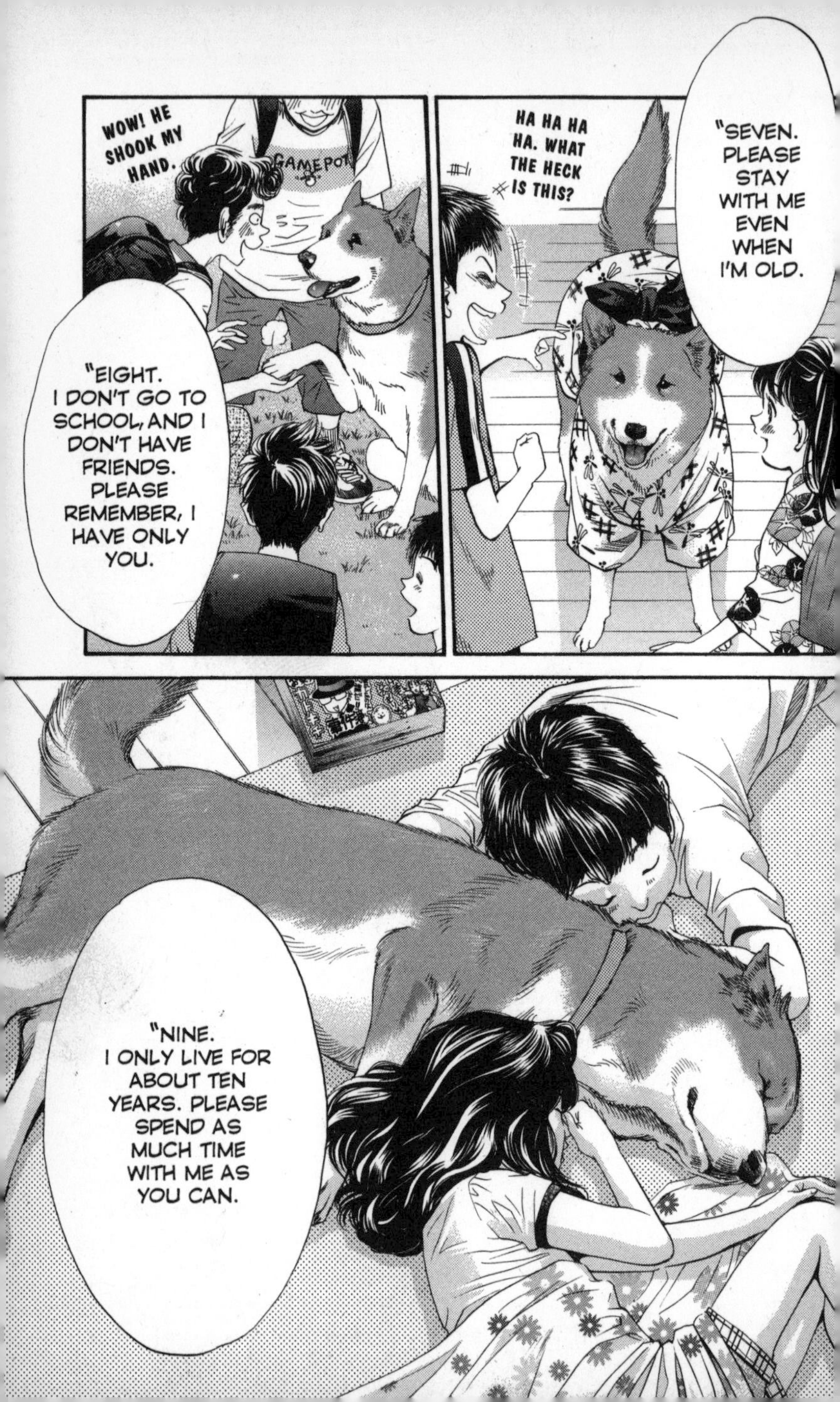
"SEVEN. PLEASE STAY WITH ME EVEN WHEN I'M OLD.
HA HA HA HA. WHAT THE HECK IS THIS?
WOW! HE SHOOK MY HAND.
GAMEPOT
"EIGHT. I DON'T GO TO SCHOOL, AND I DON'T HAVE FRIENDS. PLEASE REMEMBER, I HAVE ONLY YOU.
"NINE. I ONLY LIVE FOR ABOUT TEN YEARS. PLEASE SPEND AS MUCH TIME WITH ME AS YOU CAN.

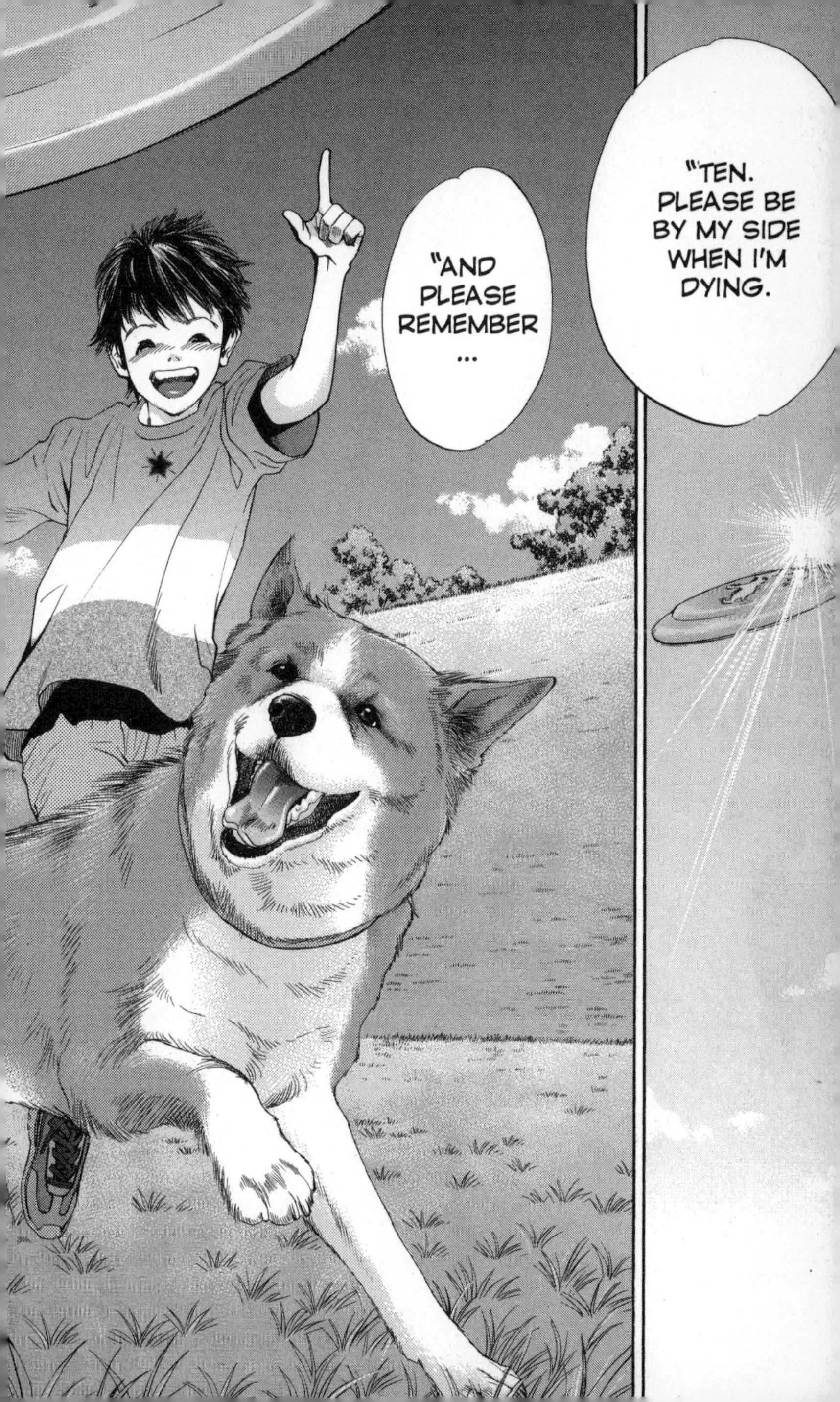
"TEN. PLEASE BE BY MY SIDE WHEN I'M DYING.
"AND PLEASE REMEMBER ...

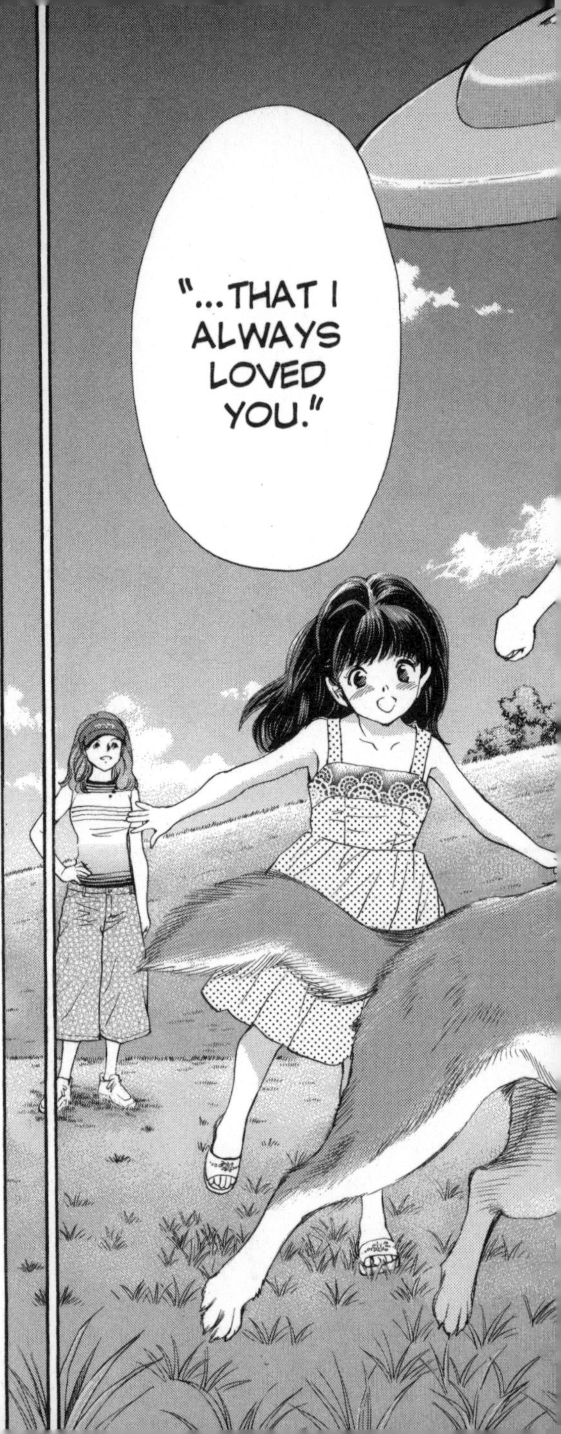
"...THAT I ALWAYS LOVED YOU."

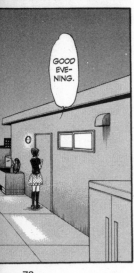

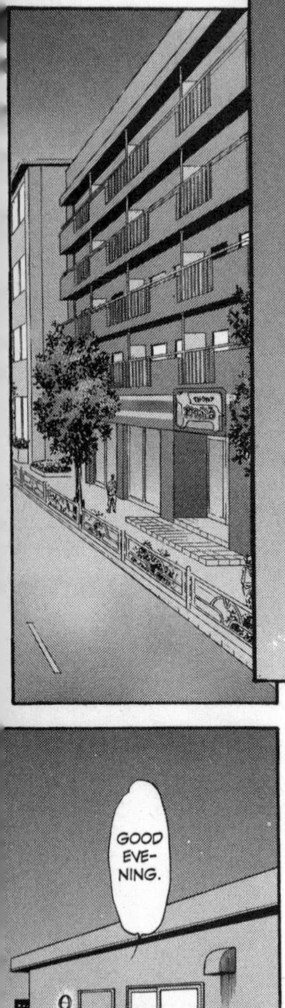
GOOD EVE-NING.

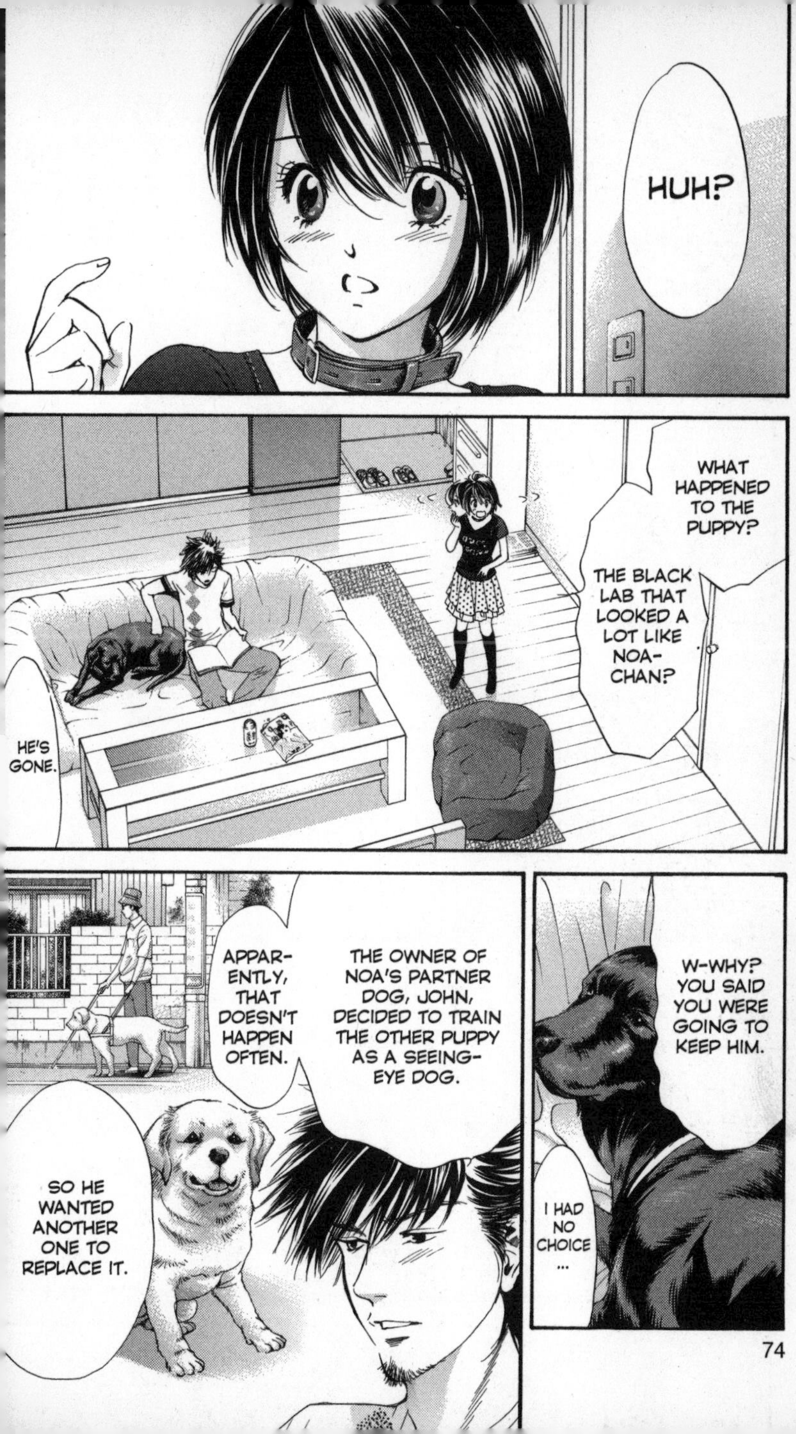
HUH?
WHAT HAPPENED TO THE PUPPY?
THE BLACK LAB THAT LOOKED A LOT LIKE NOA-CHAN?
HE'S GONE.
W-WHY? YOU SAID YOU WERE GOING TO KEEP HIM.
I HAD NO CHOICE ...
THE OWNER OF NOA'S PARTNER DOG, JOHN, DECIDED TO TRAIN THE OTHER PUPPY AS A SEEING-EYE DOG.
APPARENTLY, THAT DOESN'T HAPPEN OFTEN.
SO HE WANTED ANOTHER ONE TO REPLACE IT.

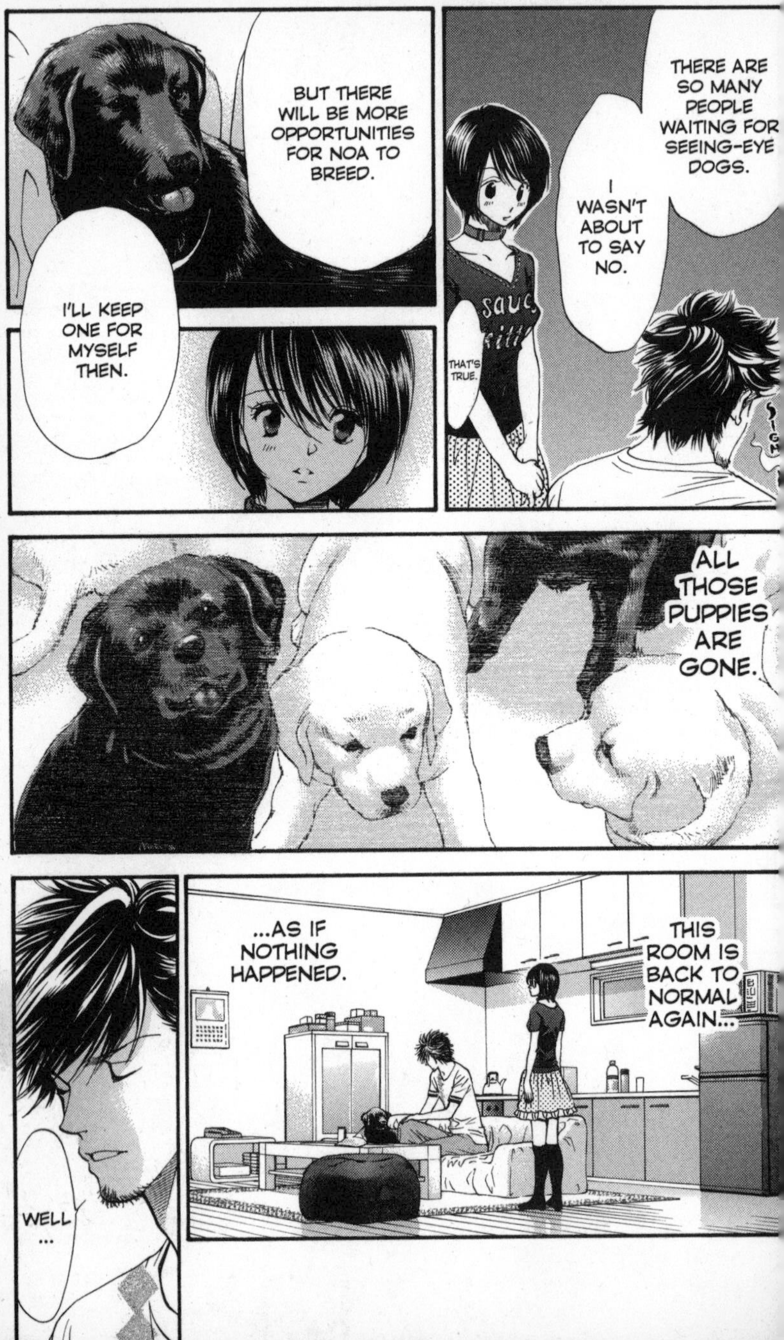
THERE ARE SO MANY PEOPLE WAITING FOR SEEING-EYE DOGS.
I WASN'T ABOUT TO SAY NO.
THAT'S TRUE.
SIGH
BUT THERE WILL BE MORE OPPORTUNITIES FOR NOA TO BREED.
I'LL KEEP ONE FOR MYSELF THEN.
ALL THOSE PUPPIES ARE GONE.
THIS ROOM IS BACK TO NORMAL AGAIN...
...AS IF NOTHING HAPPENED.
WELL ...

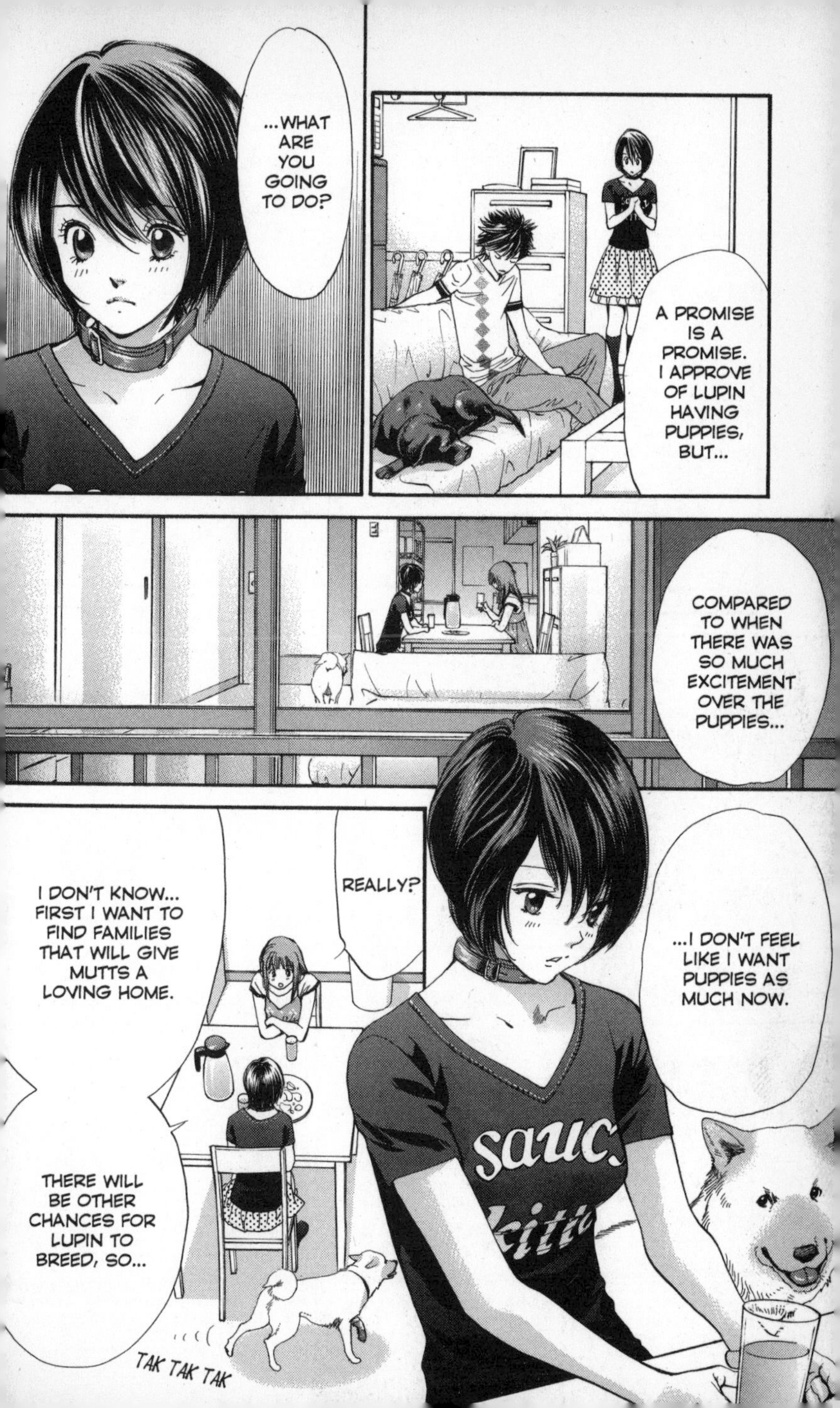
A PROMISE IS A PROMISE. I APPROVE OF LUPIN HAVING PUPPIES, BUT...
...WHAT ARE YOU GOING TO DO?
COMPARED TO WHEN THERE WAS SO MUCH EXCITEMENT OVER THE PUPPIES...
...I DON'T FEEL LIKE I WANT PUPPIES AS MUCH NOW.
REALLY?
I DON'T KNOW... FIRST I WANT TO FIND FAMILIES THAT WILL GIVE MUTTS A LOVING HOME.
THERE WILL BE OTHER CHANCES FOR LUPIN TO BREED, SO...
TAK TAK TAK

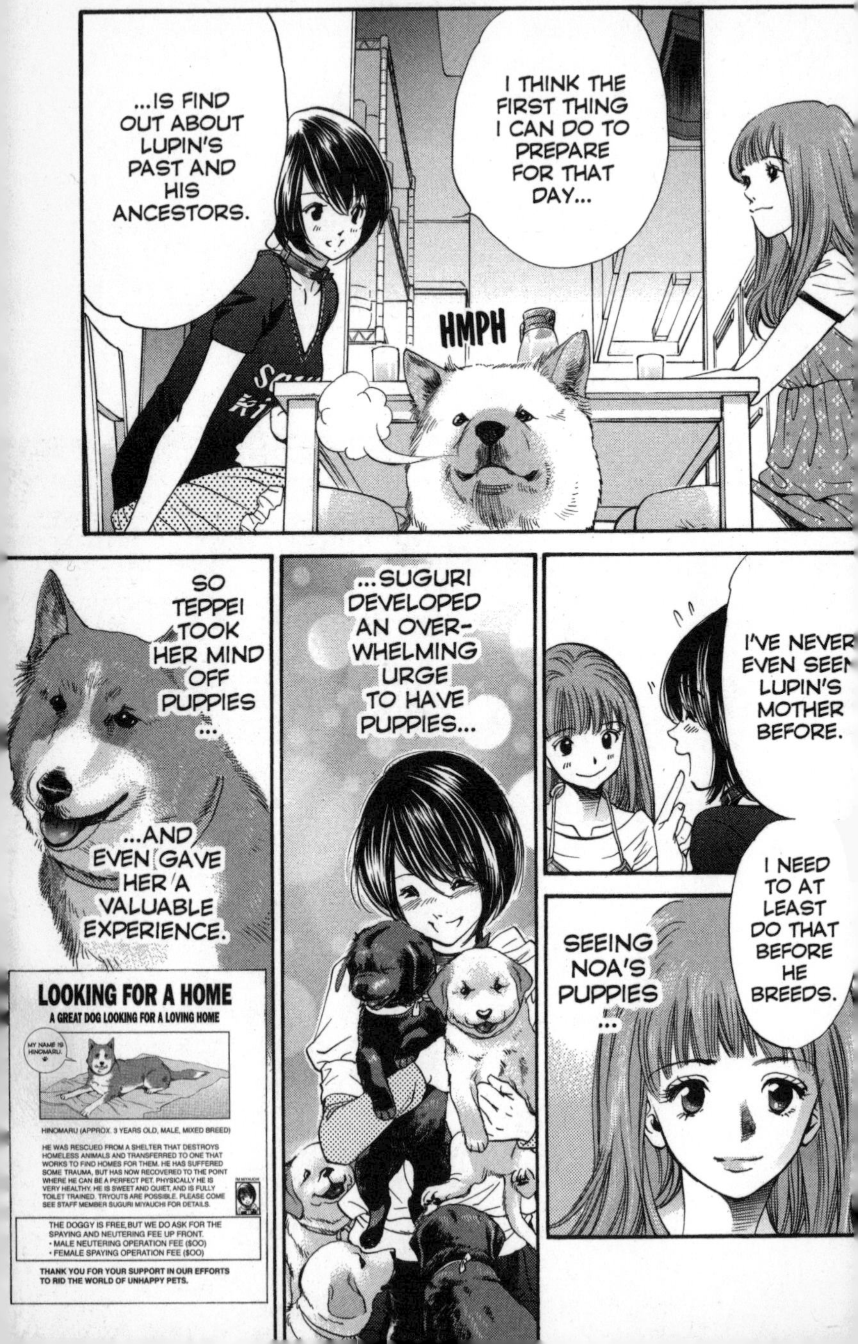
I THINK THE FIRST THING I CAN DO TO PREPARE FOR THAT DAY...
...IS FIND OUT ABOUT LUPIN'S PAST AND HIS ANCESTORS.
HMPH
I'VE NEVER EVEN SEEN LUPIN'S MOTHER BEFORE.
I NEED TO AT LEAST DO THAT BEFORE HE BREEDS.
SEEING NOA'S PUPPIES...
...SUGURI DEVELOPED AN OVER-WHELMING URGE TO HAVE PUPPIES...
SO TEPPEI TOOK HER MIND OFF PUPPIES...
...AND EVEN GAVE HER A VALUABLE EXPERIENCE.
LOOKING FOR A HOME
A GREAT DOG LOOKING FOR A LOVING HOME
MY NAME IS HINOMARU.
HINOMARU (APPROX. 3 YEARS OLD, MALE, MIXED BREED)
HE WAS RESCUED FROM A SHELTER THAT DESTROYS HOMELESS ANIMALS AND TRANSFERRED TO ONE THAT WORKS TO FIND HOMES FOR THEM. HE HAS SUFFERED SOME TRAUMA, BUT HAS NOW RECOVERED TO THE POINT WHERE HE CAN BE A PERFECT PET. PHYSICALLY HE IS VERY HEALTHY. HE IS SWEET AND QUIET, AND IS FULLY TOILET TRAINED. TRYOUTS ARE POSSIBLE. PLEASE COME SEE STAFF MEMBER SUGURI MIYAUCHI FOR DETAILS.
THE DOGGY IS FREE, BUT WE DO ASK FOR THE SPAYING AND NEUTERING FEE UP FRONT.
• MALE NEUTERING OPERATION FEE ($OO)
• FEMALE SPAYING OPERATION FEE ($OO)
THANK YOU FOR YOUR SUPPORT IN OUR EFFORTS TO RID THE WORLD OF UNHAPPY PETS.

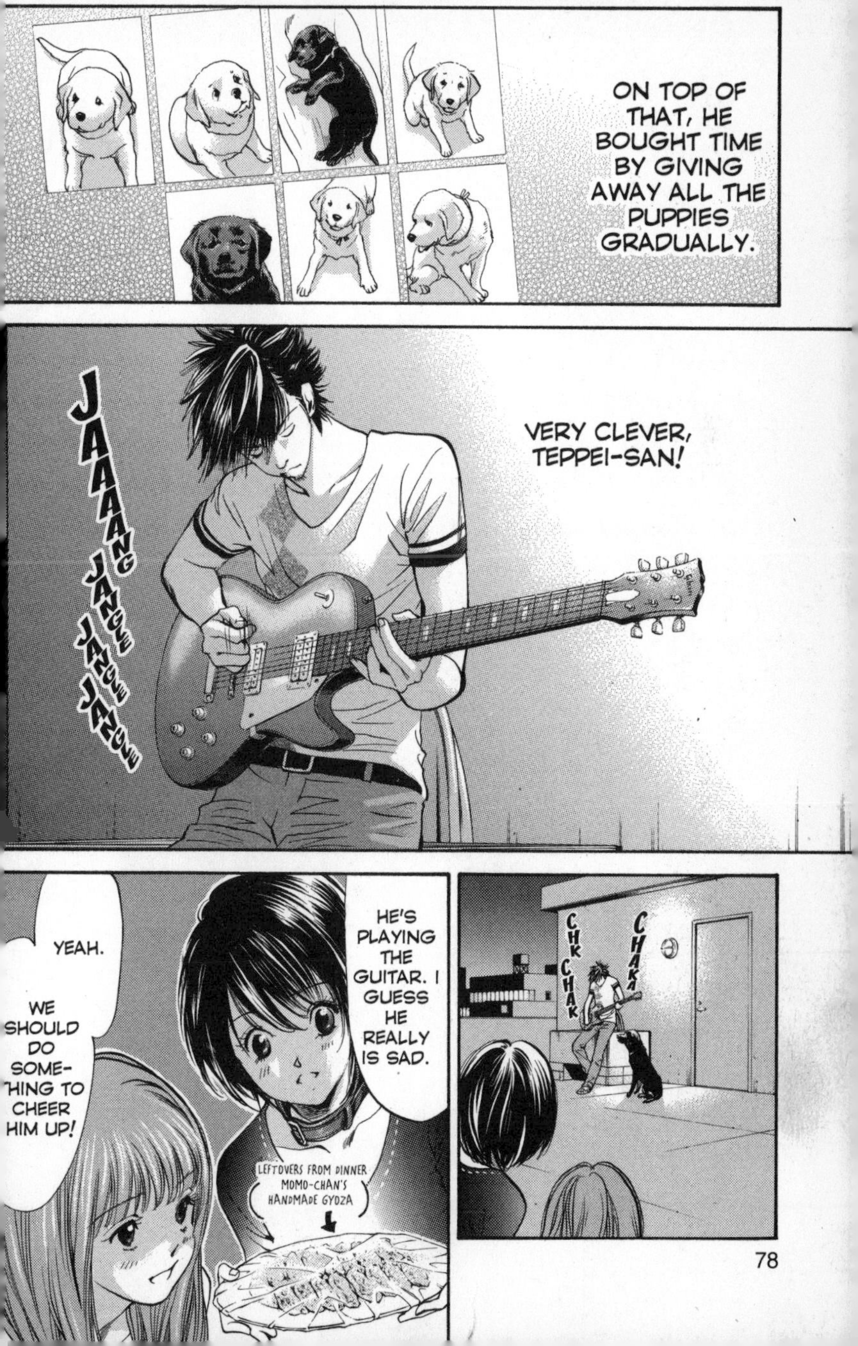
ON TOP OF THAT, HE BOUGHT TIME BY GIVING AWAY ALL THE PUPPIES GRADUALLY.
VERY CLEVER, TEPPEI-SAN!
JAAAAANG
JANGLE
JANGLE
JANGLE
CHAKA
CHK CHAK
HE'S PLAYING THE GUITAR. I GUESS HE REALLY IS SAD.
YEAH.
WE SHOULD DO SOME-THING TO CHEER HIM UP!
LEFTOVERS FROM DINNER
MOMO-CHAN'S HANDMADE GYOZA

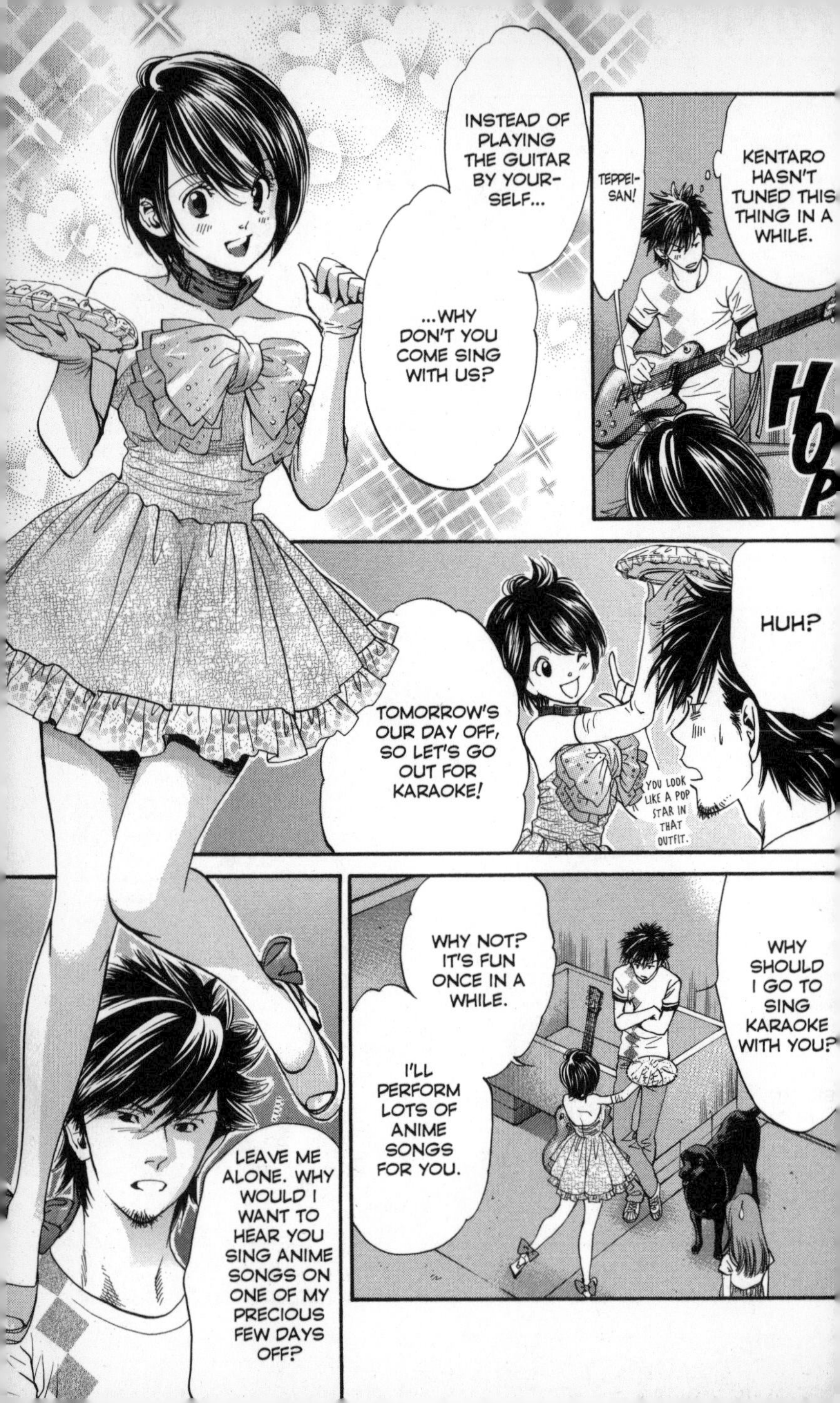
KENTARO HASN'T TUNED THIS THING IN A WHILE.
TEPPEI-SAN!
HOP
INSTEAD OF PLAYING THE GUITAR BY YOURSELF...
...WHY DON'T YOU COME SING WITH US?
HUH?
YOU LOOK LIKE A POP STAR IN THAT OUTFIT.
TOMORROW'S OUR DAY OFF, SO LET'S GO OUT FOR KARAOKE!
WHY SHOULD I GO TO SING KARAOKE WITH YOU?
WHY NOT? IT'S FUN ONCE IN A WHILE.
I'LL PERFORM LOTS OF ANIME SONGS FOR YOU.
LEAVE ME ALONE. WHY WOULD I WANT TO HEAR YOU SING ANIME SONGS ON ONE OF MY PRECIOUS FEW DAYS OFF?

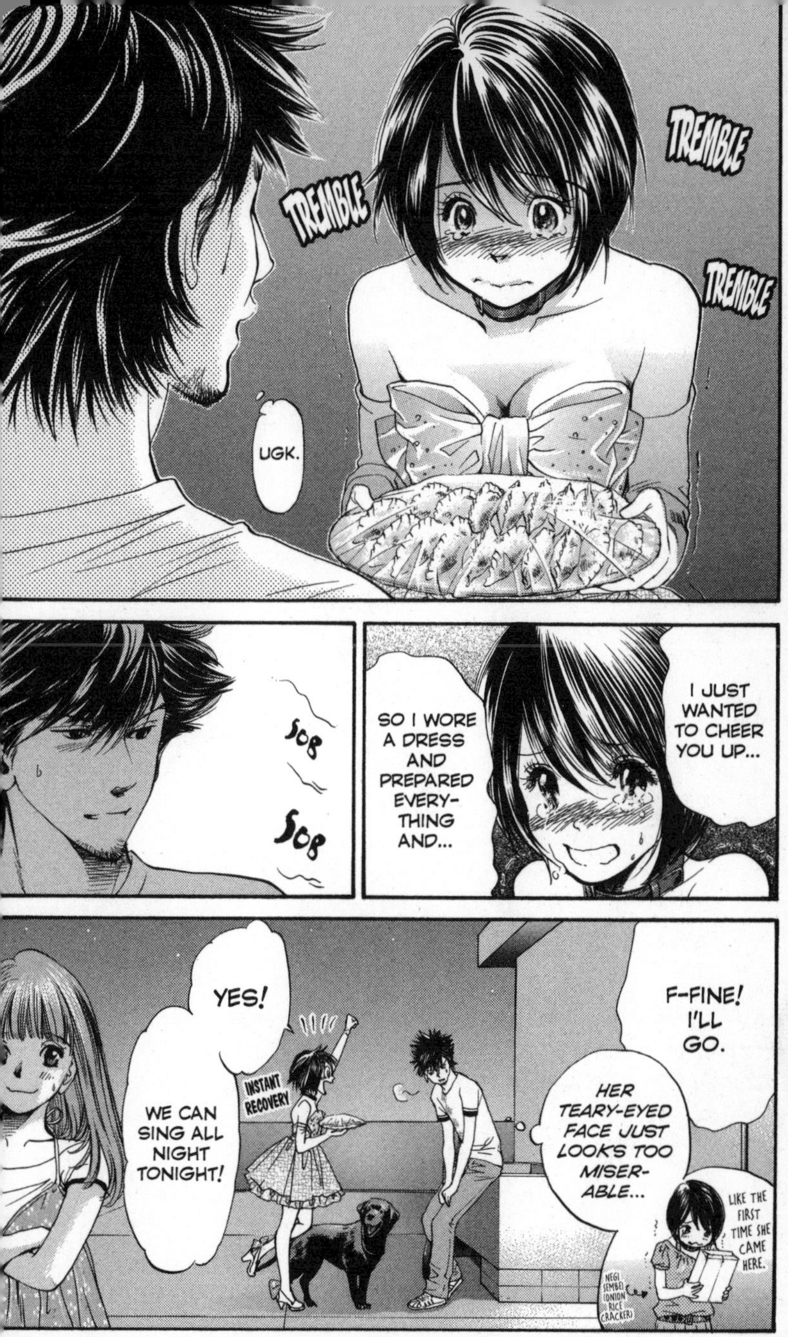

TREMBLE
TREMBLE
TREMBLE
UGK.
I JUST WANTED TO CHEER YOU UP...
SO I WORE A DRESS AND PREPARED EVERY-THING AND...
SOB
SOB
F-FINE! I'LL GO.
HER TEARY-EYED FACE JUST LOOKS TOO MISER-ABLE...
LIKE THE FIRST TIME SHE CAME HERE.
NEGI SEMBEI (ONION RICE CRACKER)
YES!
INSTANT RECOVERY
WE CAN SING ALL NIGHT TONIGHT!

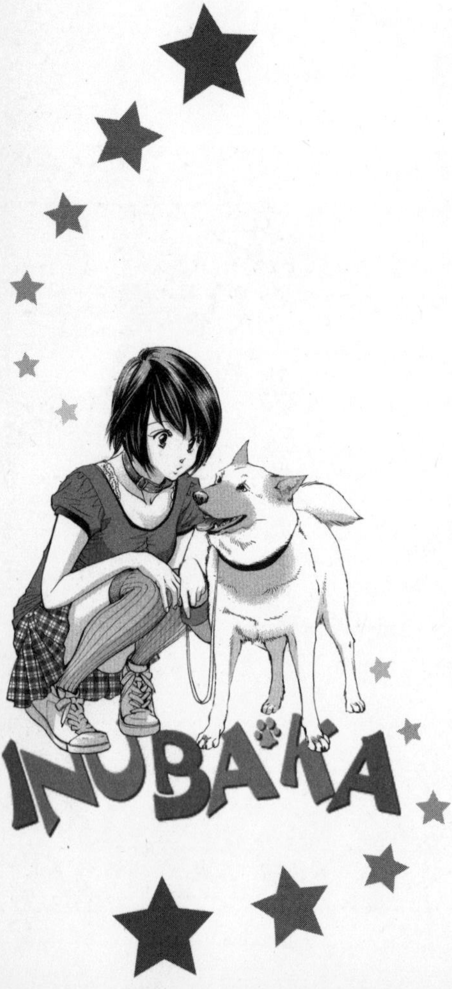
INUBAKA

INUBA*KA

CHAPTER 156: KINDA LIKE A DATE

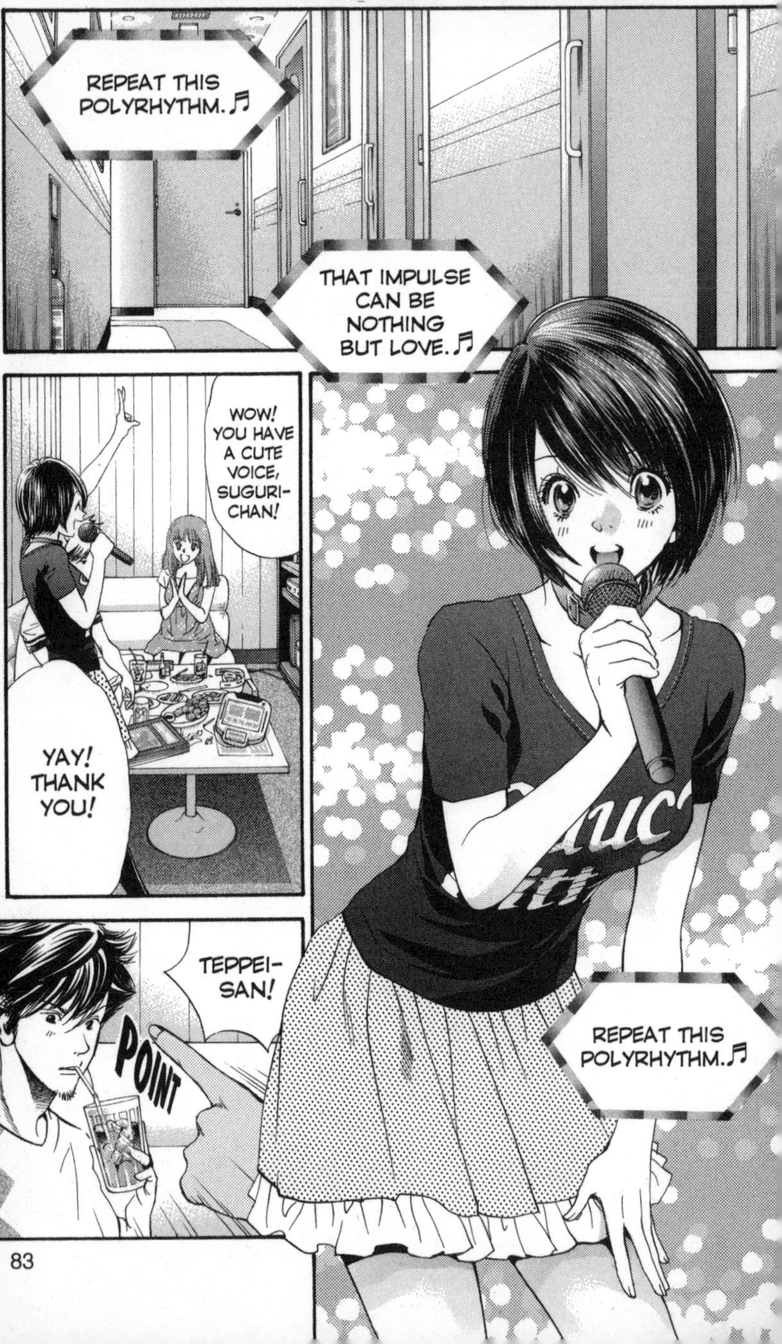

REPEAT THIS POLYRHYTHM.♬
THAT IMPULSE CAN BE NOTHING BUT LOVE.♬
REPEAT THIS POLYRHYTHM.♬
WOW! YOU HAVE A CUTE VOICE, SUGURI-CHAN!
YAY! THANK YOU!
TEPPEI-SAN!
POINT

CHAPTER 156: KINDA LIKE A DATE

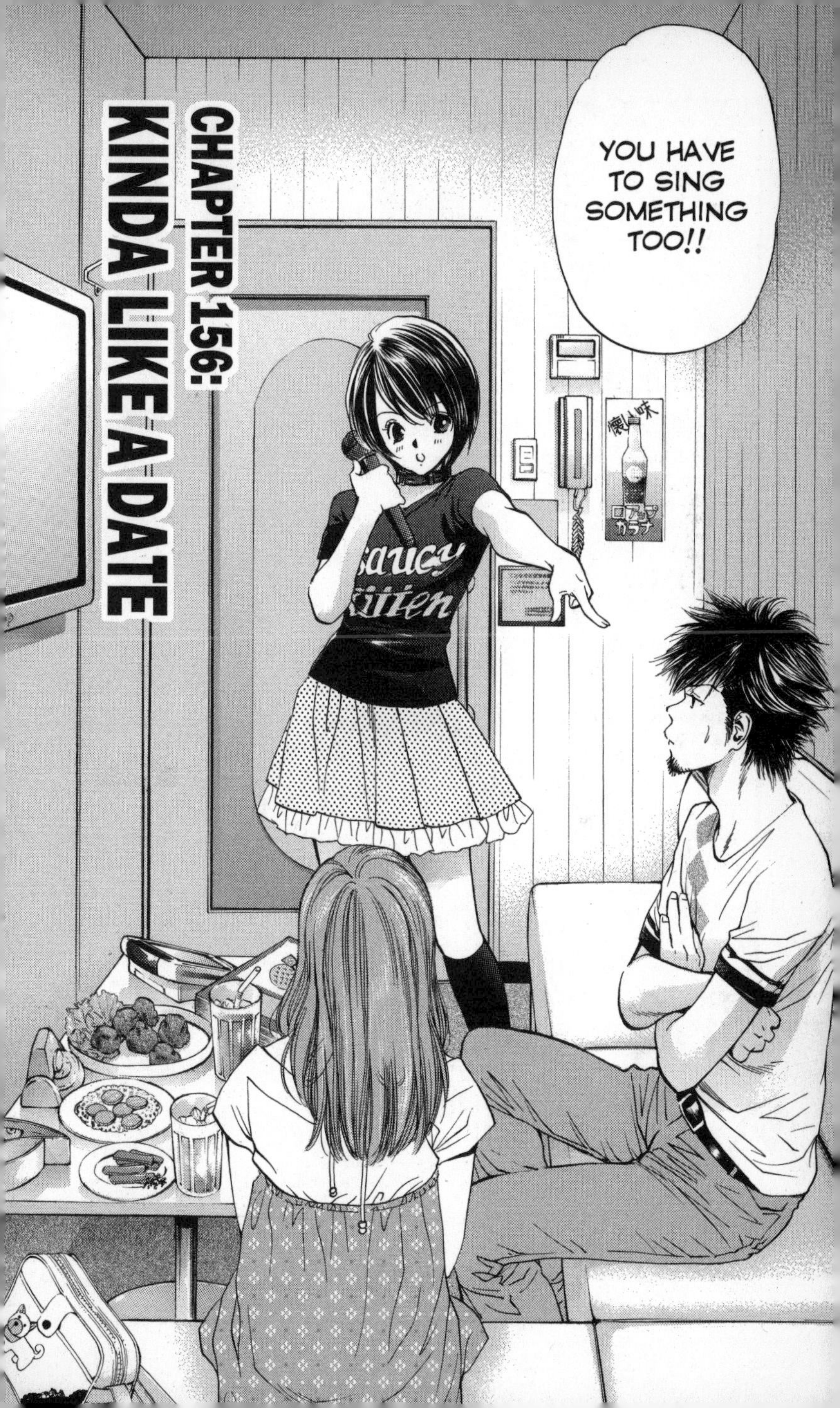
YOU HAVE TO SING SOMETHING TOO!!
saucy kitten

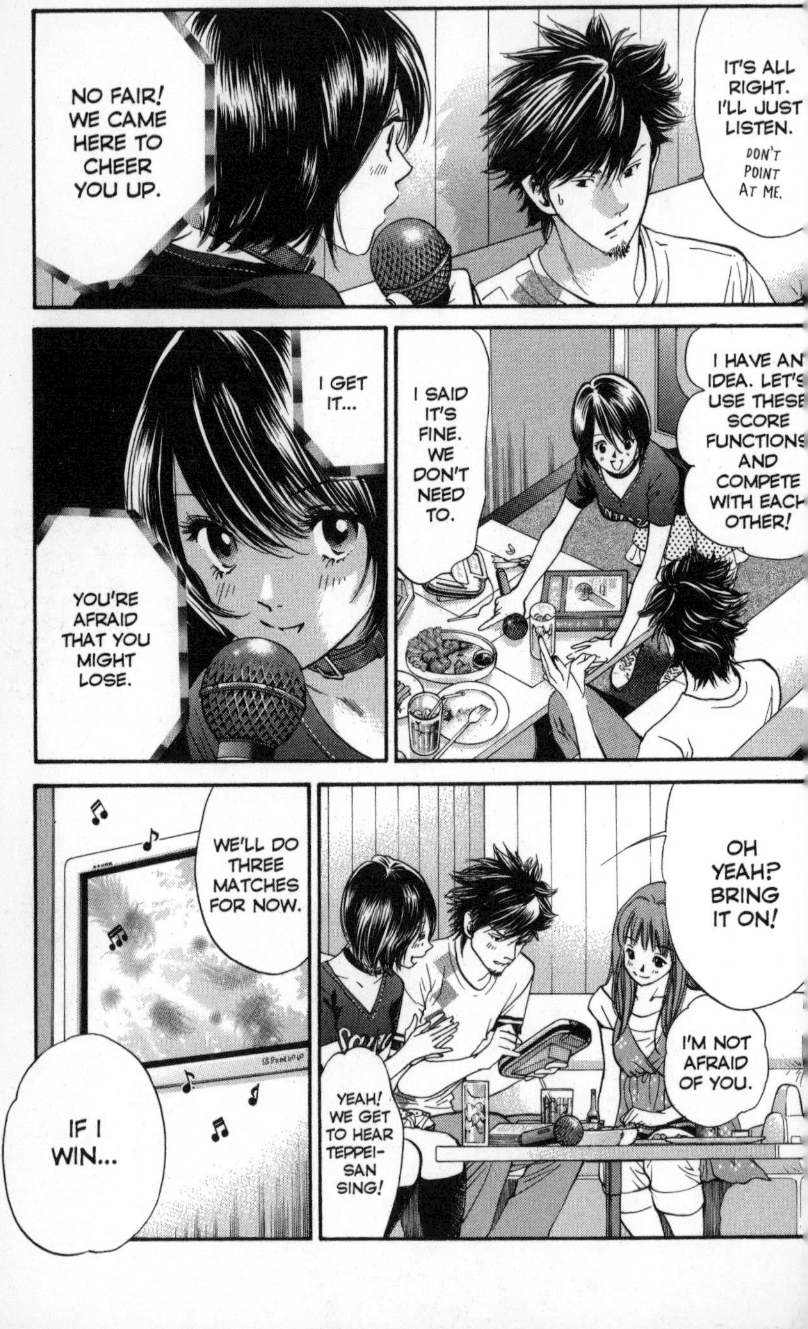

IT'S ALL RIGHT. I'LL JUST LISTEN.
DON'T POINT AT ME.
NO FAIR! WE CAME HERE TO CHEER YOU UP.
I HAVE AN IDEA. LET'S USE THESE SCORE FUNCTIONS AND COMPETE WITH EACH OTHER!
I SAID IT'S FINE. WE DON'T NEED TO.
I GET IT...
YOU'RE AFRAID THAT YOU MIGHT LOSE.
OH YEAH? BRING IT ON!
I'M NOT AFRAID OF YOU.
YEAH! WE GET TO HEAR TEPPEI-SAN SING!
WE'LL DO THREE MATCHES FOR NOW.
IF I WIN...

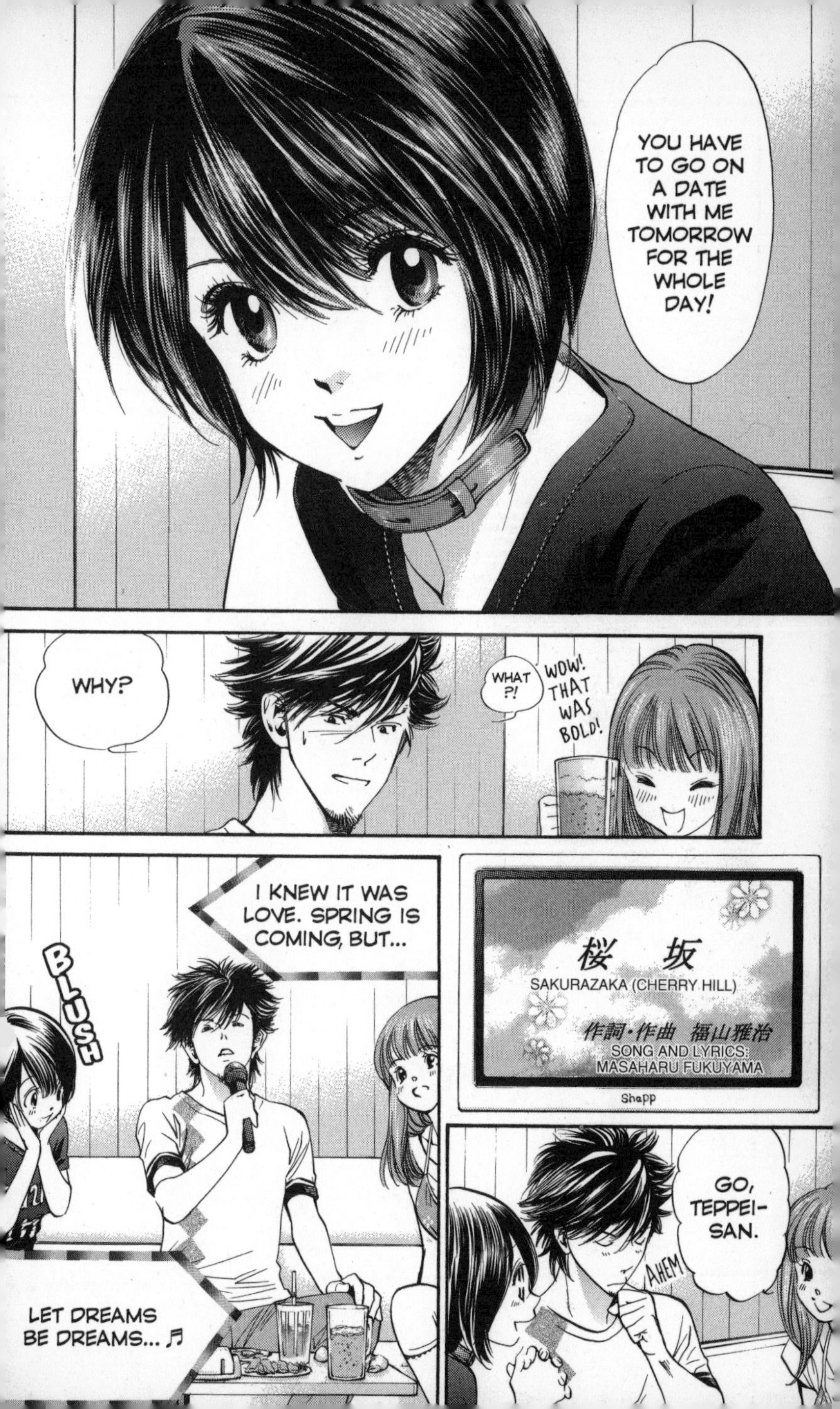
YOU HAVE TO GO ON A DATE WITH ME TOMORROW FOR THE WHOLE DAY!
WOW! THAT WAS BOLD!
WHAT ?!
WHY?
桜坂
SAKURAZAKA (CHERRY HILL)
作詞・作曲 福山雅治
SONG AND LYRICS: MASAHARU FUKUYAMA
Shapp
GO, TEPPEI-SAN.
AHEM
I KNEW IT WAS LOVE. SPRING IS COMING, BUT...
BLUSH
LET DREAMS BE DREAMS... ♬

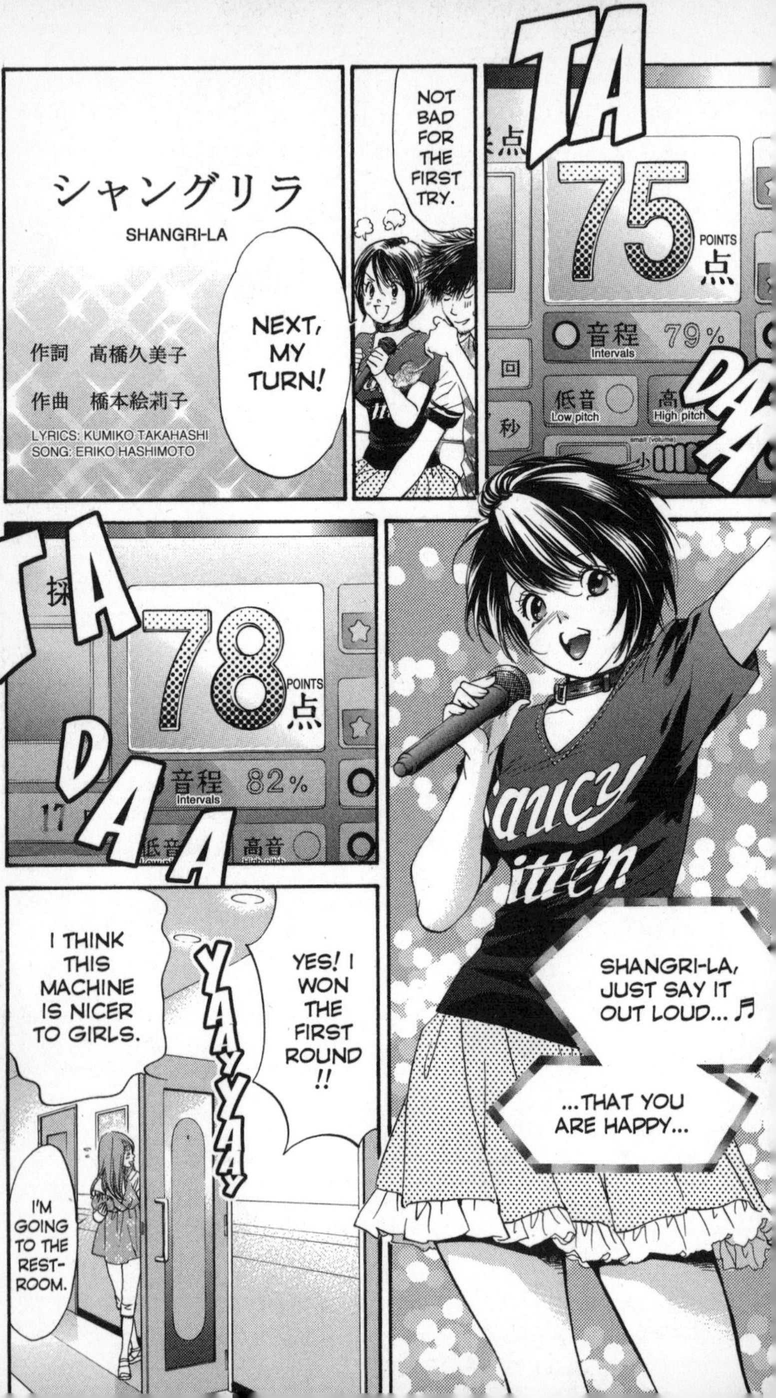
TA
75 POINTS 点
音程 79%
Intervals
低音
Low pitch
高
High pitch
small (volume)
小
回
秒
DAA
NOT BAD FOR THE FIRST TRY.
NEXT, MY TURN!
シャングリラ
SHANGRI-LA
作詞　高橋久美子
作曲　橋本絵莉子
LYRICS: KUMIKO TAKAHASHI
SONG: ERIKO HASHIMOTO
SHANGRI-LA, JUST SAY IT OUT LOUD... ♬
...THAT YOU ARE HAPPY...
TA
78 POINTS 点
音程 82%
Intervals
高音
DAA
YES! I WON THE FIRST ROUND!!
YAAYYAAY
I THINK THIS MACHINE IS NICER TO GIRLS.
I'M GOING TO THE REST-ROOM.

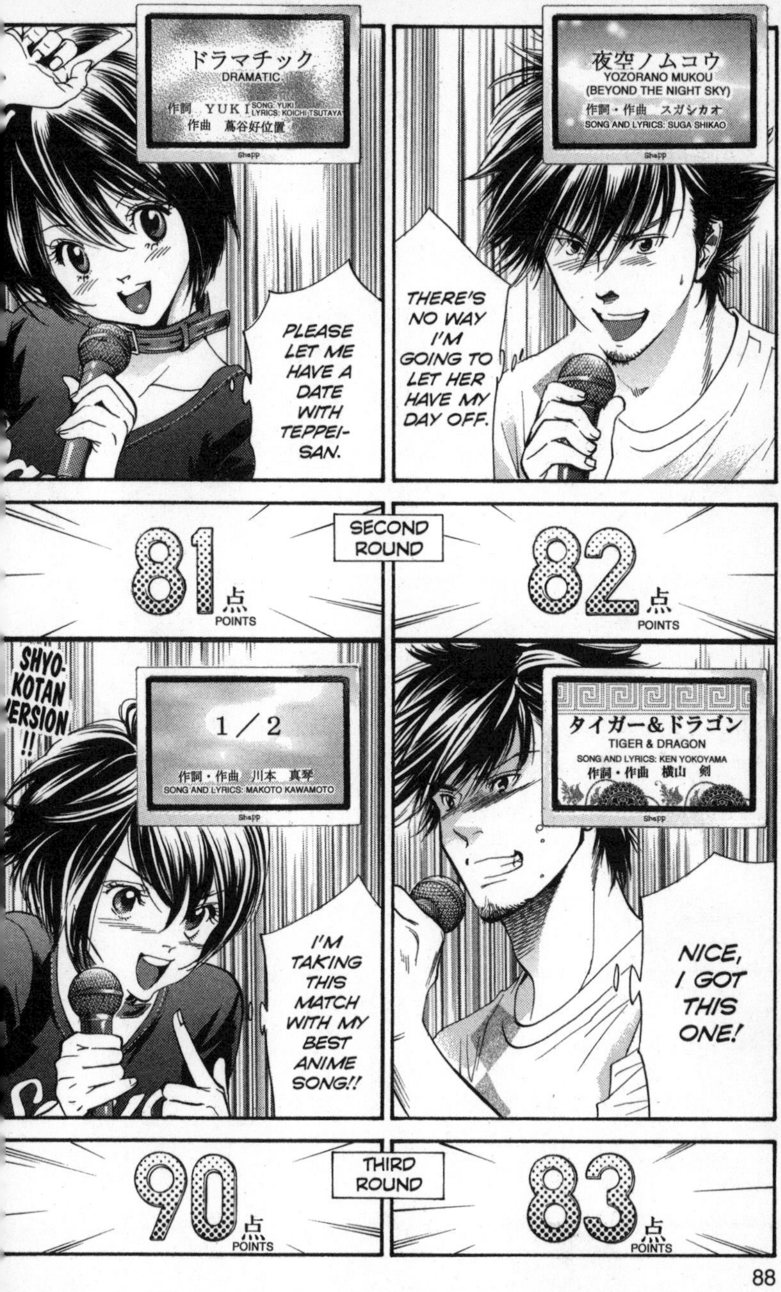

夜空ノムコウ
YOZORANO MUKOU
(BEYOND THE NIGHT SKY)
作詞・作曲 スガシカオ
SONG AND LYRICS: SUGA SHIKAO
Shapp
THERE'S NO WAY I'M GOING TO LET HER HAVE MY DAY OFF.
ドラマチック
DRAMATIC
作詞 YUKI
作曲 蔦谷好位置
SONG: YUKI
LYRICS: KOICHI TSUTAYA
Shapp
PLEASE LET ME HAVE A DATE WITH TEPPEI-SAN.
82点
POINTS
SECOND ROUND
81点
POINTS
タイガー&ドラゴン
TIGER & DRAGON
SONG AND LYRICS: KEN YOKOYAMA
作詞・作曲 横山 剣
Shapp
NICE, I GOT THIS ONE!
SHYO-KOTAN VERSION!!
1/2
作詞・作曲 川本 真琴
SONG AND LYRICS: MAKOTO KAWAMOTO
Shapp
I'M TAKING THIS MATCH WITH MY BEST ANIME SONG!!
83点
POINTS
THIRD ROUND
90点
POINTS

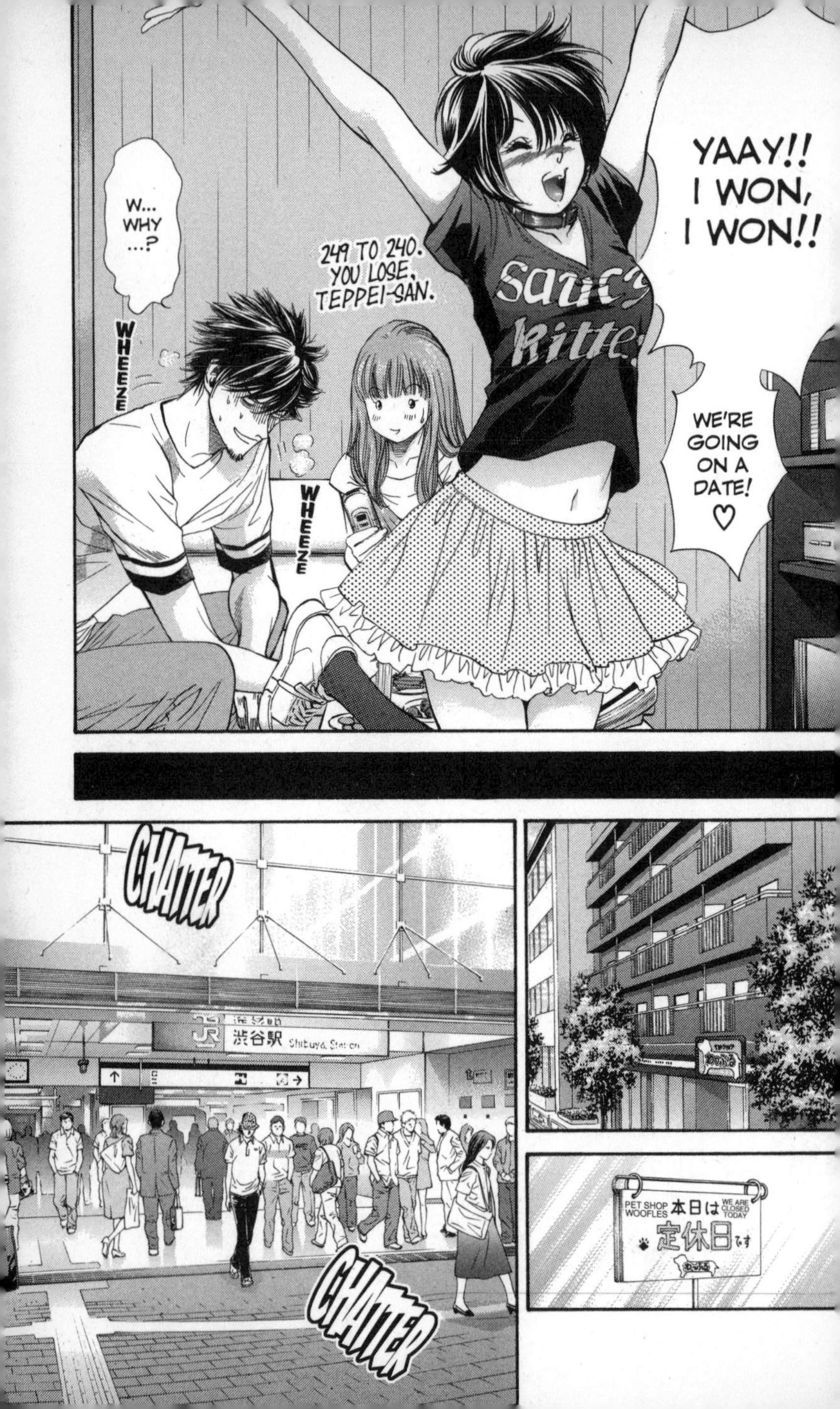
YAAY!! I WON, I WON!!
WE'RE GOING ON A DATE! ♡
249 TO 240. YOU LOSE, TEPPEI-SAN.
W... WHY ...?
WHEEZE
WHEEZE
PET SHOP WOOFLES
本日は 定休日です
WE ARE CLOSED TODAY
渋谷駅 Shibuya Station
CHATTER
CHATTER

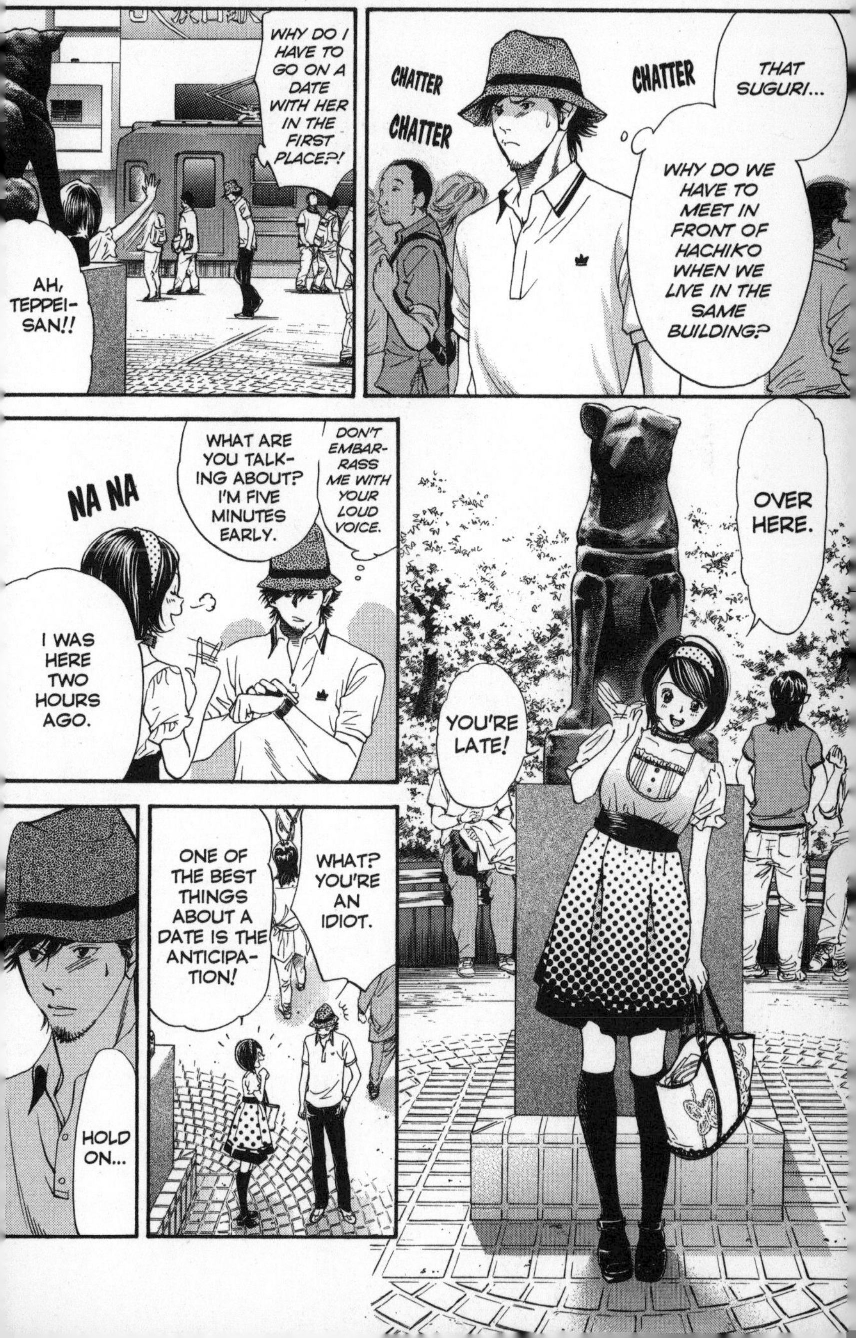

CHATTER
CHATTER
CHATTER
THAT SUGURI...
WHY DO WE HAVE TO MEET IN FRONT OF HACHIKO WHEN WE LIVE IN THE SAME BUILDING?
WHY DO I HAVE TO GO ON A DATE WITH HER IN THE FIRST PLACE?!
AH, TEPPEI-SAN!!
OVER HERE.
YOU'RE LATE!
DON'T EMBARRASS ME WITH YOUR LOUD VOICE.
WHAT ARE YOU TALKING ABOUT? I'M FIVE MINUTES EARLY.
NA NA
I WAS HERE TWO HOURS AGO.
WHAT? YOU'RE AN IDIOT.
ONE OF THE BEST THINGS ABOUT A DATE IS THE ANTICIPATION!
HOLD ON...

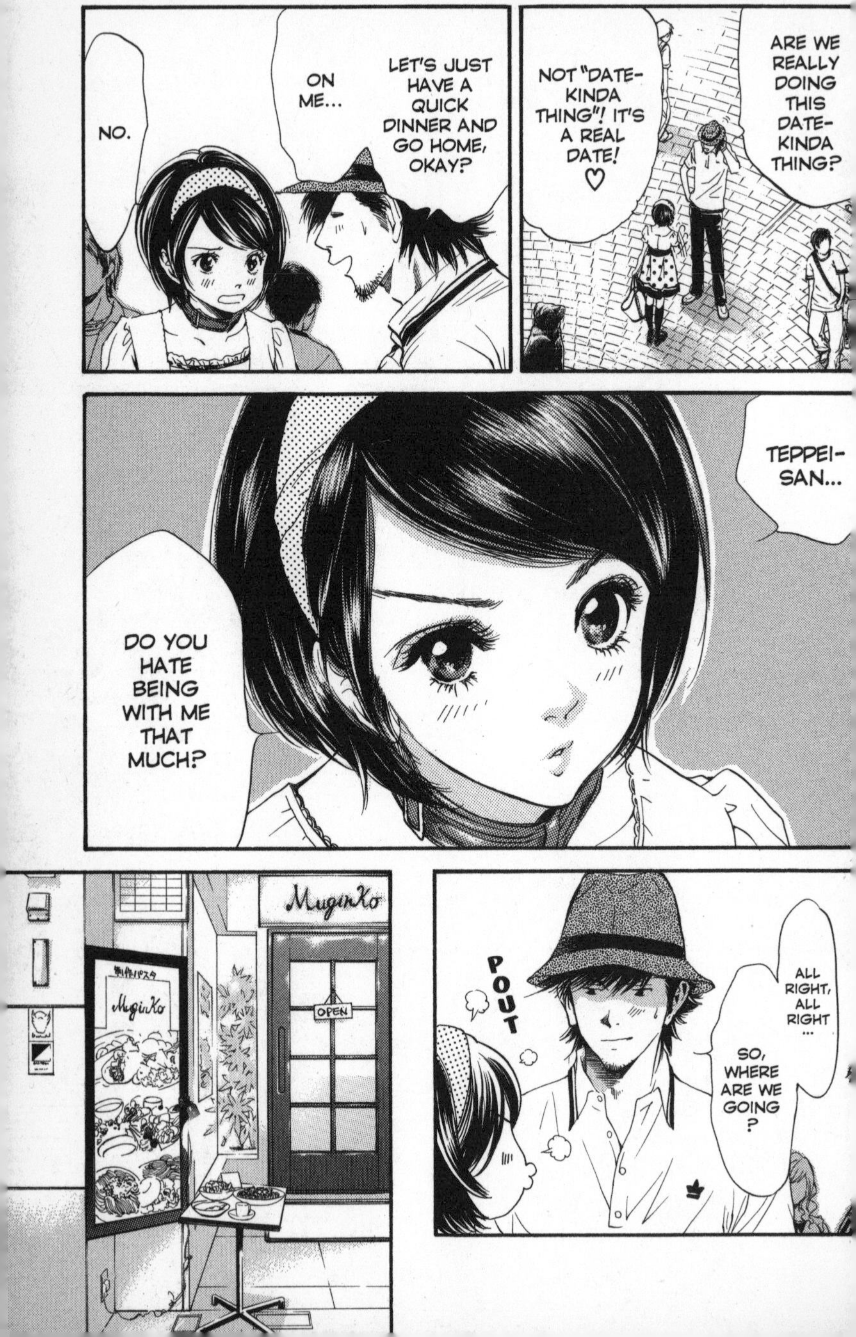
ARE WE REALLY DOING THIS DATE-KINDA THING?
NOT "DATE-KINDA THING"! IT'S A REAL DATE! ♡
LET'S JUST HAVE A QUICK DINNER AND GO HOME, OKAY?
ON ME...
NO.
TEPPEI-SAN...
DO YOU HATE BEING WITH ME THAT MUCH?
ALL RIGHT, ALL RIGHT...
SO, WHERE ARE WE GOING?
POUT
Muginko
OPEN
Muginko

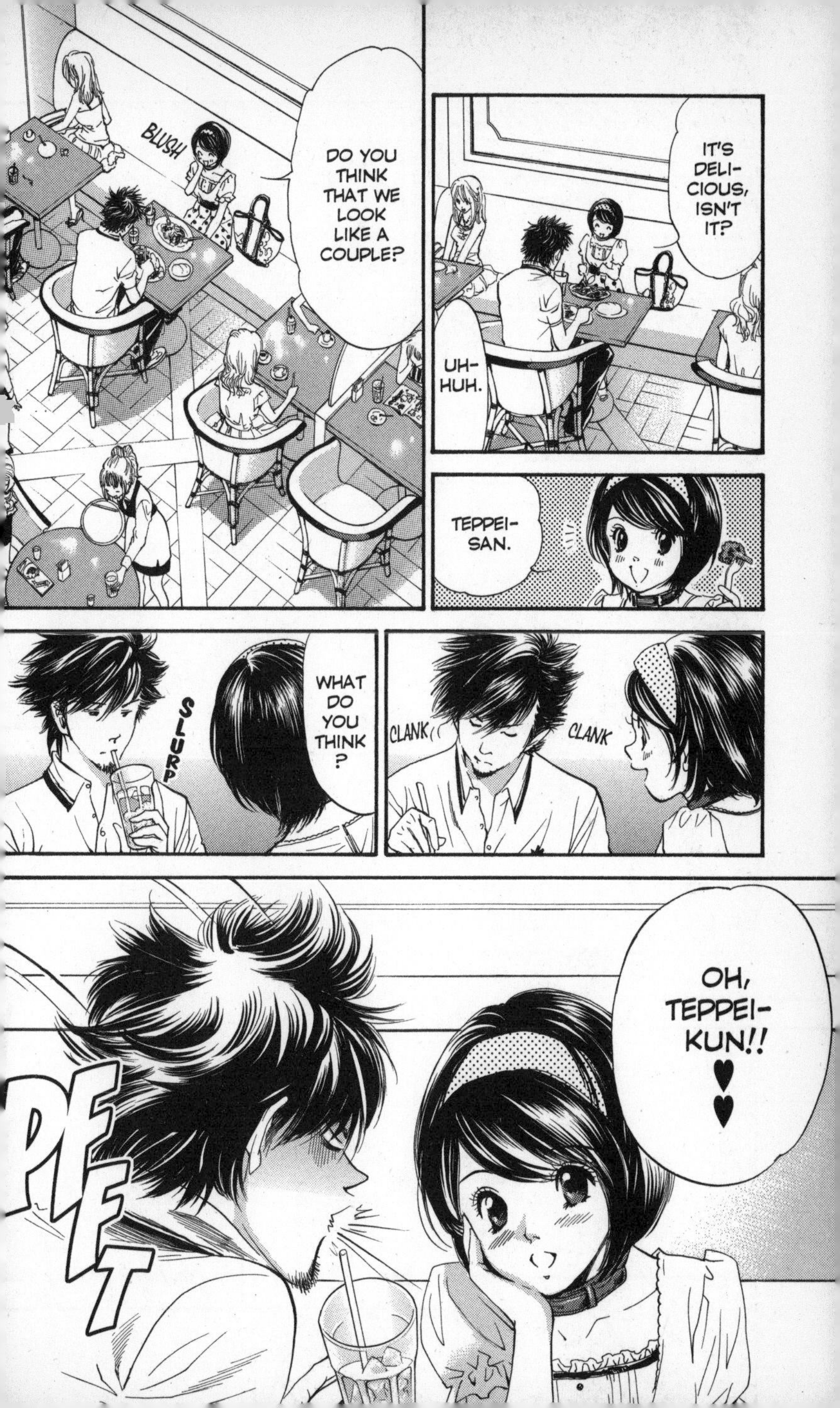
IT'S DELICIOUS, ISN'T IT?
UH-HUH.
TEPPEI-SAN.
DO YOU THINK THAT WE LOOK LIKE A COUPLE?
BLUSH
CLANK
CLANK
WHAT DO YOU THINK?
SLURP
OH, TEPPEI-KUN!! ♥ ♥
PFFT

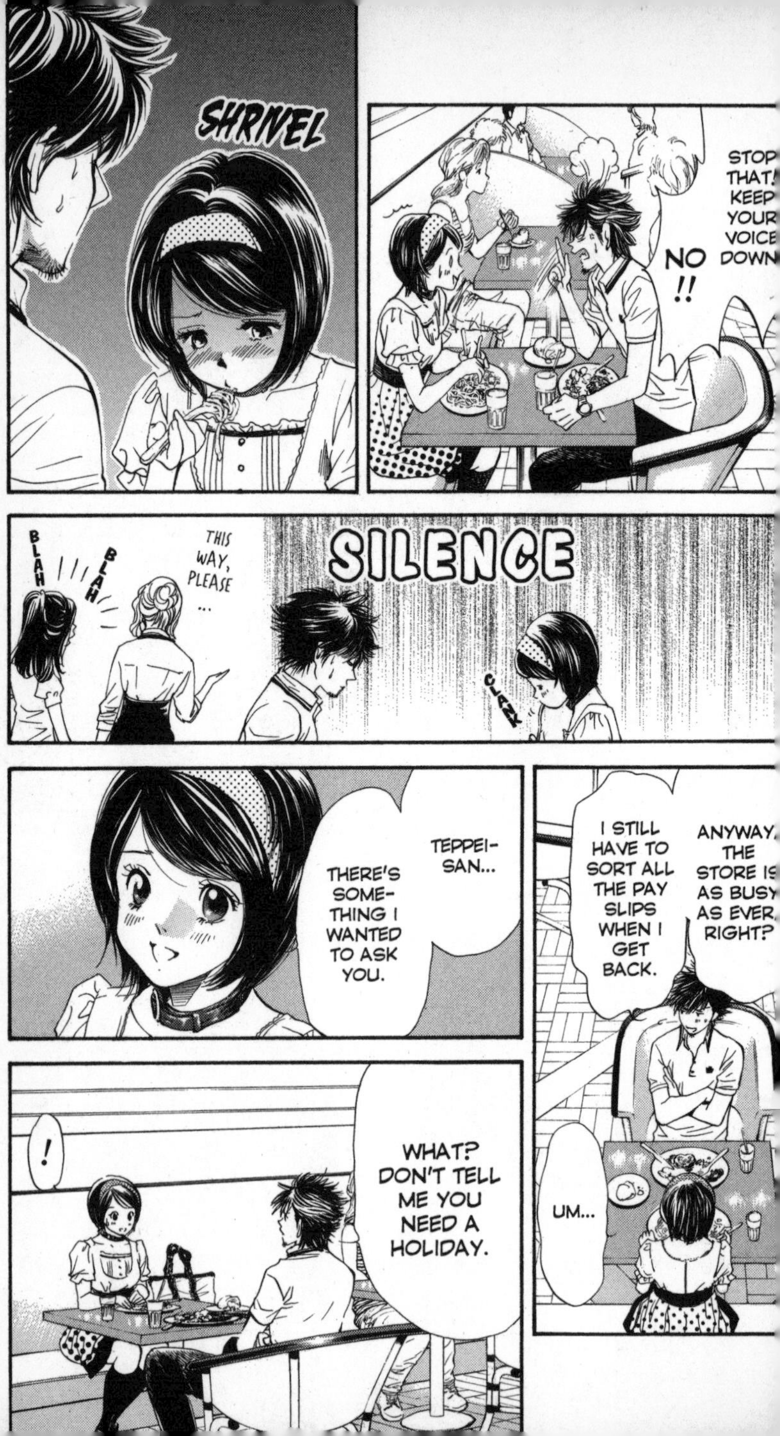
STOP THAT! KEEP YOUR VOICE DOWN
NO !!
SHRIVEL
SILENCE
CLANK
THIS WAY, PLEASE ...
BLAH BLAH
ANYWAY, THE STORE IS AS BUSY AS EVER, RIGHT?
I STILL HAVE TO SORT ALL THE PAY SLIPS WHEN I GET BACK.
UM...
TEPPEI-SAN...
THERE'S SOME-THING I WANTED TO ASK YOU.
WHAT? DON'T TELL ME YOU NEED A HOLIDAY.
!

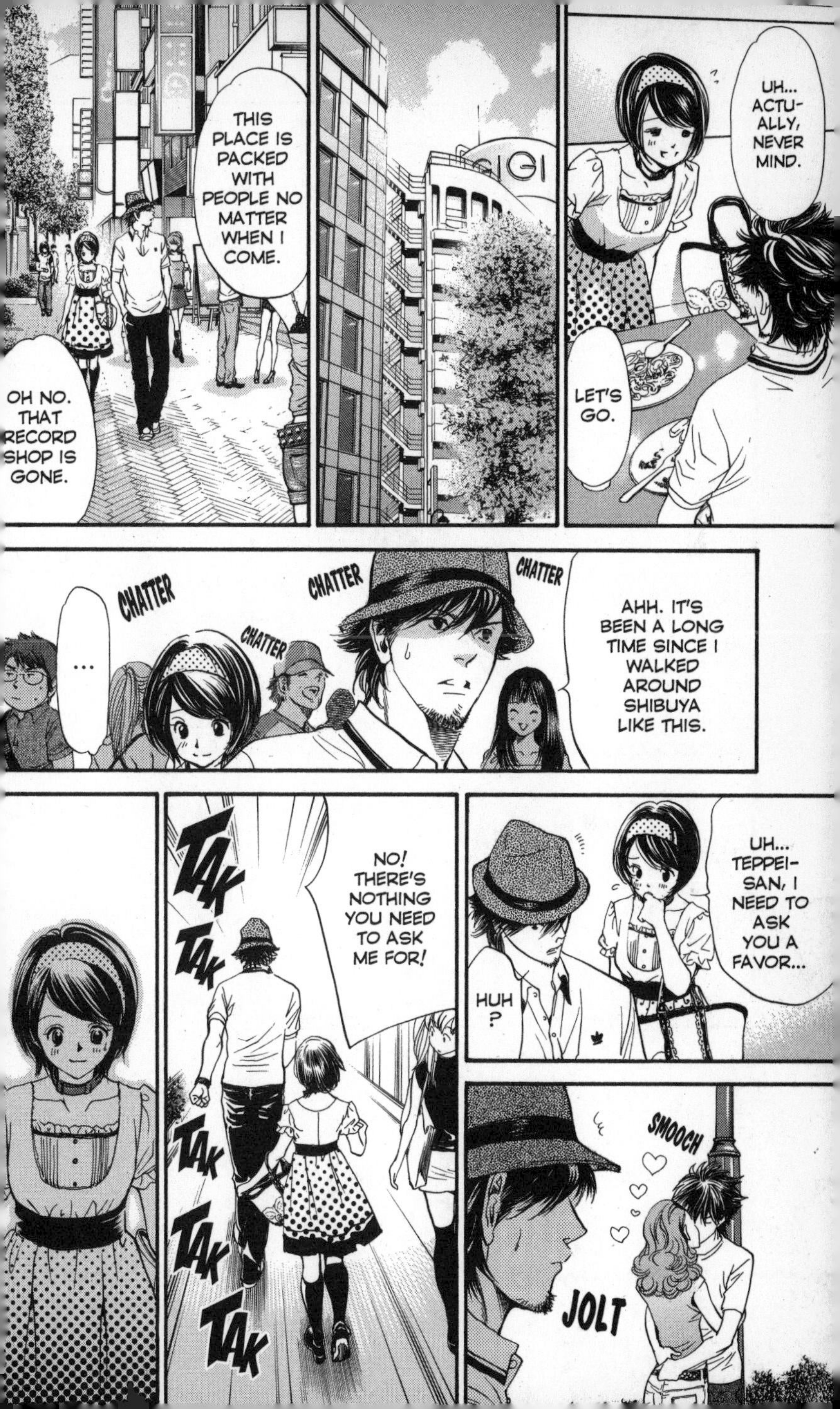
UH... ACTU-ALLY, NEVER MIND.
LET'S GO.
THIS PLACE IS PACKED WITH PEOPLE NO MATTER WHEN I COME.
OH NO. THAT RECORD SHOP IS GONE.
CHATTER
AHH. IT'S BEEN A LONG TIME SINCE I WALKED AROUND SHIBUYA LIKE THIS.
CHATTER
CHATTER
CHATTER
...
UH... TEPPEI-SAN, I NEED TO ASK YOU A FAVOR...
HUH?
SMOOCH
JOLT
NO! THERE'S NOTHING YOU NEED TO ASK ME FOR!
TAK
TAK
TAK
TAK
TAK

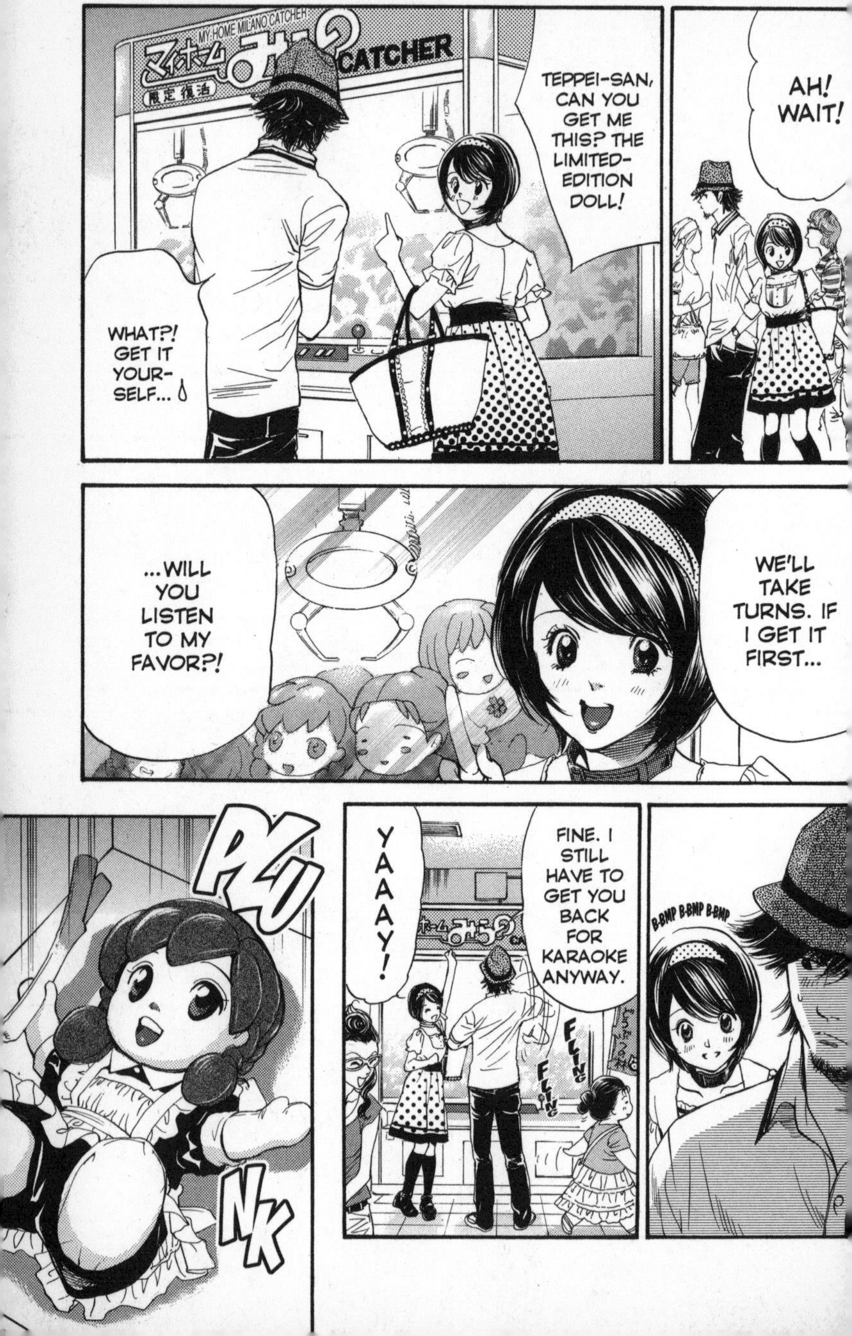
AH! WAIT!
MY-HOME MILANO CATCHER
CATCHER
限定復活
TEPPEI-SAN, CAN YOU GET ME THIS? THE LIMITED-EDITION DOLL!
WHAT?! GET IT YOURSELF...
WE'LL TAKE TURNS. IF I GET IT FIRST...
...WILL YOU LISTEN TO MY FAVOR?!
B-BMP B-BMP B-BMP
FINE. I STILL HAVE TO GET YOU BACK FOR KARAOKE ANYWAY.
YAAAAY!
FLING
FLING
PLU
NK

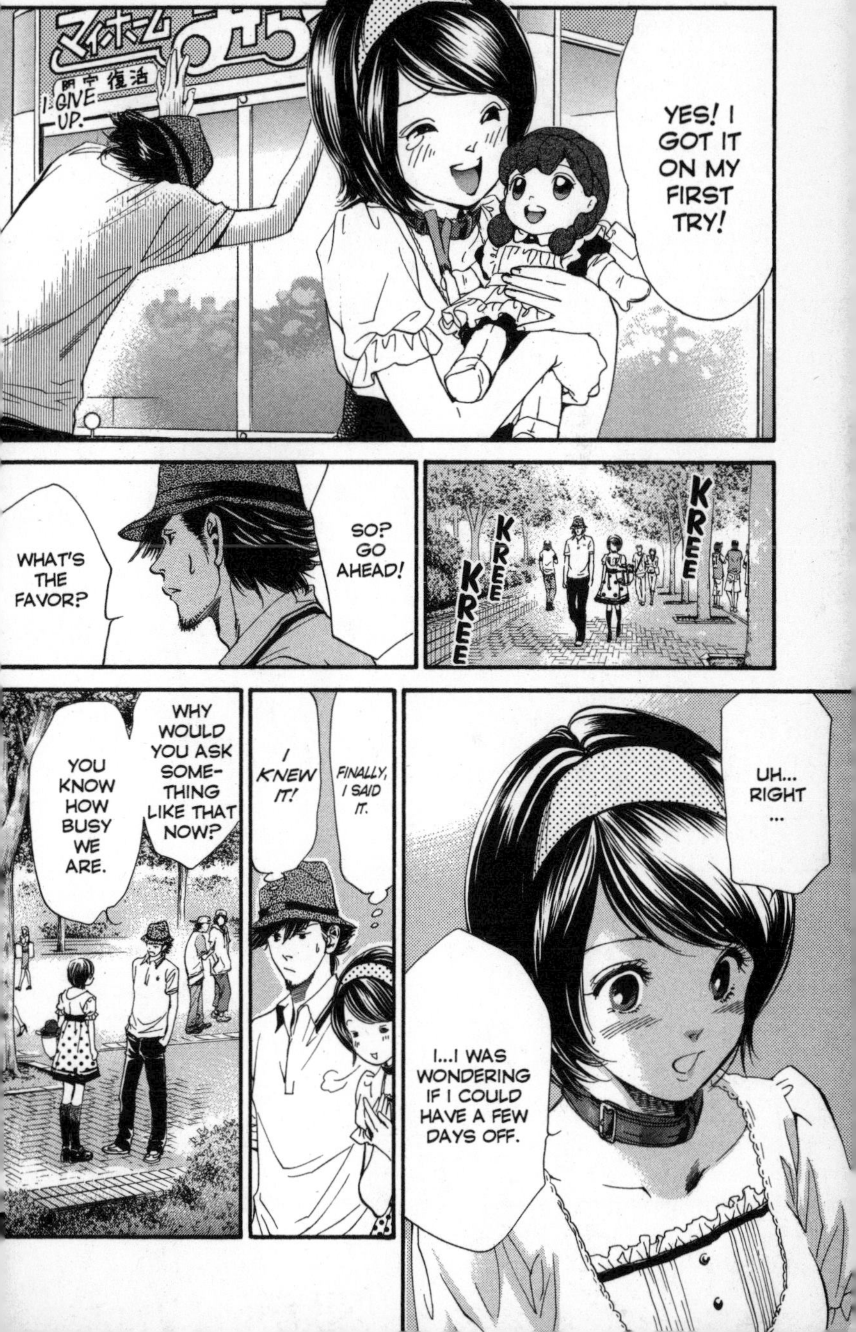
I-GIVE UP.
YES! I GOT IT ON MY FIRST TRY!
KREE
KREE
KREE
SO? GO AHEAD!
WHAT'S THE FAVOR?
UH... RIGHT ...
I...I WAS WONDERING IF I COULD HAVE A FEW DAYS OFF.
FINALLY, I SAID IT.
I KNEW IT!
WHY WOULD YOU ASK SOME-THING LIKE THAT NOW?
YOU KNOW HOW BUSY WE ARE.

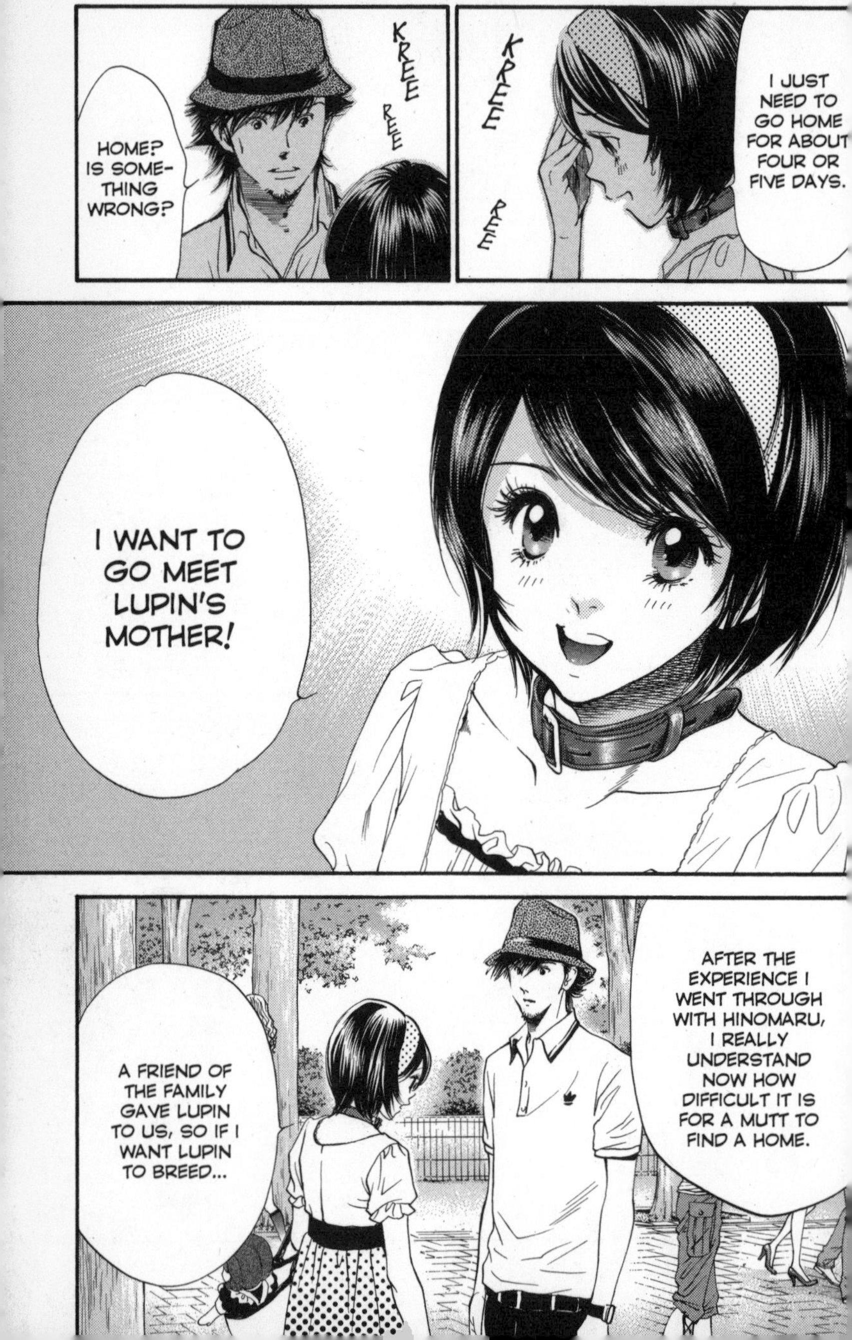
KREE REE
I JUST NEED TO GO HOME FOR ABOUT FOUR OR FIVE DAYS.
KREE REE
HOME? IS SOMETHING WRONG?
I WANT TO GO MEET LUPIN'S MOTHER!
AFTER THE EXPERIENCE I WENT THROUGH WITH HINOMARU, I REALLY UNDERSTAND NOW HOW DIFFICULT IT IS FOR A MUTT TO FIND A HOME.
A FRIEND OF THE FAMILY GAVE LUPIN TO US, SO IF I WANT LUPIN TO BREED...

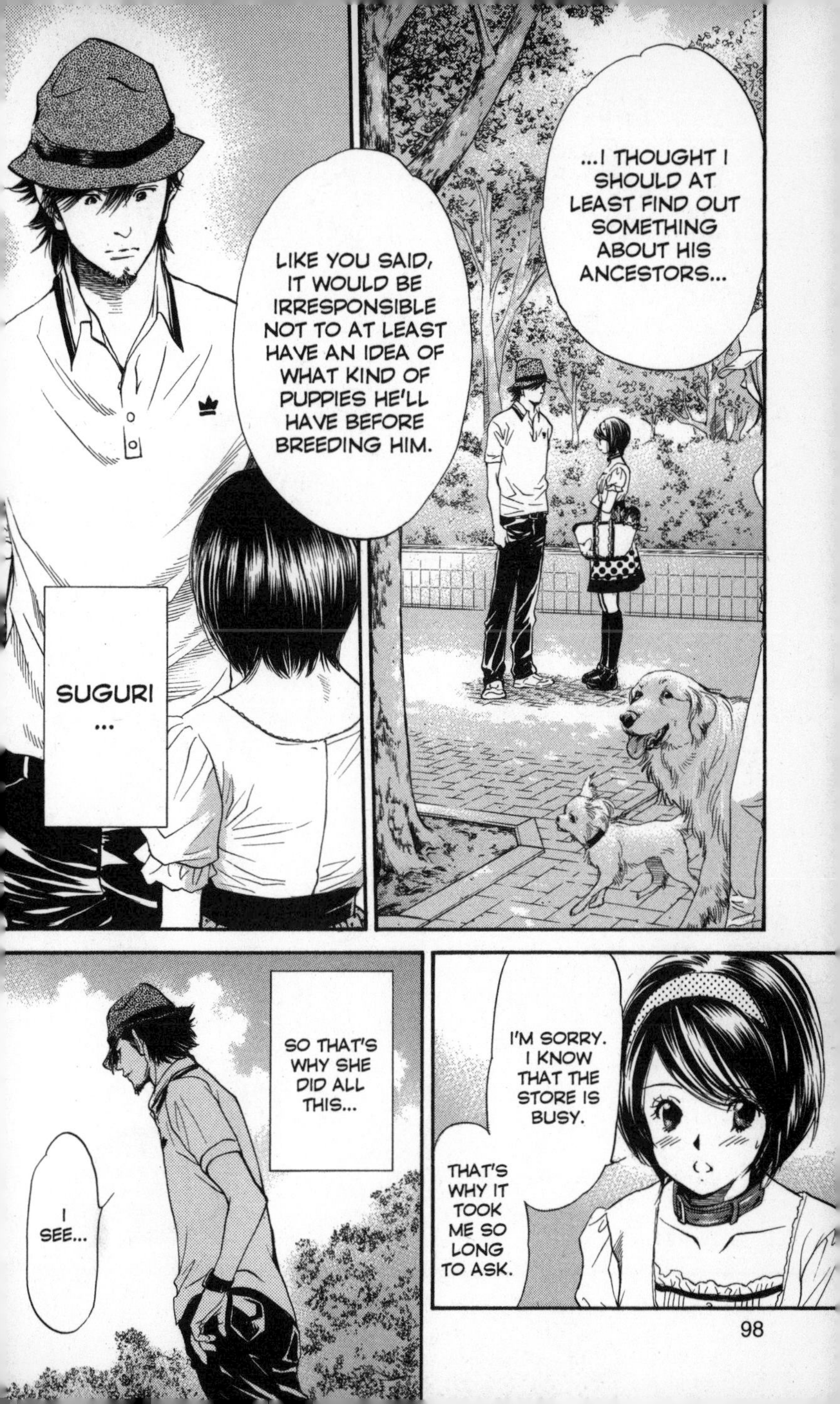
LIKE YOU SAID, IT WOULD BE IRRESPONSIBLE NOT TO AT LEAST HAVE AN IDEA OF WHAT KIND OF PUPPIES HE'LL HAVE BEFORE BREEDING HIM.
...I THOUGHT I SHOULD AT LEAST FIND OUT SOMETHING ABOUT HIS ANCESTORS...
SUGURI ...
I'M SORRY. I KNOW THAT THE STORE IS BUSY.
THAT'S WHY IT TOOK ME SO LONG TO ASK.
SO THAT'S WHY SHE DID ALL THIS...
I SEE...

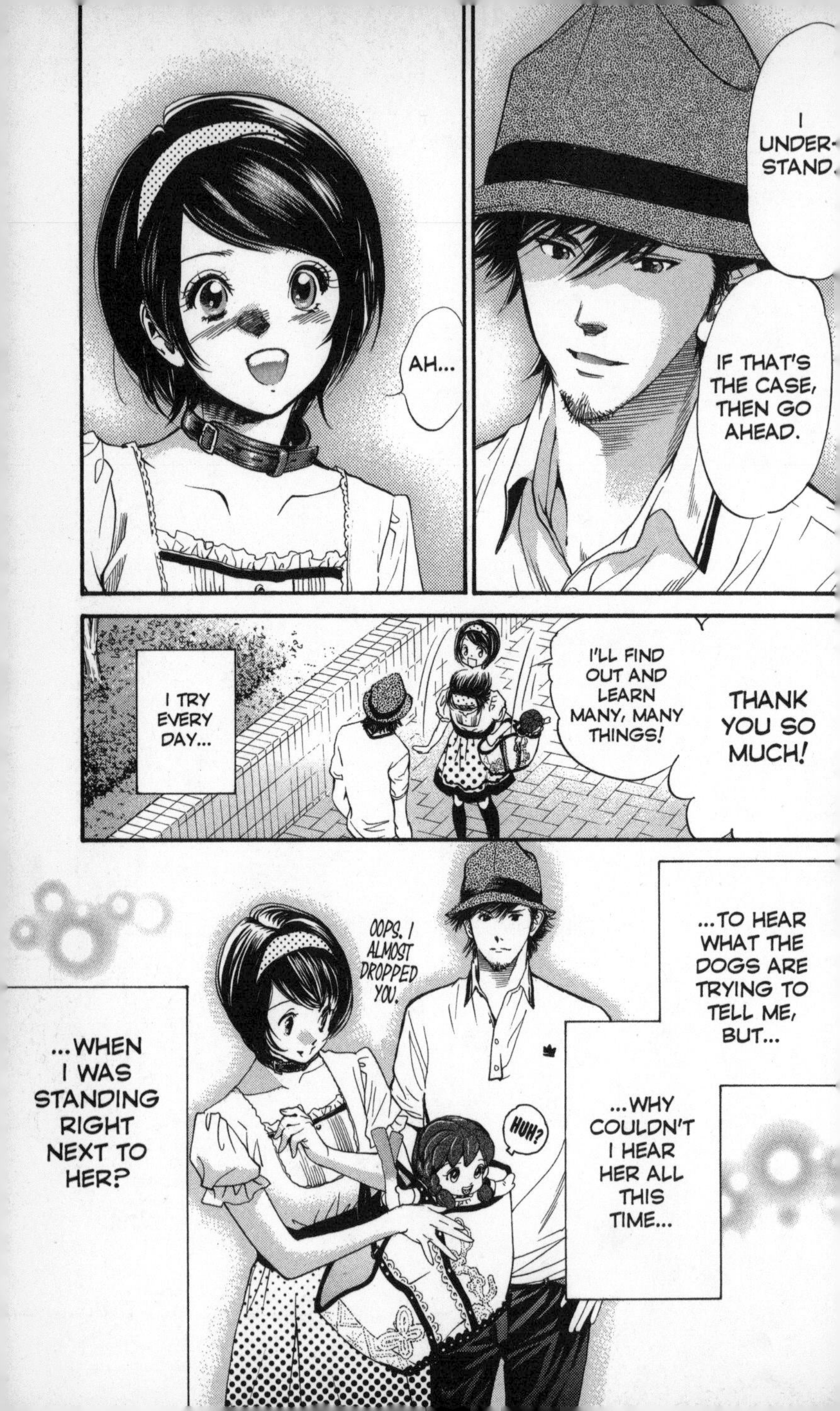
I UNDER-STAND.
IF THAT'S THE CASE, THEN GO AHEAD.
AH...
THANK YOU SO MUCH!
I'LL FIND OUT AND LEARN MANY, MANY THINGS!
I TRY EVERY DAY...
...TO HEAR WHAT THE DOGS ARE TRYING TO TELL ME, BUT...
...WHY COULDN'T I HEAR HER ALL THIS TIME...
HUH?
OOPS. I ALMOST DROPPED YOU.
...WHEN I WAS STANDING RIGHT NEXT TO HER?

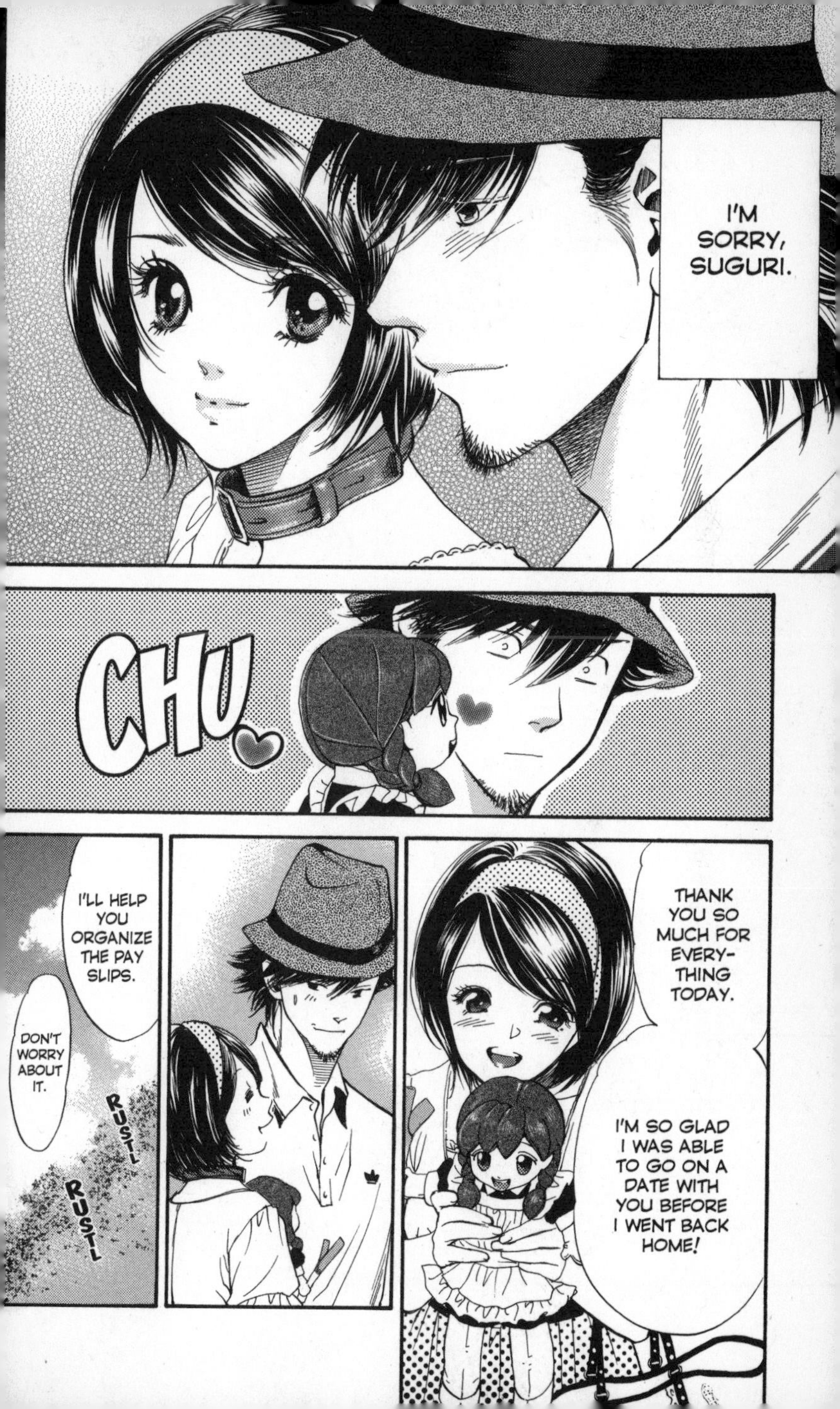
I'M SORRY, SUGURI.
CHU
THANK YOU SO MUCH FOR EVERY-THING TODAY.
I'M SO GLAD I WAS ABLE TO GO ON A DATE WITH YOU BEFORE I WENT BACK HOME!
RUSTL
RUSTL
I'LL HELP YOU ORGANIZE THE PAY SLIPS.
DON'T WORRY ABOUT IT.

CHAPTER 157: GOING HOME TO VISIT MOM

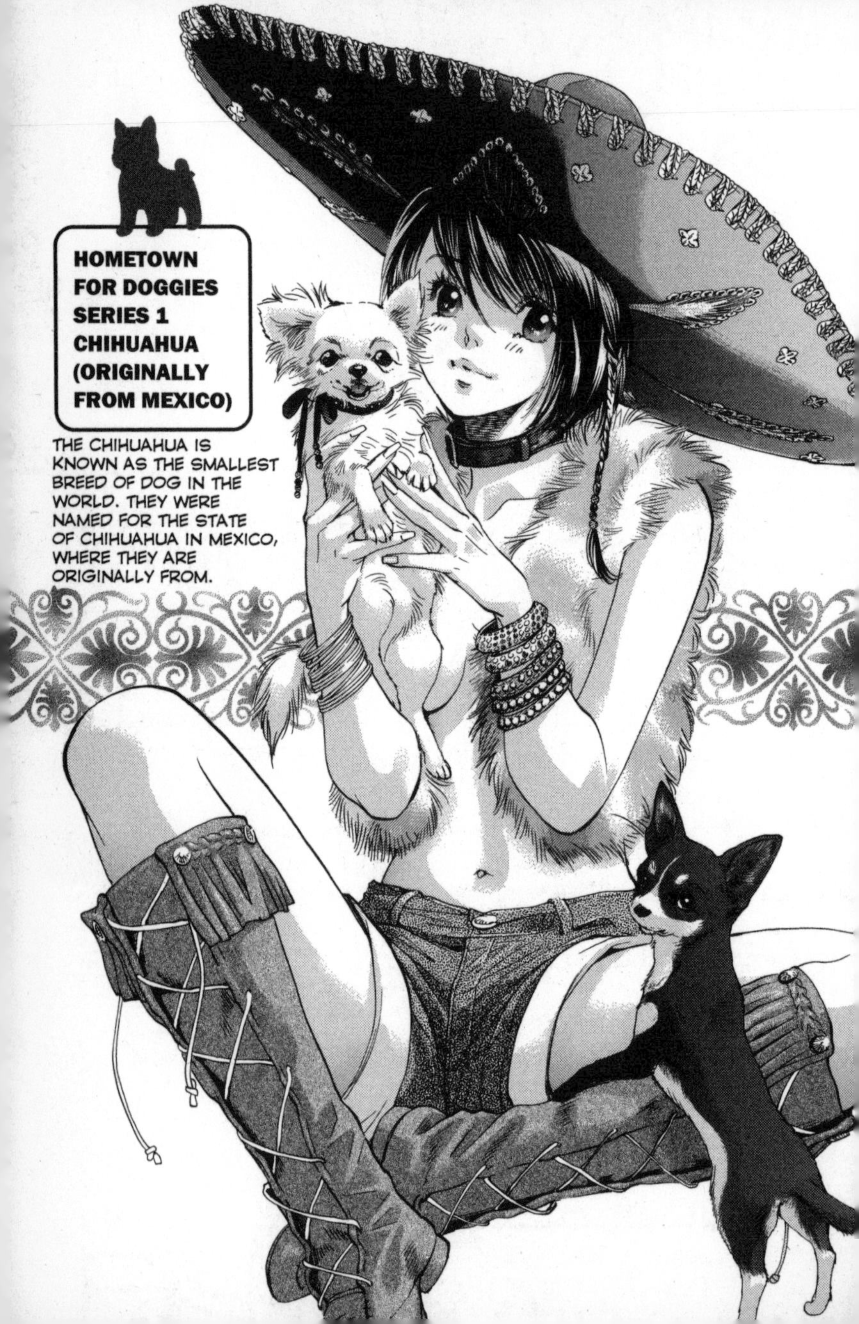
HOMETOWN FOR DOGGIES SERIES 1 CHIHUAHUA (ORIGINALLY FROM MEXICO)
THE CHIHUAHUA IS KNOWN AS THE SMALLEST BREED OF DOG IN THE WORLD. THEY WERE NAMED FOR THE STATE OF CHIHUAHUA IN MEXICO, WHERE THEY ARE ORIGINALLY FROM.

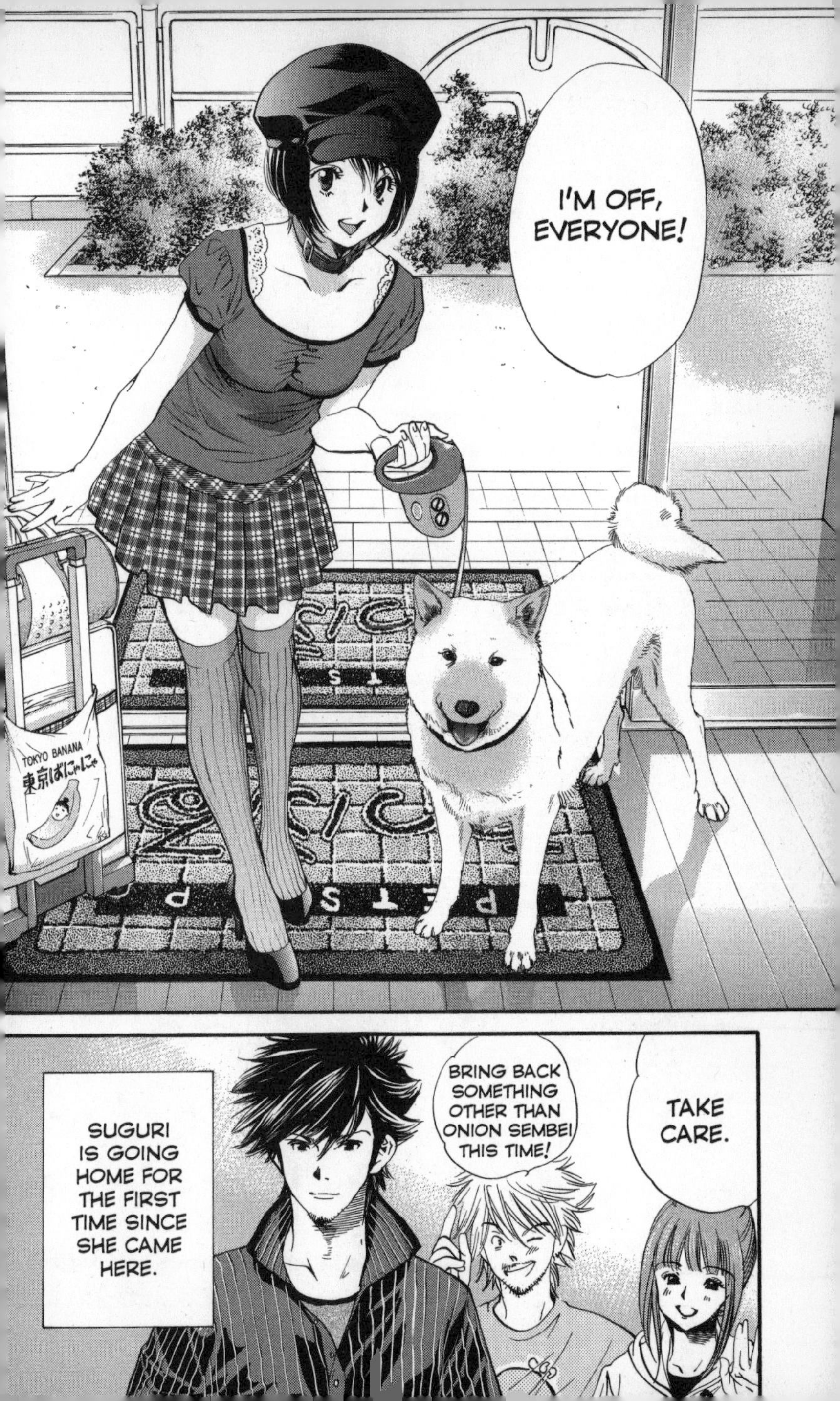
I'M OFF, EVERYONE!
TOKYO BANANA
TAKE CARE.
BRING BACK SOMETHING OTHER THAN ONION SEMBEI THIS TIME!
SUGURI IS GOING HOME FOR THE FIRST TIME SINCE SHE CAME HERE.

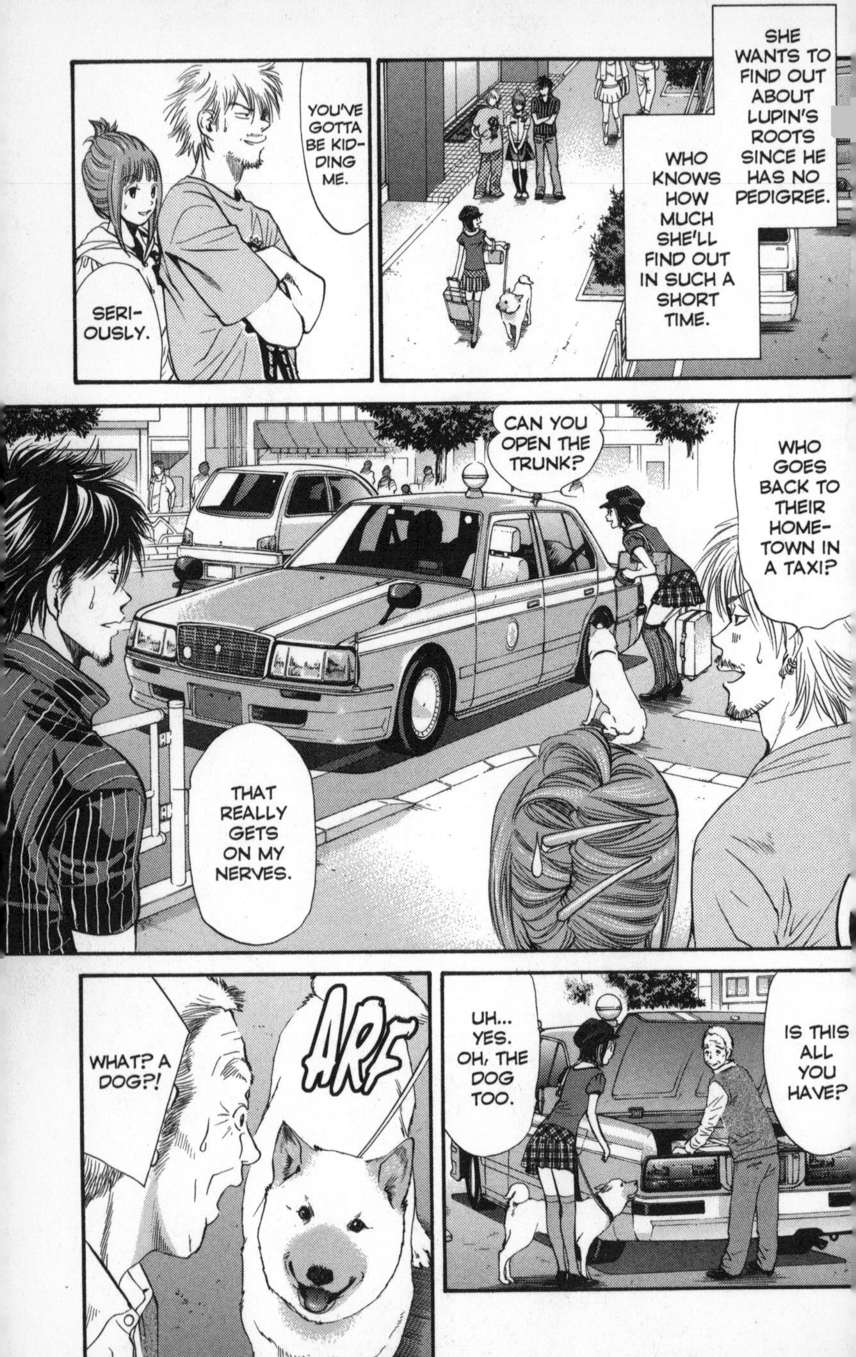
SHE WANTS TO FIND OUT ABOUT LUPIN'S ROOTS SINCE HE HAS NO PEDIGREE.
WHO KNOWS HOW MUCH SHE'LL FIND OUT IN SUCH A SHORT TIME.
YOU'VE GOTTA BE KID-DING ME.
SERI-OUSLY.
WHO GOES BACK TO THEIR HOME-TOWN IN A TAXI!?
CAN YOU OPEN THE TRUNK?
THAT REALLY GETS ON MY NERVES.
IS THIS ALL YOU HAVE?
UH... YES. OH, THE DOG TOO.
ARF
WHAT? A DOG?!

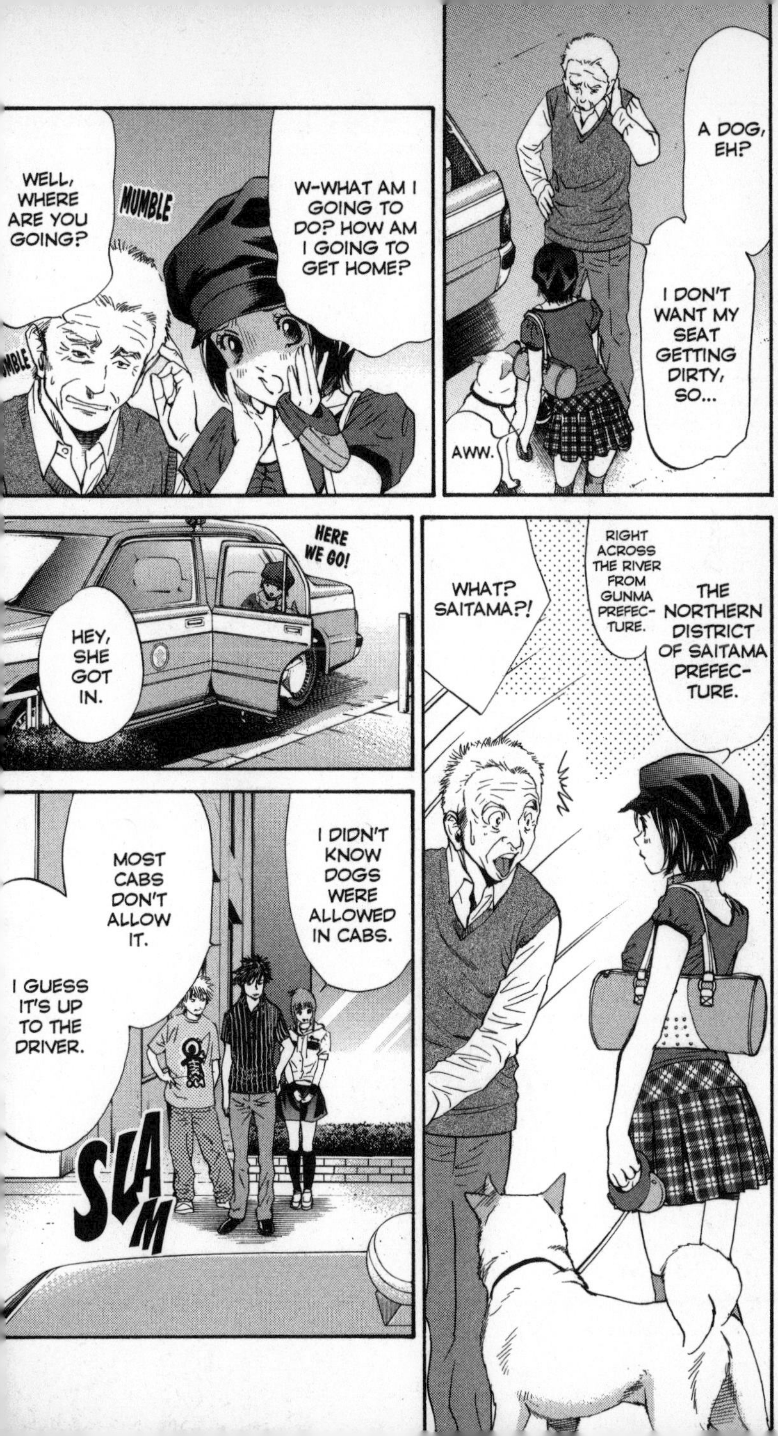
A DOG, EH?
I DON'T WANT MY SEAT GETTING DIRTY, SO...
AWW.
W-WHAT AM I GOING TO DO? HOW AM I GOING TO GET HOME?
MUMBLE
WELL, WHERE ARE YOU GOING?
THE NORTHERN DISTRICT OF SAITAMA PREFEC- TURE.
RIGHT ACROSS THE RIVER FROM GUNMA PREFEC- TURE.
WHAT? SAITAMA?!
HERE WE GO!
HEY, SHE GOT IN.
I DIDN'T KNOW DOGS WERE ALLOWED IN CABS.
MOST CABS DON'T ALLOW IT.
I GUESS IT'S UP TO THE DRIVER.
SLAM

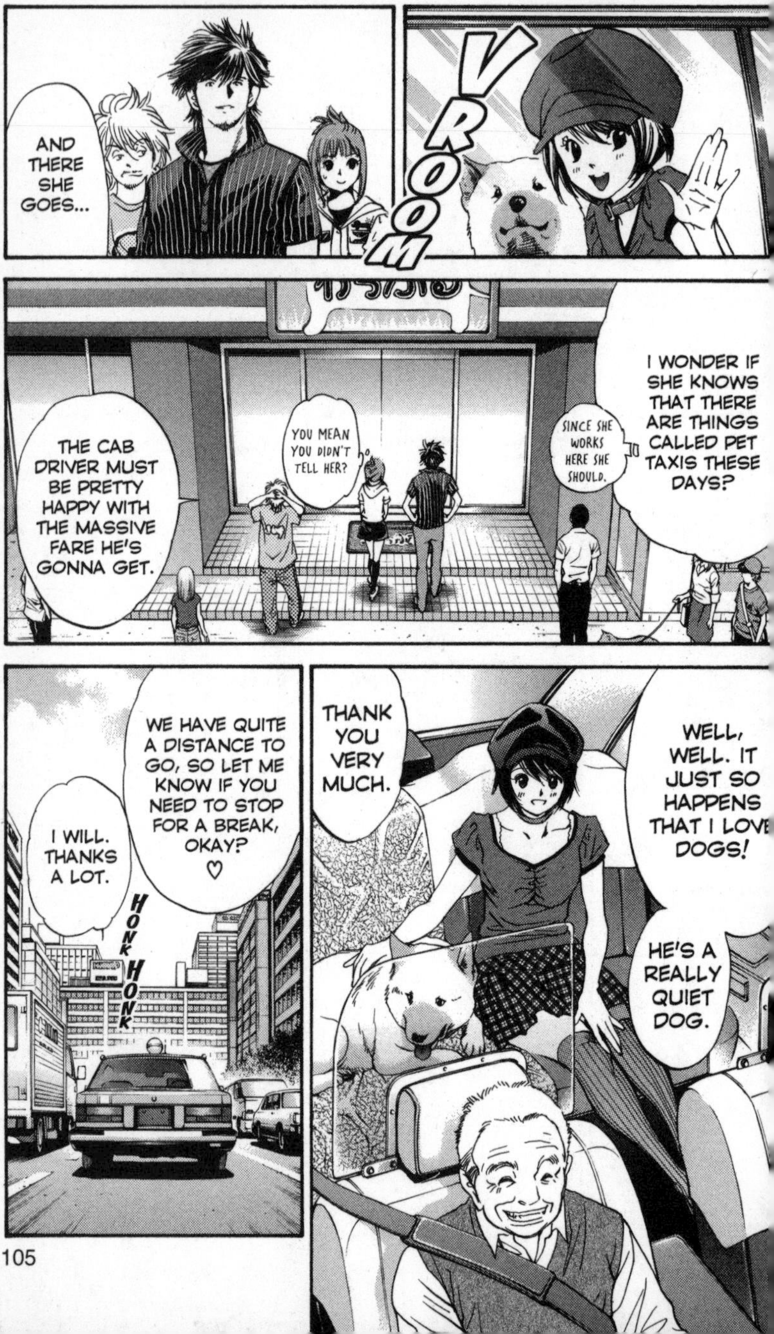
VROOOM
AND THERE SHE GOES...
I WONDER IF SHE KNOWS THAT THERE ARE THINGS CALLED PET TAXIS THESE DAYS?
SINCE SHE WORKS HERE SHE SHOULD.
YOU MEAN YOU DIDN'T TELL HER?
THE CAB DRIVER MUST BE PRETTY HAPPY WITH THE MASSIVE FARE HE'S GONNA GET.
WELL, WELL. IT JUST SO HAPPENS THAT I LOVE DOGS!
THANK YOU VERY MUCH.
HE'S A REALLY QUIET DOG.
WE HAVE QUITE A DISTANCE TO GO, SO LET ME KNOW IF YOU NEED TO STOP FOR A BREAK, OKAY? ♡
I WILL. THANKS A LOT.
HONK HONK

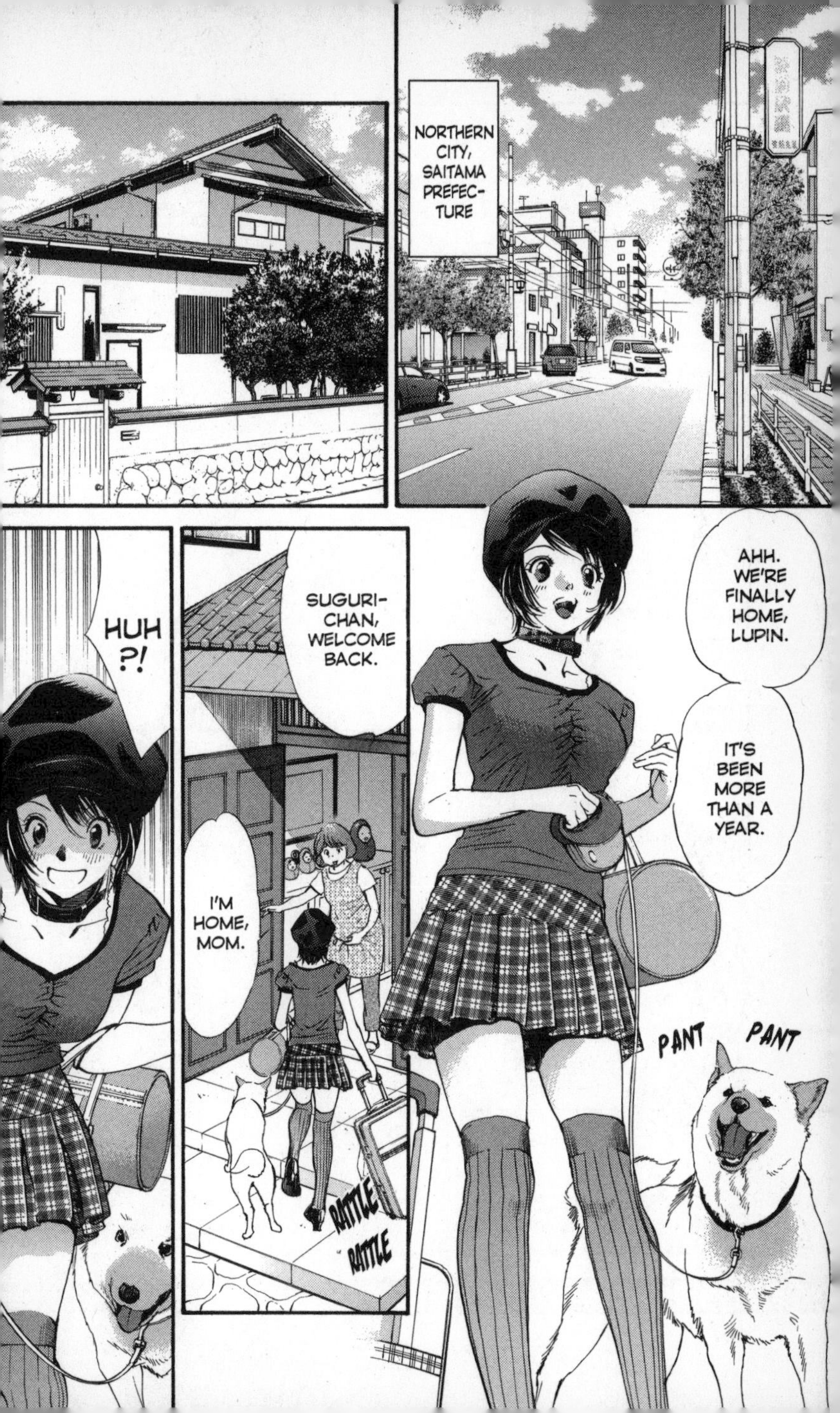
NORTHERN CITY, SAITAMA PREFECTURE
AHH. WE'RE FINALLY HOME, LUPIN.
IT'S BEEN MORE THAN A YEAR.
PANT PANT
SUGURI-CHAN, WELCOME BACK.
I'M HOME, MOM.
RATTLE RATTLE
HUH ?!

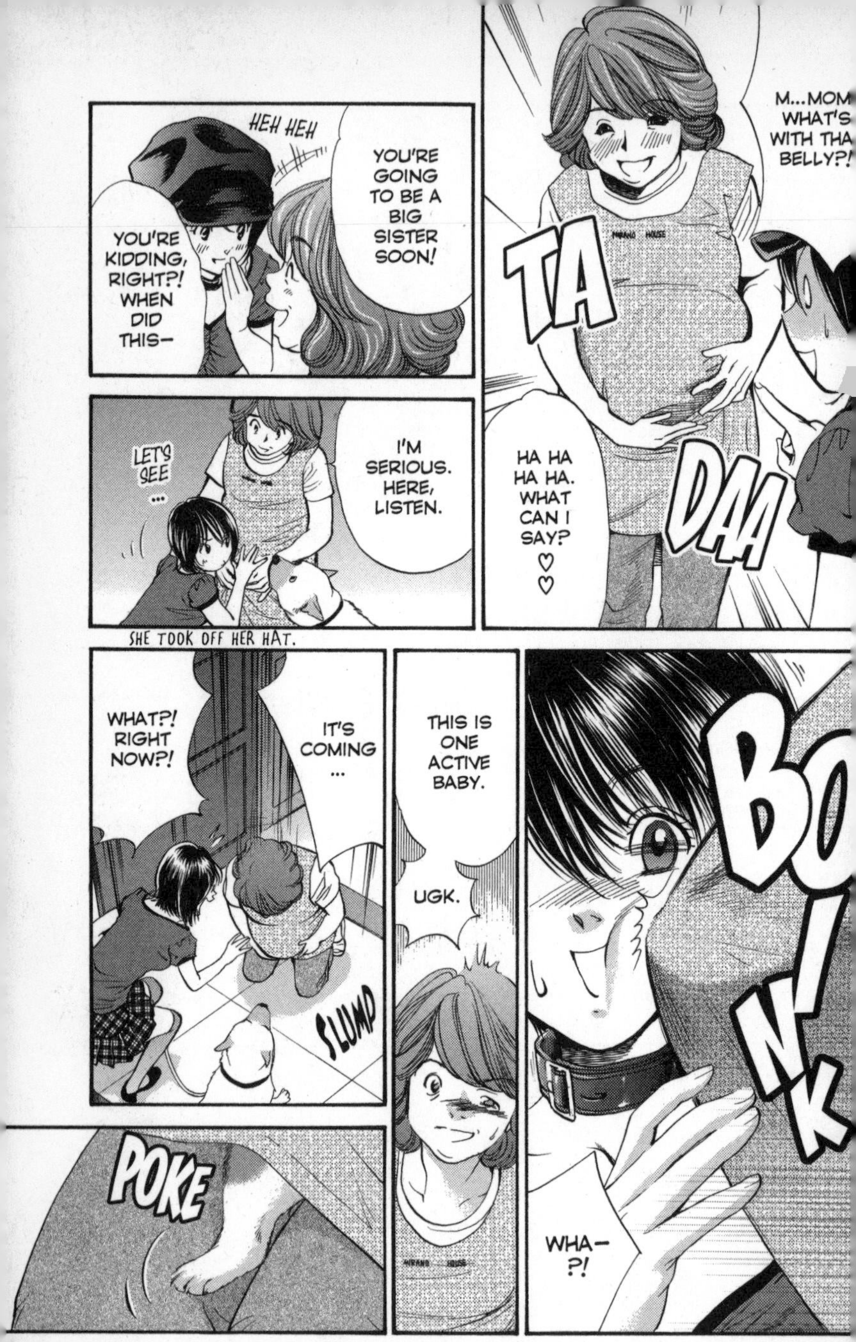
M...MOM
WHAT'S
WITH THA
BELLY?!
TA
DAA
HA HA
HA HA.
WHAT
CAN I
SAY?
♡
♡
HEH HEH
YOU'RE GOING TO BE A BIG SISTER SOON!
YOU'RE KIDDING, RIGHT?! WHEN DID THIS—
I'M SERIOUS. HERE, LISTEN.
LET'S SEE ...
SHE TOOK OFF HER HAT.
BOINK
WHA—?!
THIS IS ONE ACTIVE BABY.
UGK.
IT'S COMING ...
WHAT?! RIGHT NOW?!
SLUMP
POKE

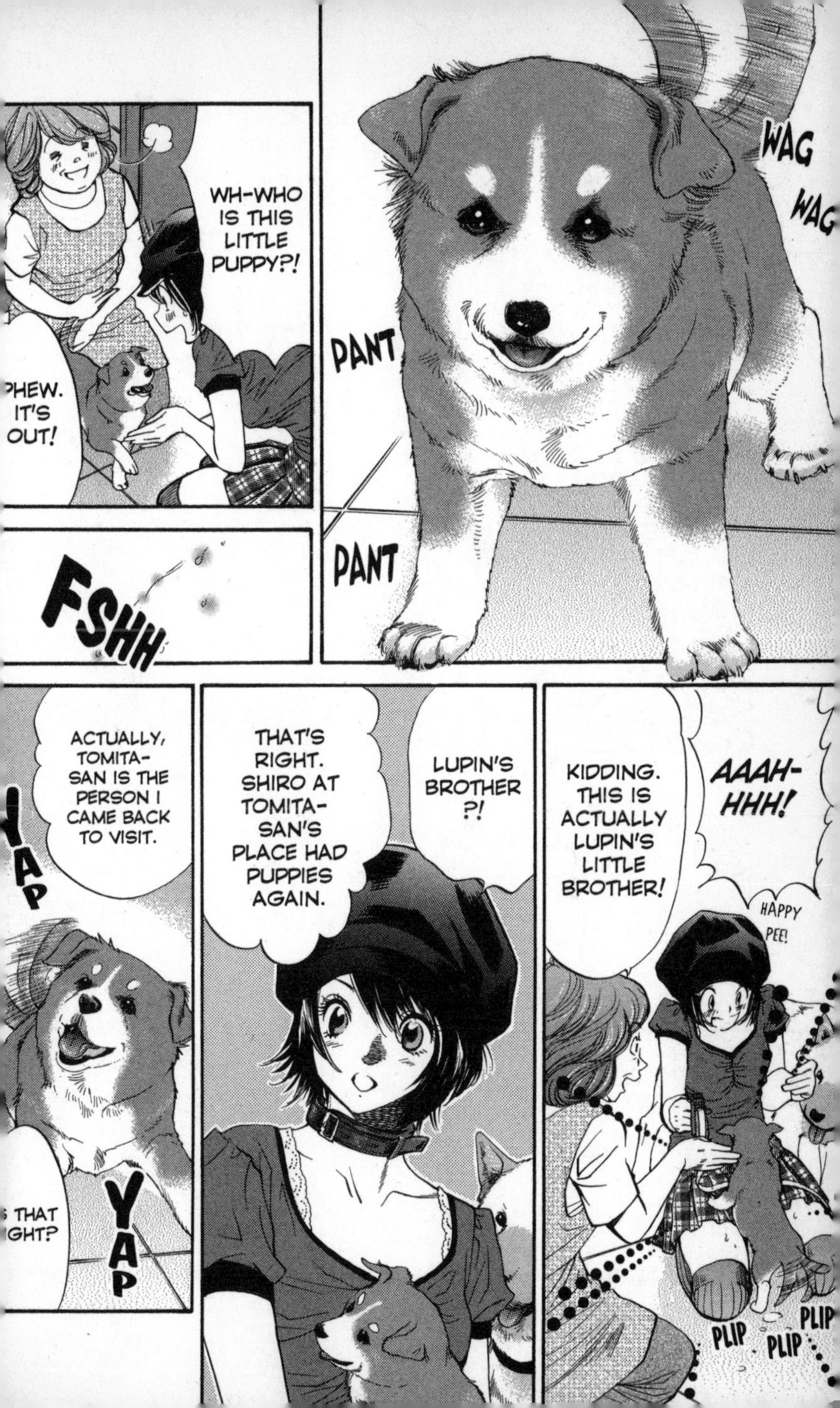
WAG
WAG
PANT
PANT
WH-WHO IS THIS LITTLE PUPPY?!
PHEW. IT'S OUT!
FSHH
AAAH-HHH!
KIDDING. THIS IS ACTUALLY LUPIN'S LITTLE BROTHER!
HAPPY PEE!
PLIP
PLIP
PLIP
LUPIN'S BROTHER ?!
THAT'S RIGHT. SHIRO AT TOMITA-SAN'S PLACE HAD PUPPIES AGAIN.
ACTUALLY, TOMITA-SAN IS THE PERSON I CAME BACK TO VISIT.
YAP
THAT
YAP
YAP

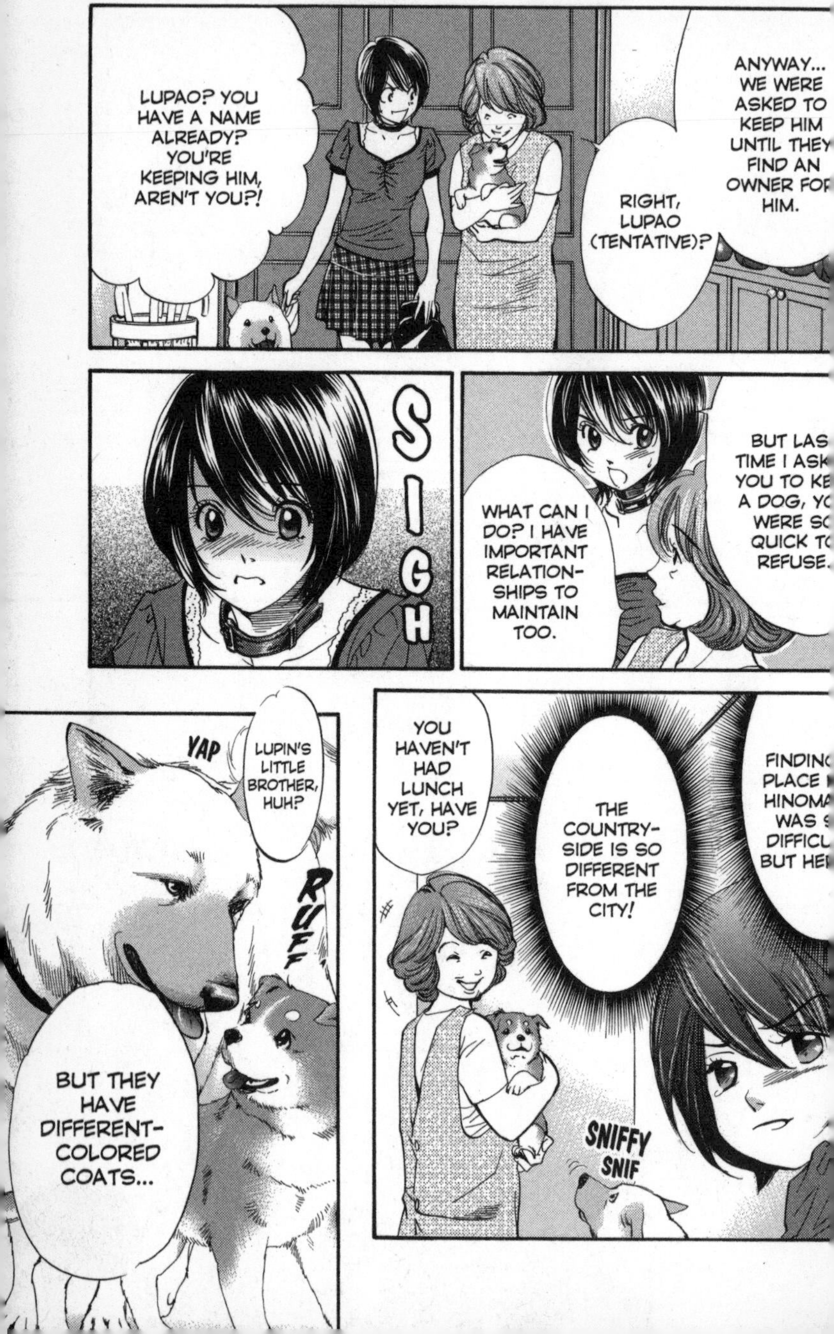

ANYWAY... WE WERE ASKED TO KEEP HIM UNTIL THEY FIND AN OWNER FOF HIM.
RIGHT, LUPAO (TENTATIVE)?
LUPAO? YOU HAVE A NAME ALREADY? YOU'RE KEEPING HIM, AREN'T YOU?!
BUT LAS TIME I ASK YOU TO KE A DOG, YO WERE SO QUICK TO REFUSE.
WHAT CAN I DO? I HAVE IMPORTANT RELATION-SHIPS TO MAINTAIN TOO.
SIGH
FINDIN PLACE HINOMA WAS DIFFICU BUT HE
THE COUNTRY-SIDE IS SO DIFFERENT FROM THE CITY!
YOU HAVEN'T HAD LUNCH YET, HAVE YOU?
SNIFFY SNIF
LUPIN'S LITTLE BROTHER, HUH?
YAP
RUFF
BUT THEY HAVE DIFFERENT-COLORED COATS...

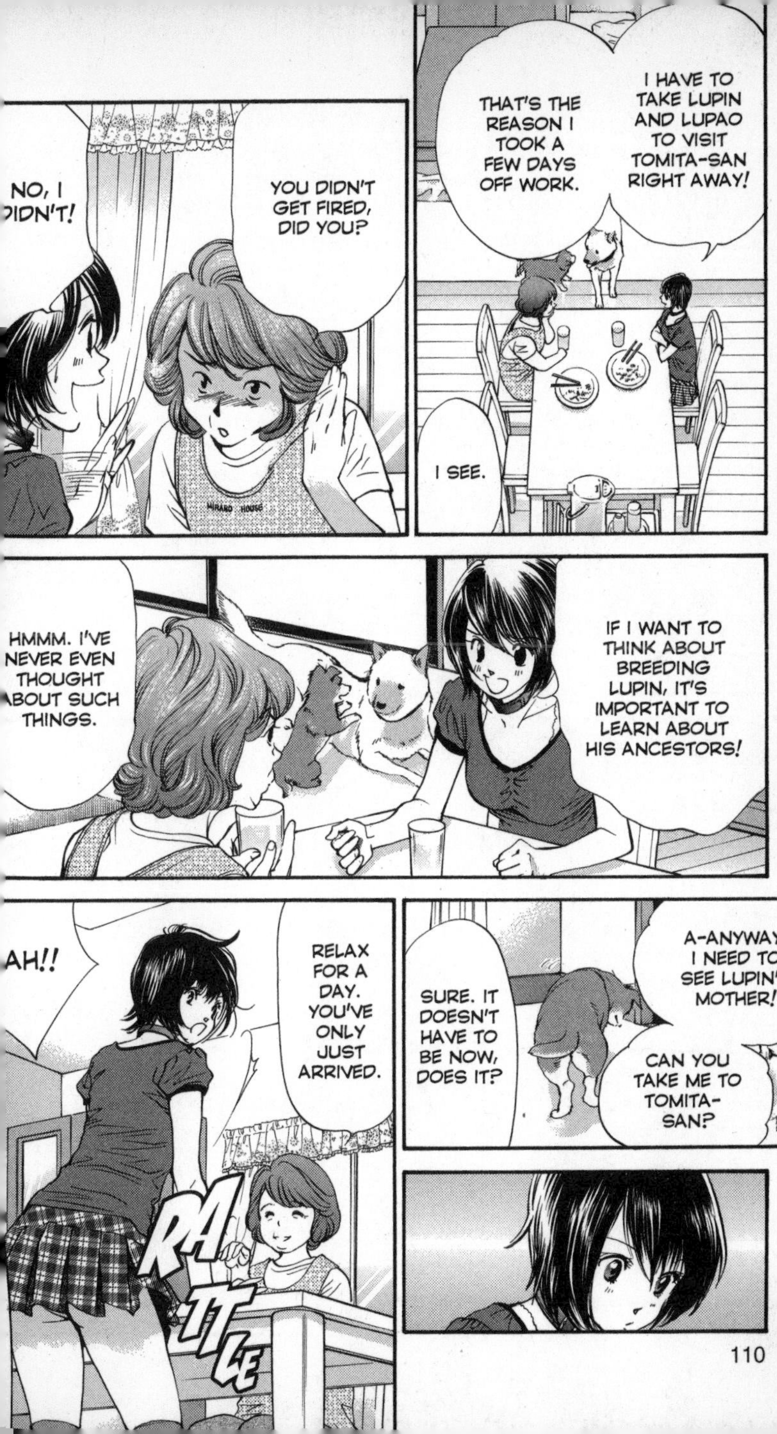
I HAVE TO TAKE LUPIN AND LUPAO TO VISIT TOMITA-SAN RIGHT AWAY!
THAT'S THE REASON I TOOK A FEW DAYS OFF WORK.
I SEE.
YOU DIDN'T GET FIRED, DID YOU?
NO, I DIDN'T!
IF I WANT TO THINK ABOUT BREEDING LUPIN, IT'S IMPORTANT TO LEARN ABOUT HIS ANCESTORS!
HMMM. I'VE NEVER EVEN THOUGHT ABOUT SUCH THINGS.
A-ANYWAY, I NEED TO SEE LUPIN'S MOTHER!
CAN YOU TAKE ME TO TOMITA-SAN?
SURE. IT DOESN'T HAVE TO BE NOW, DOES IT?
RELAX FOR A DAY. YOU'VE ONLY JUST ARRIVED.
AH!!
RATTLE

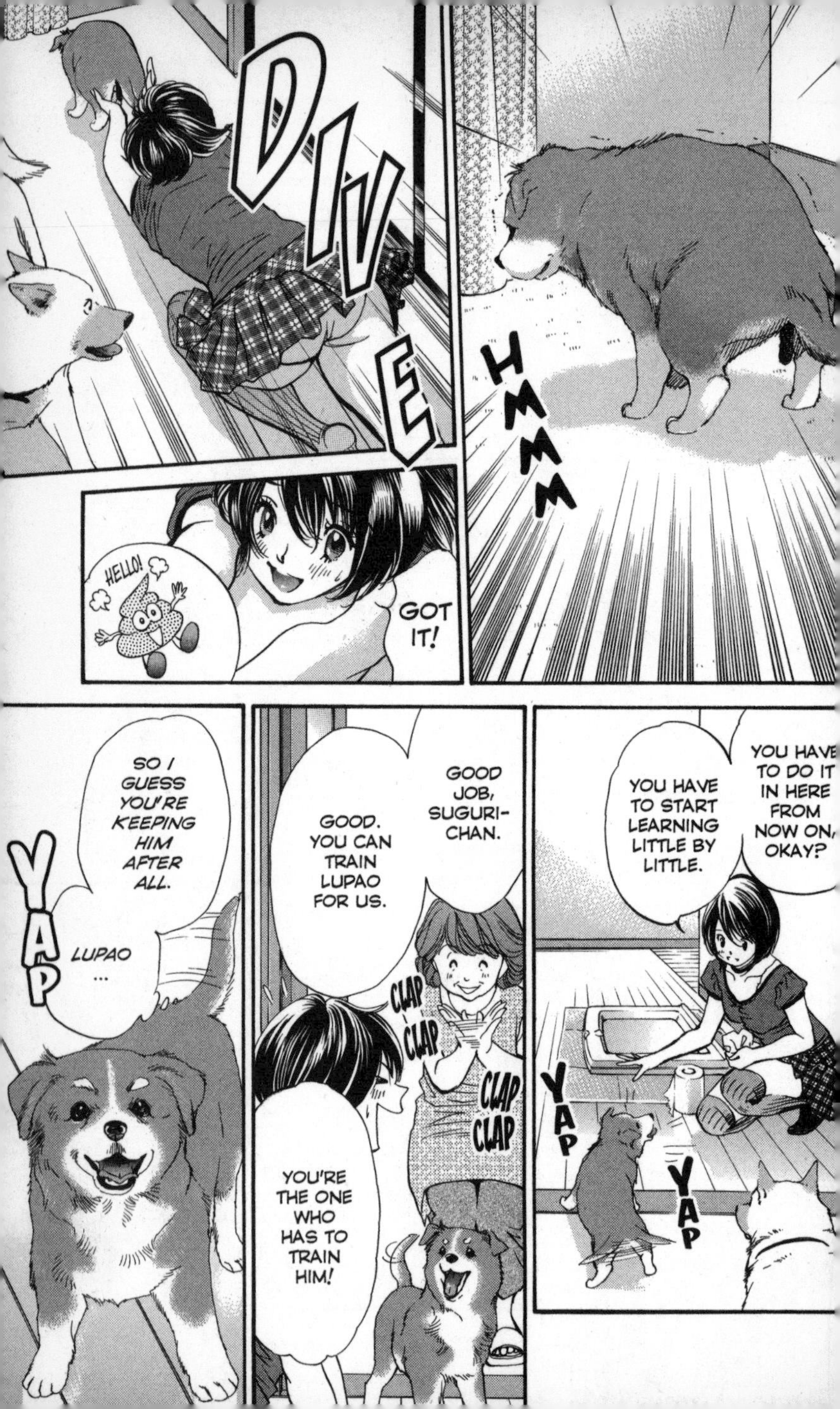
HMMM
DIVE
GOT IT!
HELLO!
YOU HAVE TO DO IT IN HERE FROM NOW ON, OKAY?
YOU HAVE TO START LEARNING LITTLE BY LITTLE.
YAP
YAP
GOOD JOB, SUGURI-CHAN.
GOOD. YOU CAN TRAIN LUPAO FOR US.
CLAP CLAP
CLAP CLAP
YOU'RE THE ONE WHO HAS TO TRAIN HIM!
SO I GUESS YOU'RE KEEPING HIM AFTER ALL.
LUPAO ...
YAP

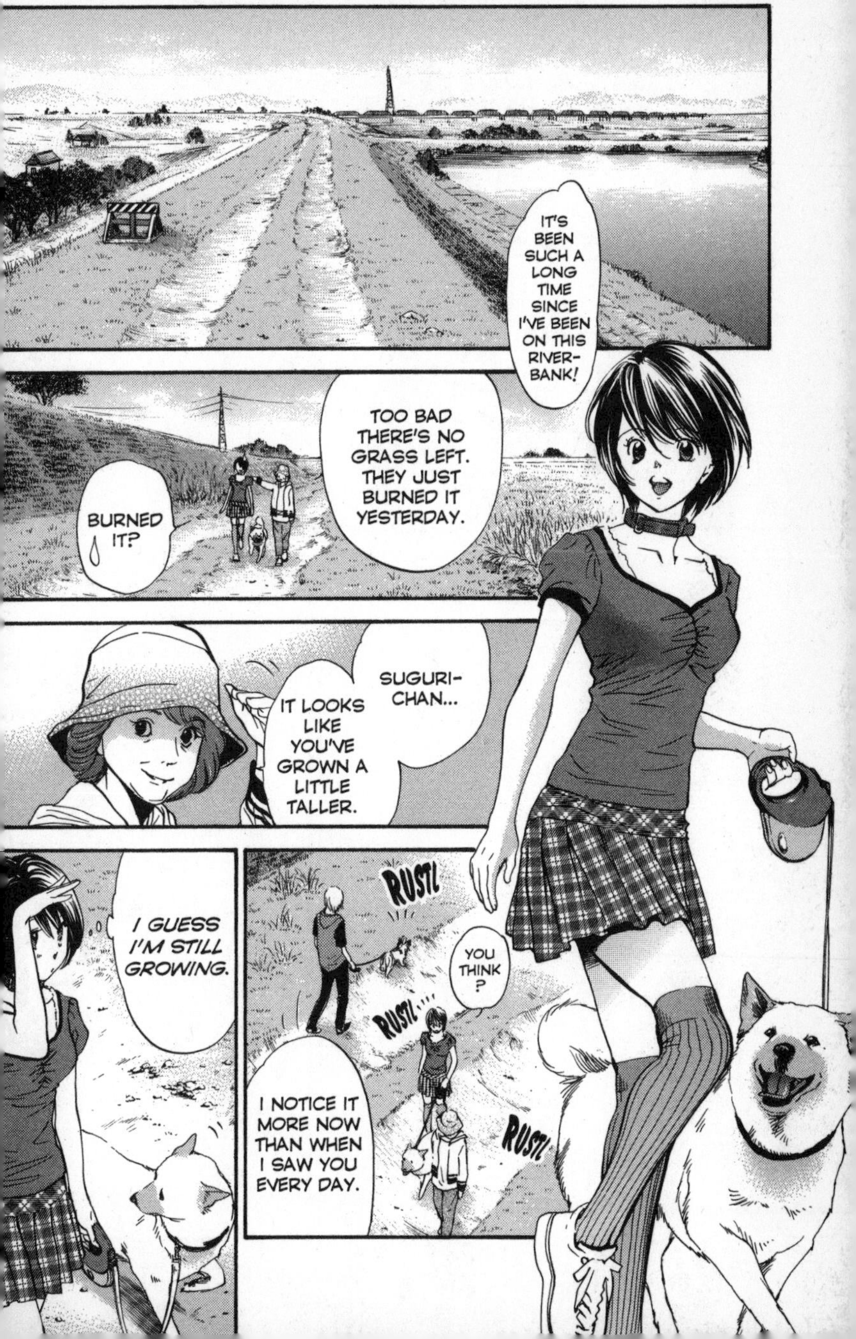

IT'S BEEN SUCH A LONG TIME SINCE I'VE BEEN ON THIS RIVER-BANK!
TOO BAD THERE'S NO GRASS LEFT. THEY JUST BURNED IT YESTERDAY.
BURNED IT?
SUGURI-CHAN...
IT LOOKS LIKE YOU'VE GROWN A LITTLE TALLER.
RUSTL
YOU THINK?
RUSTL
I NOTICE IT MORE NOW THAN WHEN I SAW YOU EVERY DAY.
RUSTL
I GUESS I'M STILL GROWING.

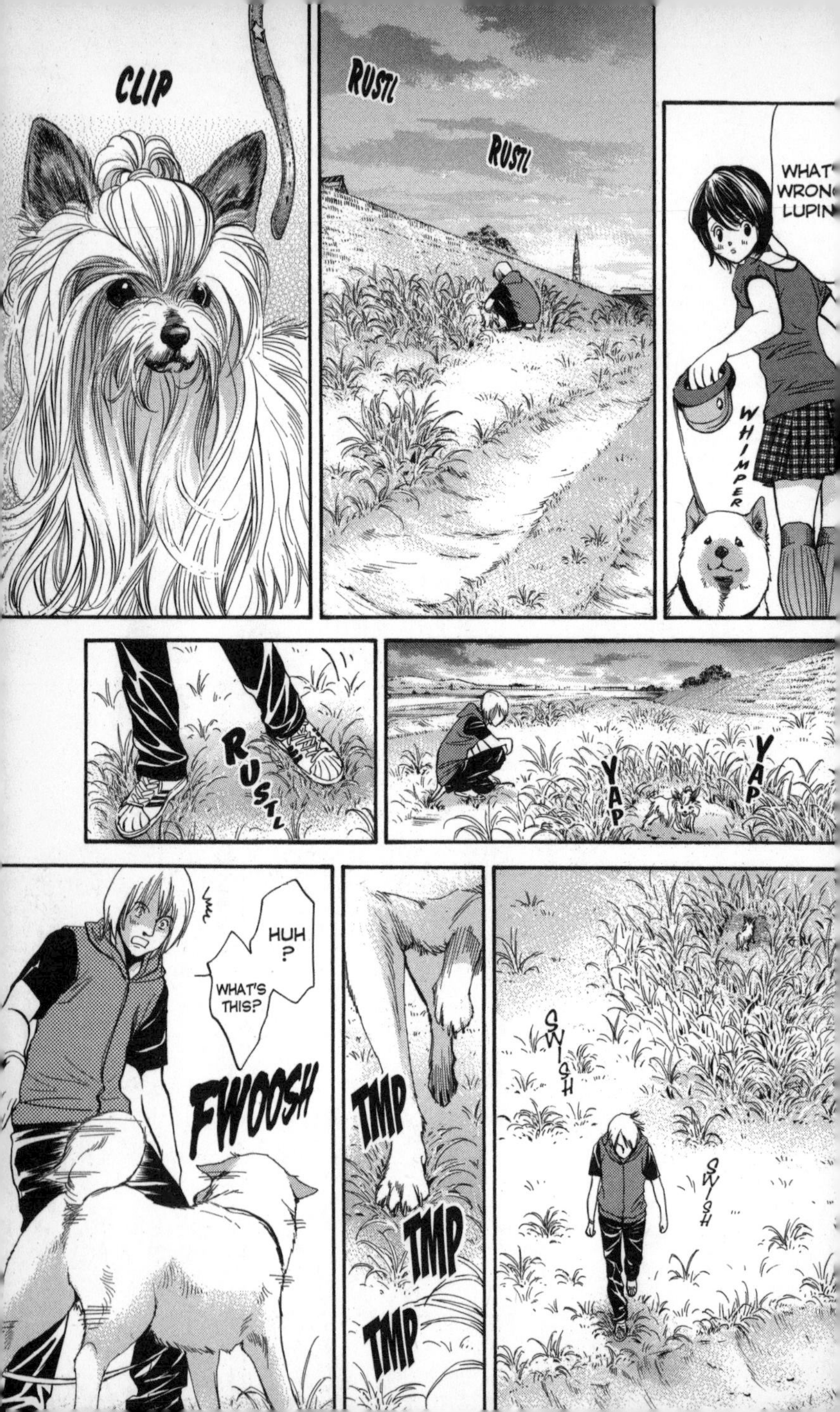
WHAT'
WRON
LUPIN
WHIMPER
RUSTL
RUSTL
CLIP
YAP
YAP
RUSTL
SWISH
SWISH
TMP
TMP
TMP
HUH?
WHAT'S THIS?
FWOOSH

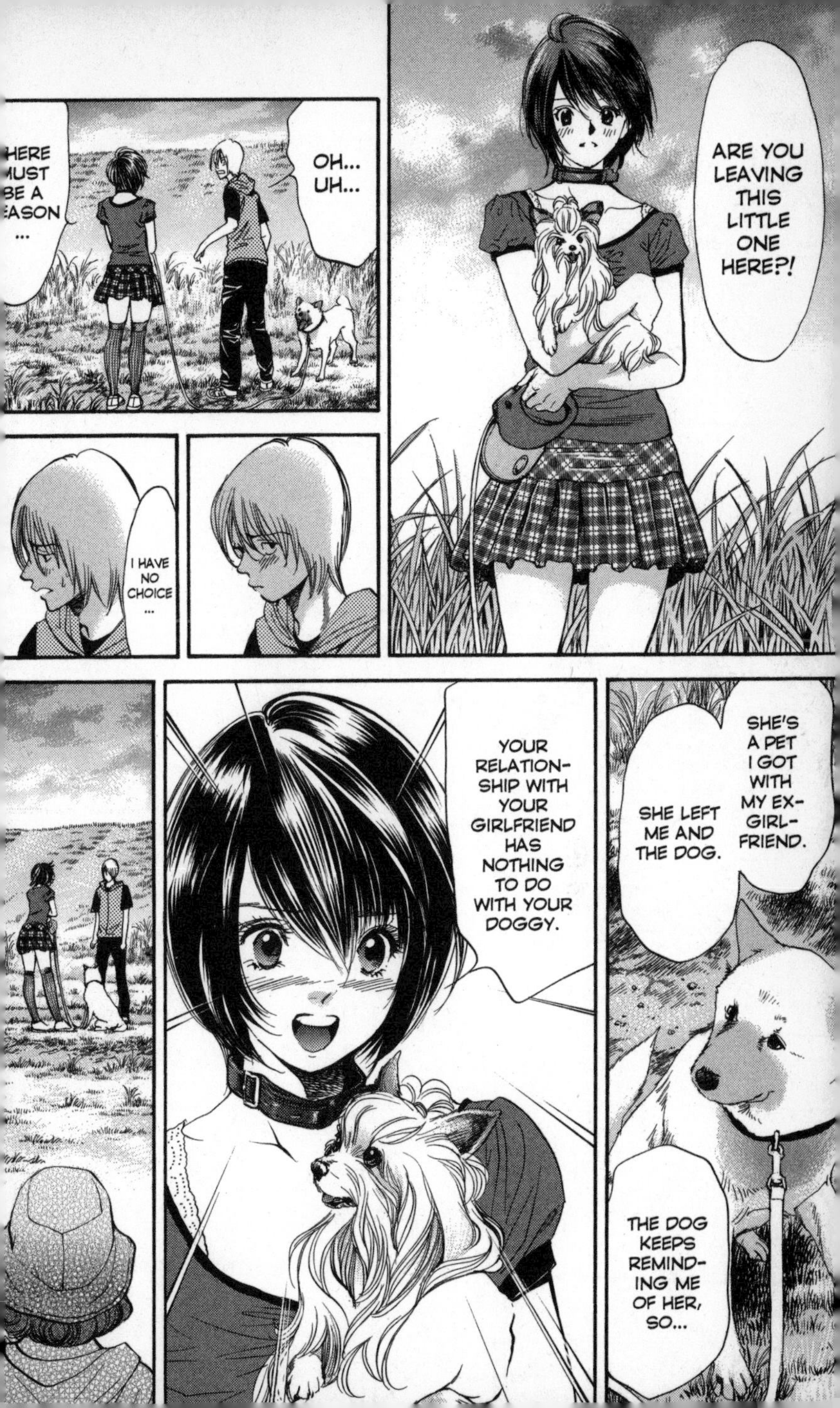
ARE YOU LEAVING THIS LITTLE ONE HERE?!
OH... UH...
HERE MUST BE A EASON ...
I HAVE NO CHOICE ...
SHE'S A PET I GOT WITH MY EX-GIRLFRIEND.
SHE LEFT ME AND THE DOG.
THE DOG KEEPS REMINDING ME OF HER, SO...
YOUR RELATIONSHIP WITH YOUR GIRLFRIEND HAS NOTHING TO DO WITH YOUR DOGGY.

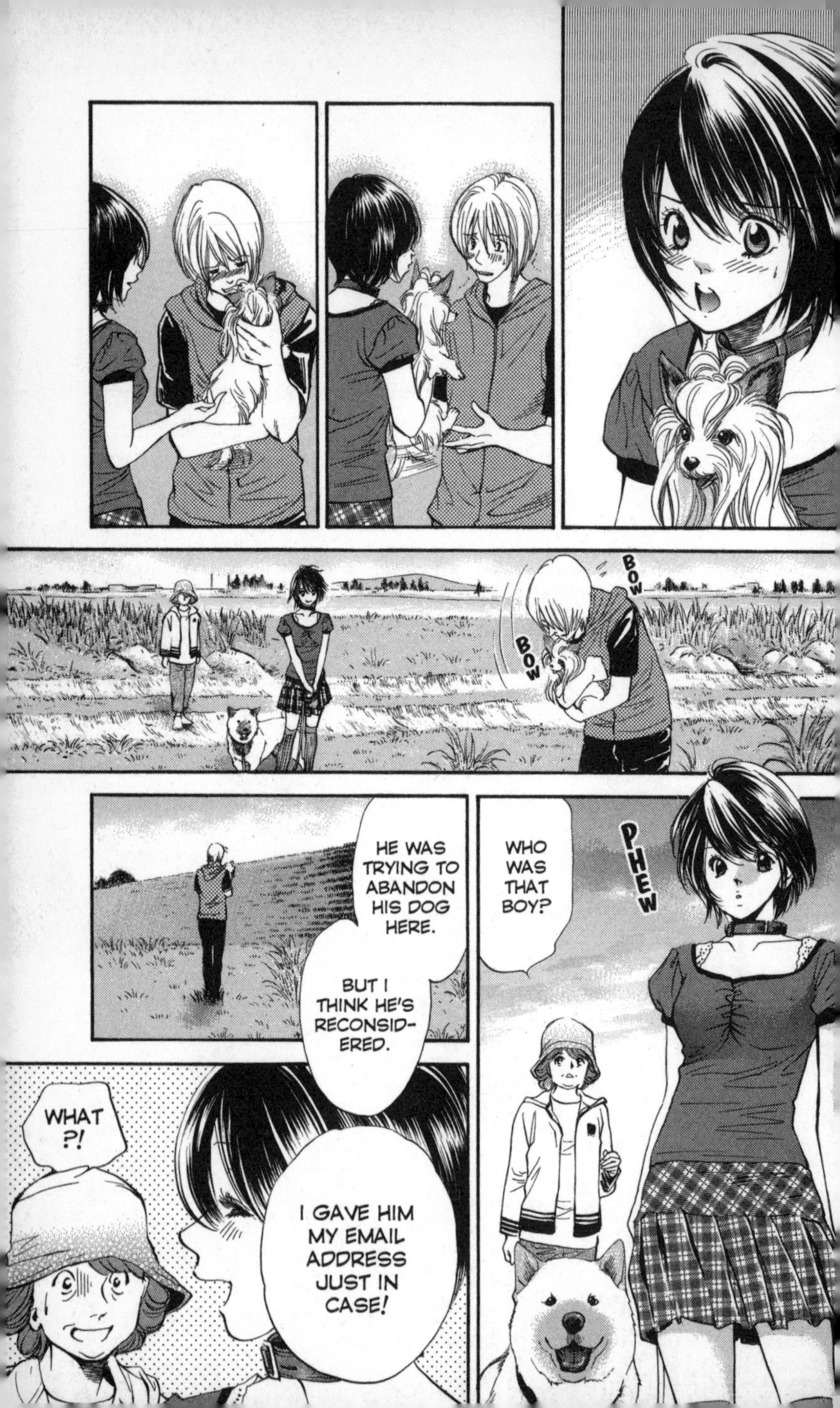
BOW
BOW
PHEW
WHO WAS THAT BOY?
HE WAS TRYING TO ABANDON HIS DOG HERE.
BUT I THINK HE'S RECONSID-ERED.
I GAVE HIM MY EMAIL ADDRESS JUST IN CASE!
WHAT?!

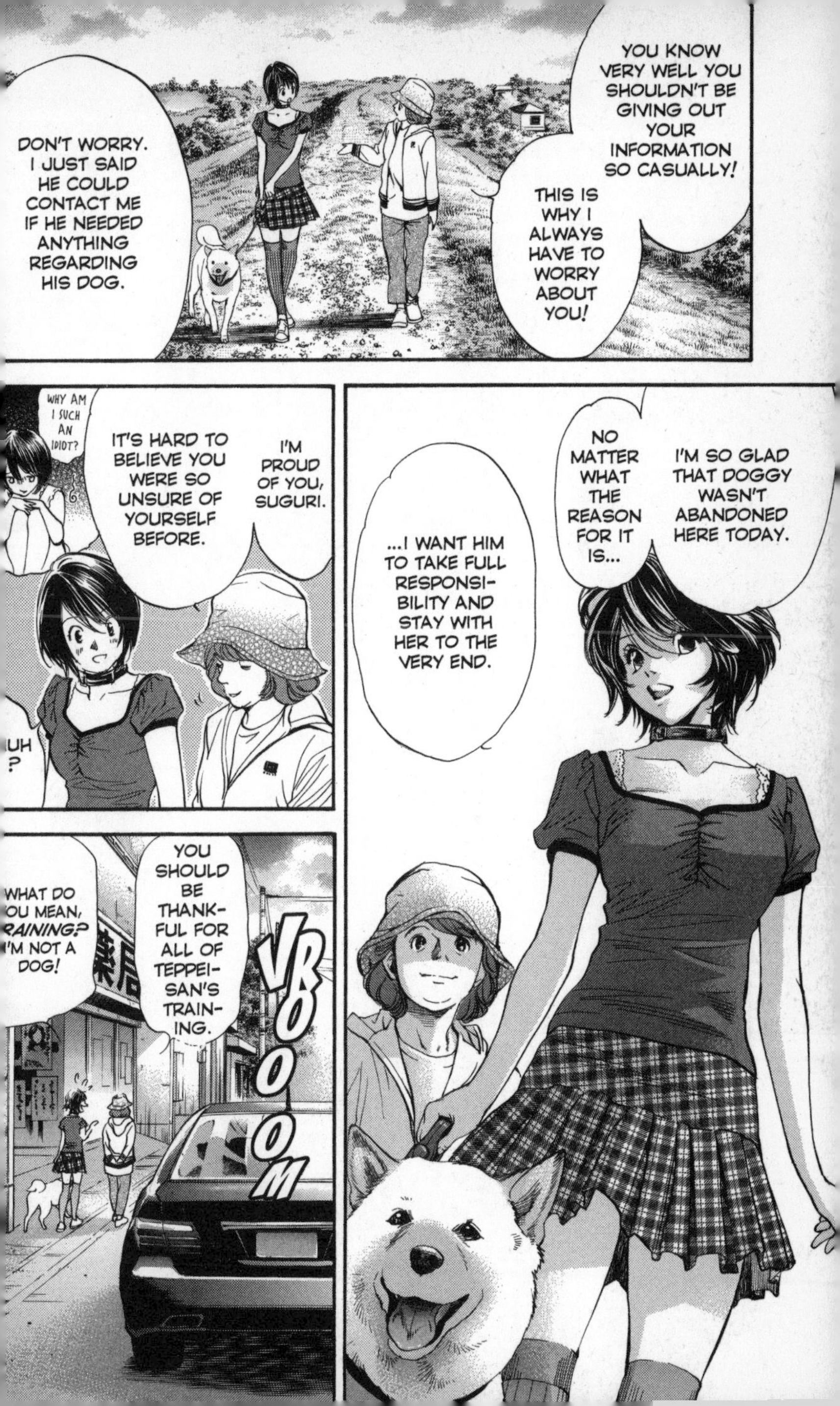
YOU KNOW VERY WELL YOU SHOULDN'T BE GIVING OUT YOUR INFORMATION SO CASUALLY!
THIS IS WHY I ALWAYS HAVE TO WORRY ABOUT YOU!
DON'T WORRY. I JUST SAID HE COULD CONTACT ME IF HE NEEDED ANYTHING REGARDING HIS DOG.
I'M SO GLAD THAT DOGGY WASN'T ABANDONED HERE TODAY.
NO MATTER WHAT THE REASON FOR IT IS...
...I WANT HIM TO TAKE FULL RESPONSI-BILITY AND STAY WITH HER TO THE VERY END.
I'M PROUD OF YOU, SUGURI.
IT'S HARD TO BELIEVE YOU WERE SO UNSURE OF YOURSELF BEFORE.
WHY AM I SUCH AN IDIOT?
UH?
YOU SHOULD BE THANK-FUL FOR ALL OF TEPPEI-SAN'S TRAIN-ING.
WHAT DO OU MEAN, RAINING? 'M NOT A DOG!
VROOOOM

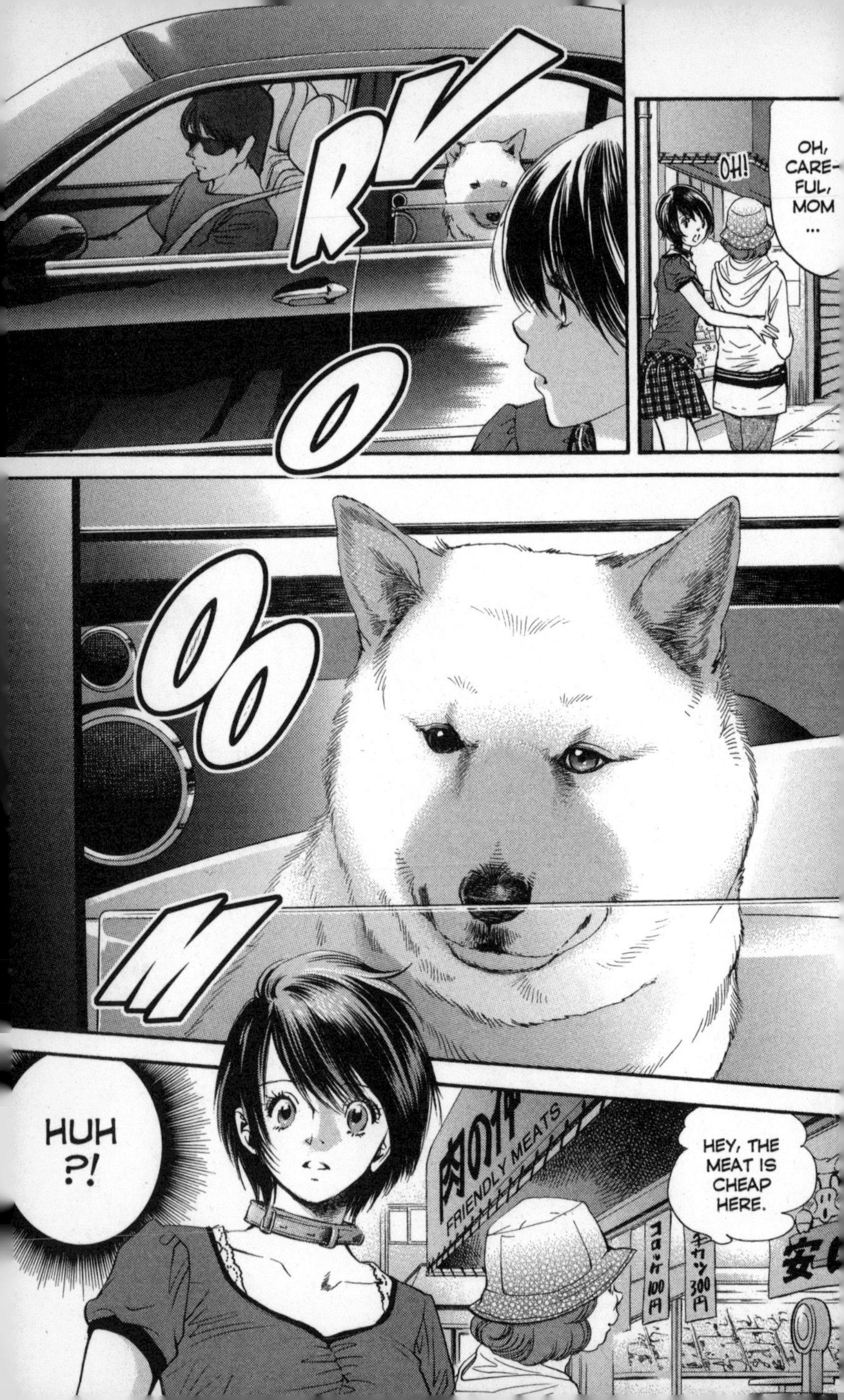
OH, CAREFUL, MOM ...
OH!
RV
O
OO
M
HEY, THE MEAT IS CHEAP HERE.
FRIENDLY MEATS
コロッケ 100円
HUH ?!

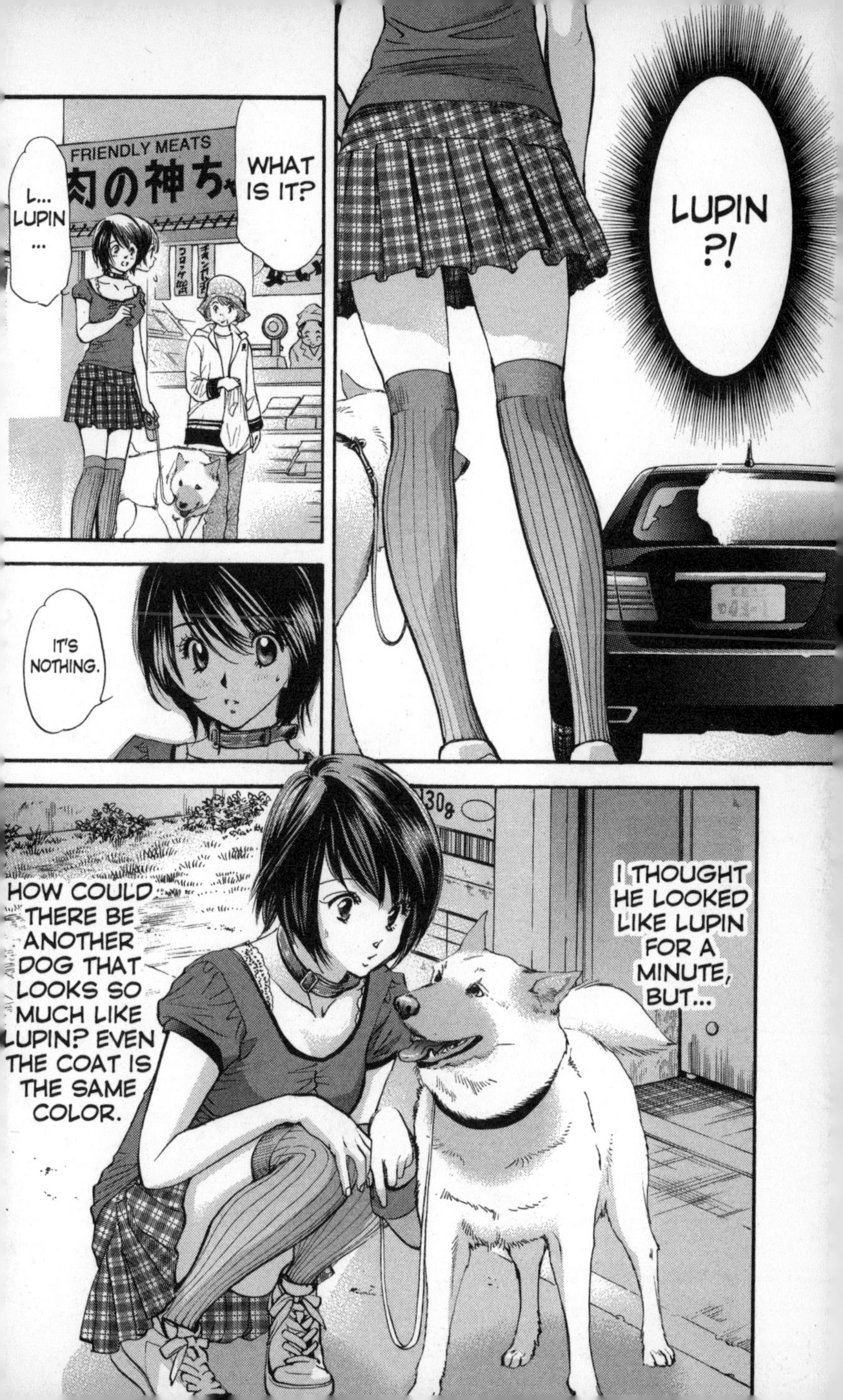

LUPIN ?!
WHAT IS IT?
FRIENDLY MEATS
L... LUPIN ...
IT'S NOTHING.
I THOUGHT HE LOOKED LIKE LUPIN FOR A MINUTE, BUT...
HOW COULD THERE BE ANOTHER DOG THAT LOOKS SO MUCH LIKE LUPIN? EVEN THE COAT IS THE SAME COLOR.

CHAPTER 158: AN EMOTIONAL REUNION?

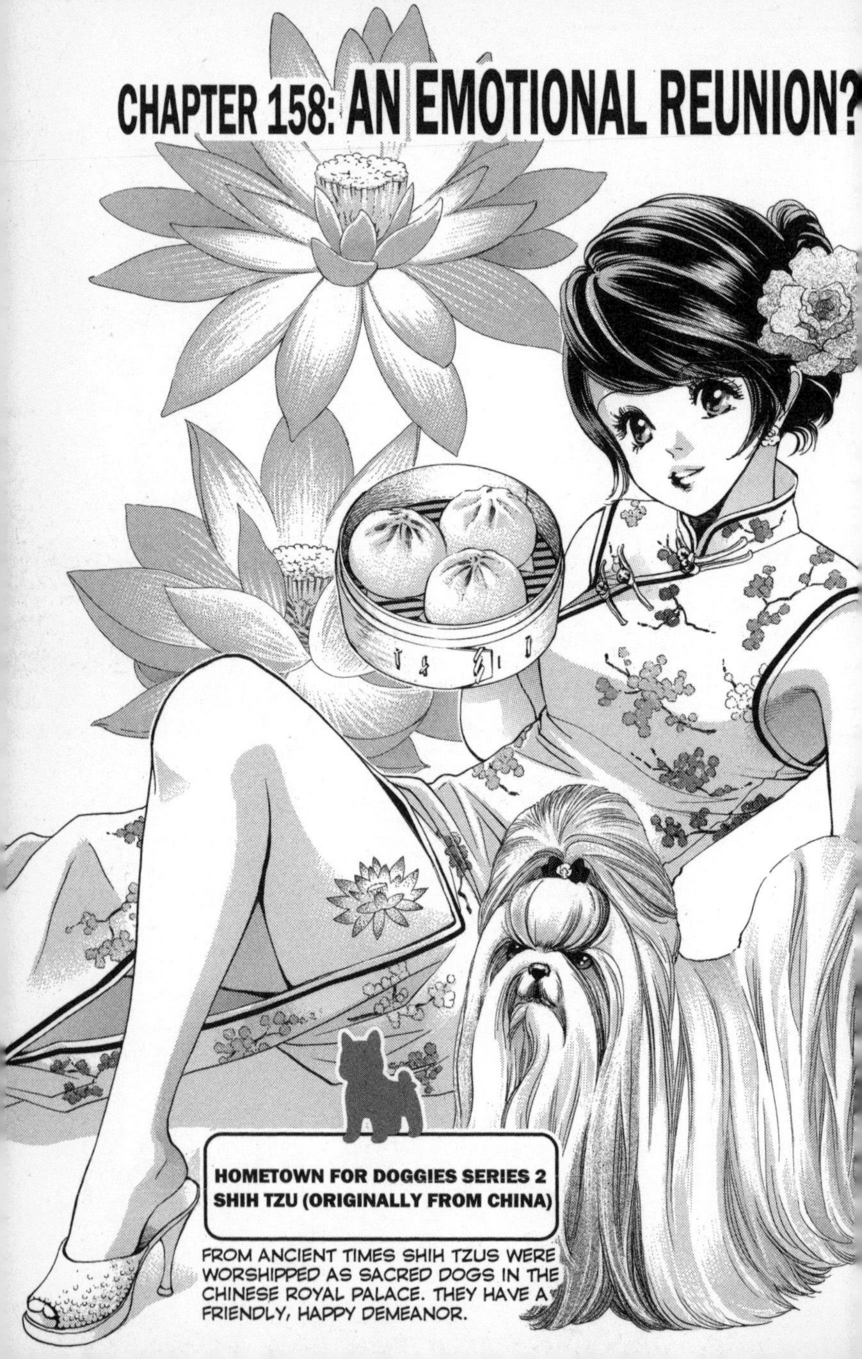
HOMETOWN FOR DOGGIES SERIES 2
SHIH TZU (ORIGINALLY FROM CHINA)
FROM ANCIENT TIMES SHIH TZUS WERE WORSHIPPED AS SACRED DOGS IN THE CHINESE ROYAL PALACE. THEY HAVE A FRIENDLY, HAPPY DEMEANOR.

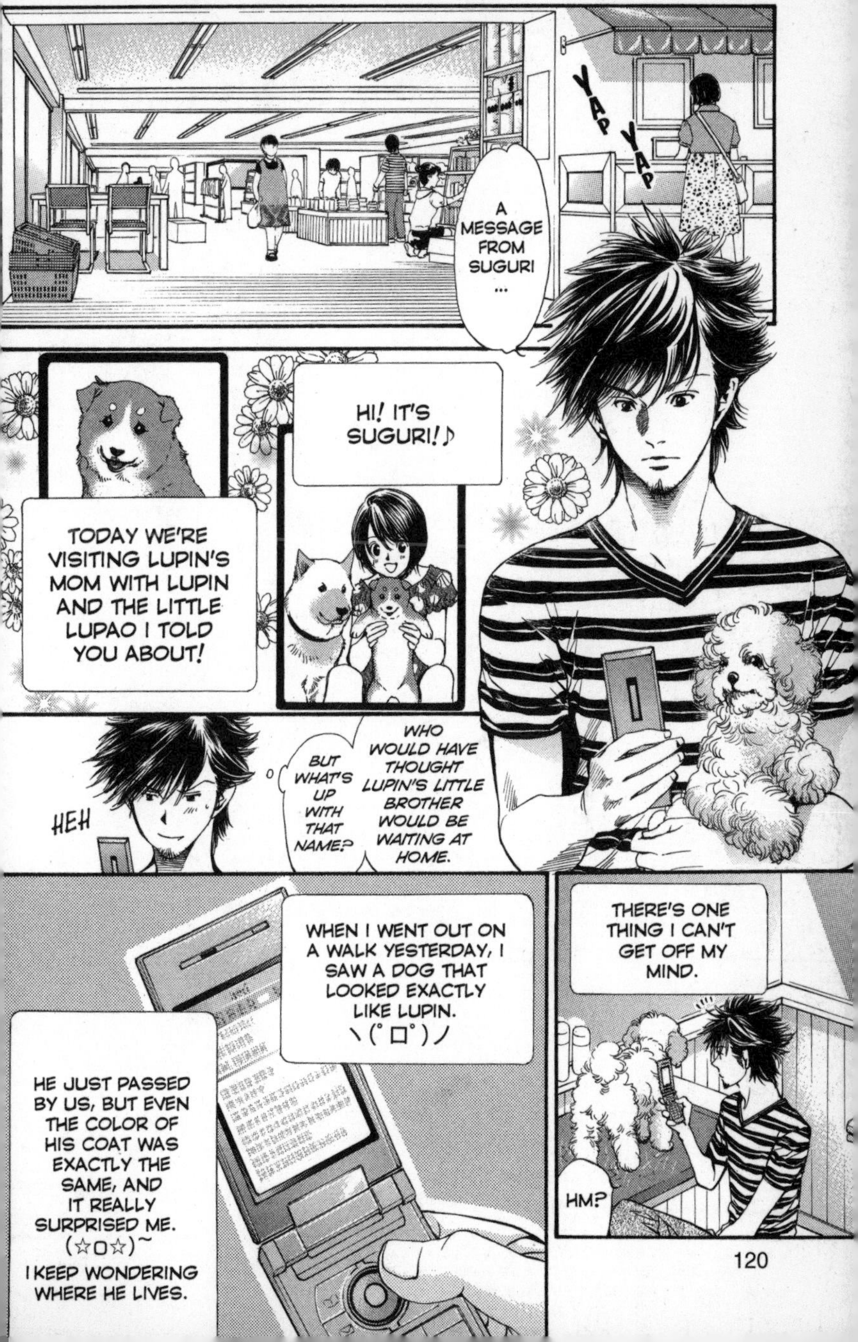
YAP YAP
A MESSAGE FROM SUGURI ...
HI! IT'S SUGURI!♪
TODAY WE'RE VISITING LUPIN'S MOM WITH LUPIN AND THE LITTLE LUPAO I TOLD YOU ABOUT!
WHO WOULD HAVE THOUGHT LUPIN'S LITTLE BROTHER WOULD BE WAITING AT HOME.
BUT WHAT'S UP WITH THAT NAME?
HEH
THERE'S ONE THING I CAN'T GET OFF MY MIND.
HM?
WHEN I WENT OUT ON A WALK YESTERDAY, I SAW A DOG THAT LOOKED EXACTLY LIKE LUPIN. ヽ(ﾟロﾟ)ノ
HE JUST PASSED BY US, BUT EVEN THE COLOR OF HIS COAT WAS EXACTLY THE SAME, AND IT REALLY SURPRISED ME. (☆ロ☆)~ I KEEP WONDERING WHERE HE LIVES.

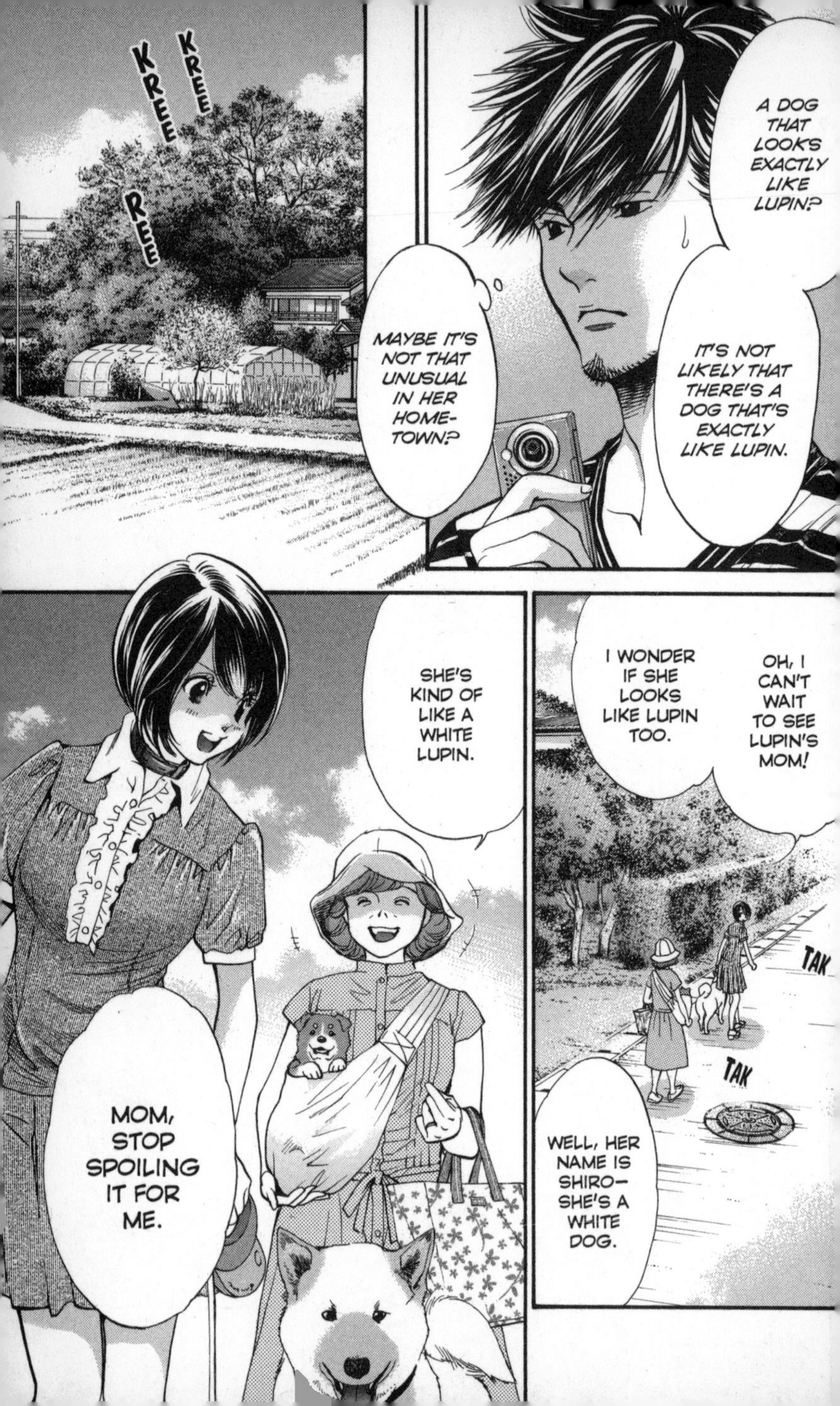

A DOG THAT LOOKS EXACTLY LIKE LUPIN?
IT'S NOT LIKELY THAT THERE'S A DOG THAT'S EXACTLY LIKE LUPIN.
MAYBE IT'S NOT THAT UNUSUAL IN HER HOME-TOWN?
KREE KREE
REE REE
OH, I CAN'T WAIT TO SEE LUPIN'S MOM!
I WONDER IF SHE LOOKS LIKE LUPIN TOO.
TAK
TAK
WELL, HER NAME IS SHIRO—SHE'S A WHITE DOG.
SHE'S KIND OF LIKE A WHITE LUPIN.
MOM, STOP SPOILING IT FOR ME.

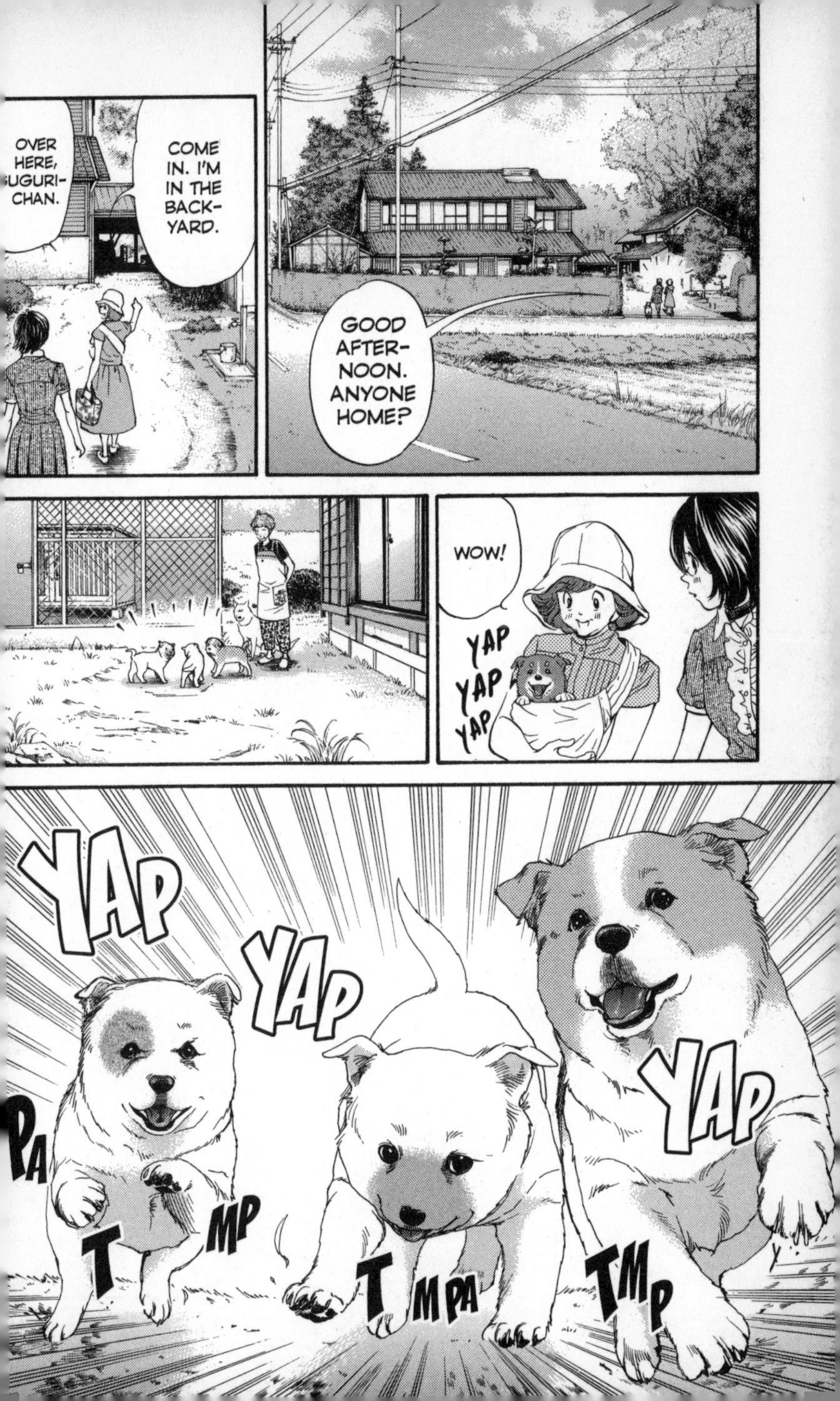
GOOD AFTERNOON. ANYONE HOME?
COME IN. I'M IN THE BACKYARD.
OVER HERE, SUGURI-CHAN.
WOW!
YAP YAP YAP
YAP
YAP
YAP
TMP
TMPA
PA
TMP

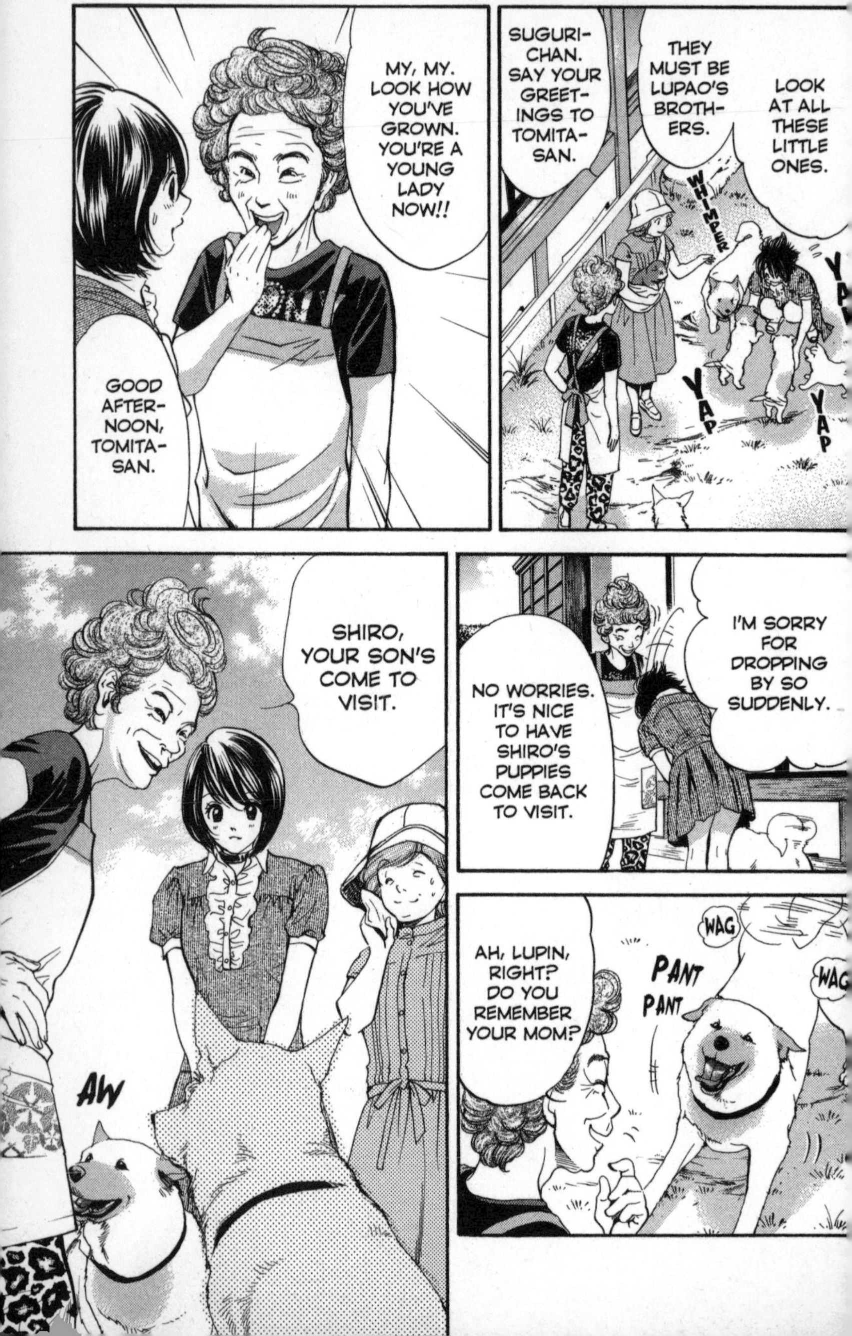
LOOK AT ALL THESE LITTLE ONES.
THEY MUST BE LUPAO'S BROTHERS.
SUGURI-CHAN. SAY YOUR GREETINGS TO TOMITA-SAN.
WHIMPER
YAP
YAP
YAP
MY, MY. LOOK HOW YOU'VE GROWN. YOU'RE A YOUNG LADY NOW!!
GOOD AFTERNOON, TOMITA-SAN.
I'M SORRY FOR DROPPING BY SO SUDDENLY.
NO WORRIES. IT'S NICE TO HAVE SHIRO'S PUPPIES COME BACK TO VISIT.
WAG
WAG
PANT PANT
AH, LUPIN, RIGHT? DO YOU REMEMBER YOUR MOM?
SHIRO, YOUR SON'S COME TO VISIT.
AW

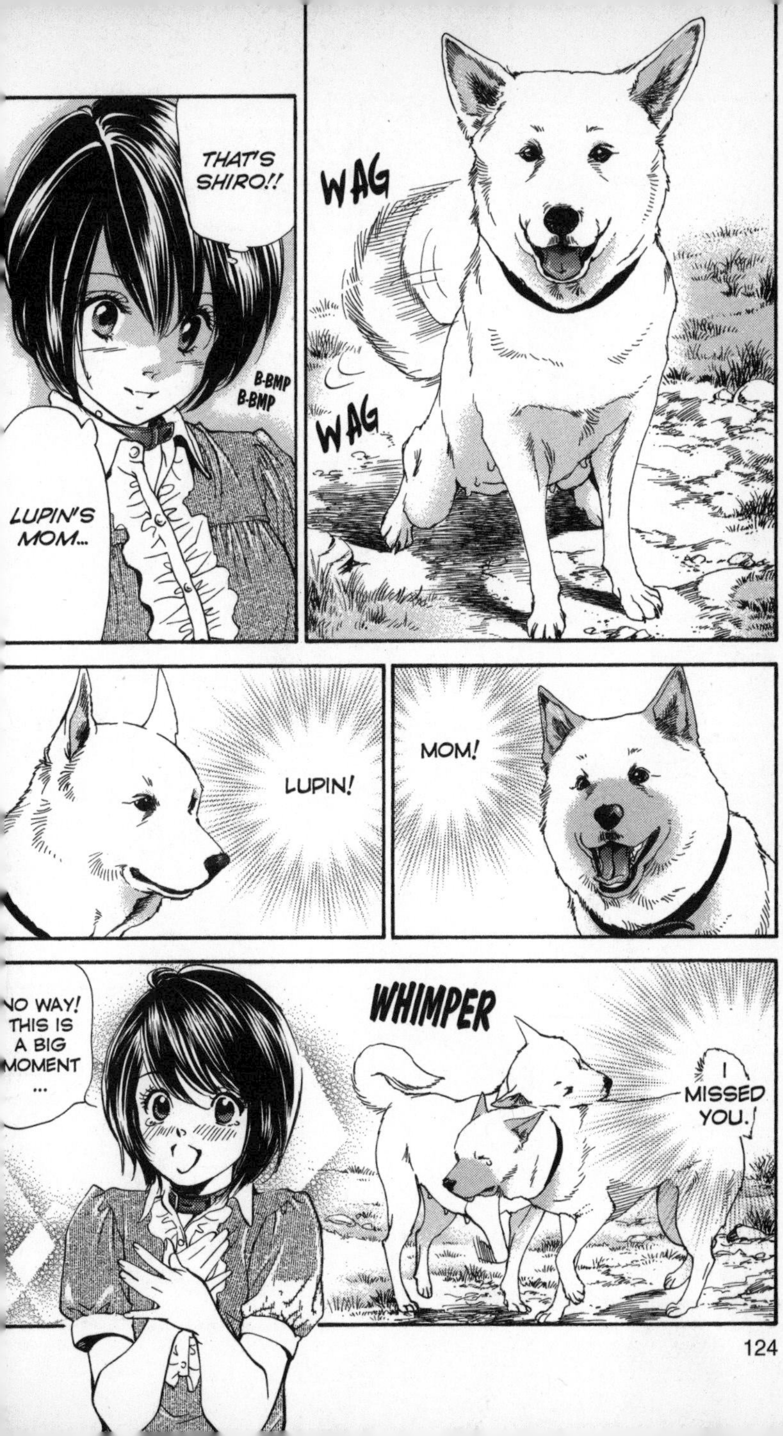
WAG
WAG
THAT'S SHIRO!!
B-BMP B-BMP
LUPIN'S MOM...
MOM!
LUPIN!
I MISSED YOU.
WHIMPER
NO WAY! THIS IS A BIG MOMENT ...

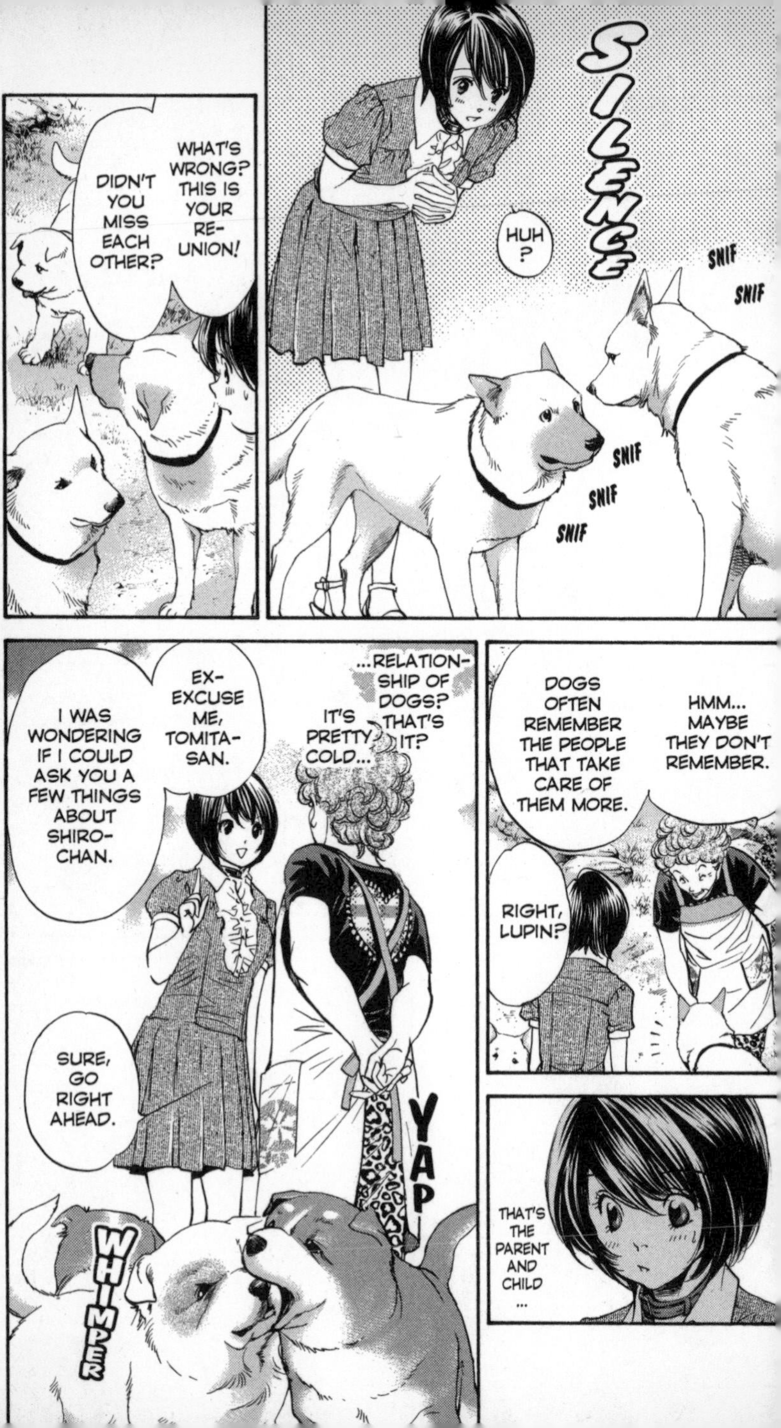
SILENCE
HUH?
SNIF
SNIF
SNIF
SNIF
SNIF
WHAT'S WRONG? THIS IS YOUR RE-UNION!
DIDN'T YOU MISS EACH OTHER?
HMM... MAYBE THEY DON'T REMEMBER.
DOGS OFTEN REMEMBER THE PEOPLE THAT TAKE CARE OF THEM MORE.
RIGHT, LUPIN?
THAT'S THE PARENT AND CHILD ...
...RELATION-SHIP OF DOGS? THAT'S IT?
IT'S PRETTY COLD...
EX-EXCUSE ME, TOMITA-SAN.
I WAS WONDERING IF I COULD ASK YOU A FEW THINGS ABOUT SHIRO-CHAN.
YAP
SURE, GO RIGHT AHEAD.
WHIMPER

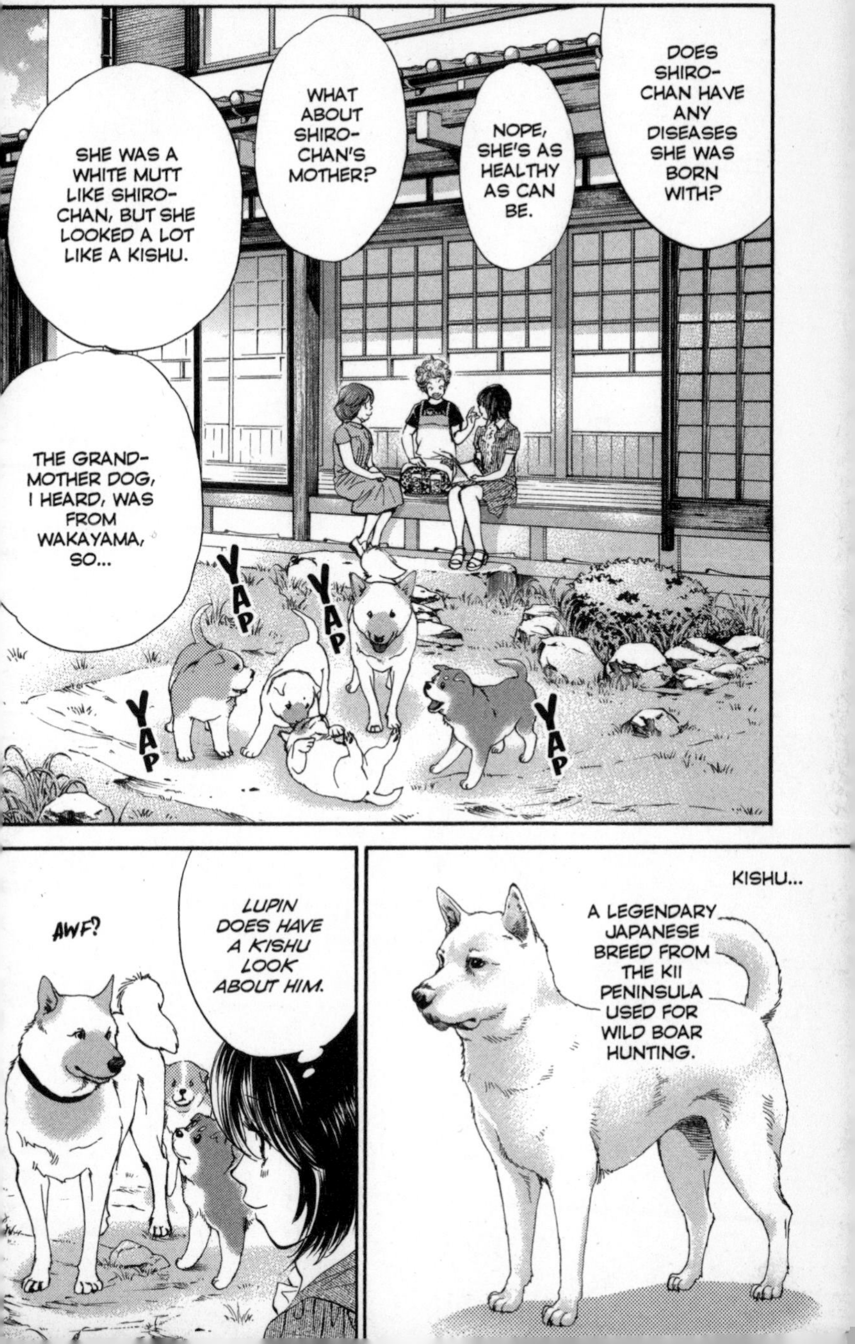
DOES SHIRO-CHAN HAVE ANY DISEASES SHE WAS BORN WITH?
NOPE, SHE'S AS HEALTHY AS CAN BE.
WHAT ABOUT SHIRO-CHAN'S MOTHER?
SHE WAS A WHITE MUTT LIKE SHIRO-CHAN, BUT SHE LOOKED A LOT LIKE A KISHU.
THE GRAND-MOTHER DOG, I HEARD, WAS FROM WAKAYAMA, SO...
YAP
YAP
YAP
YAP
KISHU...
A LEGENDARY JAPANESE BREED FROM THE KII PENINSULA USED FOR WILD BOAR HUNTING.
LUPIN DOES HAVE A KISHU LOOK ABOUT HIM.
AWF?

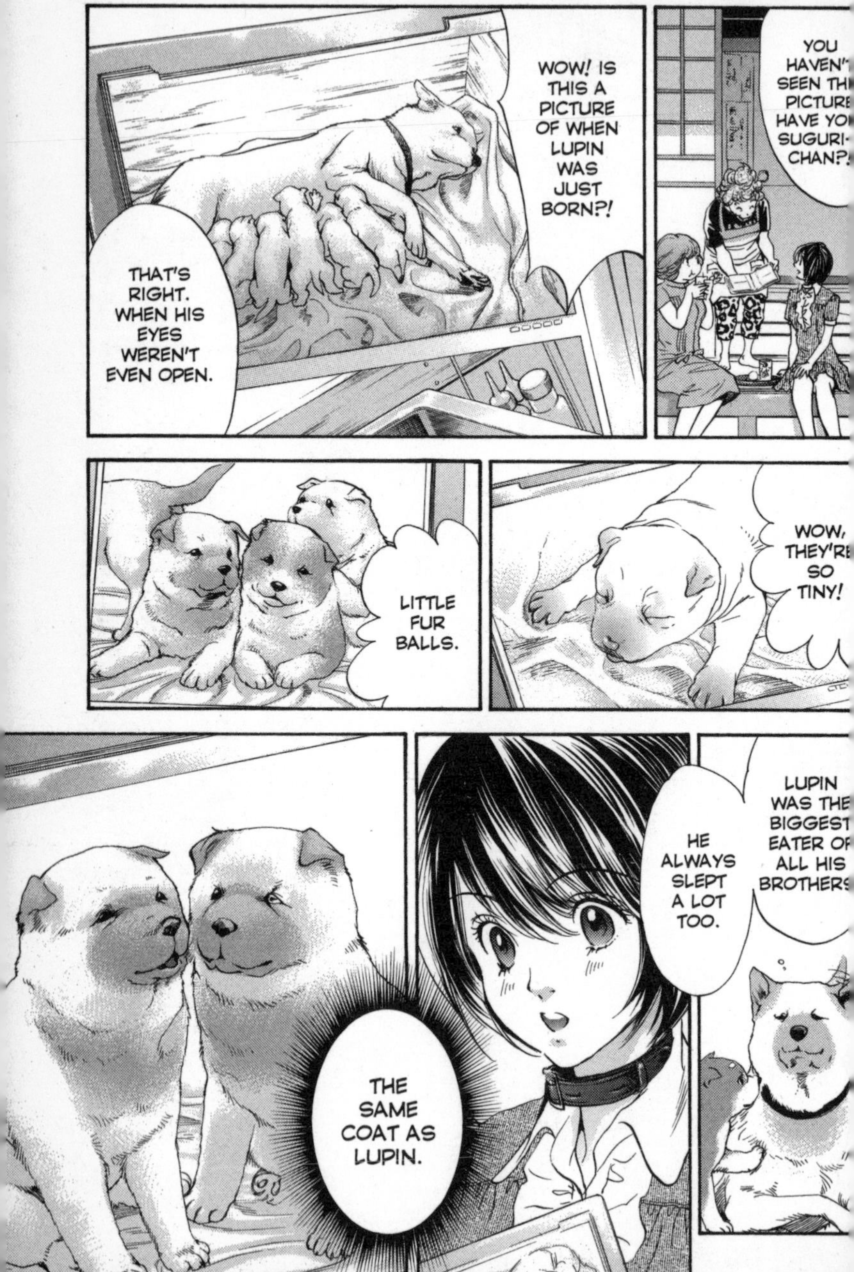
YOU HAVEN' SEEN TH PICTUR HAVE YO SUGURI- CHAN?
WOW! IS THIS A PICTURE OF WHEN LUPIN WAS JUST BORN?!
THAT'S RIGHT. WHEN HIS EYES WEREN'T EVEN OPEN.
WOW, THEY'R SO TINY!
LITTLE FUR BALLS.
LUPIN WAS THE BIGGEST EATER O ALL HIS BROTHERS
HE ALWAYS SLEPT A LOT TOO.
THE SAME COAT AS LUPIN.

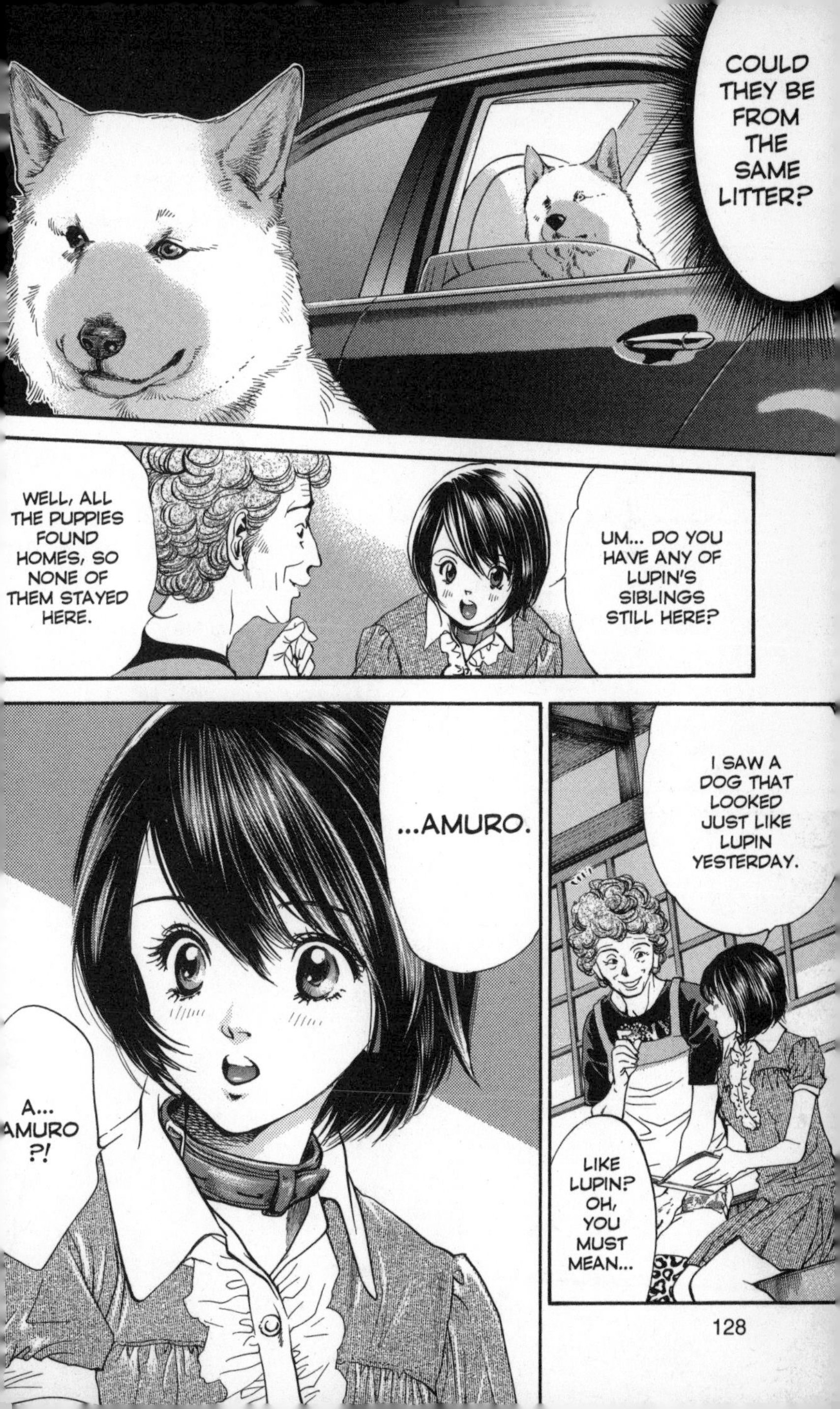
COULD THEY BE FROM THE SAME LITTER?
UM... DO YOU HAVE ANY OF LUPIN'S SIBLINGS STILL HERE?
WELL, ALL THE PUPPIES FOUND HOMES, SO NONE OF THEM STAYED HERE.
I SAW A DOG THAT LOOKED JUST LIKE LUPIN YESTERDAY.
LIKE LUPIN? OH, YOU MUST MEAN...
...AMURO.
A... AMURO ?!

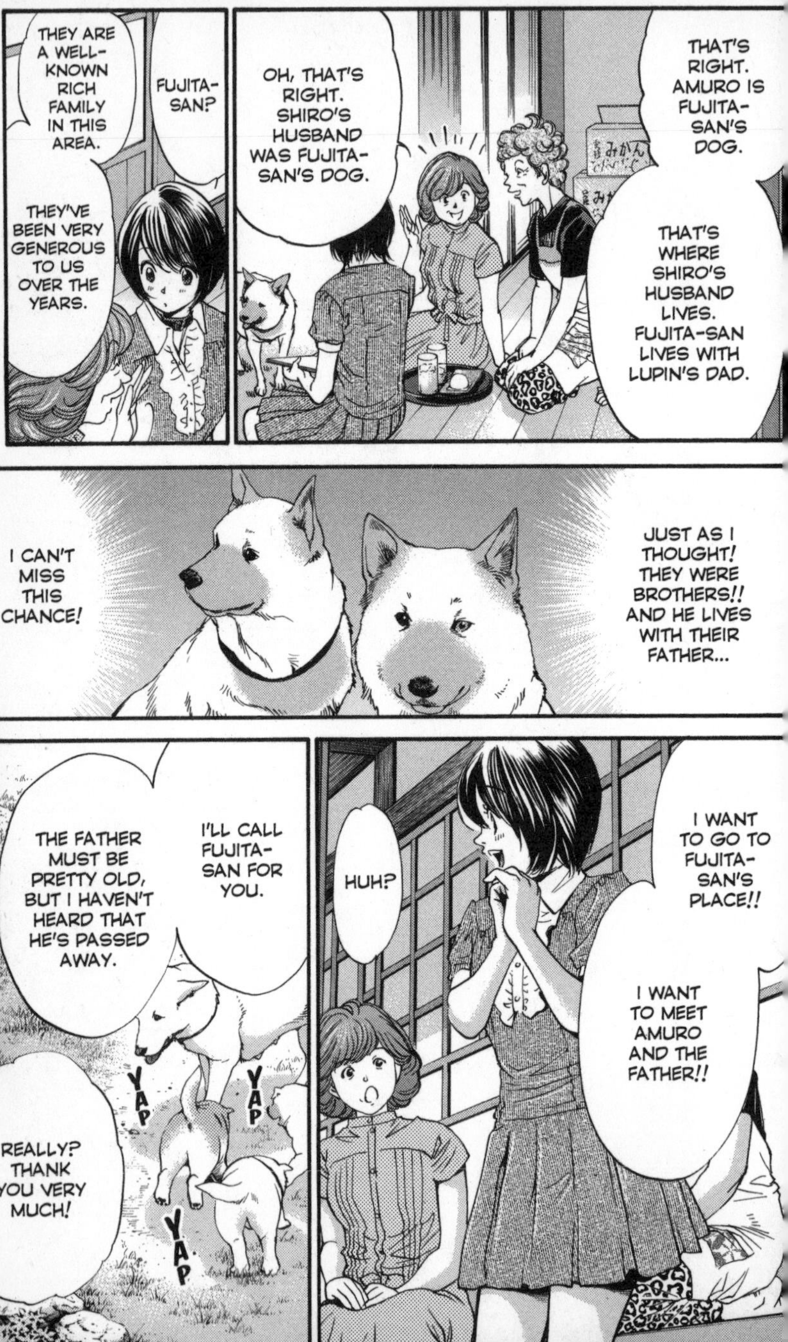
THAT'S RIGHT. AMURO IS FUJITA-SAN'S DOG.
THAT'S WHERE SHIRO'S HUSBAND LIVES. FUJITA-SAN LIVES WITH LUPIN'S DAD.
OH, THAT'S RIGHT. SHIRO'S HUSBAND WAS FUJITA-SAN'S DOG.
FUJITA-SAN?
THEY ARE A WELL-KNOWN RICH FAMILY IN THIS AREA.
THEY'VE BEEN VERY GENEROUS TO US OVER THE YEARS.
JUST AS I THOUGHT! THEY WERE BROTHERS!! AND HE LIVES WITH THEIR FATHER...
I CAN'T MISS THIS CHANCE!
I WANT TO GO TO FUJITA-SAN'S PLACE!!
I WANT TO MEET AMURO AND THE FATHER!!
HUH?
I'LL CALL FUJITA-SAN FOR YOU.
THE FATHER MUST BE PRETTY OLD, BUT I HAVEN'T HEARD THAT HE'S PASSED AWAY.
YAP
YAP
YAP
REALLY? THANK YOU VERY MUCH!

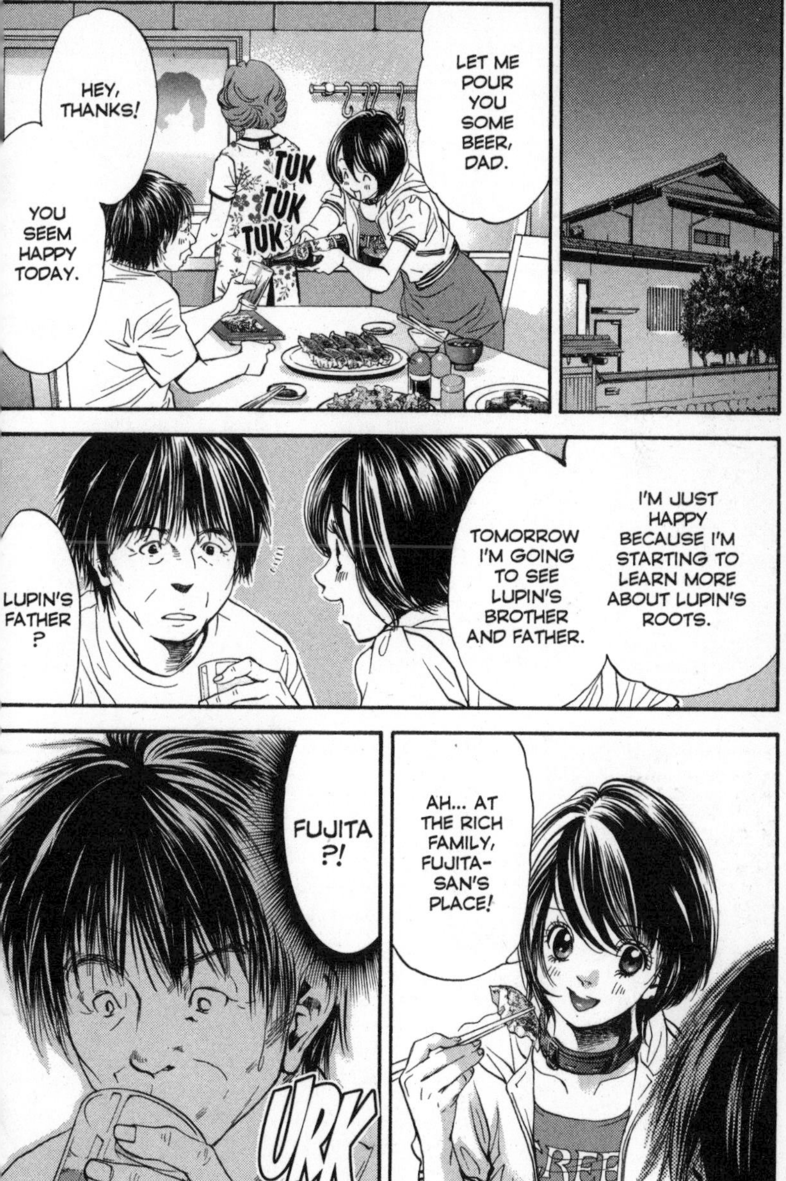
LET ME POUR YOU SOME BEER, DAD.
TUK TUK TUK
HEY, THANKS!
YOU SEEM HAPPY TODAY.
I'M JUST HAPPY BECAUSE I'M STARTING TO LEARN MORE ABOUT LUPIN'S ROOTS.
TOMORROW I'M GOING TO SEE LUPIN'S BROTHER AND FATHER.
LUPIN'S FATHER?
AH... AT THE RICH FAMILY, FUJITA-SAN'S PLACE!
FUJITA?!
URK

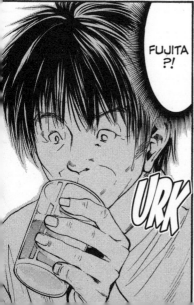

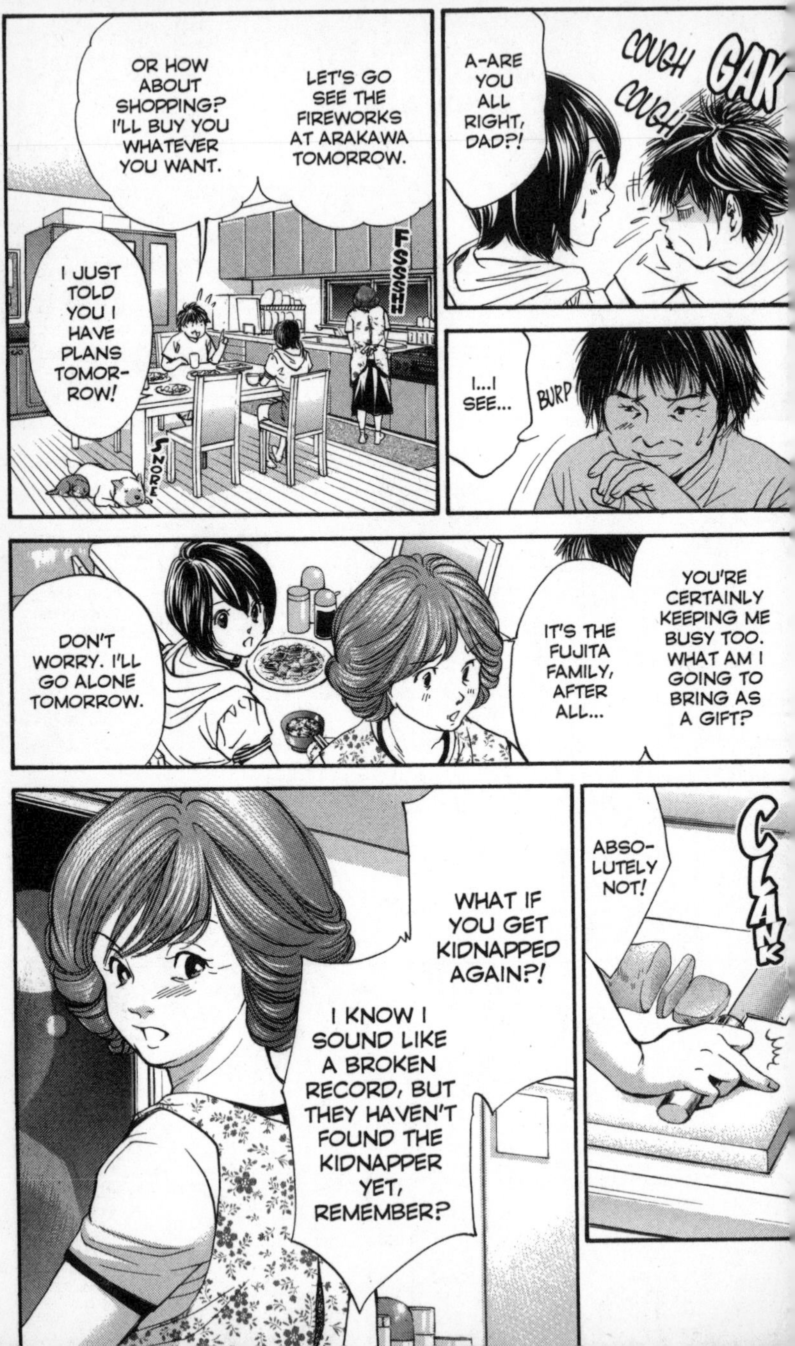
COUGH
GAK
COUGH
A-ARE YOU ALL RIGHT, DAD?!
BURP
I...I SEE...
LET'S GO SEE THE FIREWORKS AT ARAKAWA TOMORROW.
OR HOW ABOUT SHOPPING? I'LL BUY YOU WHATEVER YOU WANT.
FSSSHH
I JUST TOLD YOU I HAVE PLANS TOMOR-ROW!
SNORE
YOU'RE CERTAINLY KEEPING ME BUSY TOO. WHAT AM I GOING TO BRING AS A GIFT?
IT'S THE FUJITA FAMILY, AFTER ALL...
DON'T WORRY. I'LL GO ALONE TOMORROW.
CLANK
ABSO-LUTELY NOT!
WHAT IF YOU GET KIDNAPPED AGAIN?!
I KNOW I SOUND LIKE A BROKEN RECORD, BUT THEY HAVEN'T FOUND THE KIDNAPPER YET, REMEMBER?

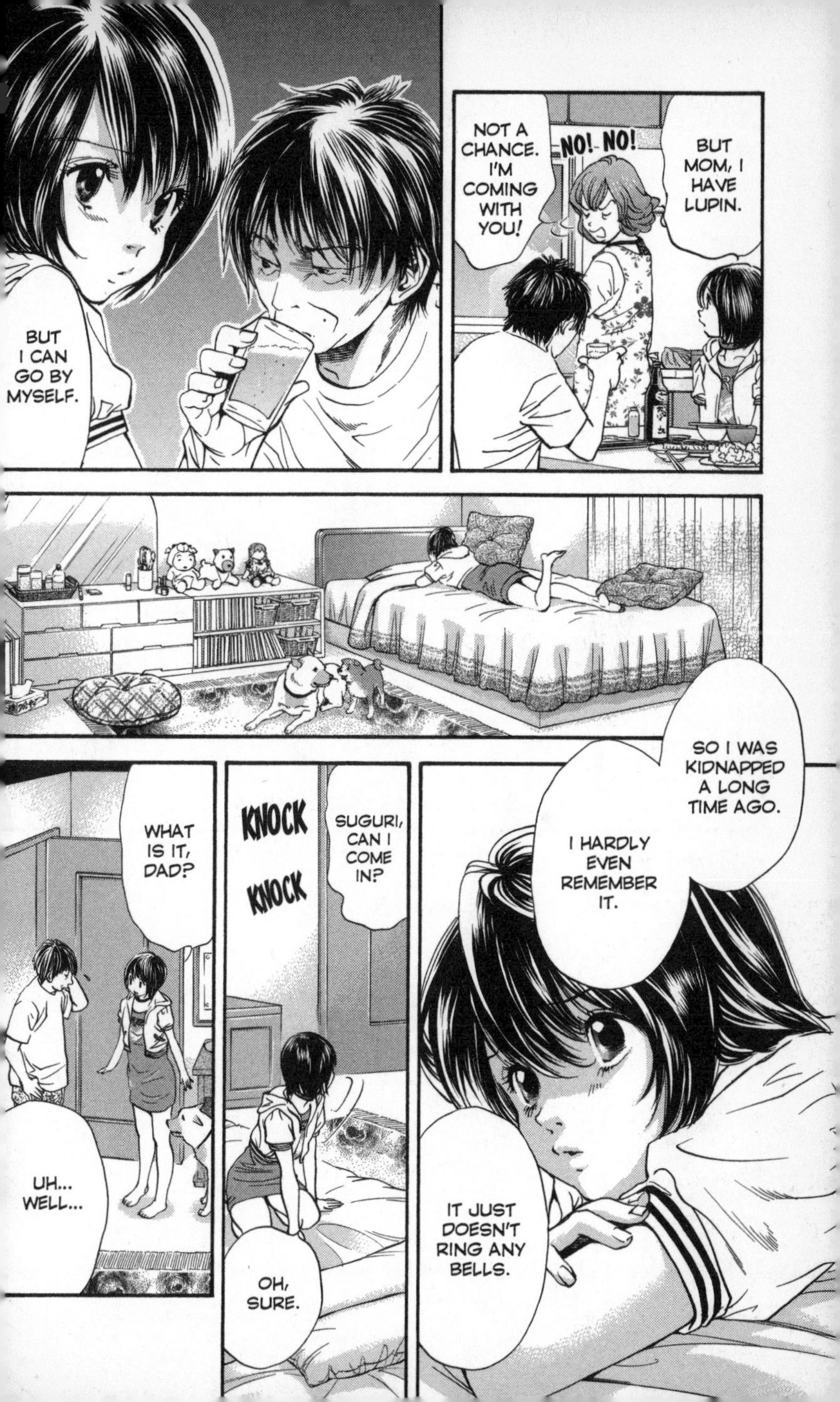
BUT MOM, I HAVE LUPIN.
NO! NO!
NOT A CHANCE. I'M COMING WITH YOU!
BUT I CAN GO BY MYSELF.
SO I WAS KIDNAPPED A LONG TIME AGO.
I HARDLY EVEN REMEMBER IT.
IT JUST DOESN'T RING ANY BELLS.
SUGURI, CAN I COME IN?
KNOCK
KNOCK
OH, SURE.
WHAT IS IT, DAD?
UH... WELL...

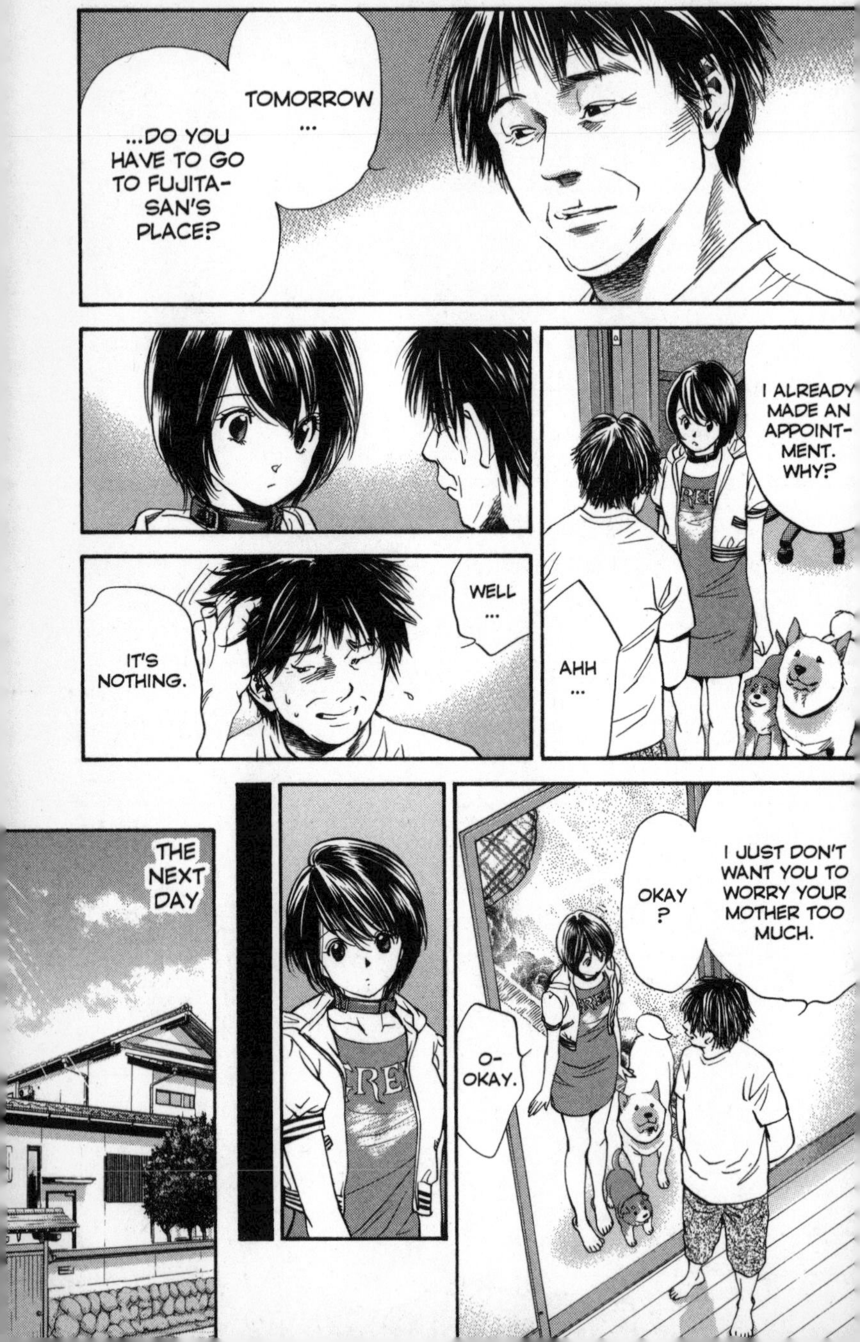
TOMORROW ...
...DO YOU HAVE TO GO TO FUJITA-SAN'S PLACE?
I ALREADY MADE AN APPOINTMENT. WHY?
AHH ...
WELL ...
IT'S NOTHING.
I JUST DON'T WANT YOU TO WORRY YOUR MOTHER TOO MUCH.
OKAY ?
O-OKAY.
THE NEXT DAY

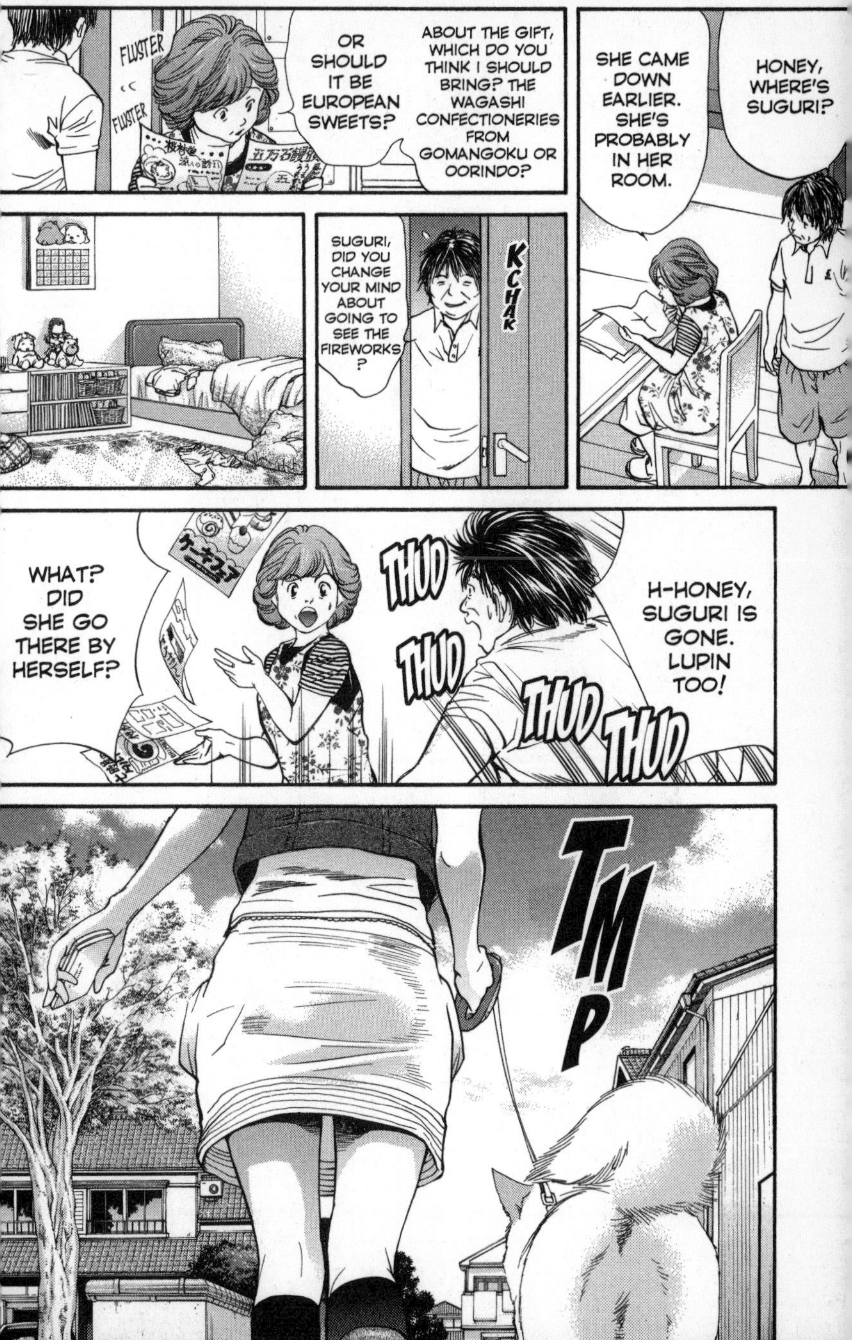
HONEY, WHERE'S SUGURI?
SHE CAME DOWN EARLIER. SHE'S PROBABLY IN HER ROOM.
ABOUT THE GIFT, WHICH DO YOU THINK I SHOULD BRING? THE WAGASHI CONFECTIONERIES FROM GOMANGOKU OR OORINDO?
OR SHOULD IT BE EUROPEAN SWEETS?
FLUSTER
FLUSTER
KCHAK
SUGURI, DID YOU CHANGE YOUR MIND ABOUT GOING TO SEE THE FIREWORKS?
H-HONEY, SUGURI IS GONE. LUPIN TOO!
THUD
THUD
THUD
THUD
WHAT? DID SHE GO THERE BY HERSELF?
TMP

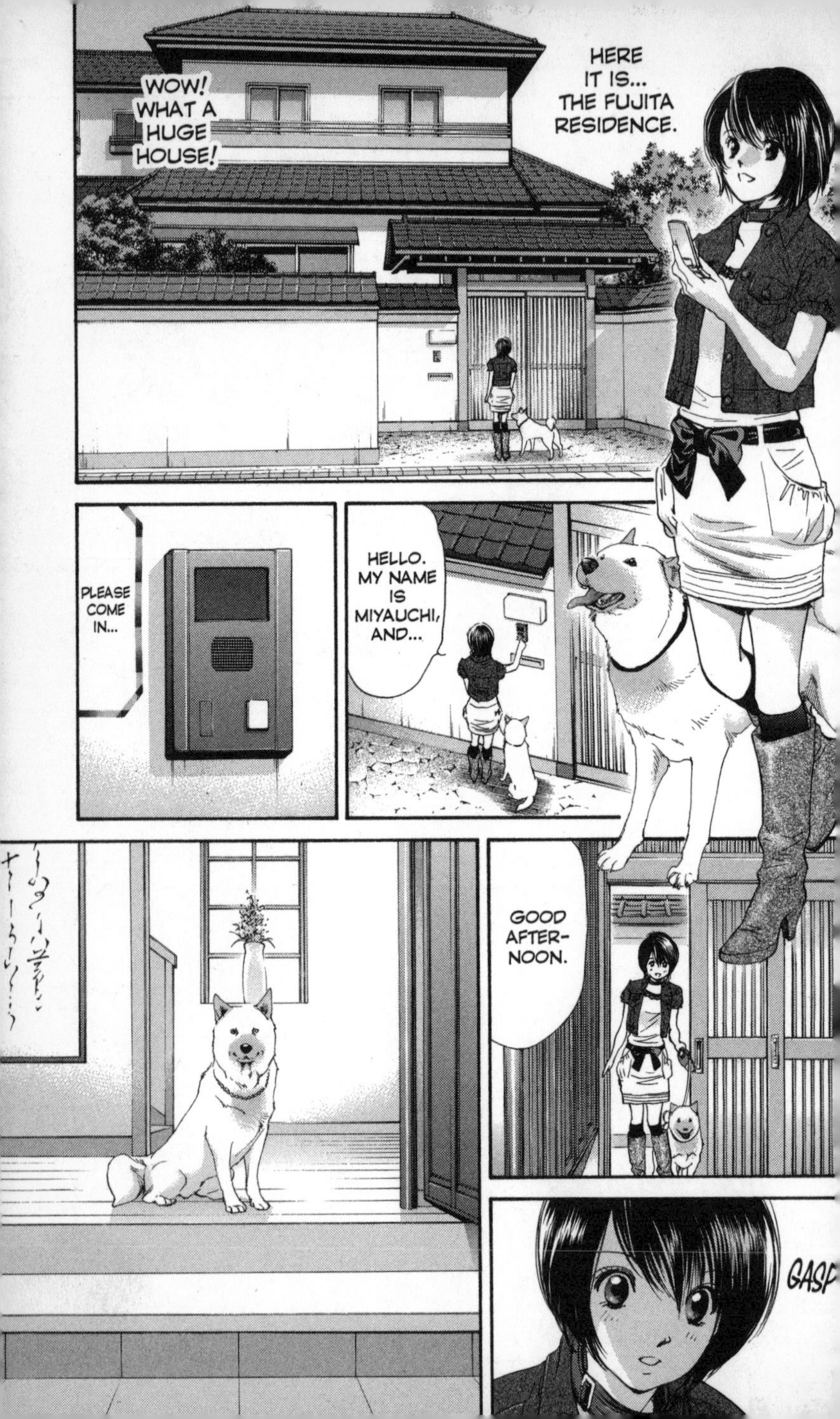
HERE IT IS... THE FUJITA RESIDENCE.
WOW! WHAT A HUGE HOUSE!
HELLO. MY NAME IS MIYAUCHI, AND...
PLEASE COME IN...
GOOD AFTER-NOON.
GASP

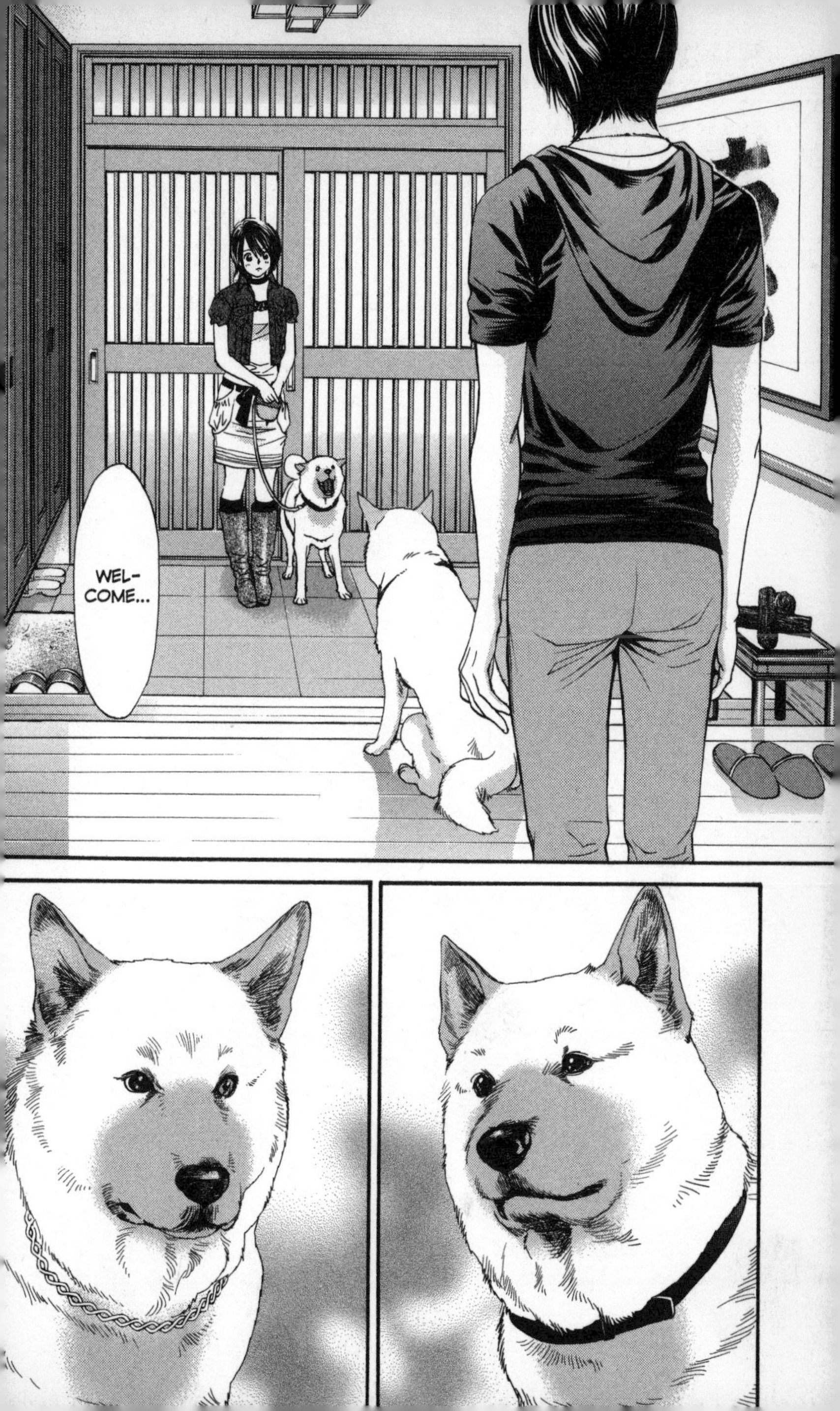
WEL-
COME...

CHAPTER 159: CHEER UP, FATHER...

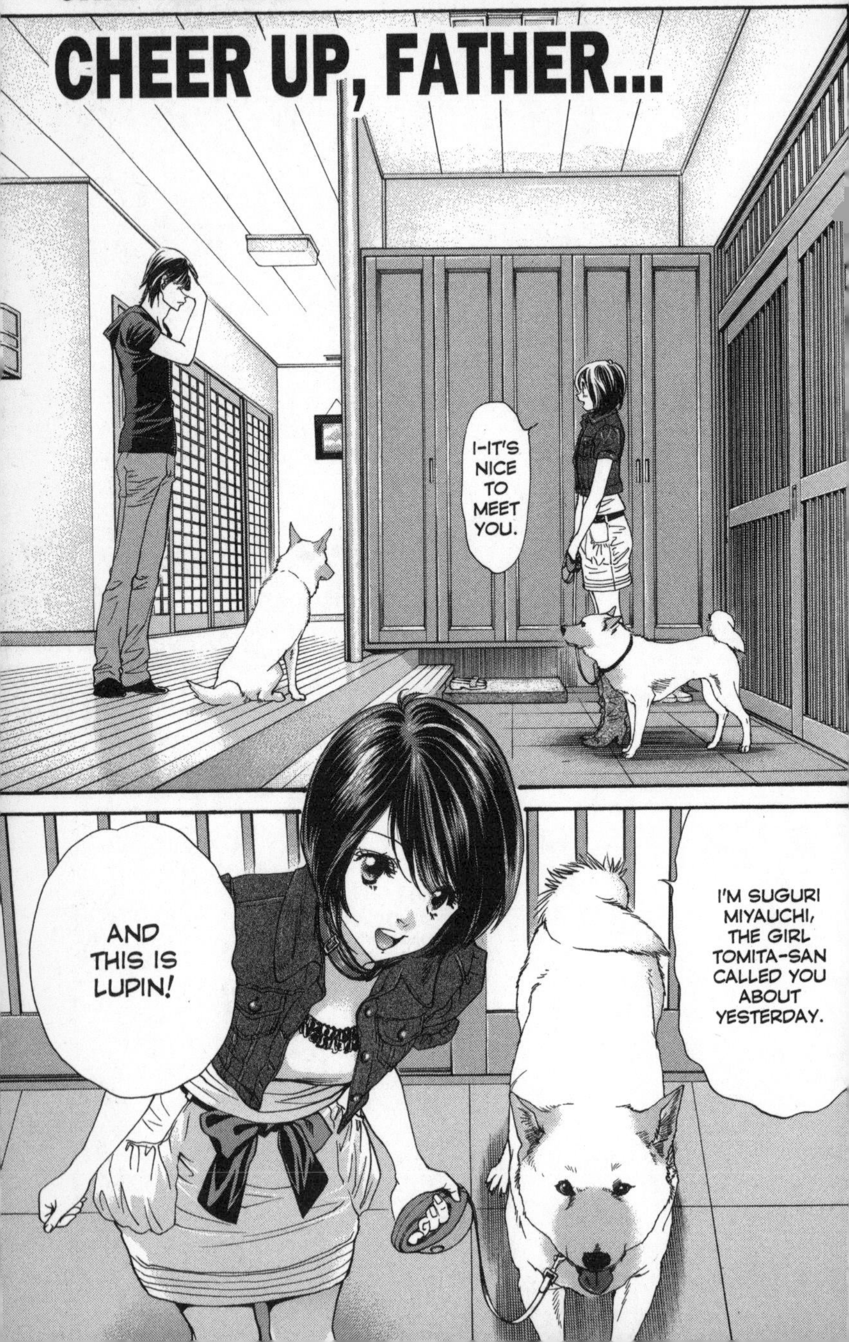
I-IT'S NICE TO MEET YOU.
I'M SUGURI MIYAUCHI, THE GIRL TOMITA-SAN CALLED YOU ABOUT YESTERDAY.
AND THIS IS LUPIN!

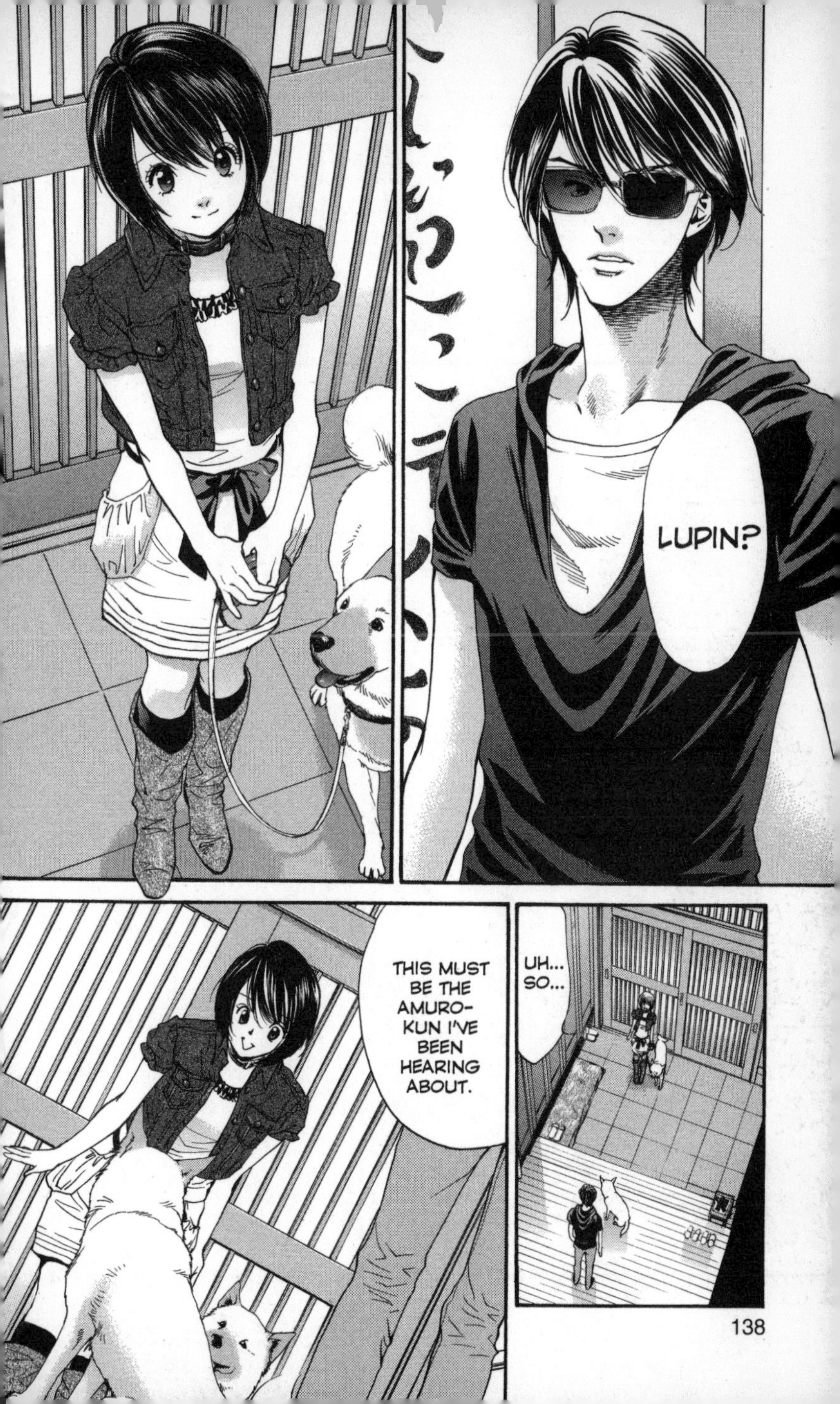
LUPIN?
UH... SO...
THIS MUST BE THE AMURO-KUN I'VE BEEN HEARING ABOUT.

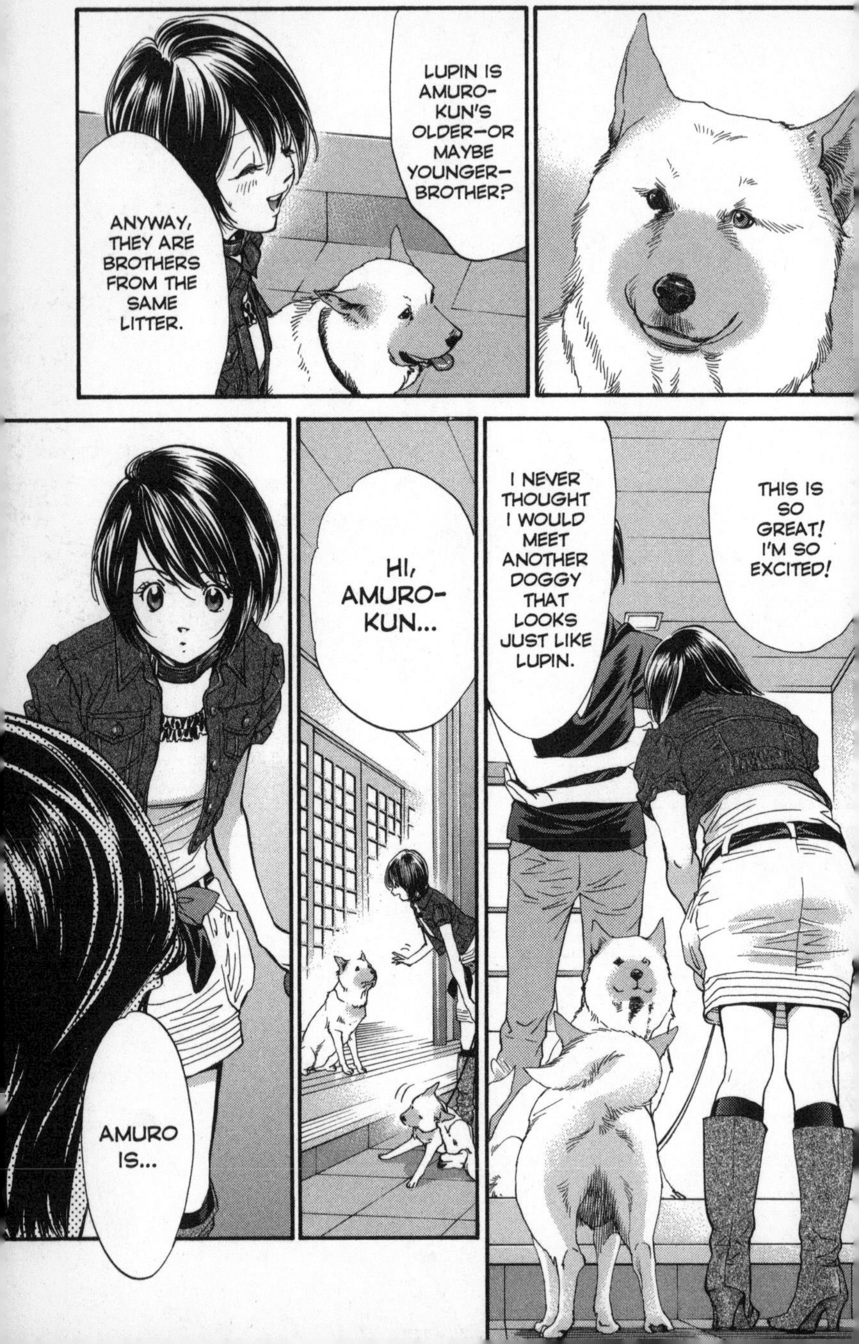
LUPIN IS AMURO-KUN'S OLDER—OR MAYBE YOUNGER—BROTHER?
ANYWAY, THEY ARE BROTHERS FROM THE SAME LITTER.
THIS IS SO GREAT! I'M SO EXCITED!
I NEVER THOUGHT I WOULD MEET ANOTHER DOGGY THAT LOOKS JUST LIKE LUPIN.
HI, AMURO-KUN...
AMURO IS...

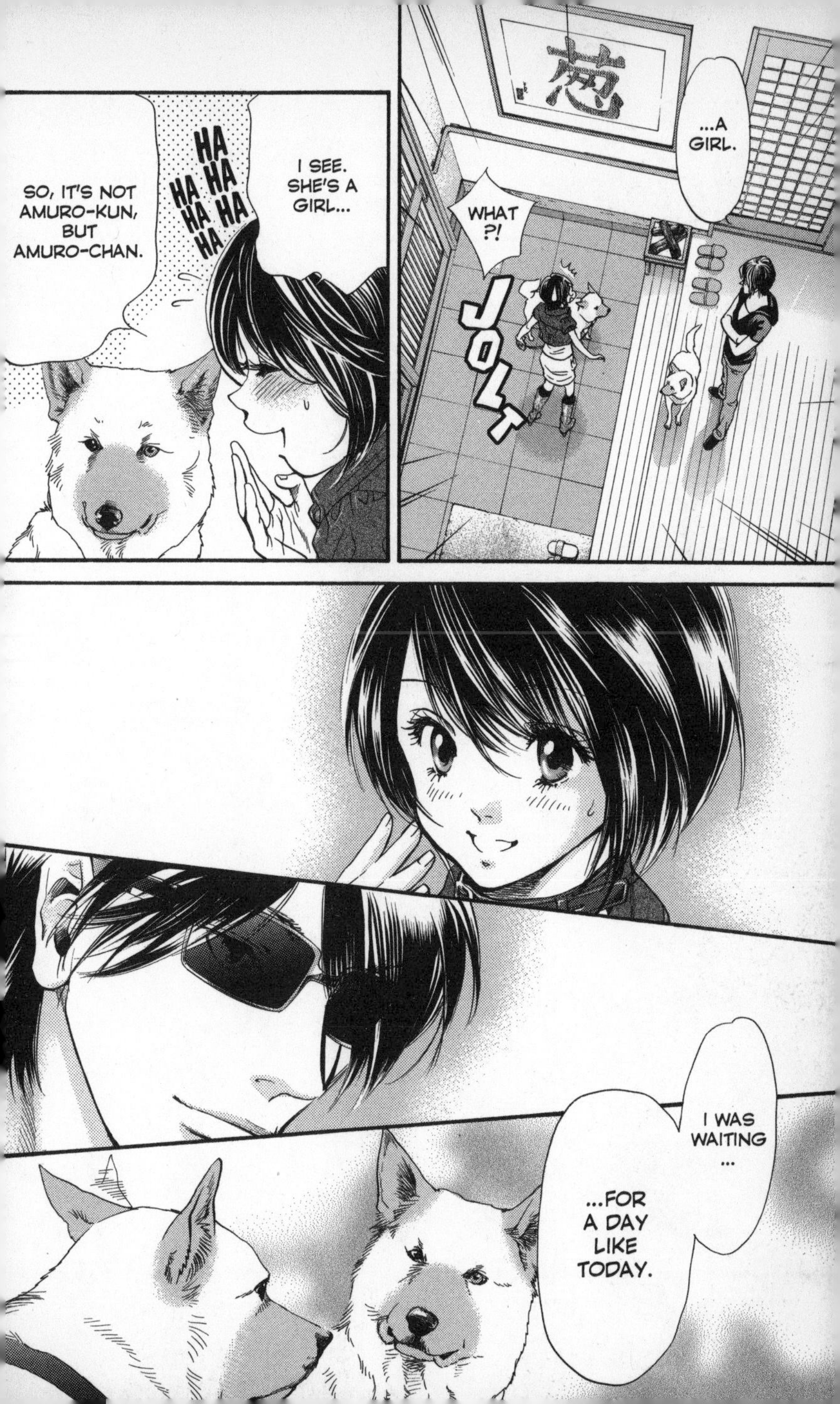
...A GIRL.
WHAT?!
JOLT
I SEE. SHE'S A GIRL...
HA HA HA HA HA HA HA
SO, IT'S NOT AMURO-KUN, BUT AMURO-CHAN.
I WAS WAITING ...
...FOR A DAY LIKE TODAY.

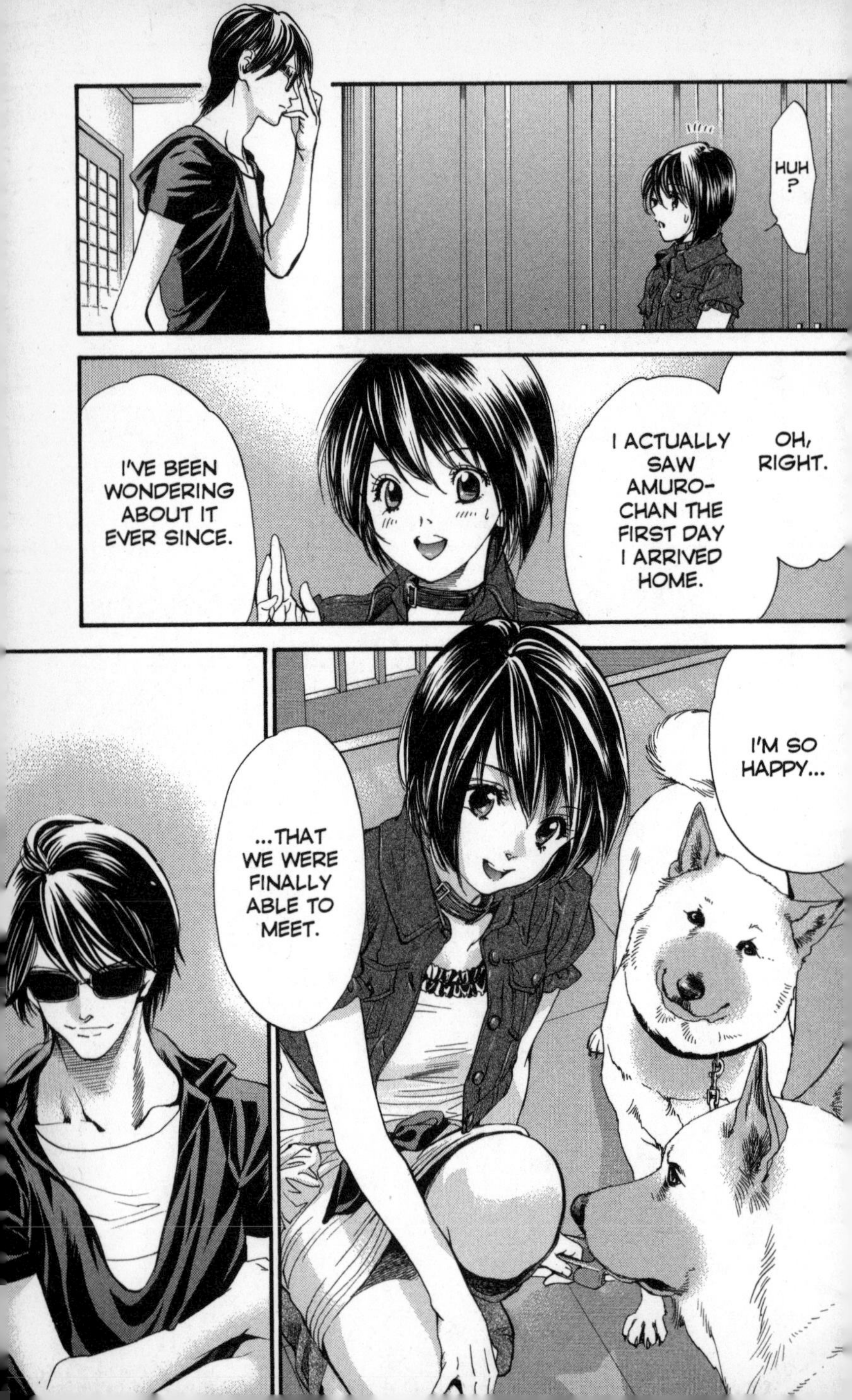
HUH ?
OH, RIGHT.
I ACTUALLY SAW AMURO-CHAN THE FIRST DAY I ARRIVED HOME.
I'VE BEEN WONDERING ABOUT IT EVER SINCE.
I'M SO HAPPY...
...THAT WE WERE FINALLY ABLE TO MEET.

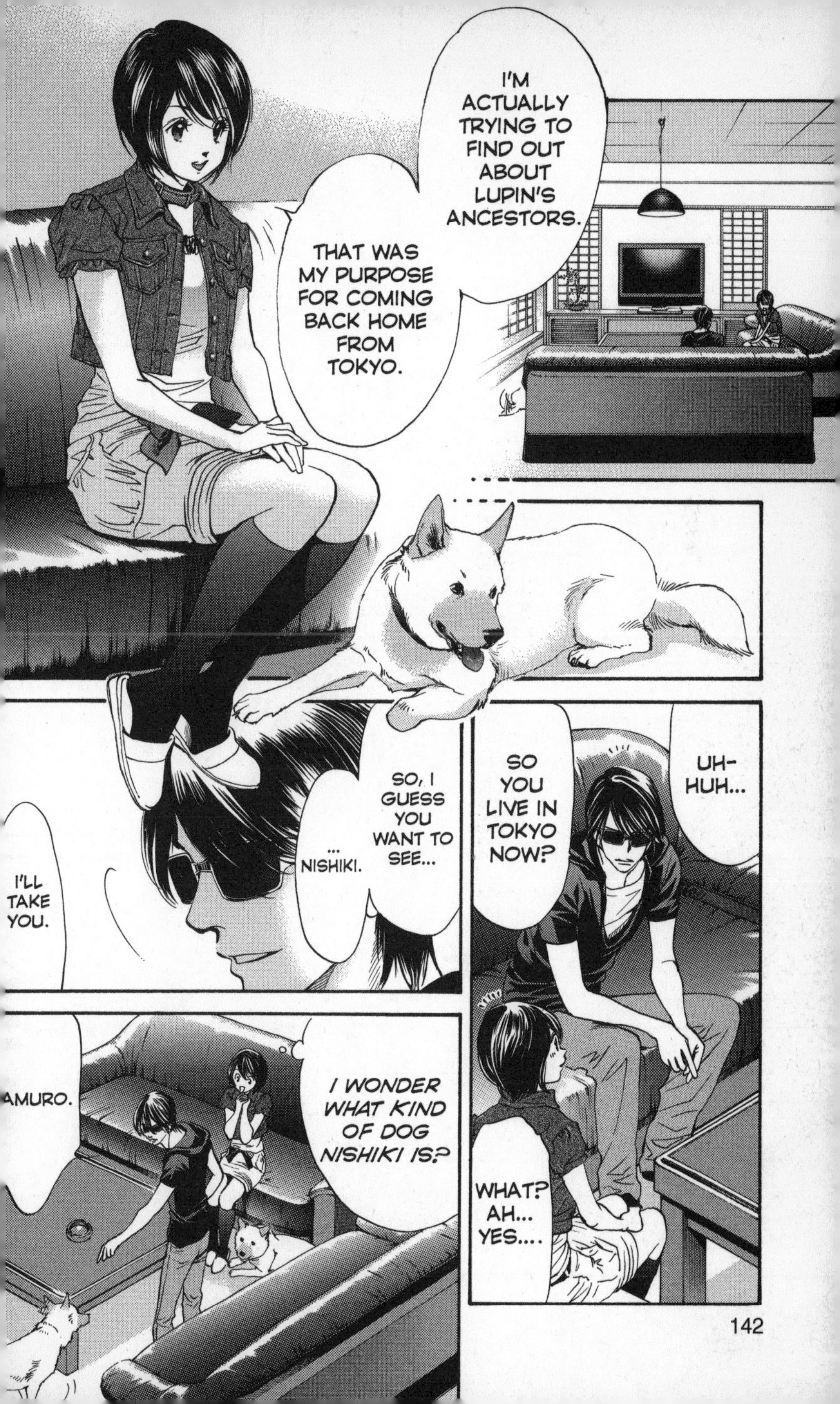
I'M ACTUALLY TRYING TO FIND OUT ABOUT LUPIN'S ANCESTORS.
THAT WAS MY PURPOSE FOR COMING BACK HOME FROM TOKYO.
UH-HUH...
SO YOU LIVE IN TOKYO NOW?
WHAT? AH... YES....
SO, I GUESS YOU WANT TO SEE...
... NISHIKI.
I'LL TAKE YOU.
I WONDER WHAT KIND OF DOG NISHIKI IS?
AMURO.

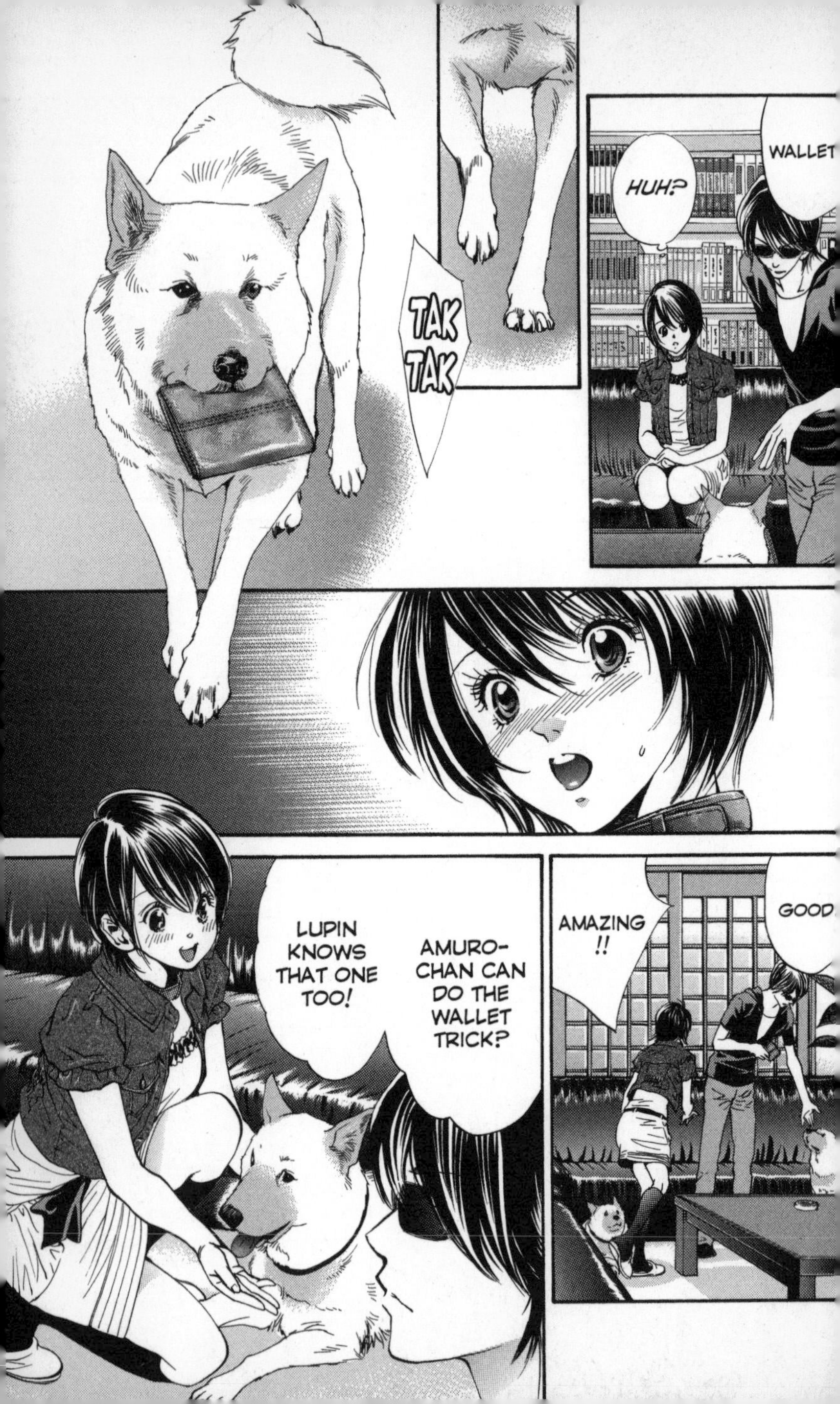
WALLET
HUH?
TAK TAK
GOOD.
AMAZING !!
AMURO-CHAN CAN DO THE WALLET TRICK?
LUPIN KNOWS THAT ONE TOO!

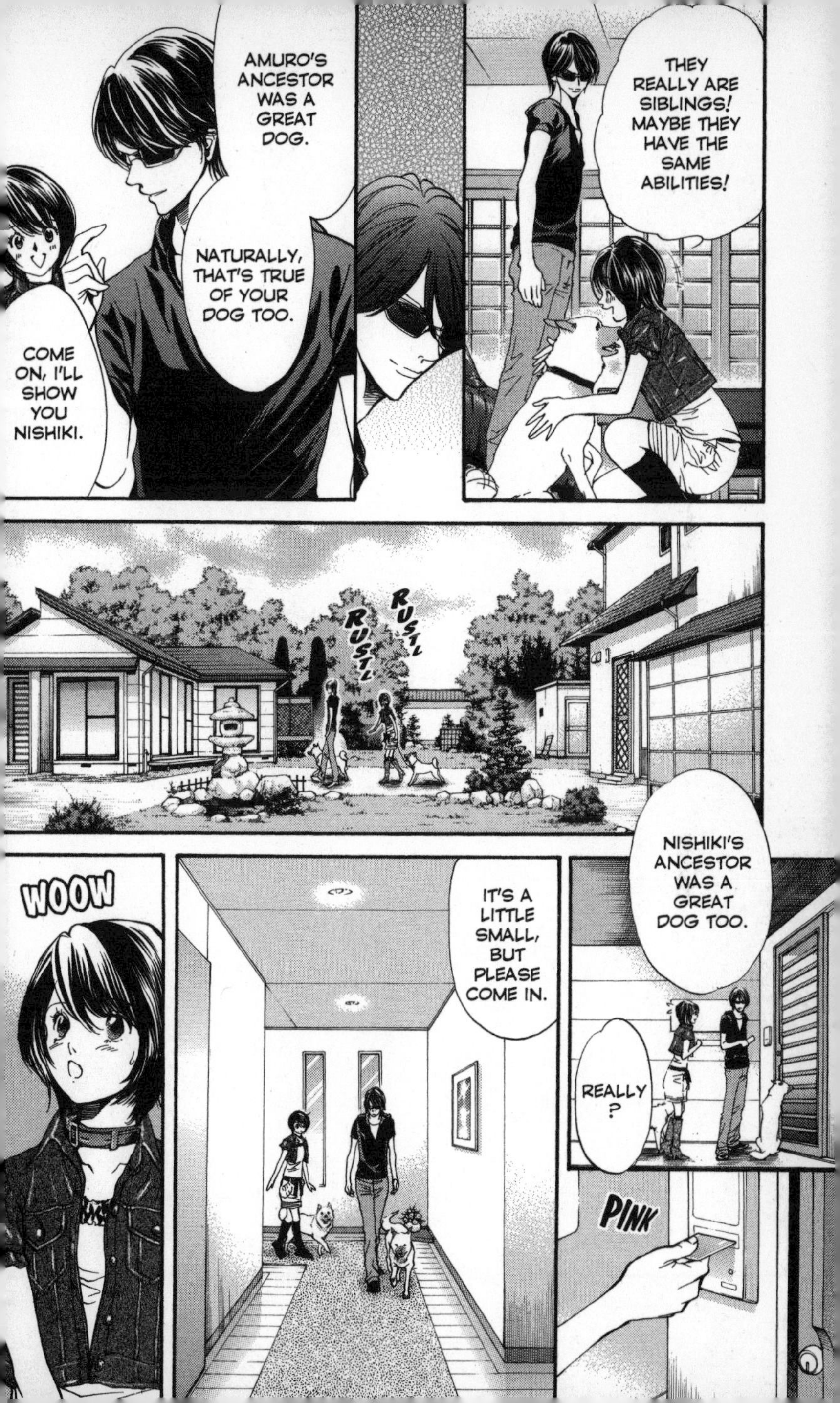
THEY REALLY ARE SIBLINGS! MAYBE THEY HAVE THE SAME ABILITIES!
AMURO'S ANCESTOR WAS A GREAT DOG.
NATURALLY, THAT'S TRUE OF YOUR DOG TOO.
COME ON, I'LL SHOW YOU NISHIKI.
RUSTL
RUSTL
NISHIKI'S ANCESTOR WAS A GREAT DOG TOO.
REALLY?
PINK
IT'S A LITTLE SMALL, BUT PLEASE COME IN.
WOOW

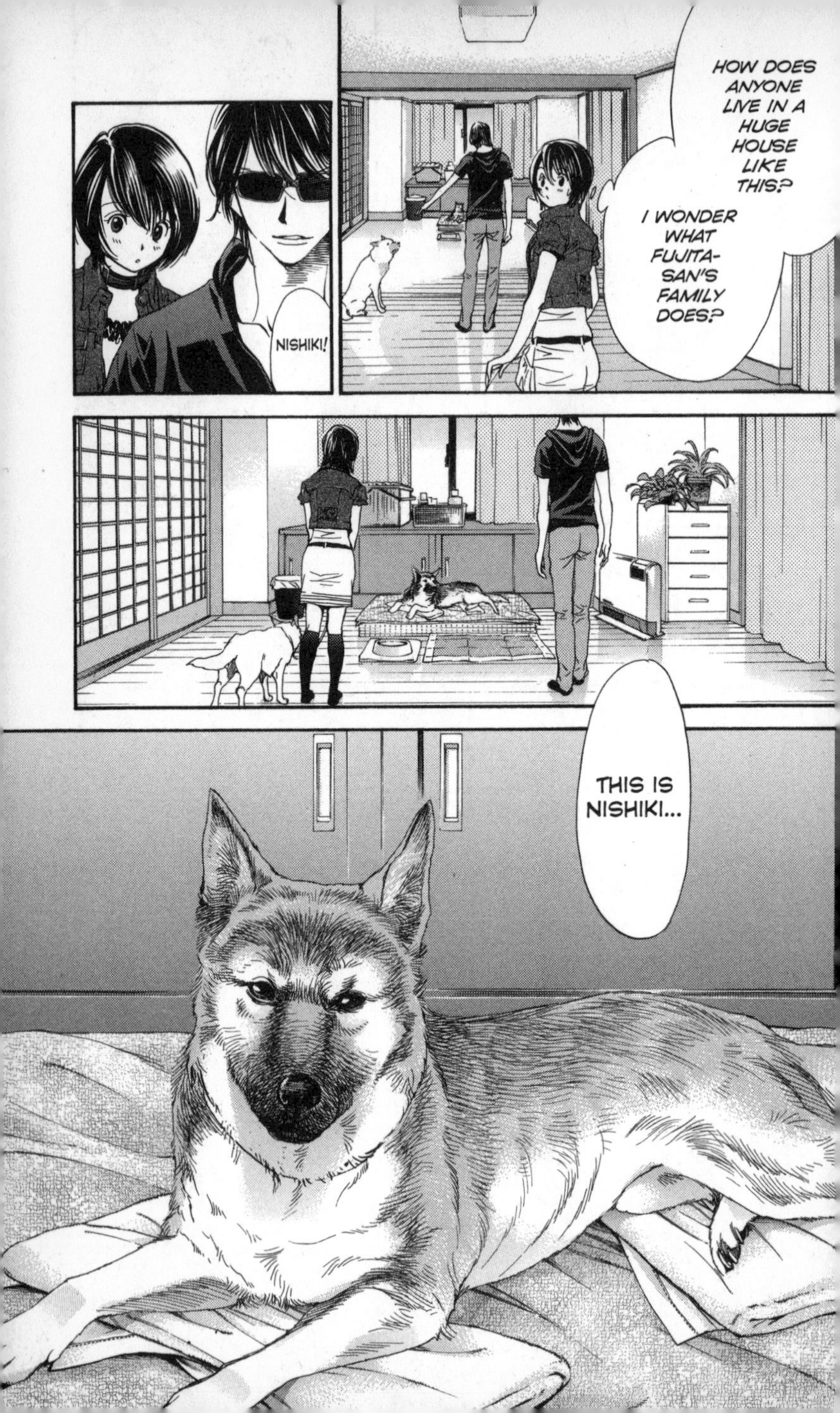
HOW DOES ANYONE LIVE IN A HUGE HOUSE LIKE THIS?
I WONDER WHAT FUJITA-SAN'S FAMILY DOES?
NISHIKI!
THIS IS NISHIKI...

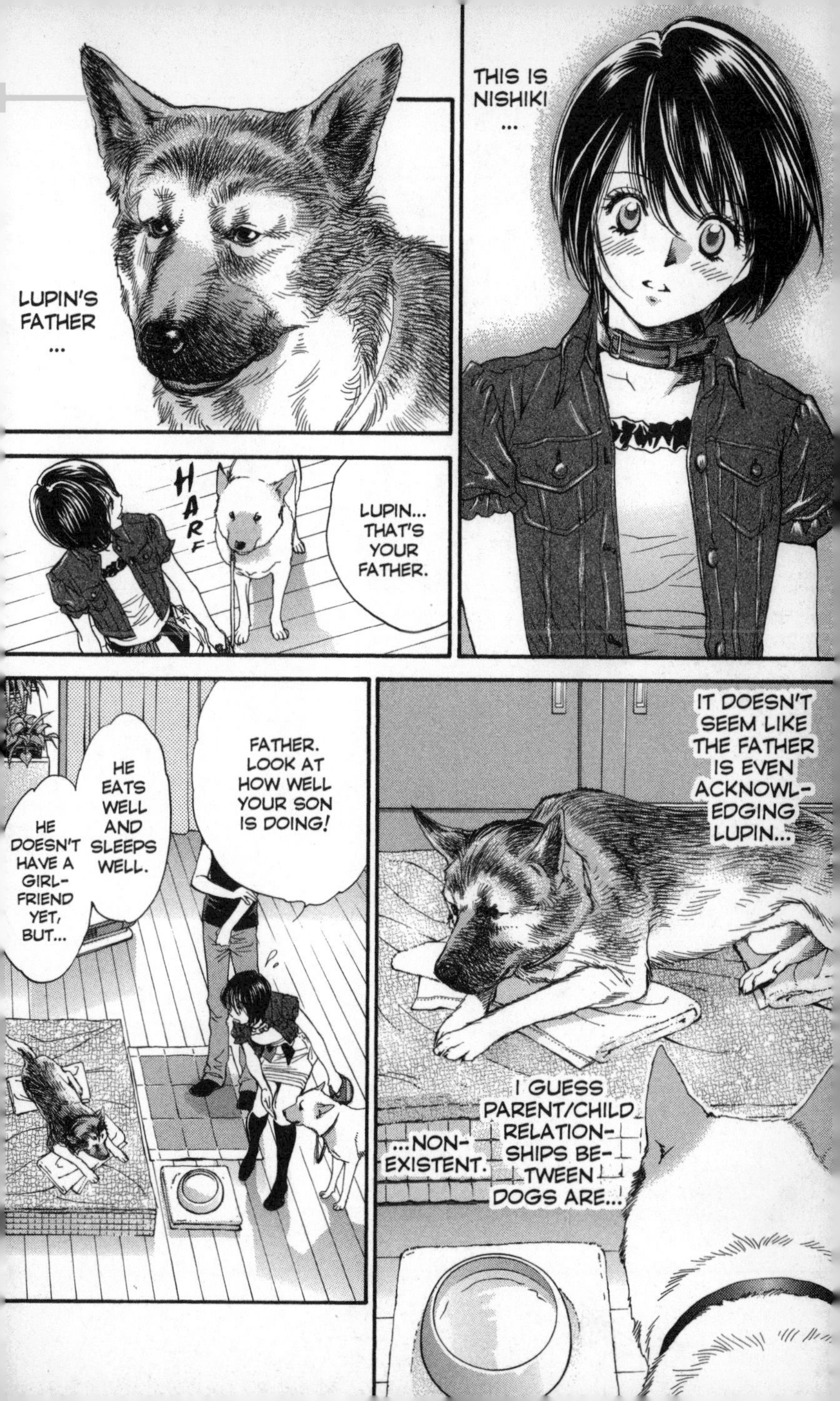
THIS IS NISHIKI ...
LUPIN'S FATHER ...
HARF
LUPIN... THAT'S YOUR FATHER.
IT DOESN'T SEEM LIKE THE FATHER IS EVEN ACKNOWLEDGING LUPIN...
I GUESS PARENT/CHILD RELATIONSHIPS BETWEEN DOGS ARE...
...NON-EXISTENT.
FATHER. LOOK AT HOW WELL YOUR SON IS DOING!
HE EATS WELL AND SLEEPS WELL.
HE DOESN'T HAVE A GIRLFRIEND YET, BUT...

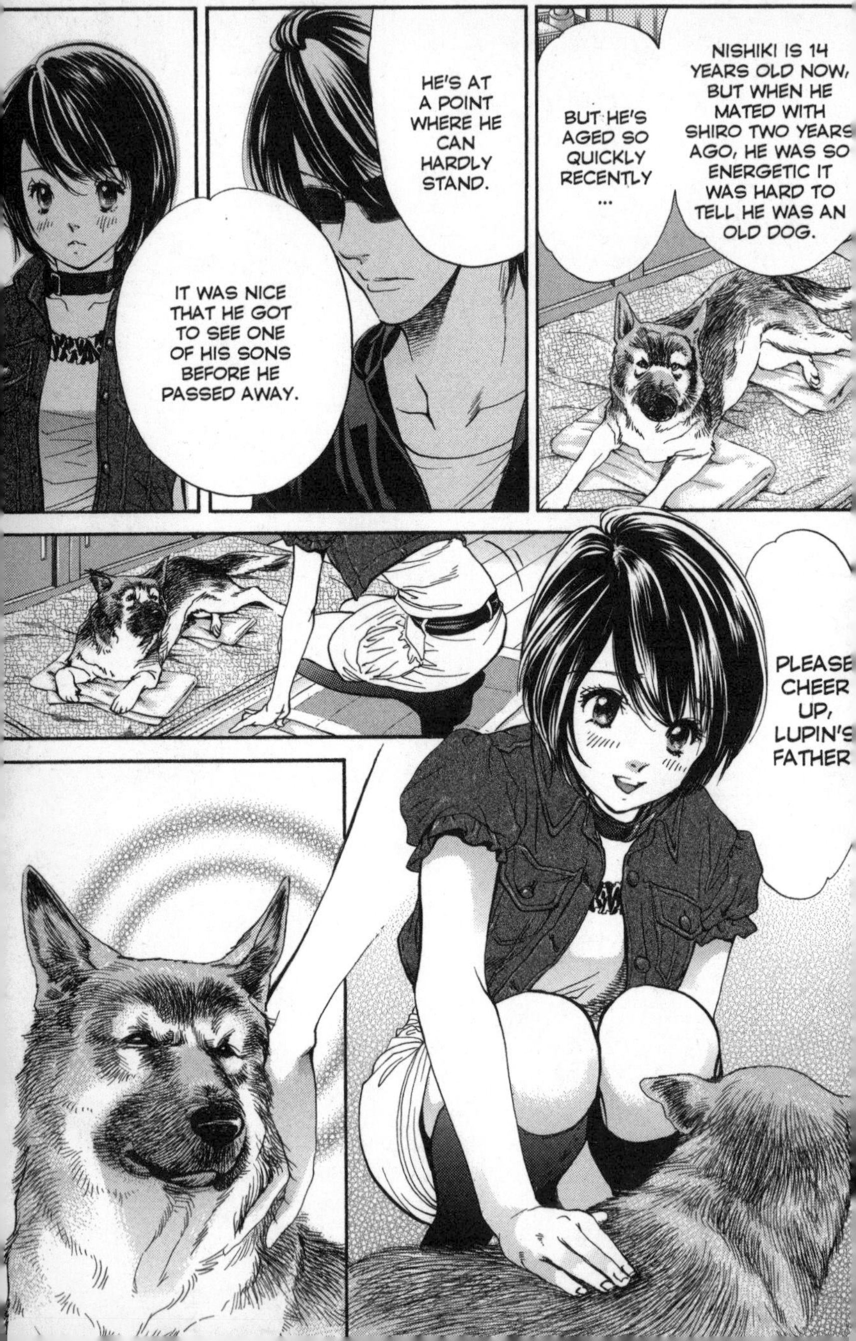

NISHIKI IS 14 YEARS OLD NOW, BUT WHEN HE MATED WITH SHIRO TWO YEARS AGO, HE WAS SO ENERGETIC IT WAS HARD TO TELL HE WAS AN OLD DOG.
BUT HE'S AGED SO QUICKLY RECENTLY ...
HE'S AT A POINT WHERE HE CAN HARDLY STAND.
IT WAS NICE THAT HE GOT TO SEE ONE OF HIS SONS BEFORE HE PASSED AWAY.
PLEASE CHEER UP, LUPIN'S FATHER

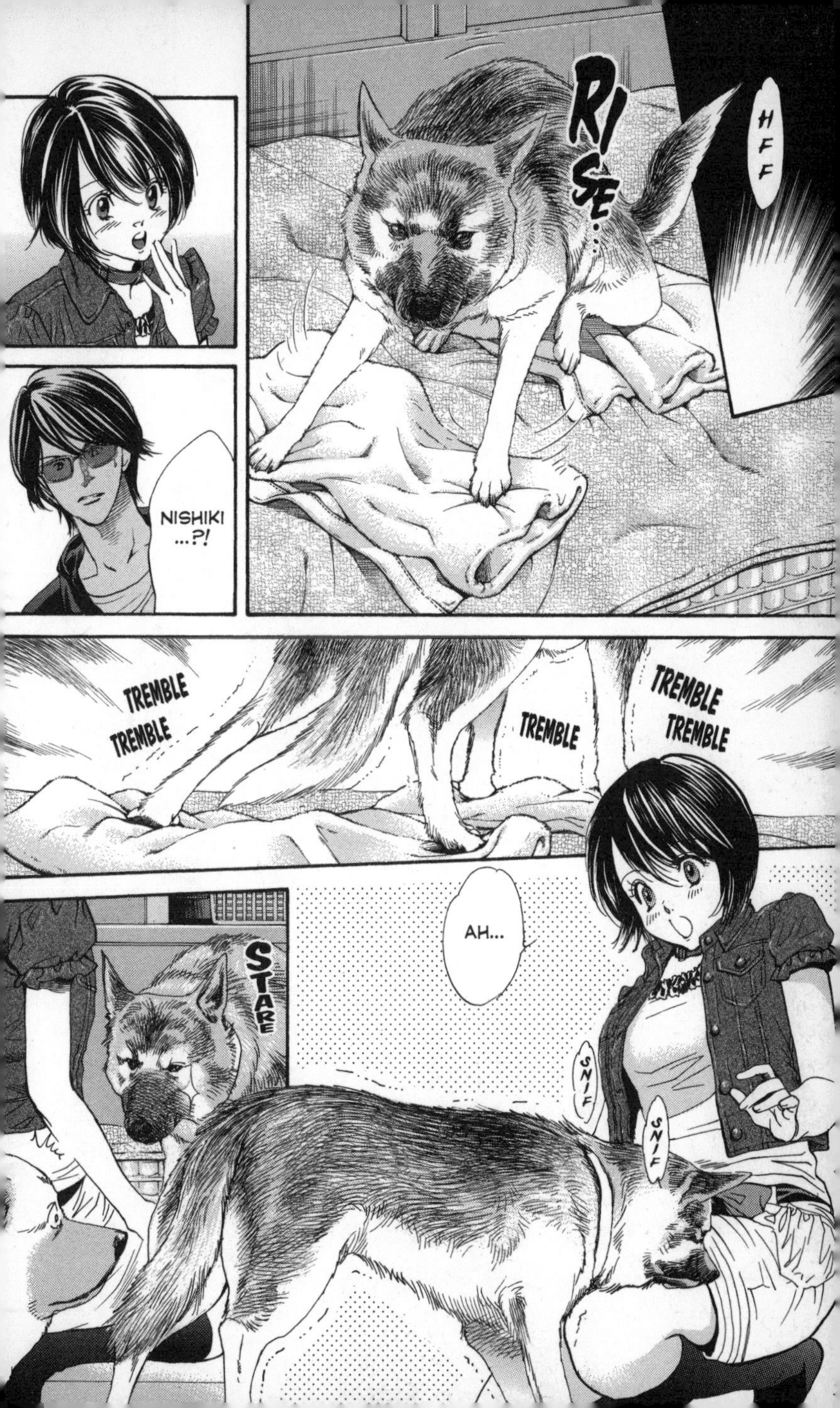
HFF
RISE...
NISHIKI ...?!
TREMBLE TREMBLE
TREMBLE
TREMBLE TREMBLE
AH...
SNIF
SNIF
STARE

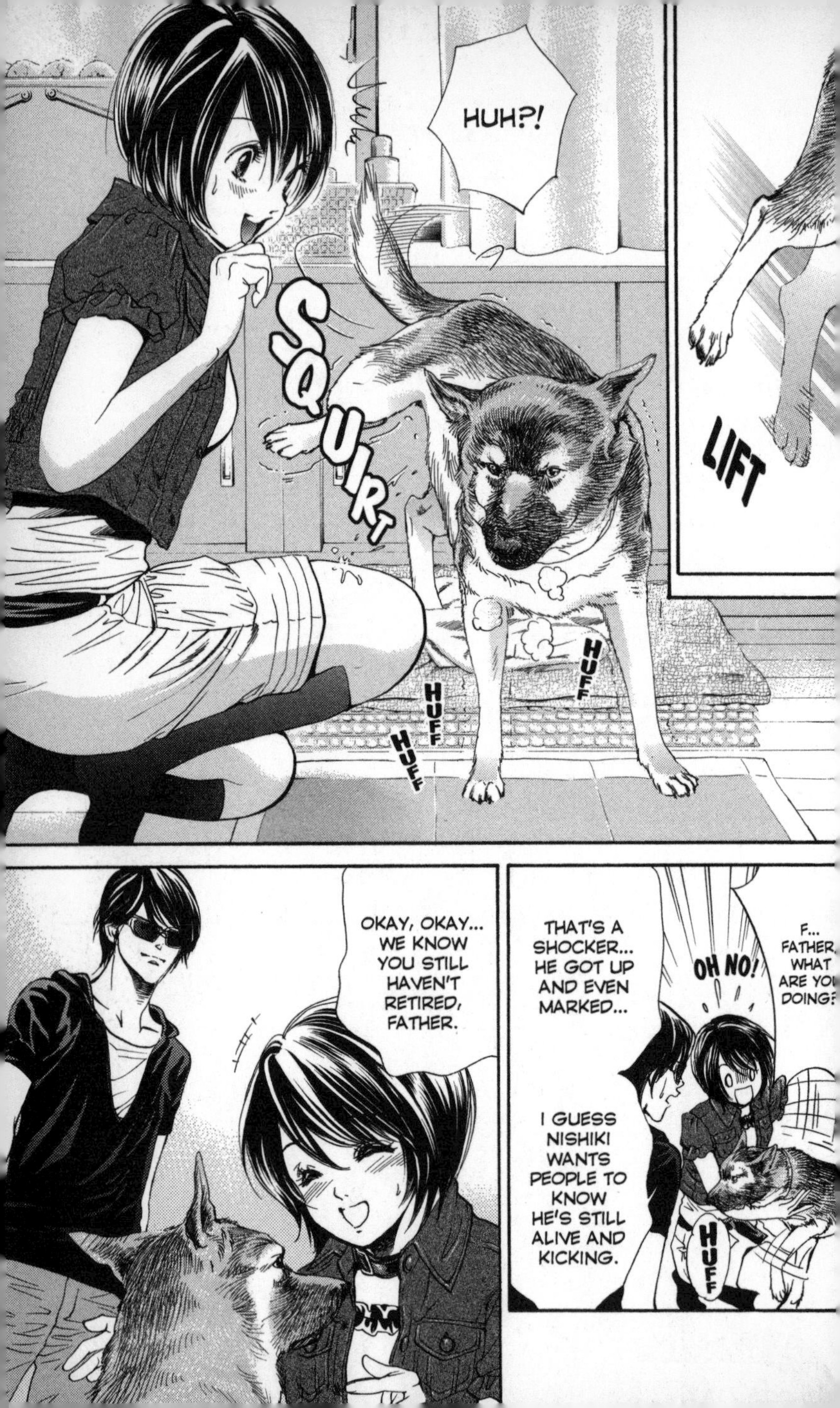
LIFT
HUH?!
SQUIRT
HUFF
HUFF
HUFF
F... FATHER, WHAT ARE YO DOING?
OH NO!
THAT'S A SHOCKER... HE GOT UP AND EVEN MARKED...
I GUESS NISHIKI WANTS PEOPLE TO KNOW HE'S STILL ALIVE AND KICKING.
HUFF
OKAY, OKAY... WE KNOW YOU STILL HAVEN'T RETIRED, FATHER.

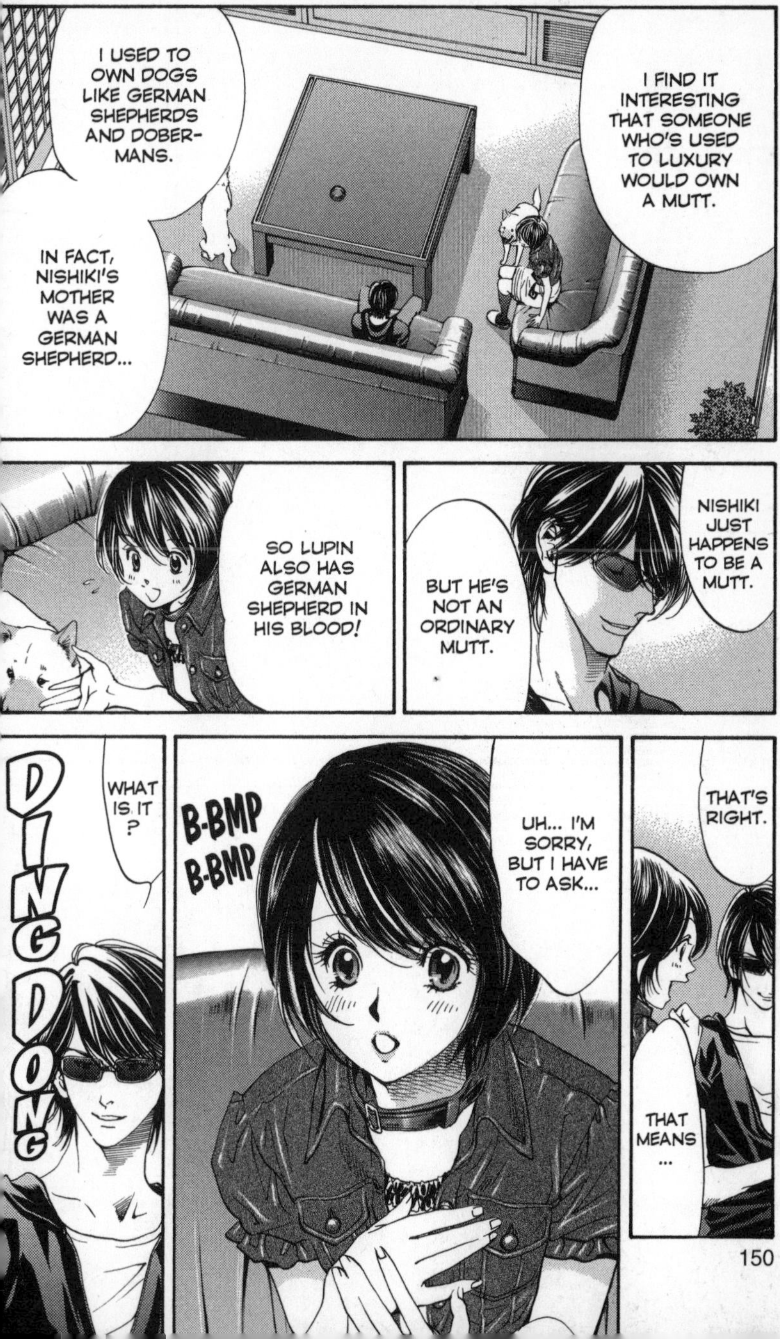

I FIND IT INTERESTING THAT SOMEONE WHO'S USED TO LUXURY WOULD OWN A MUTT.
I USED TO OWN DOGS LIKE GERMAN SHEPHERDS AND DOBER-MANS.
IN FACT, NISHIKI'S MOTHER WAS A GERMAN SHEPHERD...
NISHIKI JUST HAPPENS TO BE A MUTT.
BUT HE'S NOT AN ORDINARY MUTT.
SO LUPIN ALSO HAS GERMAN SHEPHERD IN HIS BLOOD!
THAT'S RIGHT.
THAT MEANS ...
B-BMP
B-BMP
UH... I'M SORRY, BUT I HAVE TO ASK...
WHAT IS IT ?
DING DONG

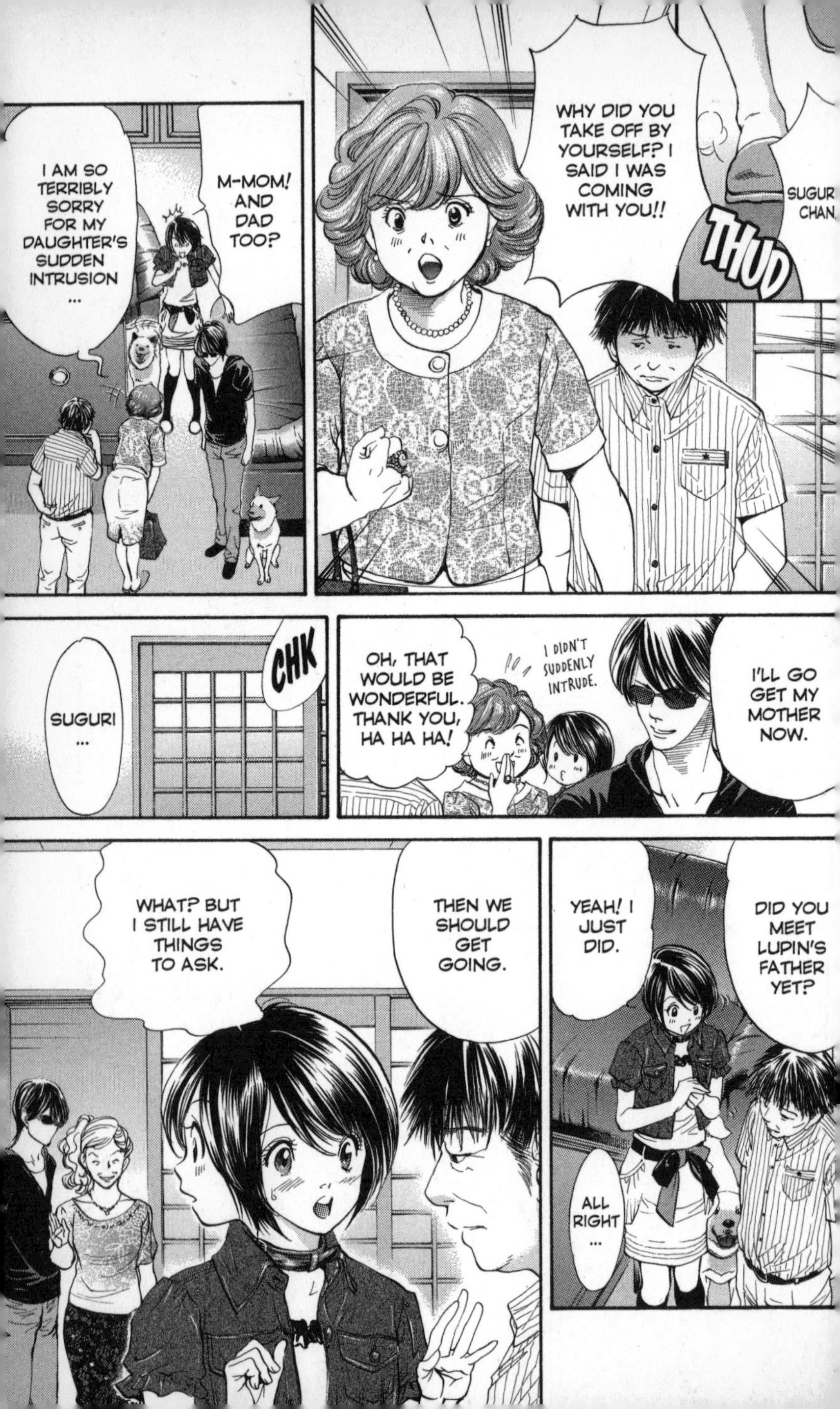
SUGUR CHAN
THUD
WHY DID YOU TAKE OFF BY YOURSELF? I SAID I WAS COMING WITH YOU!!
M-MOM! AND DAD TOO?
I AM SO TERRIBLY SORRY FOR MY DAUGHTER'S SUDDEN INTRUSION ...
I'LL GO GET MY MOTHER NOW.
OH, THAT WOULD BE WONDERFUL. THANK YOU, HA HA HA!
I DIDN'T SUDDENLY INTRUDE.
CHK
SUGURI ...
DID YOU MEET LUPIN'S FATHER YET?
YEAH! I JUST DID.
ALL RIGHT ...
THEN WE SHOULD GET GOING.
WHAT? BUT I STILL HAVE THINGS TO ASK.

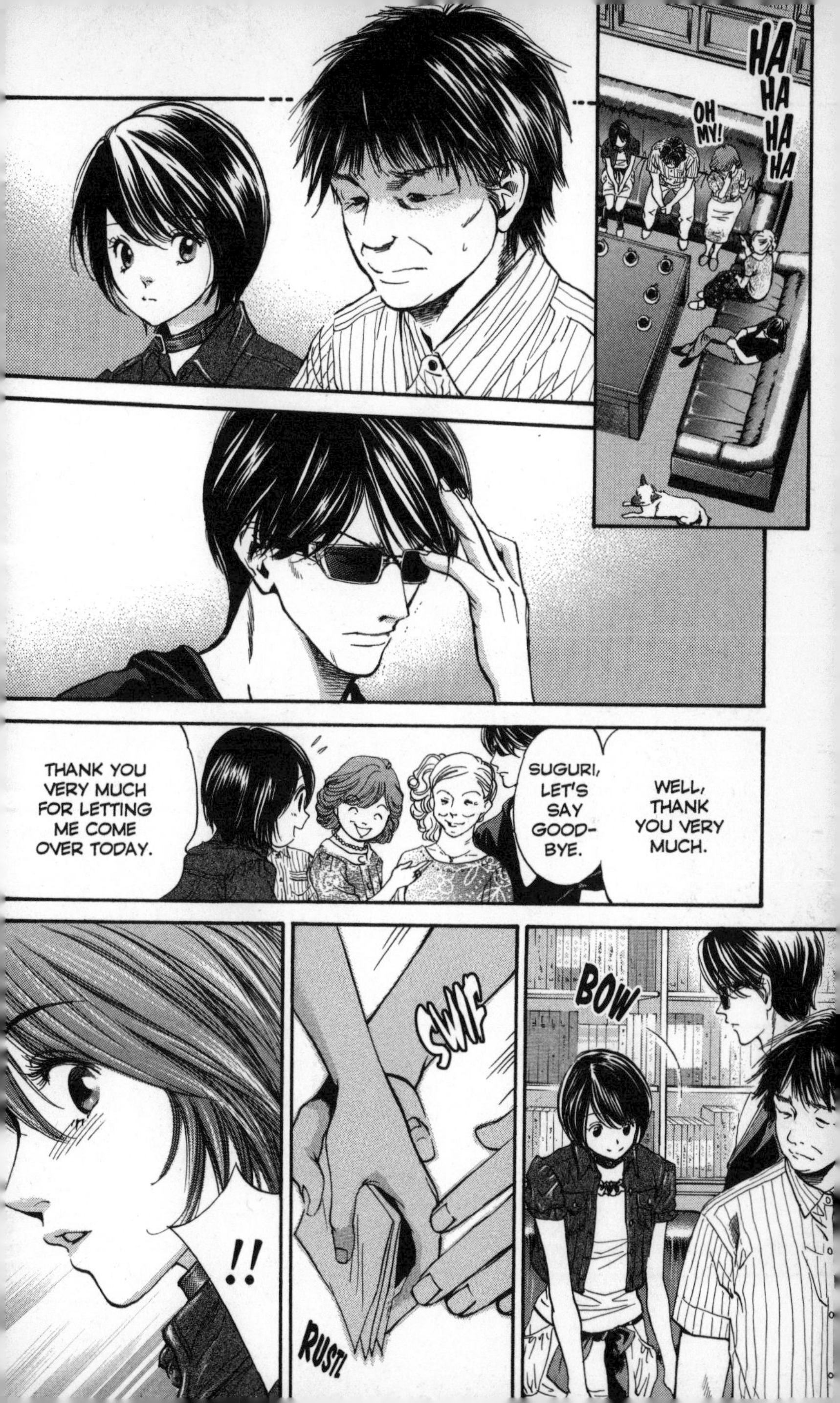
HA HA HA HA
OH MY!
WELL, THANK YOU VERY MUCH.
SUGURI, LET'S SAY GOOD-BYE.
THANK YOU VERY MUCH FOR LETTING ME COME OVER TODAY.
BOW
SWIF
RUST!
!!

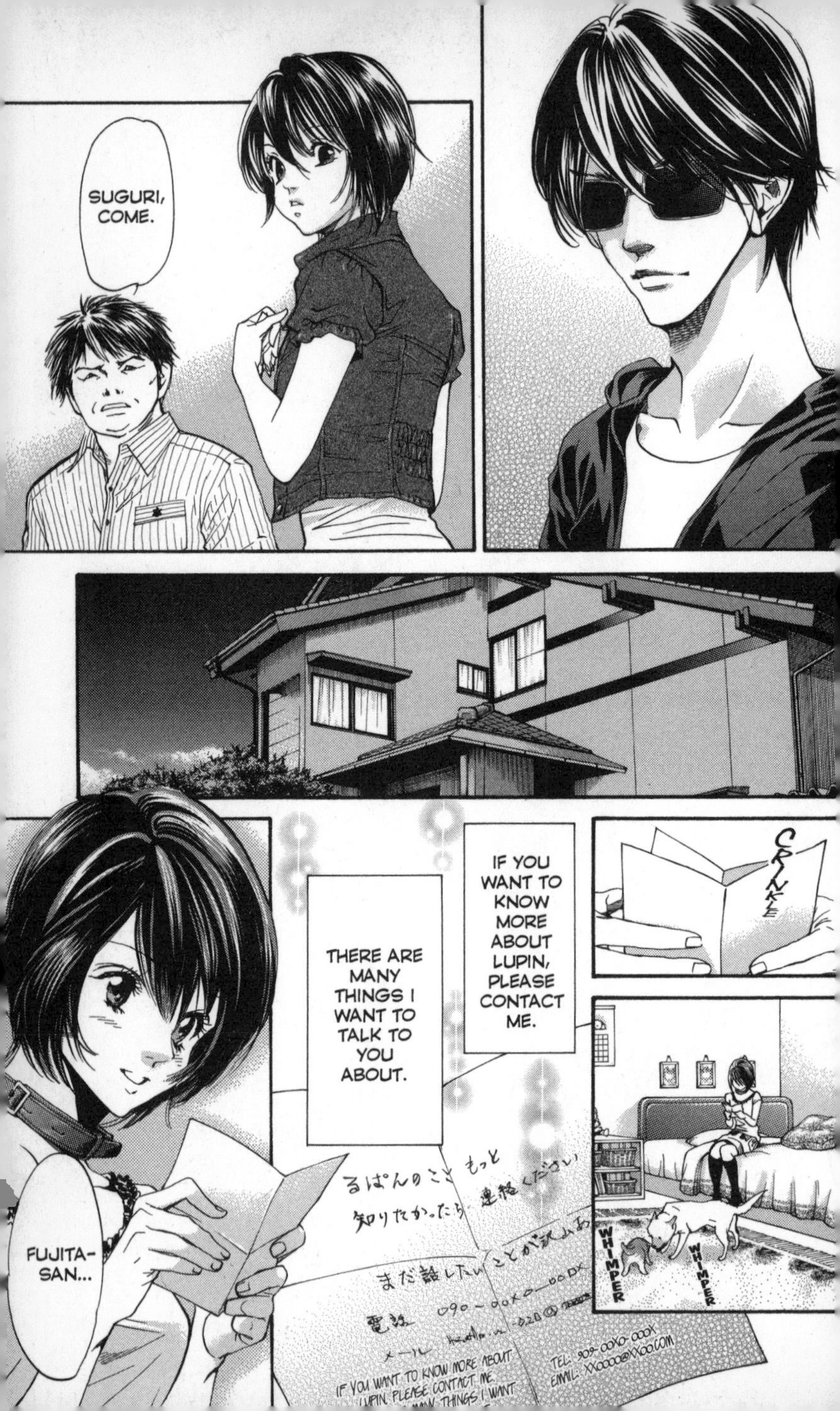
SUGURI, COME.
CRINKLE
WHIMPER
WHIMPER
IF YOU WANT TO KNOW MORE ABOUT LUPIN, PLEASE CONTACT ME.
THERE ARE MANY THINGS I WANT TO TALK TO YOU ABOUT.
るぱんのこと もっと
知りたかったら 連絡ください
まだ話したいことが沢山あ
電話
メール
IF YOU WANT TO KNOW MORE ABOUT
LUPIN, PLEASE CONTACT ME.
TEL: 909-OOXO-OOOX
EMAIL: XXOOOO@XXOO.COM
FUJITA-SAN...

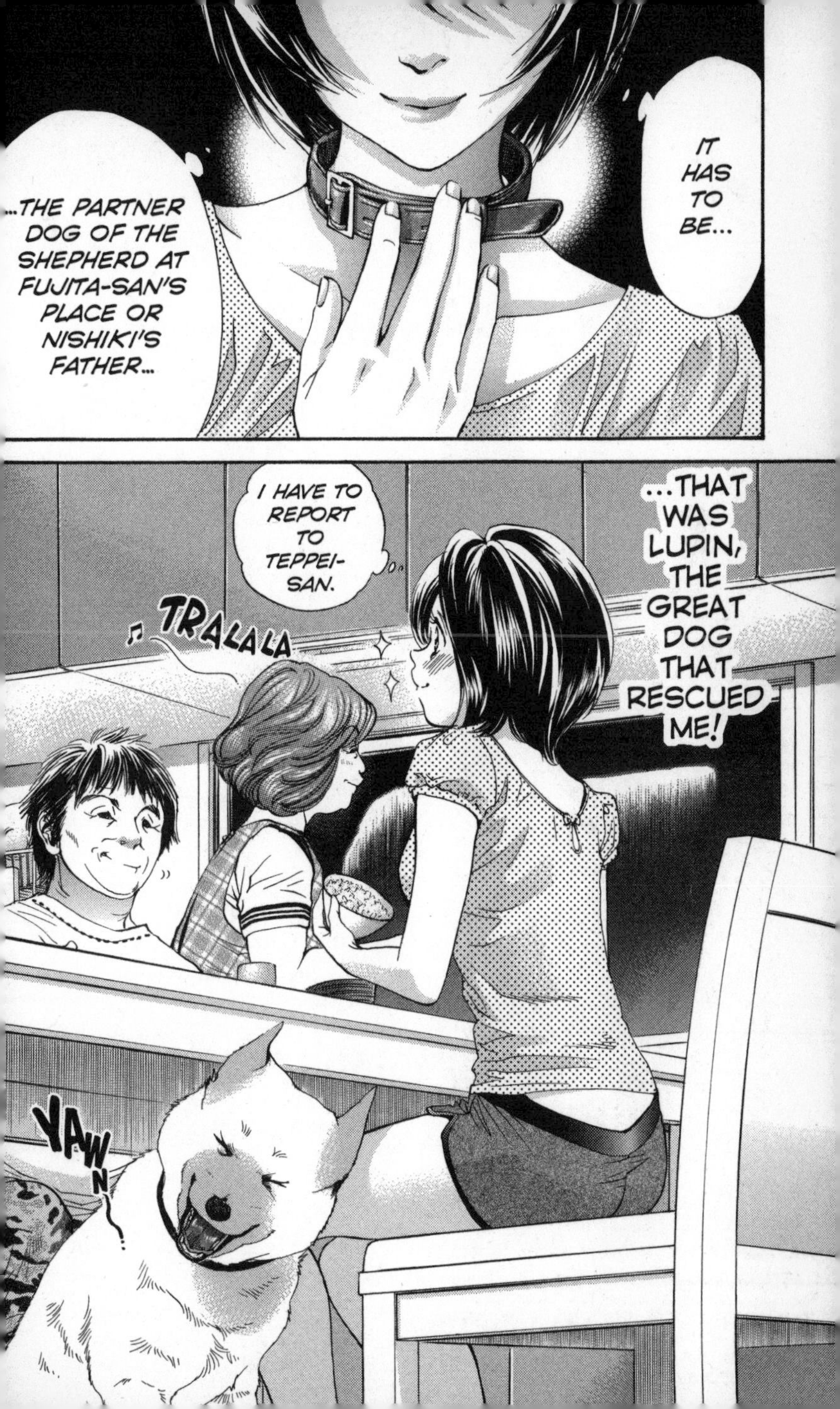
IT HAS TO BE...
...THE PARTNER DOG OF THE SHEPHERD AT FUJITA-SAN'S PLACE OR NISHIKI'S FATHER...
...THAT WAS LUPIN, THE GREAT DOG THAT RESCUED ME!
I HAVE TO REPORT TO TEPPEI-SAN.
TRALALA
YAWN

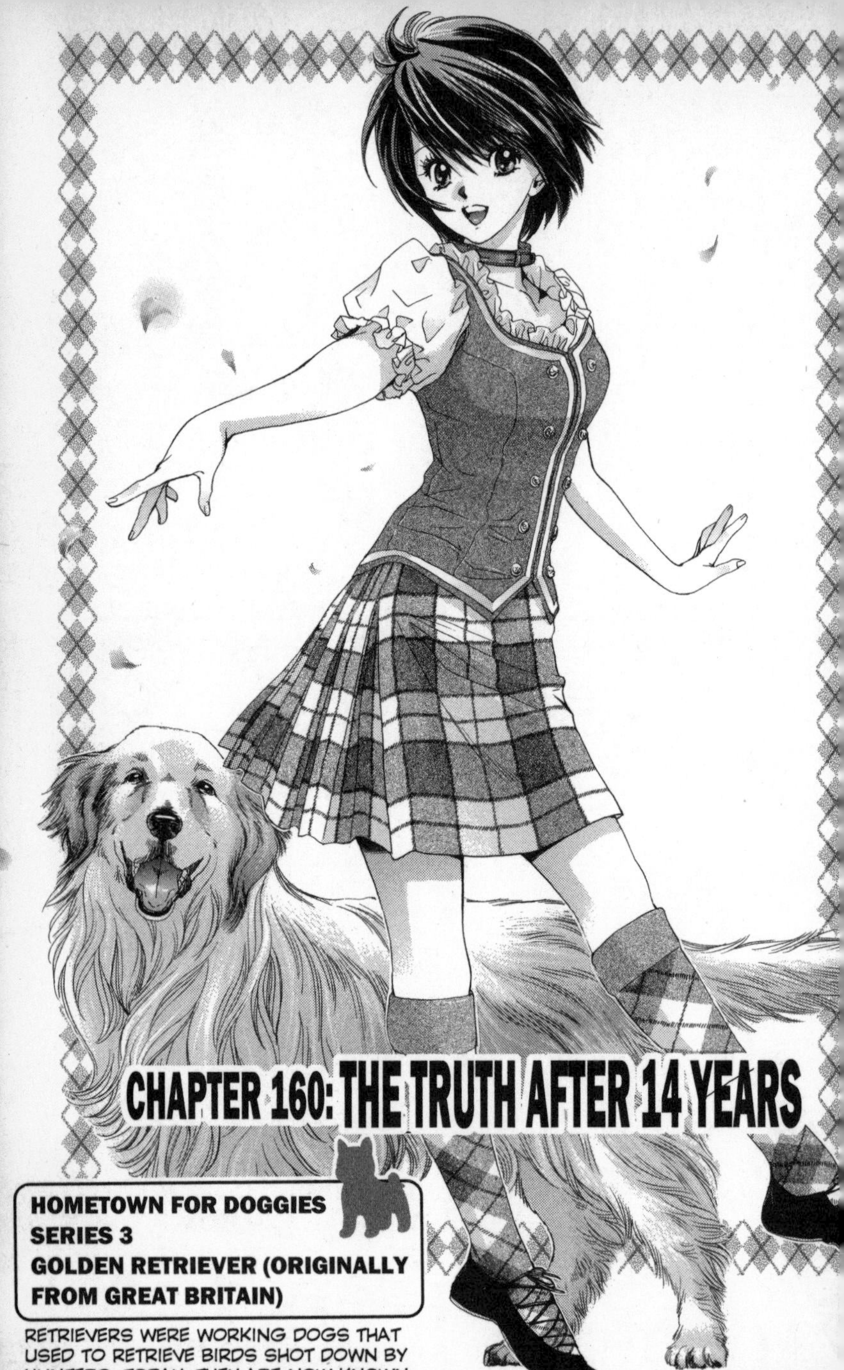
CHAPTER 160: THE TRUTH AFTER 14 YEARS
HOMETOWN FOR DOGGIES
SERIES 3
GOLDEN RETRIEVER (ORIGINALLY FROM GREAT BRITAIN)
RETRIEVERS WERE WORKING DOGS THAT USED TO RETRIEVE BIRDS SHOT DOWN BY HUNTERS. TODAY, THEY ARE NOW KNOWN AND LOVED AS A FAMILY-FRIENDLY DOG.

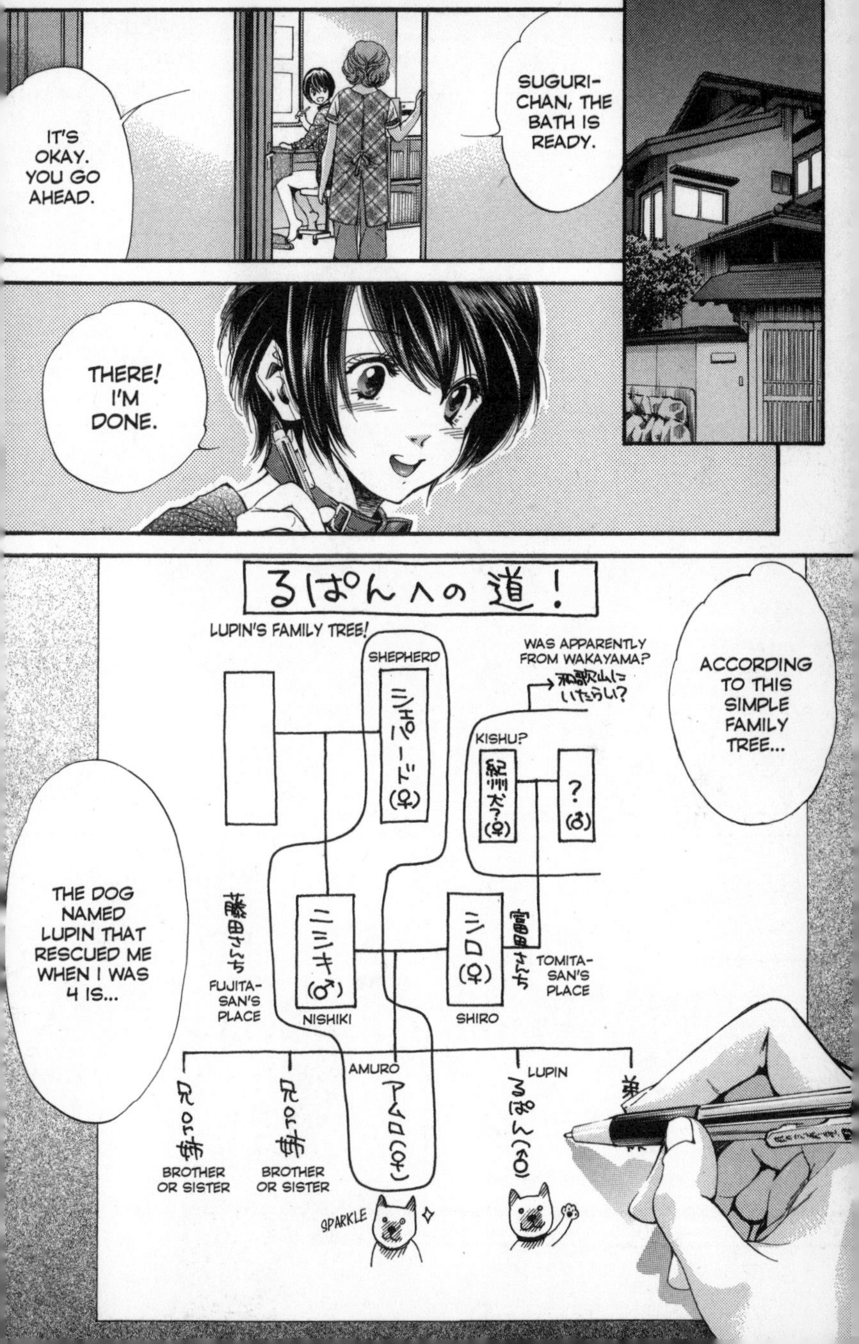
SUGURI-CHAN, THE BATH IS READY.
IT'S OKAY. YOU GO AHEAD.
THERE! I'M DONE.
ACCORDING TO THIS SIMPLE FAMILY TREE...
るぱんへの道！
LUPIN'S FAMILY TREE!
WAS APPARENTLY FROM WAKAYAMA?
和歌山にいたらしい?
SHEPHERD
シェパード(♀)
KISHU?
紀州犬?(♀)
?(♂)
藤田さんち
FUJITA-SAN'S PLACE
ニシキ(♂)
NISHIKI
シロ(♀)
SHIRO
富田さんち
TOMITA-SAN'S PLACE
兄or姉
BROTHER OR SISTER
兄or姉
BROTHER OR SISTER
AMURO
アムロ(♀)
SPARKLE
LUPIN
るぱん(♂)
THE DOG NAMED LUPIN THAT RESCUED ME WHEN I WAS 4 IS...

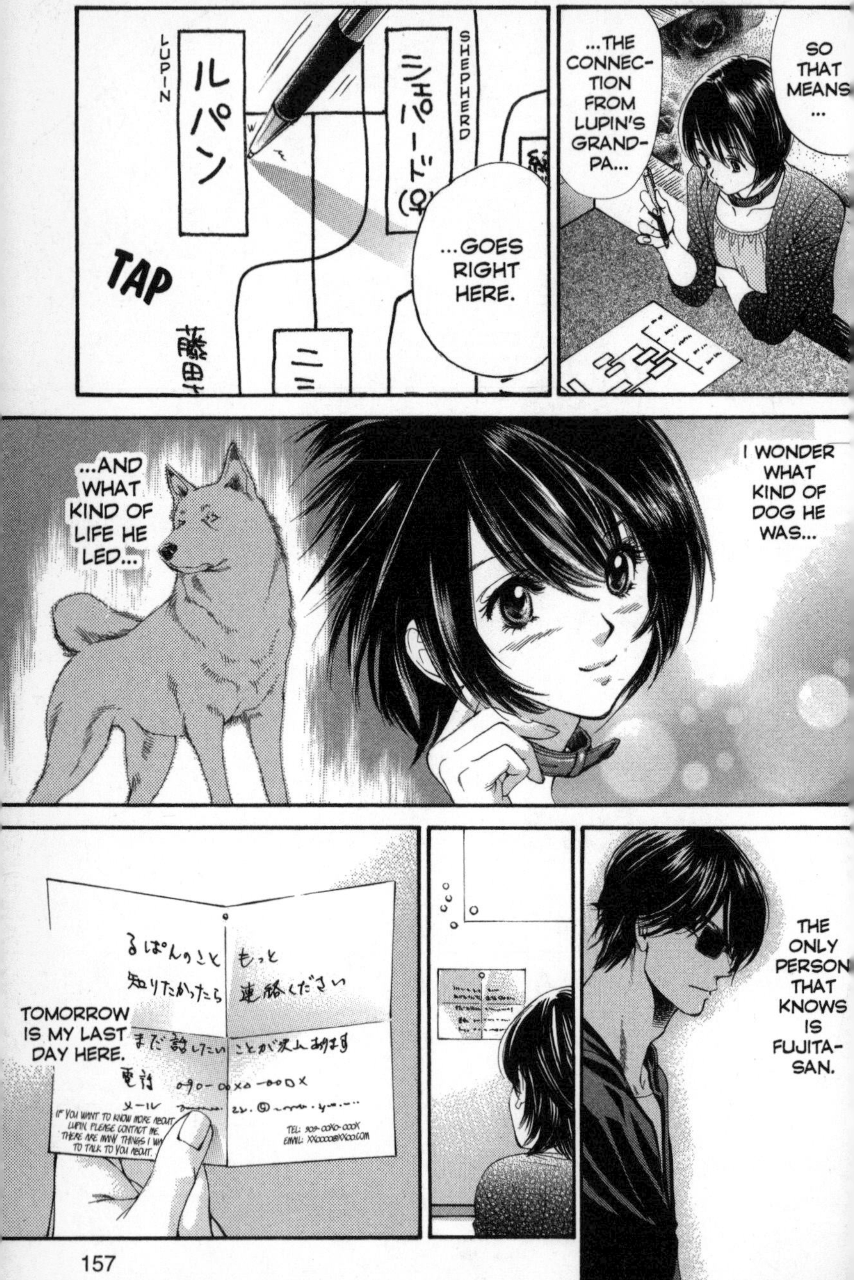
SO THAT MEANS...
...THE CONNECTION FROM LUPIN'S GRANDPA...
SHEPHERD
シェパード(♀)
LUPIN
ルパン
...GOES RIGHT HERE.
TAP
I WONDER WHAT KIND OF DOG HE WAS...
...AND WHAT KIND OF LIFE HE LED...
THE ONLY PERSON THAT KNOWS IS FUJITA-SAN.
るぱんのこと もっと
知りたかったら 連絡ください
まだ話したいことが沢山あります
TOMORROW IS MY LAST DAY HERE.
IF YOU WANT TO KNOW MORE ABOUT LUPIN, PLEASE CONTACT ME. THERE ARE MANY THINGS I W
TO TALK TO YOU ABOUT.
TEL: 909-00X0-000X
EMAIL: XX0000@XX00.COM

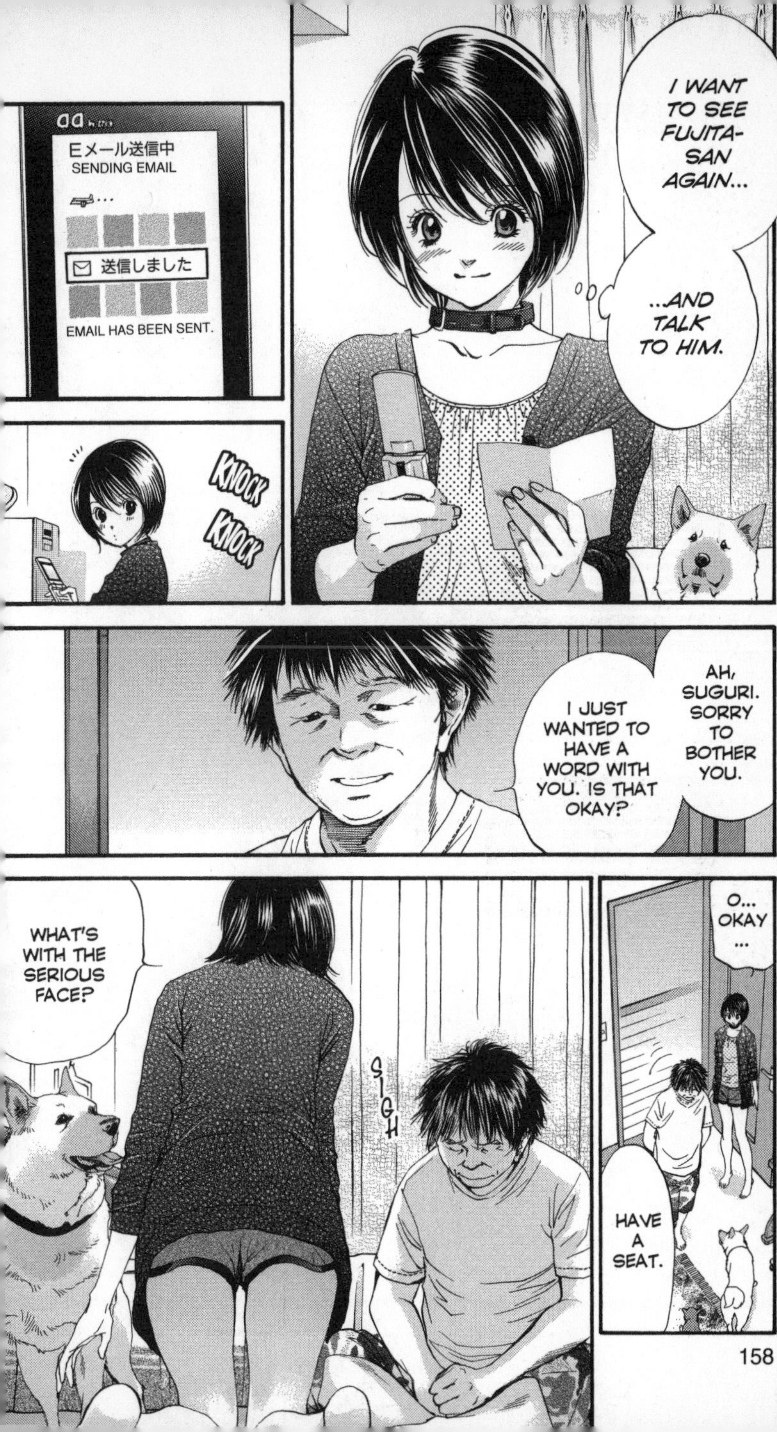
I WANT TO SEE FUJITA-SAN AGAIN...
...AND TALK TO HIM.
Eメール送信中
SENDING EMAIL
送信しました
EMAIL HAS BEEN SENT.
KNOCK
KNOCK
AH, SUGURI. SORRY TO BOTHER YOU.
I JUST WANTED TO HAVE A WORD WITH YOU. IS THAT OKAY?
O... OKAY ...
HAVE A SEAT.
WHAT'S WITH THE SERIOUS FACE?
SIGH

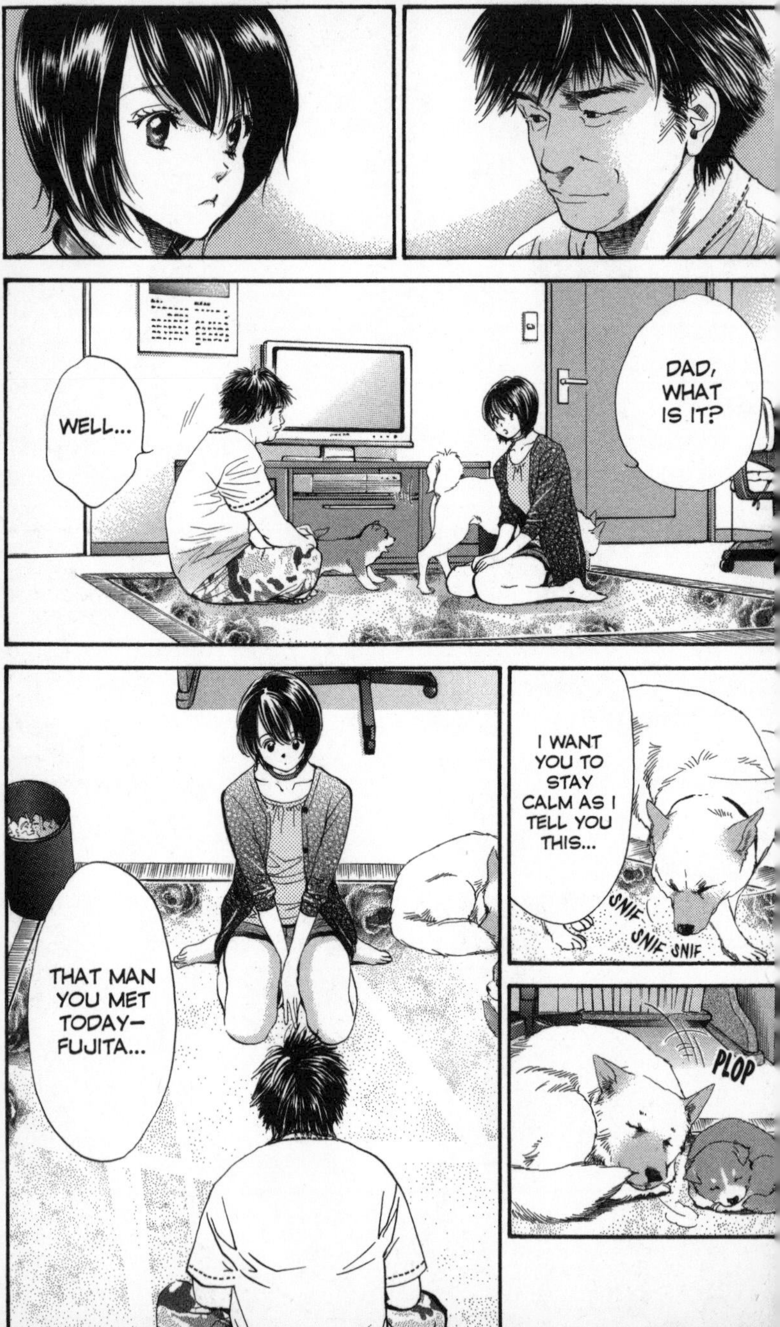
DAD, WHAT IS IT?
WELL...
I WANT YOU TO STAY CALM AS I TELL YOU THIS...
SNIF SNIF SNIF
PLOP
THAT MAN YOU MET TODAY—FUJITA...

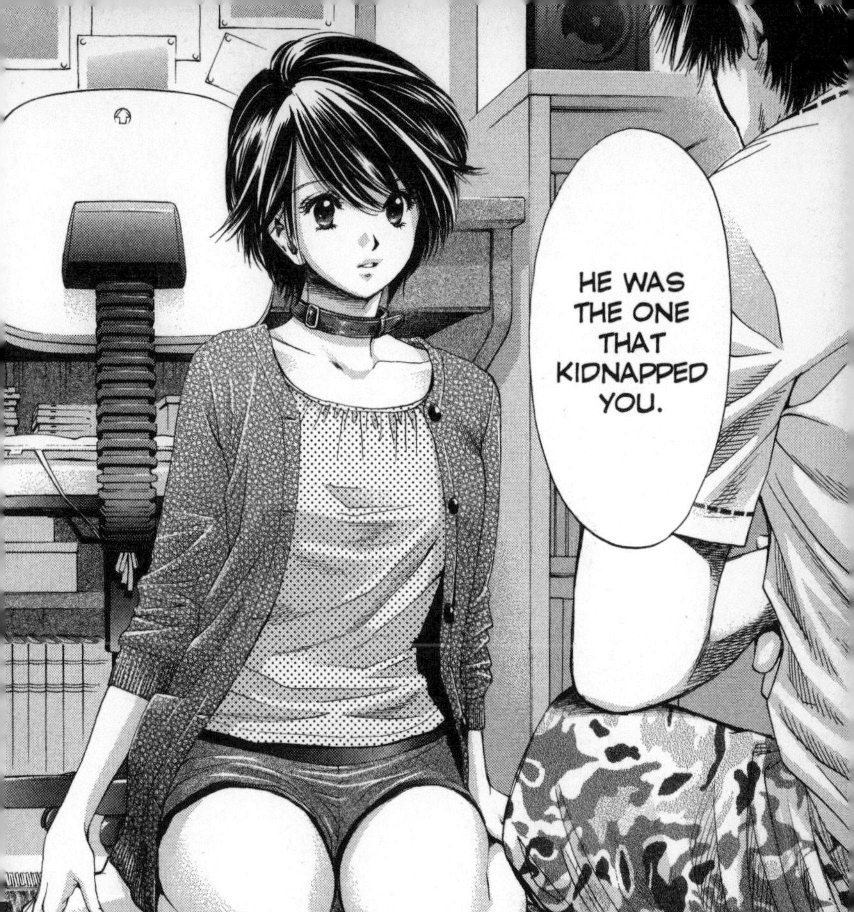
HE WAS THE ONE THAT KIDNAPPED YOU.
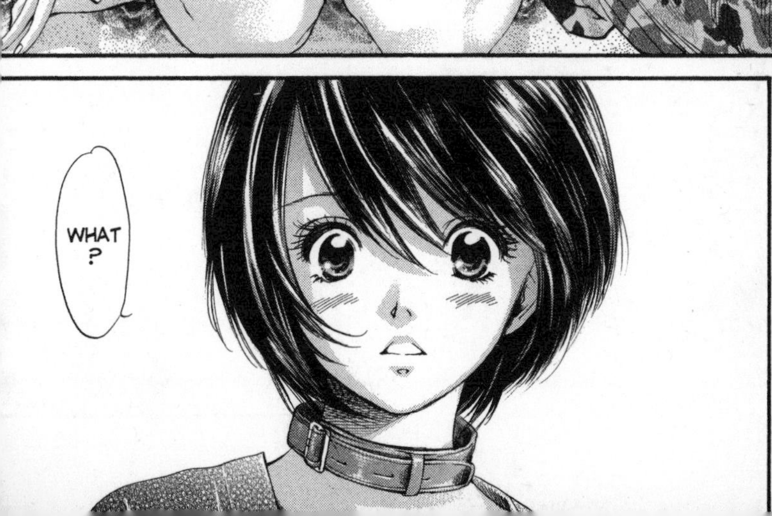
WHAT ?

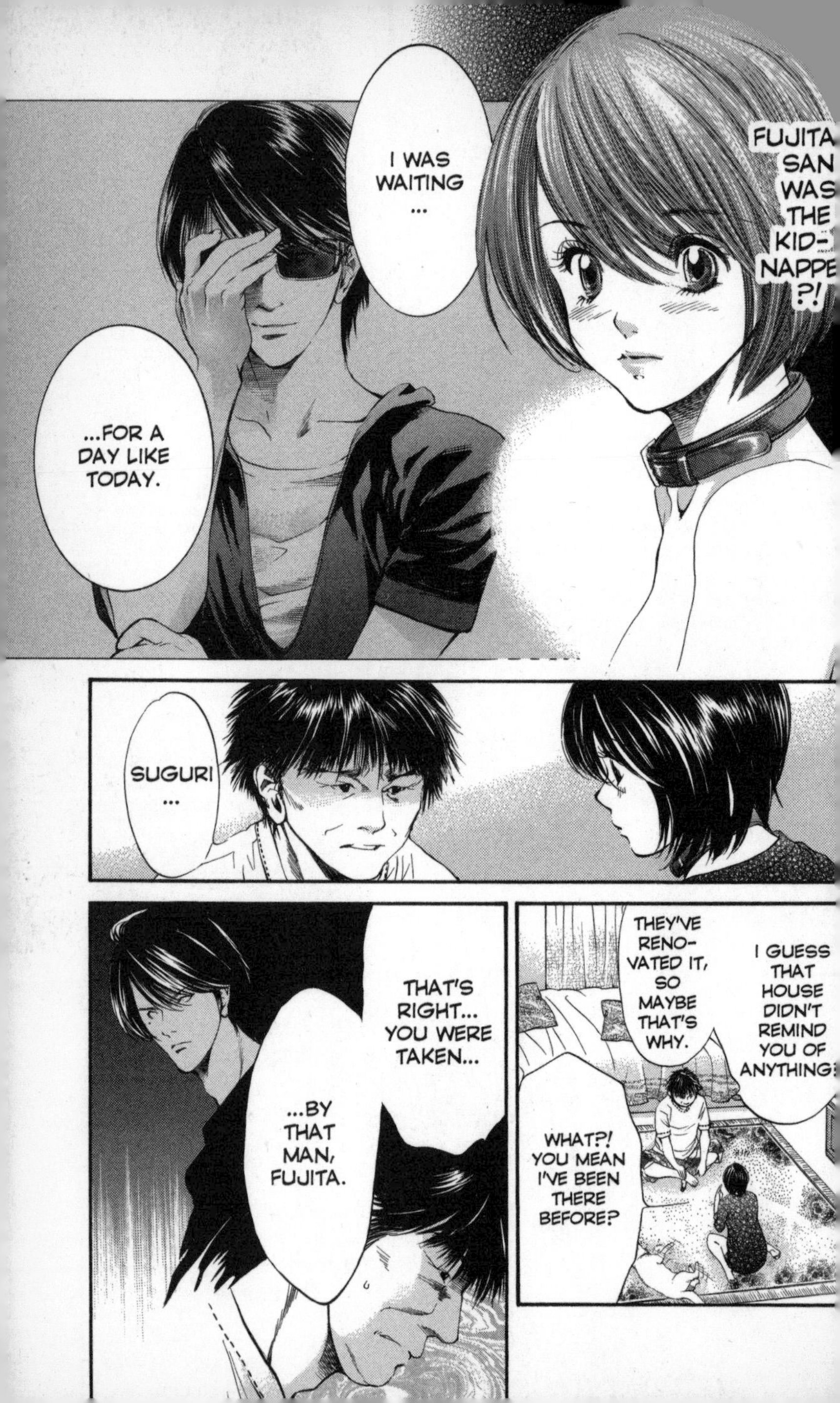
FUJITA SAN WAS THE KID-NAPPE ?!
I WAS WAITING ...
...FOR A DAY LIKE TODAY.
SUGURI ...
I GUESS THAT HOUSE DIDN'T REMIND YOU OF ANYTHING
THEY'VE RENO-VATED IT, SO MAYBE THAT'S WHY.
WHAT?! YOU MEAN I'VE BEEN THERE BEFORE?
THAT'S RIGHT... YOU WERE TAKEN...
...BY THAT MAN, FUJITA.

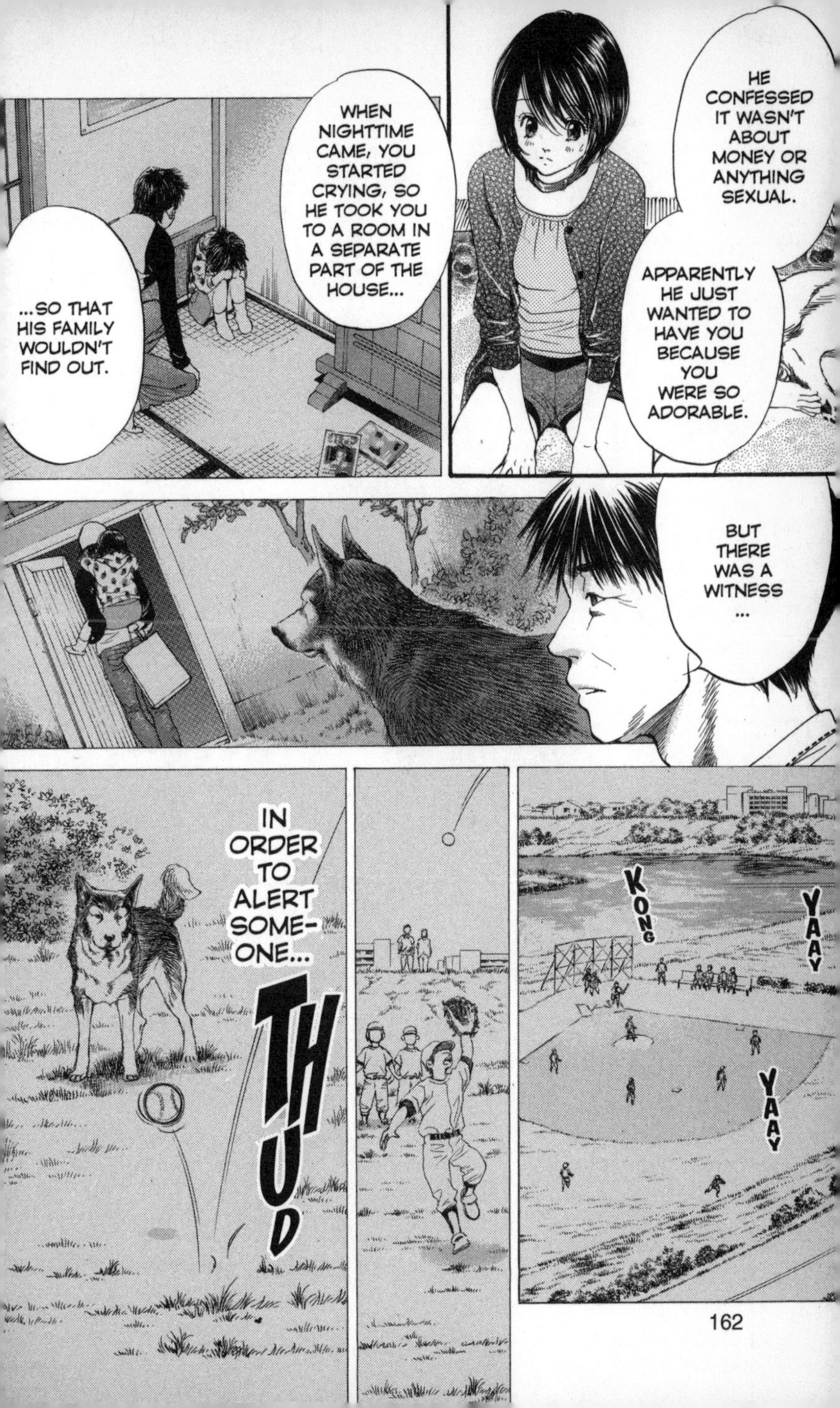
HE CONFESSED IT WASN'T ABOUT MONEY OR ANYTHING SEXUAL.
APPARENTLY HE JUST WANTED TO HAVE YOU BECAUSE YOU WERE SO ADORABLE.
WHEN NIGHTTIME CAME, YOU STARTED CRYING, SO HE TOOK YOU TO A ROOM IN A SEPARATE PART OF THE HOUSE...
...SO THAT HIS FAMILY WOULDN'T FIND OUT.
BUT THERE WAS A WITNESS ...
KONG
YAAY
YAAY
IN ORDER TO ALERT SOME-ONE...
THUD

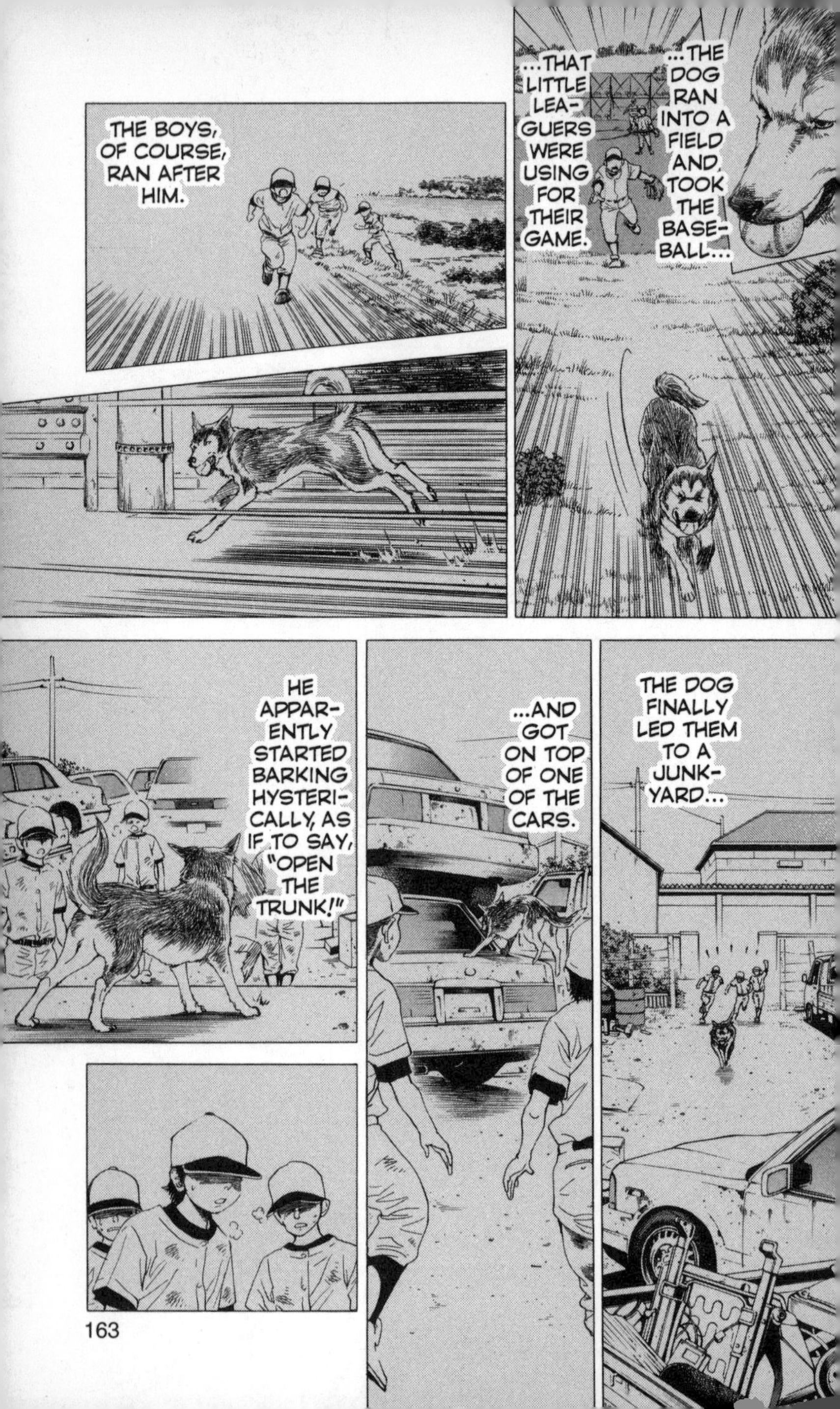
...THE DOG RAN INTO A FIELD AND TOOK THE BASEBALL...
...THAT LITTLE LEAGUERS WERE USING FOR THEIR GAME.
THE BOYS, OF COURSE, RAN AFTER HIM.
THE DOG FINALLY LED THEM TO A JUNKYARD...
...AND GOT ON TOP OF ONE OF THE CARS.
HE APPARENTLY STARTED BARKING HYSTERICALLY, AS IF TO SAY, "OPEN THE TRUNK!"

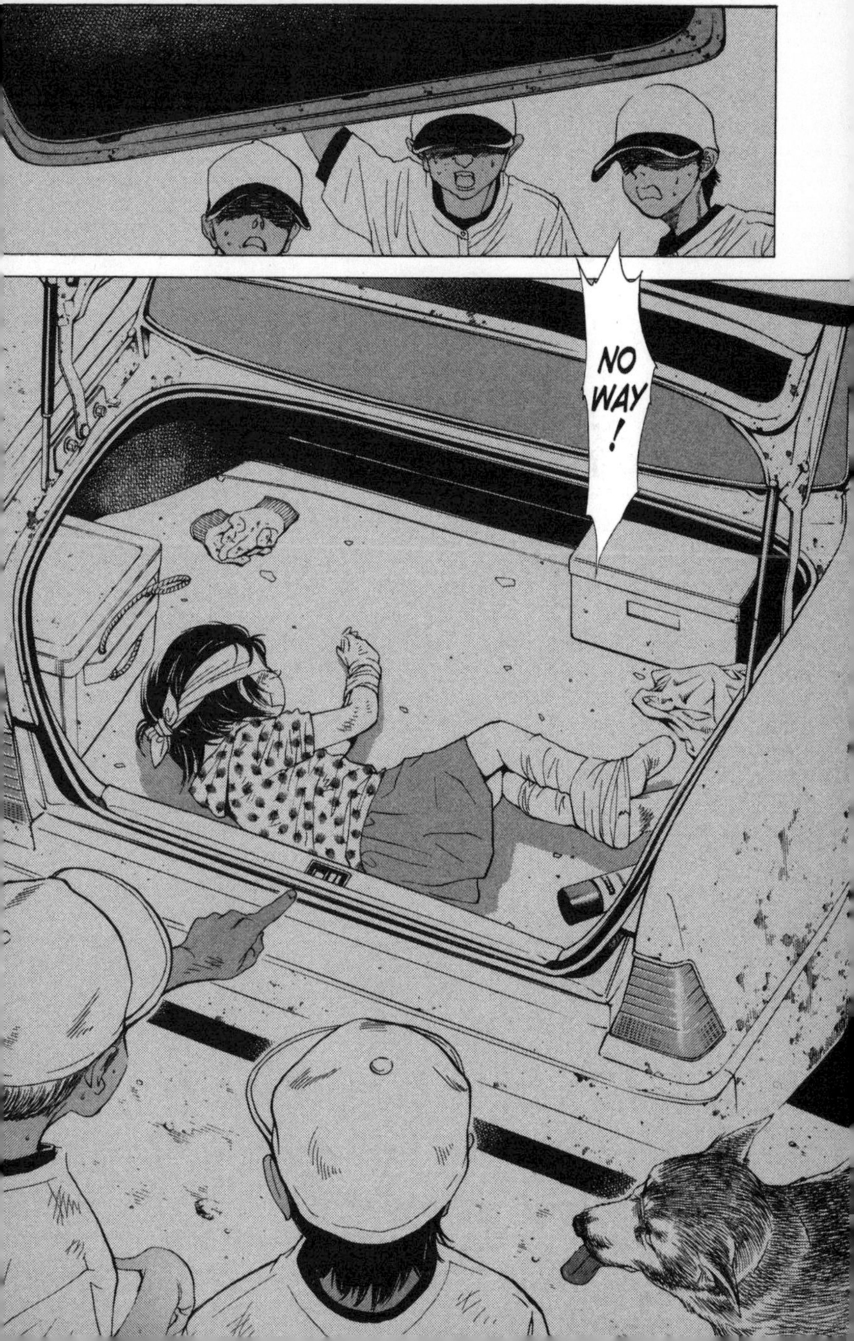
NO WAY!

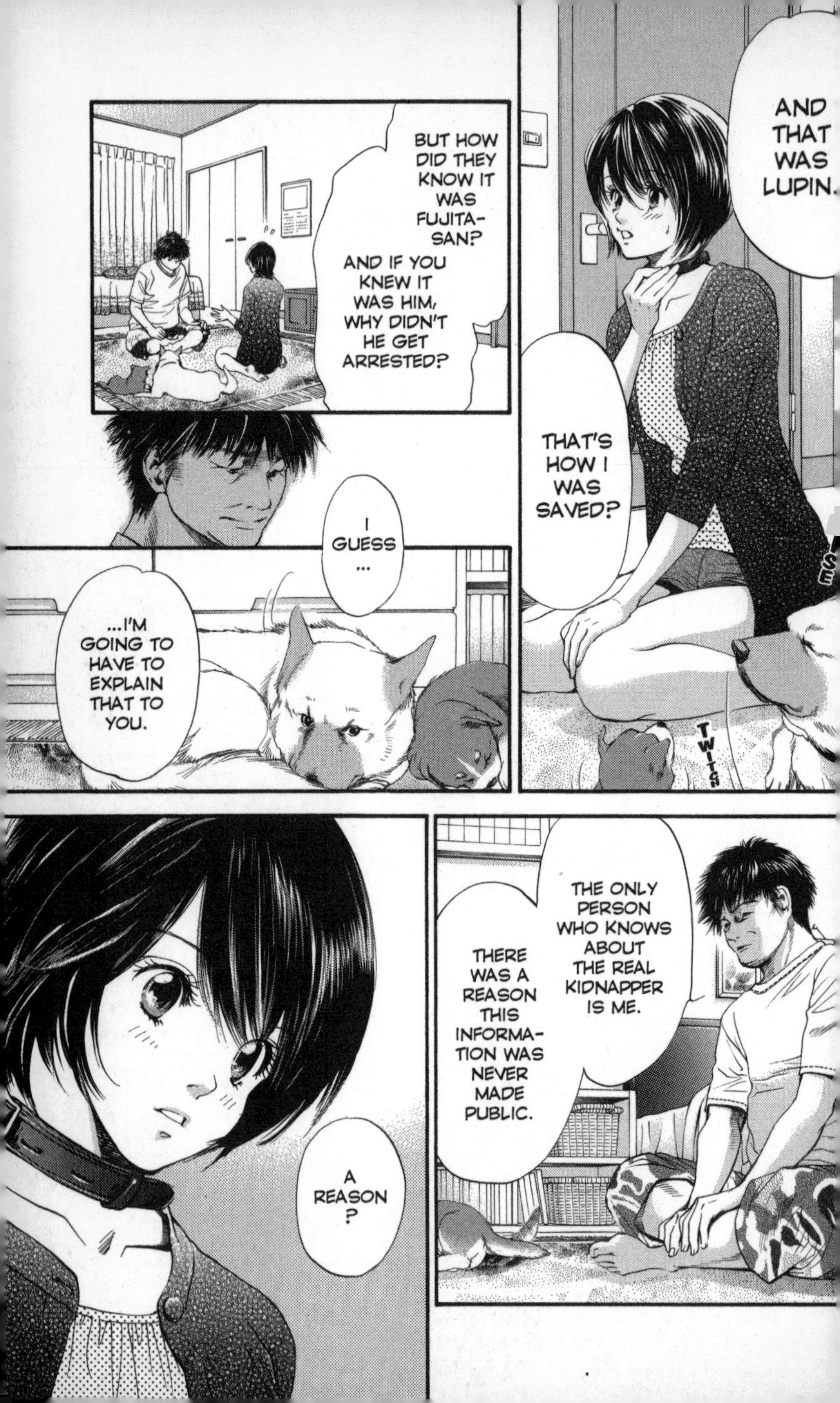
AND THAT WAS LUPIN.
THAT'S HOW I WAS SAVED?
SE
TWITCH
BUT HOW DID THEY KNOW IT WAS FUJITA-SAN?
AND IF YOU KNEW IT WAS HIM, WHY DIDN'T HE GET ARRESTED?
I GUESS ...
...I'M GOING TO HAVE TO EXPLAIN THAT TO YOU.
THE ONLY PERSON WHO KNOWS ABOUT THE REAL KIDNAPPER IS ME.
THERE WAS A REASON THIS INFORMATION WAS NEVER MADE PUBLIC.
A REASON?

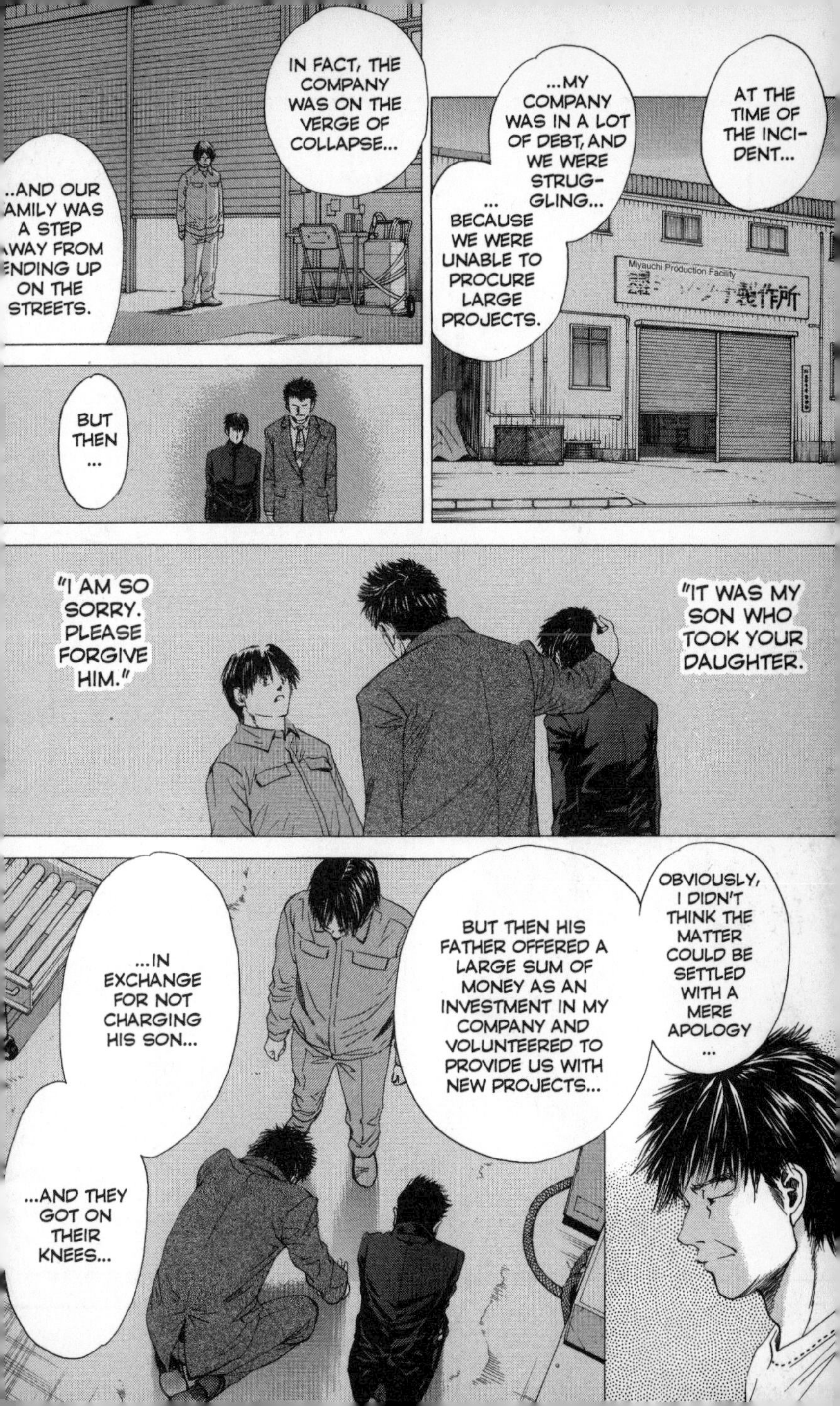
AT THE TIME OF THE INCIDENT...
...MY COMPANY WAS IN A LOT OF DEBT, AND WE WERE STRUGGLING...
...BECAUSE WE WERE UNABLE TO PROCURE LARGE PROJECTS.
Miyauchi Production Facility
IN FACT, THE COMPANY WAS ON THE VERGE OF COLLAPSE...
..AND OUR AMILY WAS A STEP AWAY FROM ENDING UP ON THE STREETS.
BUT THEN...
"IT WAS MY SON WHO TOOK YOUR DAUGHTER.
"I AM SO SORRY. PLEASE FORGIVE HIM."
OBVIOUSLY, I DIDN'T THINK THE MATTER COULD BE SETTLED WITH A MERE APOLOGY...
BUT THEN HIS FATHER OFFERED A LARGE SUM OF MONEY AS AN INVESTMENT IN MY COMPANY AND VOLUNTEERED TO PROVIDE US WITH NEW PROJECTS...
...IN EXCHANGE FOR NOT CHARGING HIS SON...
...AND THEY GOT ON THEIR KNEES...

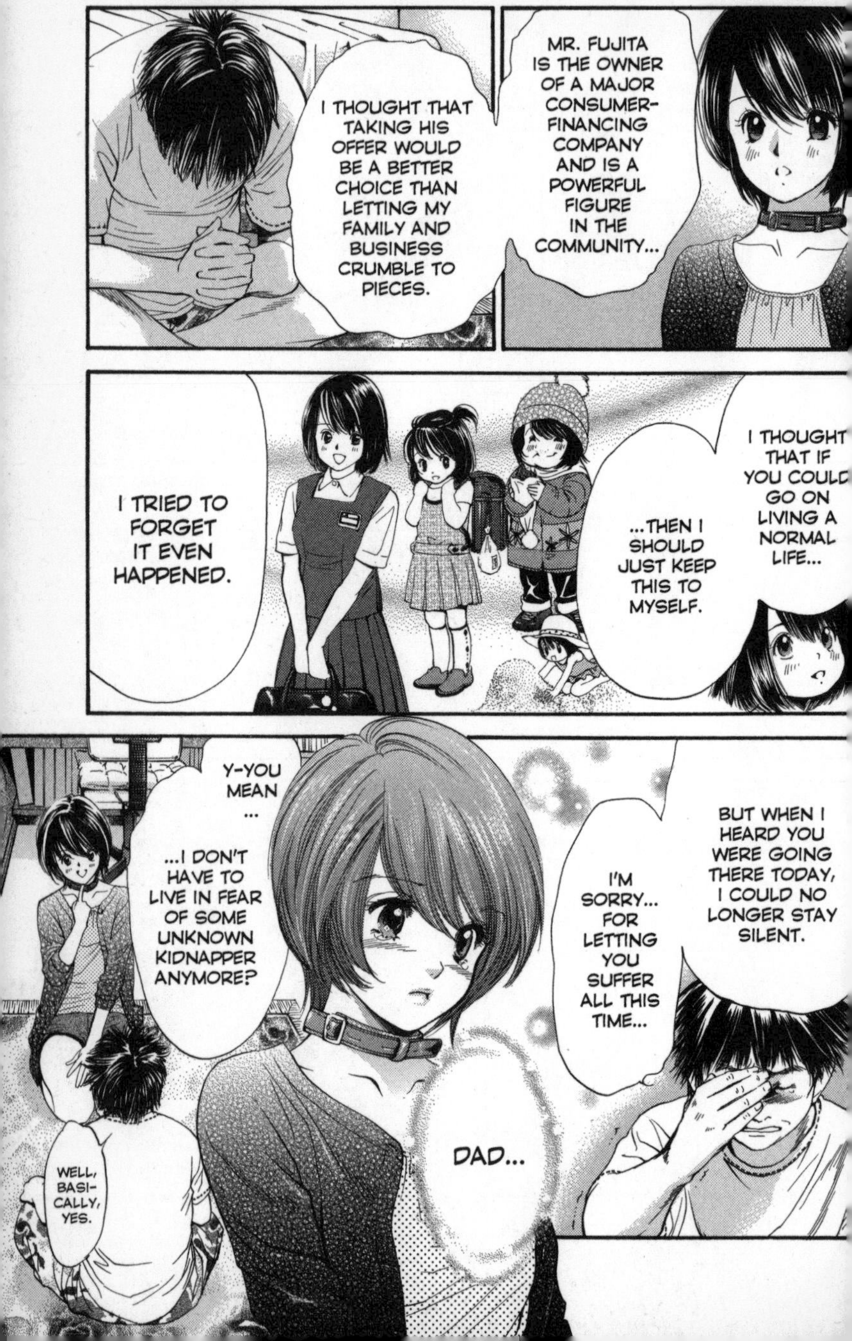
MR. FUJITA IS THE OWNER OF A MAJOR CONSUMER-FINANCING COMPANY AND IS A POWERFUL FIGURE IN THE COMMUNITY...
I THOUGHT THAT TAKING HIS OFFER WOULD BE A BETTER CHOICE THAN LETTING MY FAMILY AND BUSINESS CRUMBLE TO PIECES.
I THOUGHT THAT IF YOU COULD GO ON LIVING A NORMAL LIFE...
...THEN I SHOULD JUST KEEP THIS TO MYSELF.
I TRIED TO FORGET IT EVEN HAPPENED.
BUT WHEN I HEARD YOU WERE GOING THERE TODAY, I COULD NO LONGER STAY SILENT.
I'M SORRY... FOR LETTING YOU SUFFER ALL THIS TIME...
DAD...
Y-YOU MEAN ...
...I DON'T HAVE TO LIVE IN FEAR OF SOME UNKNOWN KIDNAPPER ANYMORE?
WELL, BASI-CALLY, YES.

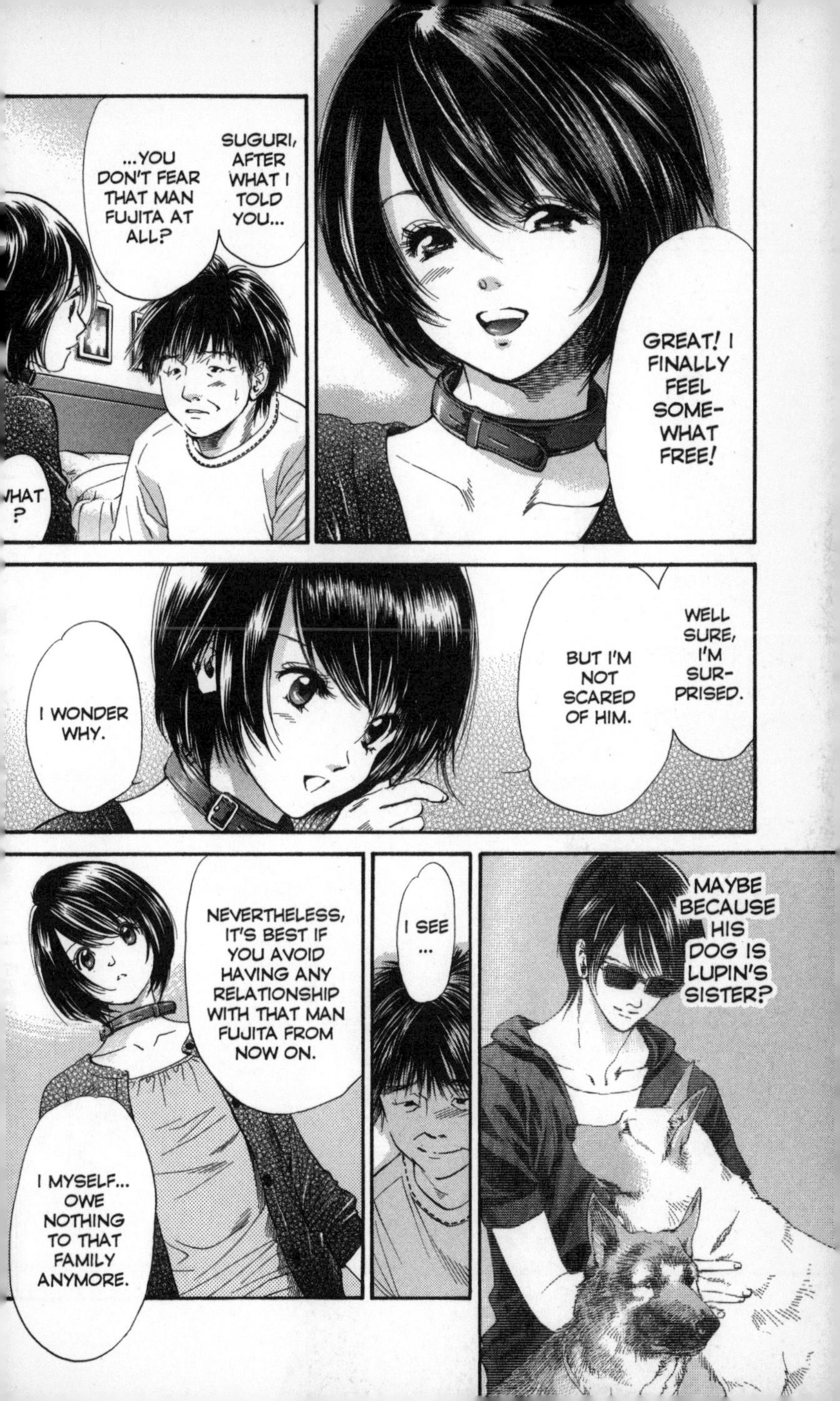
GREAT! I FINALLY FEEL SOMEWHAT FREE!
SUGURI, AFTER WHAT I TOLD YOU...
...YOU DON'T FEAR THAT MAN FUJITA AT ALL?
HAT ?
WELL SURE, I'M SURPRISED.
BUT I'M NOT SCARED OF HIM.
I WONDER WHY.
MAYBE BECAUSE HIS DOG IS LUPIN'S SISTER?
I SEE ...
NEVERTHELESS, IT'S BEST IF YOU AVOID HAVING ANY RELATIONSHIP WITH THAT MAN FUJITA FROM NOW ON.
I MYSELF... OWE NOTHING TO THAT FAMILY ANYMORE.

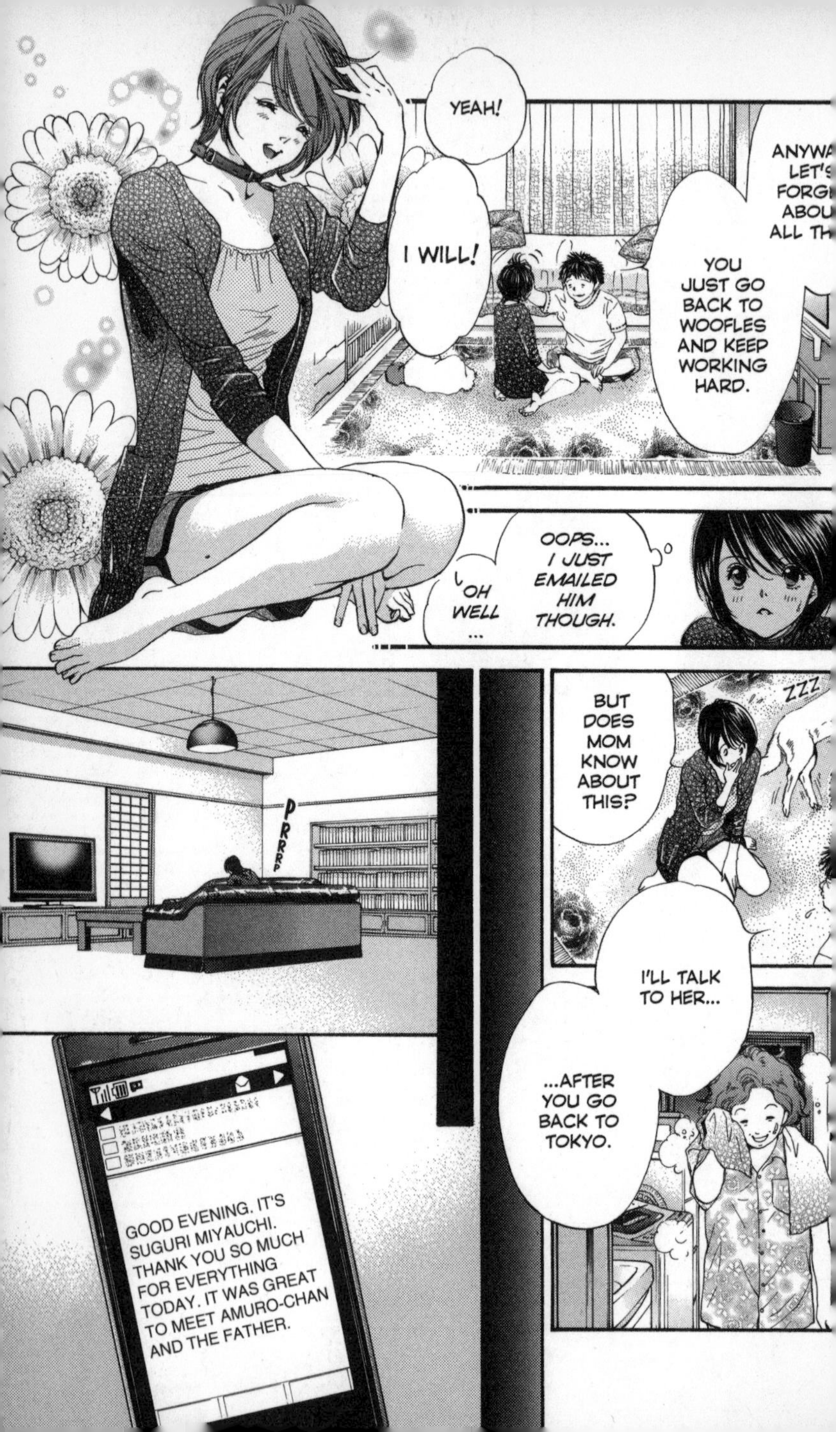

ANYWA
LET'S
FORG
ABOU
ALL TH
YOU JUST GO BACK TO WOOFLES AND KEEP WORKING HARD.
YEAH!
I WILL!
OOPS... I JUST EMAILED HIM THOUGH.
OH WELL ...
BUT DOES MOM KNOW ABOUT THIS?
I'LL TALK TO HER...
...AFTER YOU GO BACK TO TOKYO.
PRRRP
GOOD EVENING. IT'S SUGURI MIYAUCHI. THANK YOU SO MUCH FOR EVERYTHING TODAY. IT WAS GREAT TO MEET AMURO-CHAN AND THE FATHER.

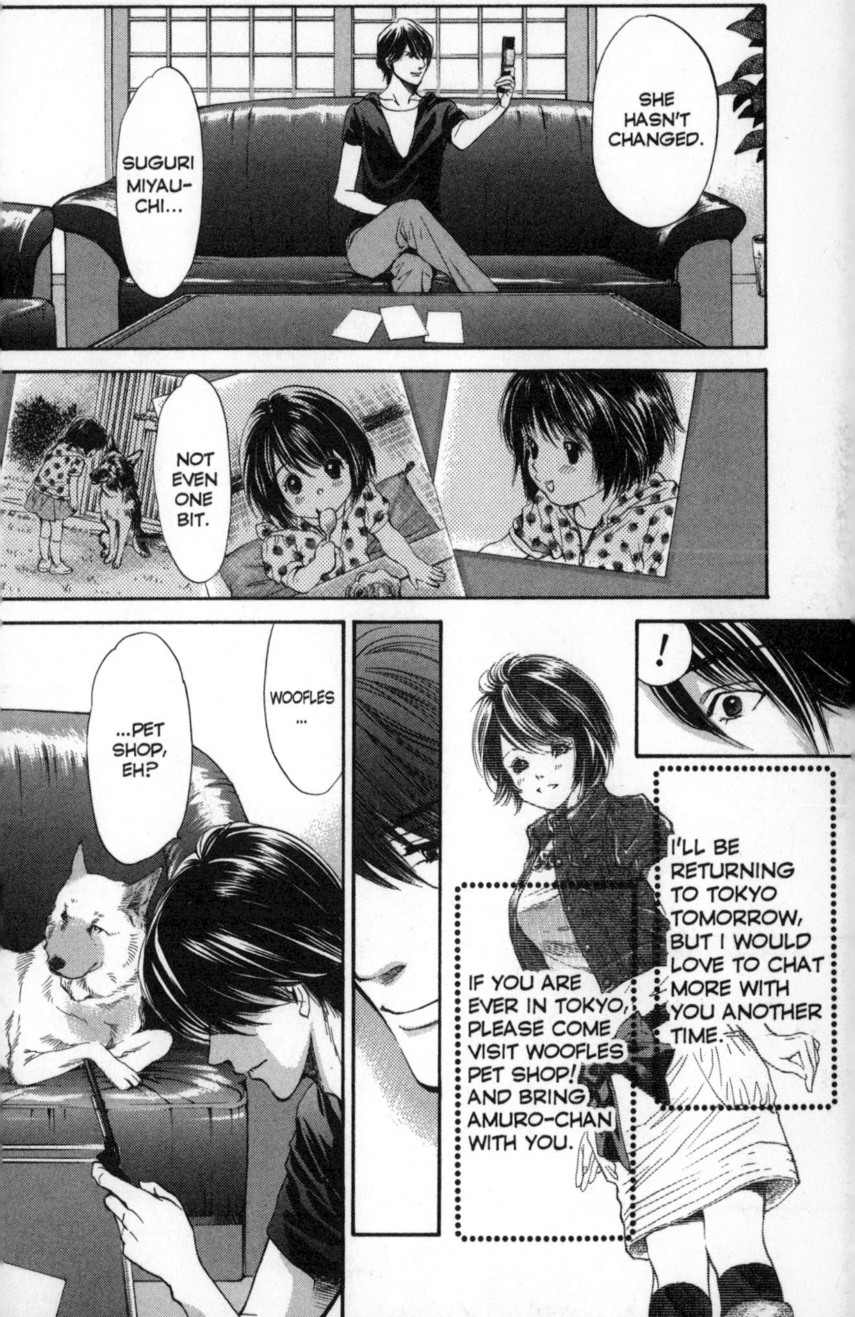
SHE HASN'T CHANGED.
SUGURI MIYAU-CHI...
NOT EVEN ONE BIT.
!
I'LL BE RETURNING TO TOKYO TOMORROW, BUT I WOULD LOVE TO CHAT MORE WITH YOU ANOTHER TIME.
IF YOU ARE EVER IN TOKYO, PLEASE COME VISIT WOOFLES PET SHOP! AND BRING AMURO-CHAN WITH YOU.
WOOFLES ...
...PET SHOP, EH?

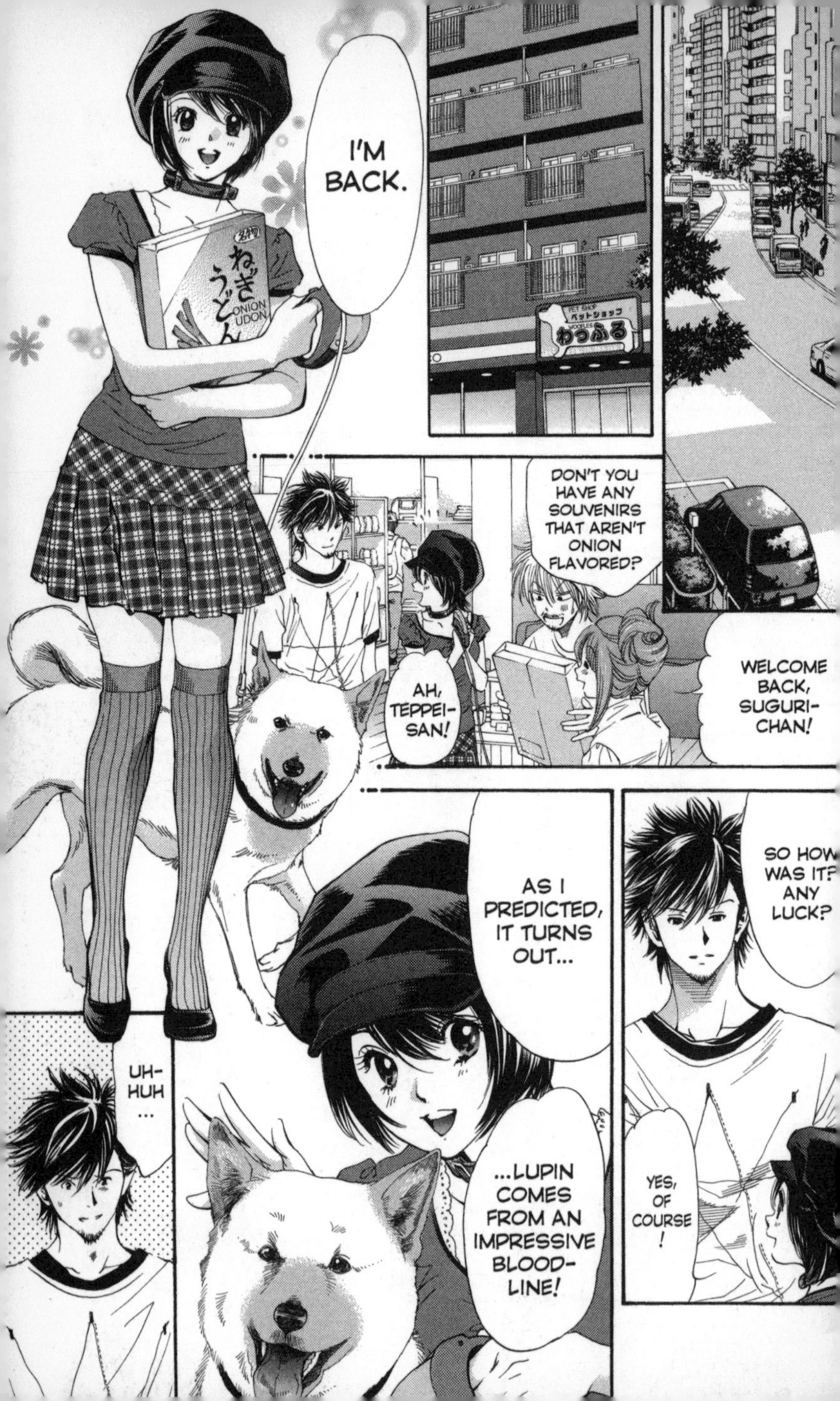

ペットショップ
わっふる
ねぎうどん
ONION UDON
I'M BACK.
WELCOME BACK, SUGURI-CHAN!
DON'T YOU HAVE ANY SOUVENIRS THAT AREN'T ONION FLAVORED?
AH, TEPPEI-SAN!
SO HOW WAS IT? ANY LUCK?
YES, OF COURSE!
AS I PREDICTED, IT TURNS OUT...
...LUPIN COMES FROM AN IMPRESSIVE BLOOD-LINE!
UH-HUH...

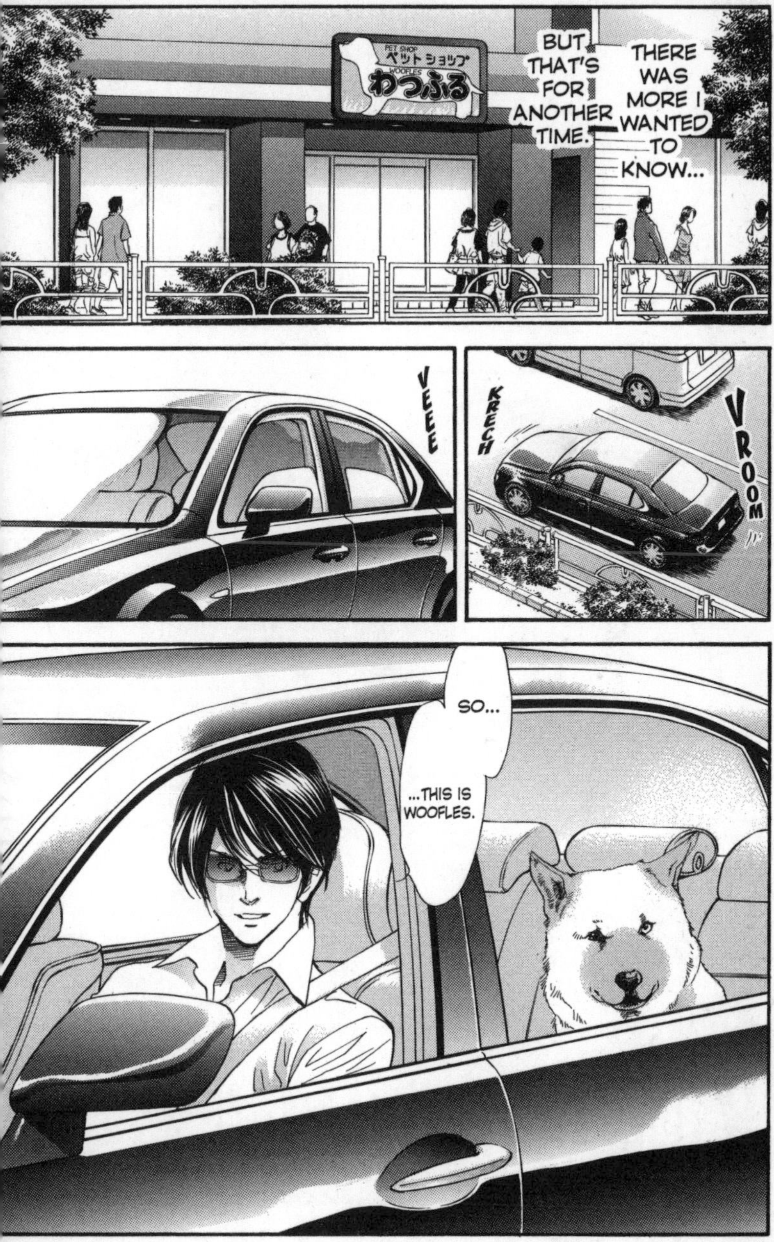
PET SHOP
ペットショップ
WOOFLES
わっふる
THERE WAS MORE I WANTED TO KNOW...
BUT THAT'S FOR ANOTHER TIME.
VROOM
KRECH
VEEE
SO...
...THIS IS WOOFLES.

CHAPTER 161: THE EYES SAY JUST AS MUCH AS THE MOUTH?!

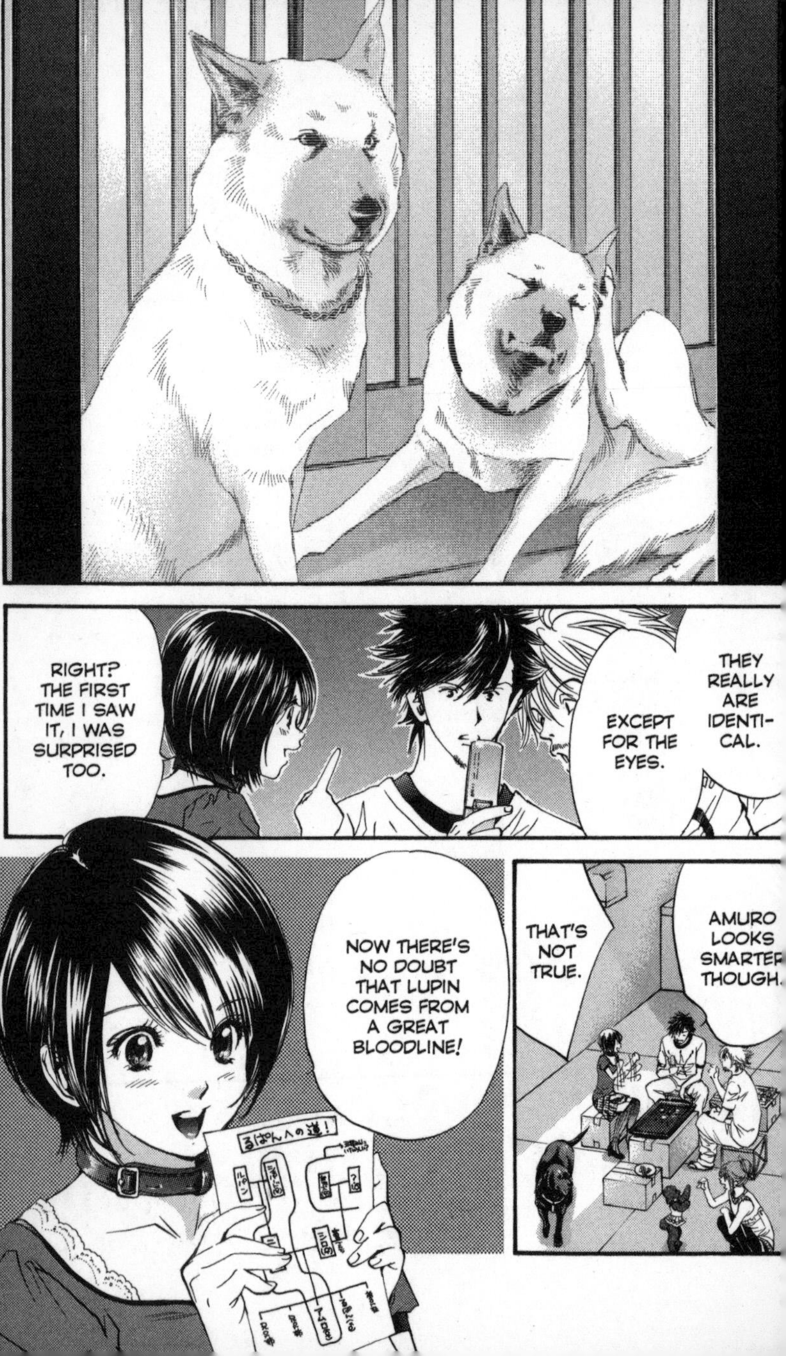
THEY REALLY ARE IDENTICAL.
EXCEPT FOR THE EYES.
RIGHT? THE FIRST TIME I SAW IT, I WAS SURPRISED TOO.
AMURO LOOKS SMARTER THOUGH.
THAT'S NOT TRUE.
NOW THERE'S NO DOUBT THAT LUPIN COMES FROM A GREAT BLOODLINE!
るぱんへの道！

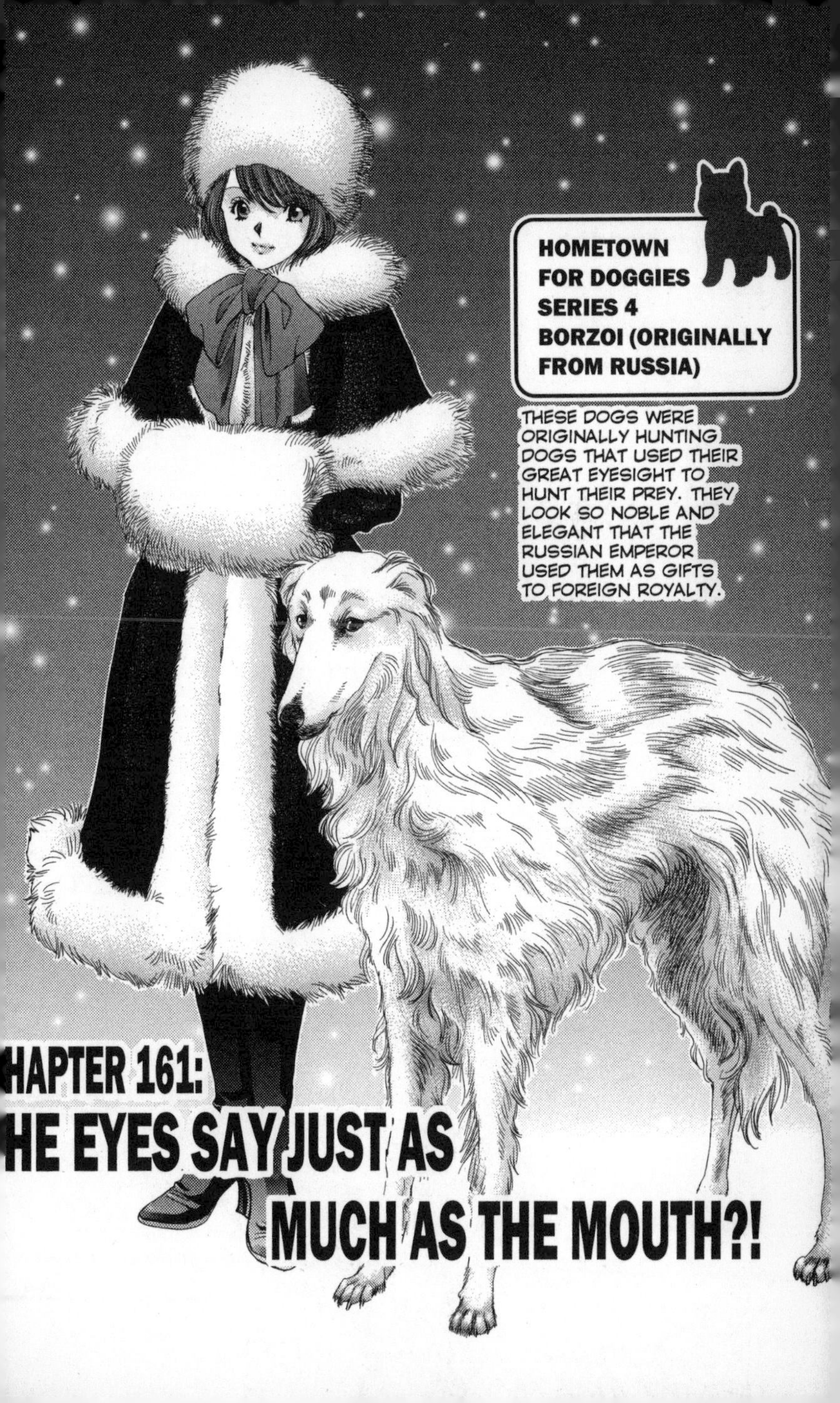
HOMETOWN FOR DOGGIES SERIES 4
BORZOI (ORIGINALLY FROM RUSSIA)
THESE DOGS WERE ORIGINALLY HUNTING DOGS THAT USED THEIR GREAT EYESIGHT TO HUNT THEIR PREY. THEY LOOK SO NOBLE AND ELEGANT THAT THE RUSSIAN EMPEROR USED THEM AS GIFTS TO FOREIGN ROYALTY.
HAPTER 161:
HE EYES SAY JUST AS MUCH AS THE MOUTH?!

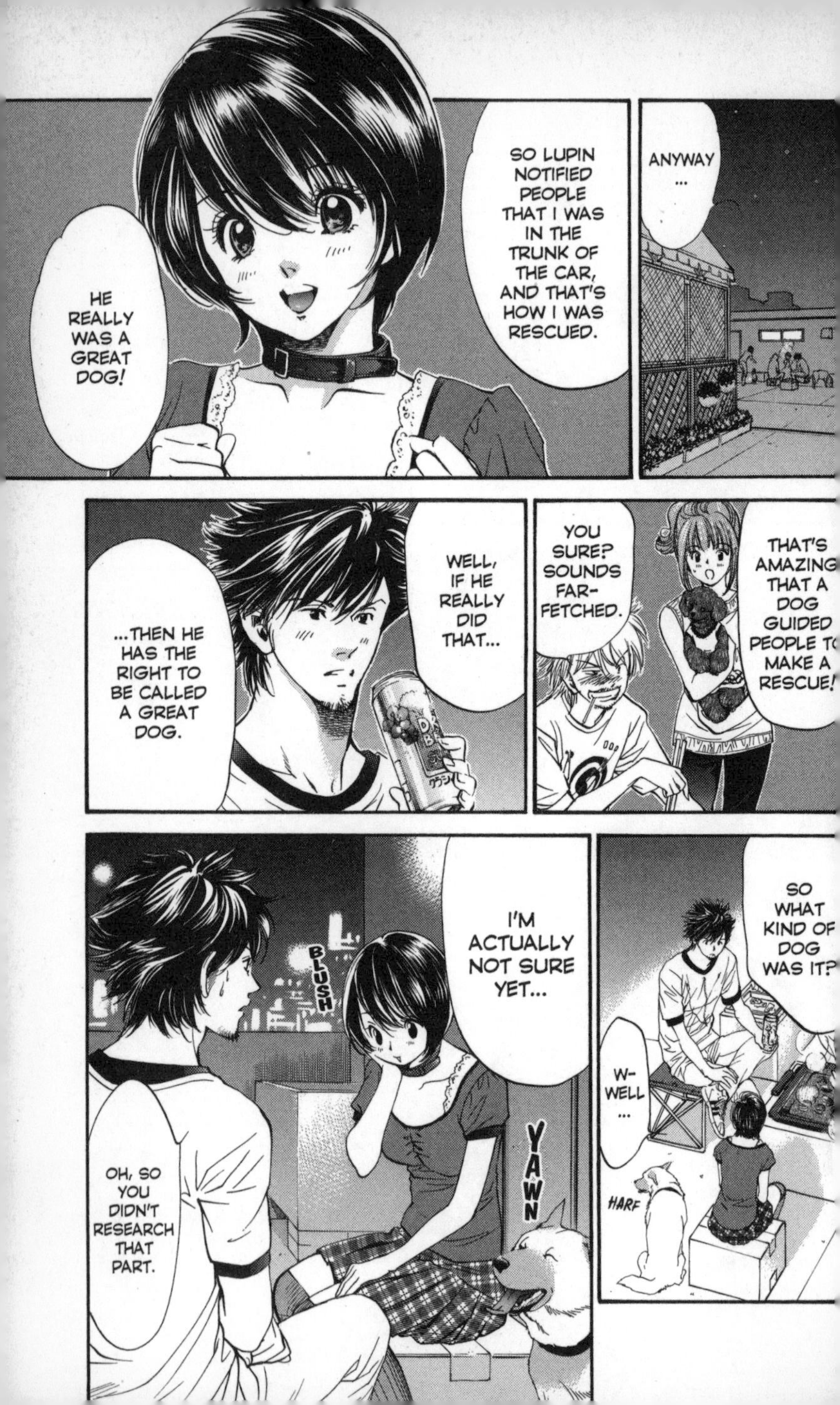
ANYWAY ...
SO LUPIN NOTIFIED PEOPLE THAT I WAS IN THE TRUNK OF THE CAR, AND THAT'S HOW I WAS RESCUED.
HE REALLY WAS A GREAT DOG!
THAT'S AMAZING THAT A DOG GUIDED PEOPLE T MAKE A RESCUE!
YOU SURE? SOUNDS FAR-FETCHED.
WELL, IF HE REALLY DID THAT...
...THEN HE HAS THE RIGHT TO BE CALLED A GREAT DOG.
SO WHAT KIND OF DOG WAS IT?
W-WELL ...
HARF
I'M ACTUALLY NOT SURE YET...
BLUSH
YAWN
OH, SO YOU DIDN'T RESEARCH THAT PART.

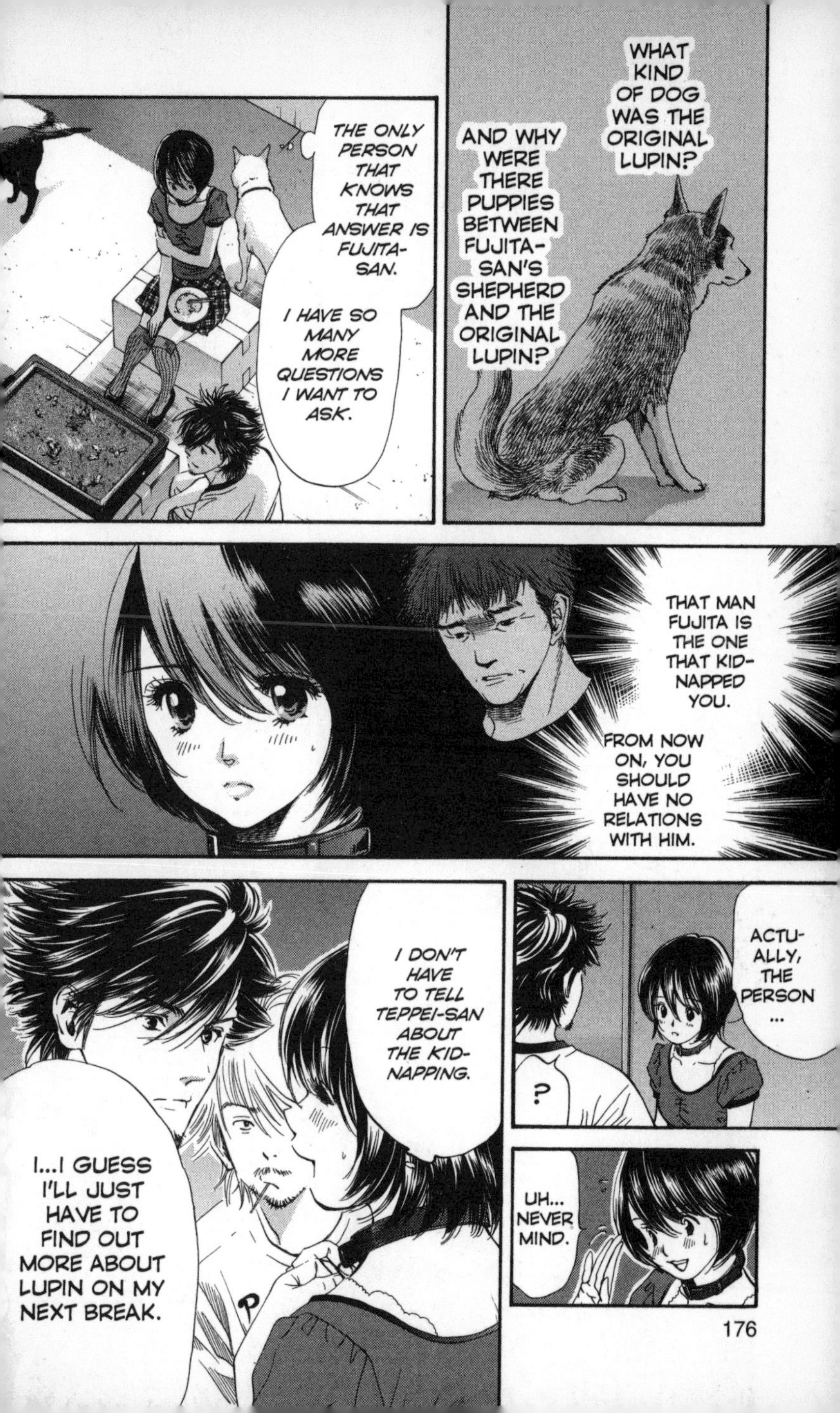
WHAT KIND OF DOG WAS THE ORIGINAL LUPIN?
AND WHY WERE THERE PUPPIES BETWEEN FUJITA-SAN'S SHEPHERD AND THE ORIGINAL LUPIN?
THE ONLY PERSON THAT KNOWS THAT ANSWER IS FUJITA-SAN.
I HAVE SO MANY MORE QUESTIONS I WANT TO ASK.
THAT MAN FUJITA IS THE ONE THAT KID-NAPPED YOU.
FROM NOW ON, YOU SHOULD HAVE NO RELATIONS WITH HIM.
ACTU-ALLY, THE PERSON...
?
UH... NEVER MIND.
I DON'T HAVE TO TELL TEPPEI-SAN ABOUT THE KID-NAPPING.
I...I GUESS I'LL JUST HAVE TO FIND OUT MORE ABOUT LUPIN ON MY NEXT BREAK.

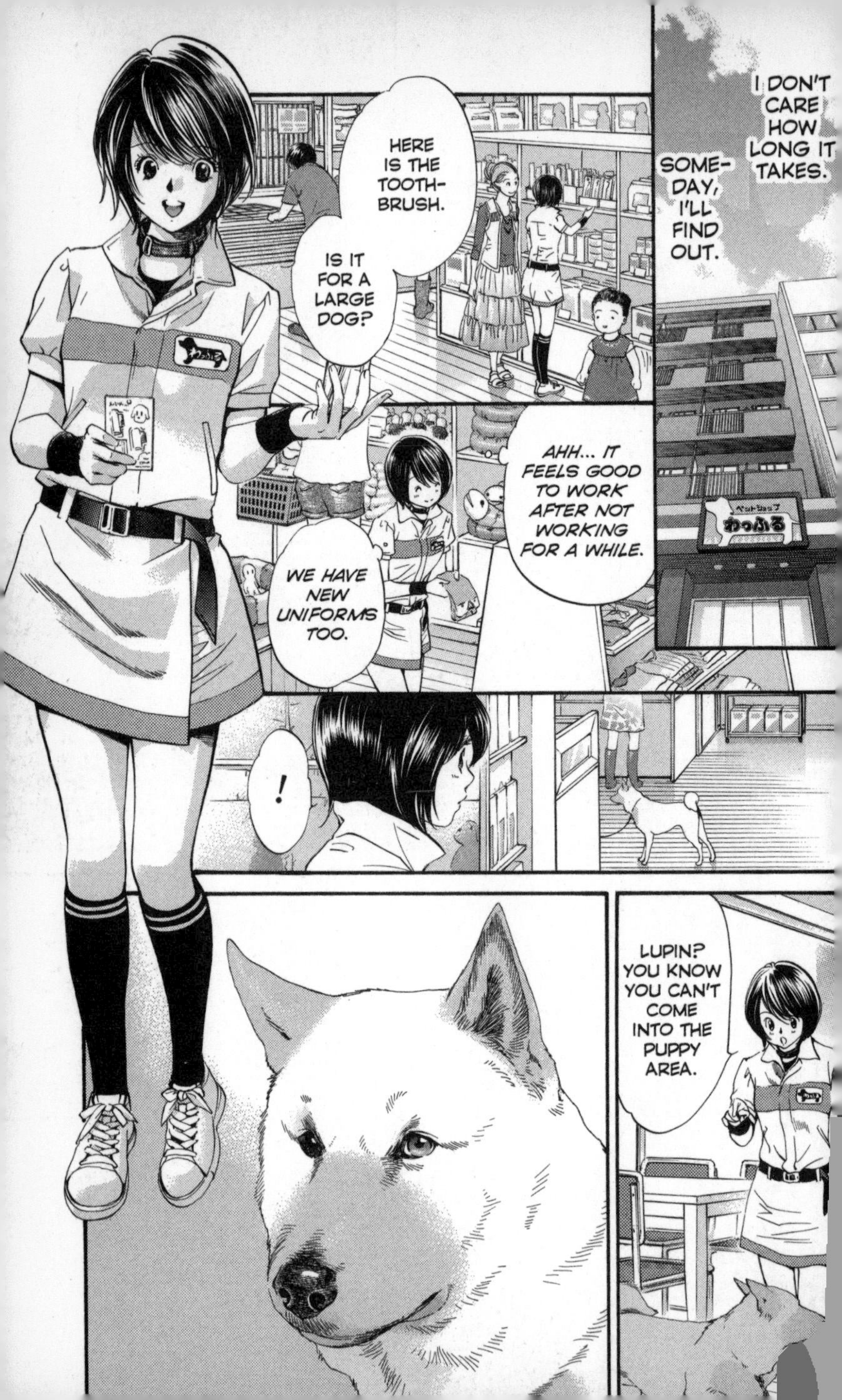
I DON'T CARE HOW LONG IT TAKES.
SOME-DAY, I'LL FIND OUT.
ペットショップ
わっふる
HERE IS THE TOOTH-BRUSH.
IS IT FOR A LARGE DOG?
AHH... IT FEELS GOOD TO WORK AFTER NOT WORKING FOR A WHILE.
WE HAVE NEW UNIFORMS TOO.
!
LUPIN? YOU KNOW YOU CAN'T COME INTO THE PUPPY AREA.

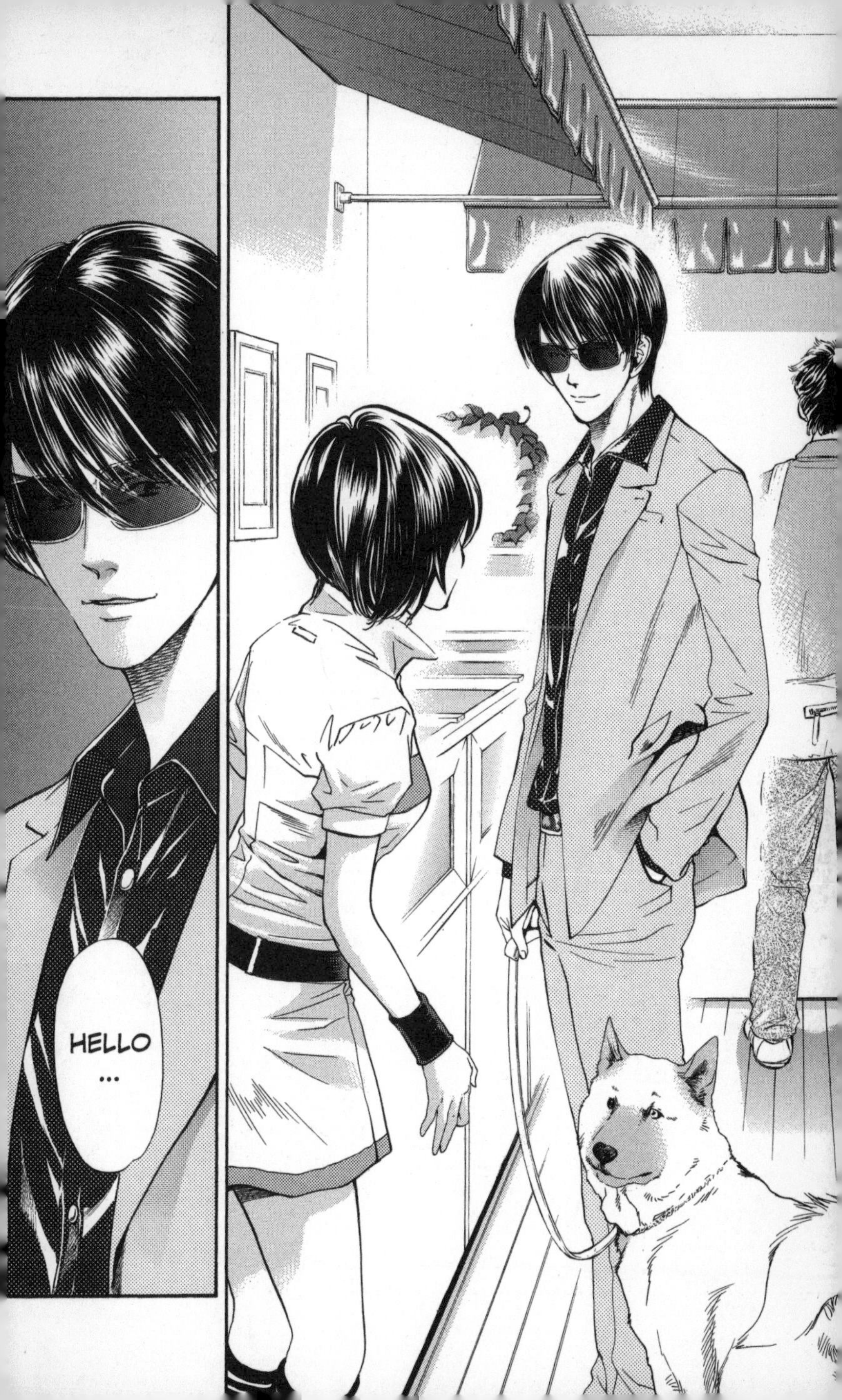
HELLO ...

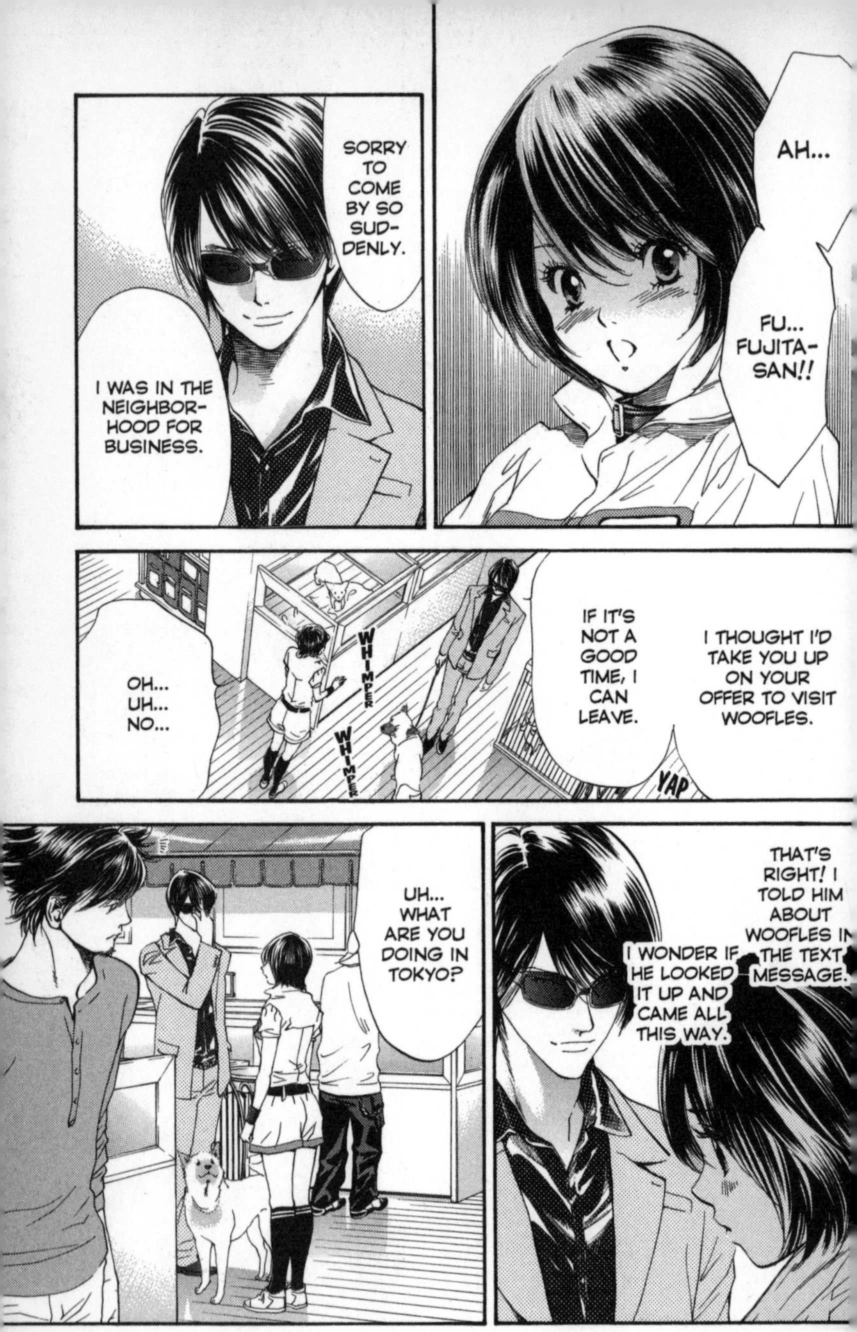
AH...
FU... FUJITA-SAN!!
SORRY TO COME BY SO SUD-DENLY.
I WAS IN THE NEIGHBOR-HOOD FOR BUSINESS.
I THOUGHT I'D TAKE YOU UP ON YOUR OFFER TO VISIT WOOFLES.
IF IT'S NOT A GOOD TIME, I CAN LEAVE.
YAP
WHIMPER
WHIMPER
OH... UH... NO...
THAT'S RIGHT! I TOLD HIM ABOUT WOOFLES IN THE TEXT MESSAGE.
I WONDER IF HE LOOKED IT UP AND CAME ALL THIS WAY.
UH... WHAT ARE YOU DOING IN TOKYO?

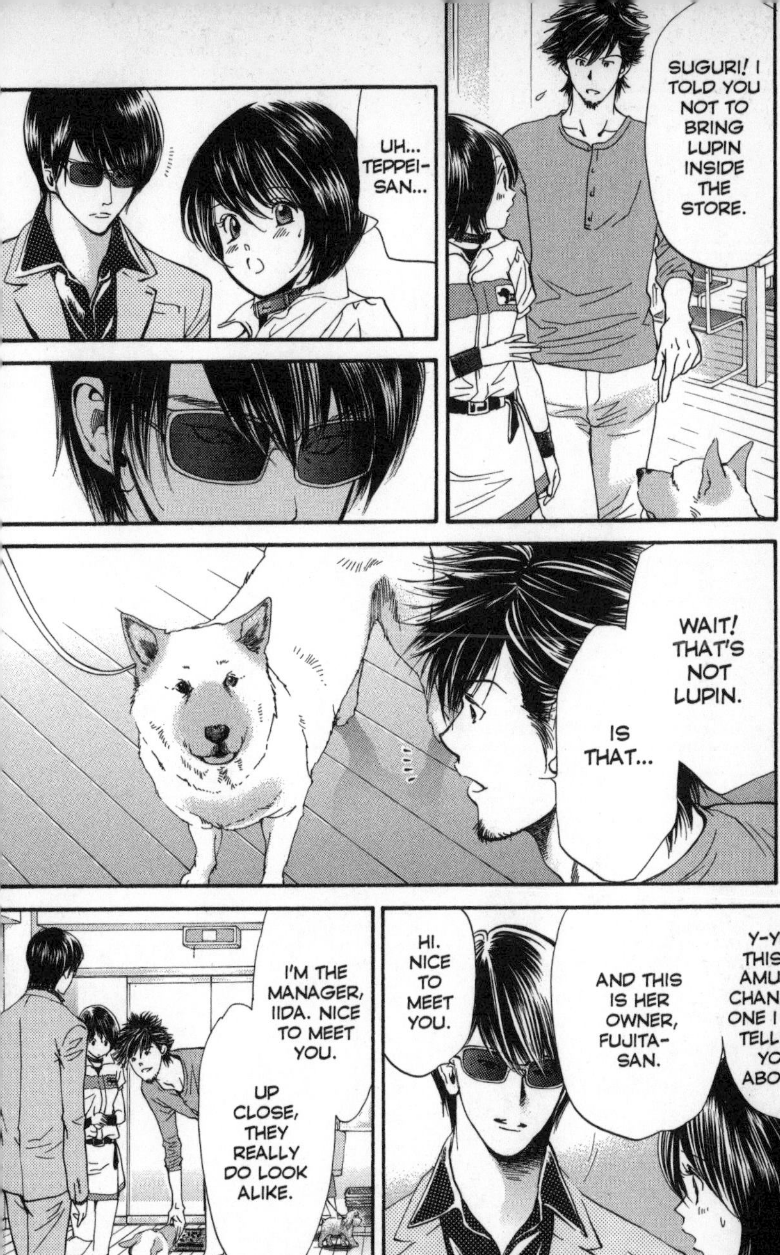
SUGURI! I TOLD YOU NOT TO BRING LUPIN INSIDE THE STORE.
UH... TEPPEI-SAN...
WAIT! THAT'S NOT LUPIN.
IS THAT...
Y-YES. THIS IS AMURO-CHAN, THE ONE I WAS TELLING YOU ABOUT.
AND THIS IS HER OWNER, FUJITA-SAN.
HI. NICE TO MEET YOU.
I'M THE MANAGER, IIDA. NICE TO MEET YOU.
UP CLOSE, THEY REALLY DO LOOK ALIKE.

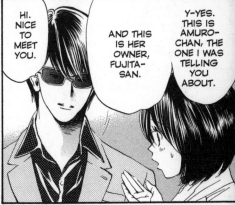

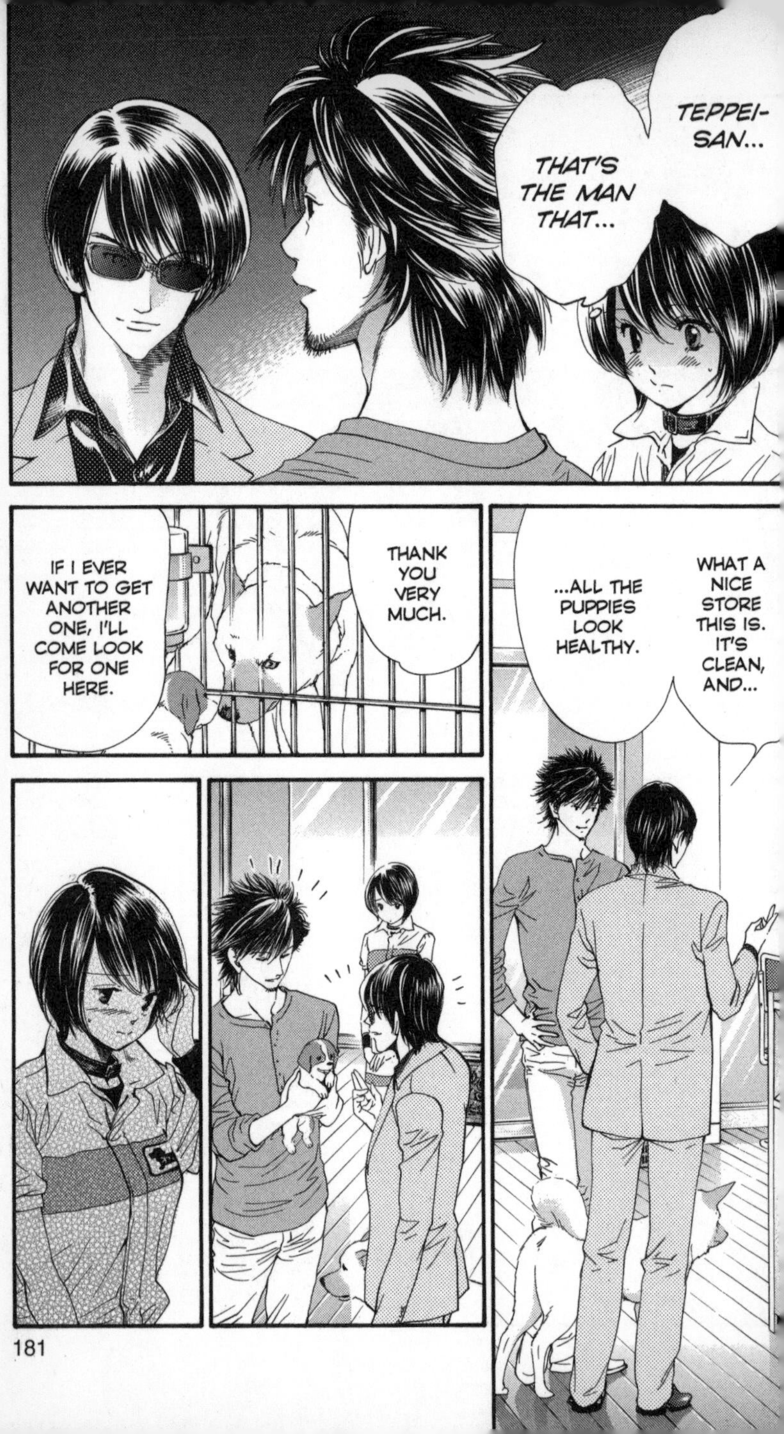
TEPPEI-SAN...
THAT'S THE MAN THAT...
WHAT A NICE STORE THIS IS. IT'S CLEAN, AND...
...ALL THE PUPPIES LOOK HEALTHY.
THANK YOU VERY MUCH.
IF I EVER WANT TO GET ANOTHER ONE, I'LL COME LOOK FOR ONE HERE.

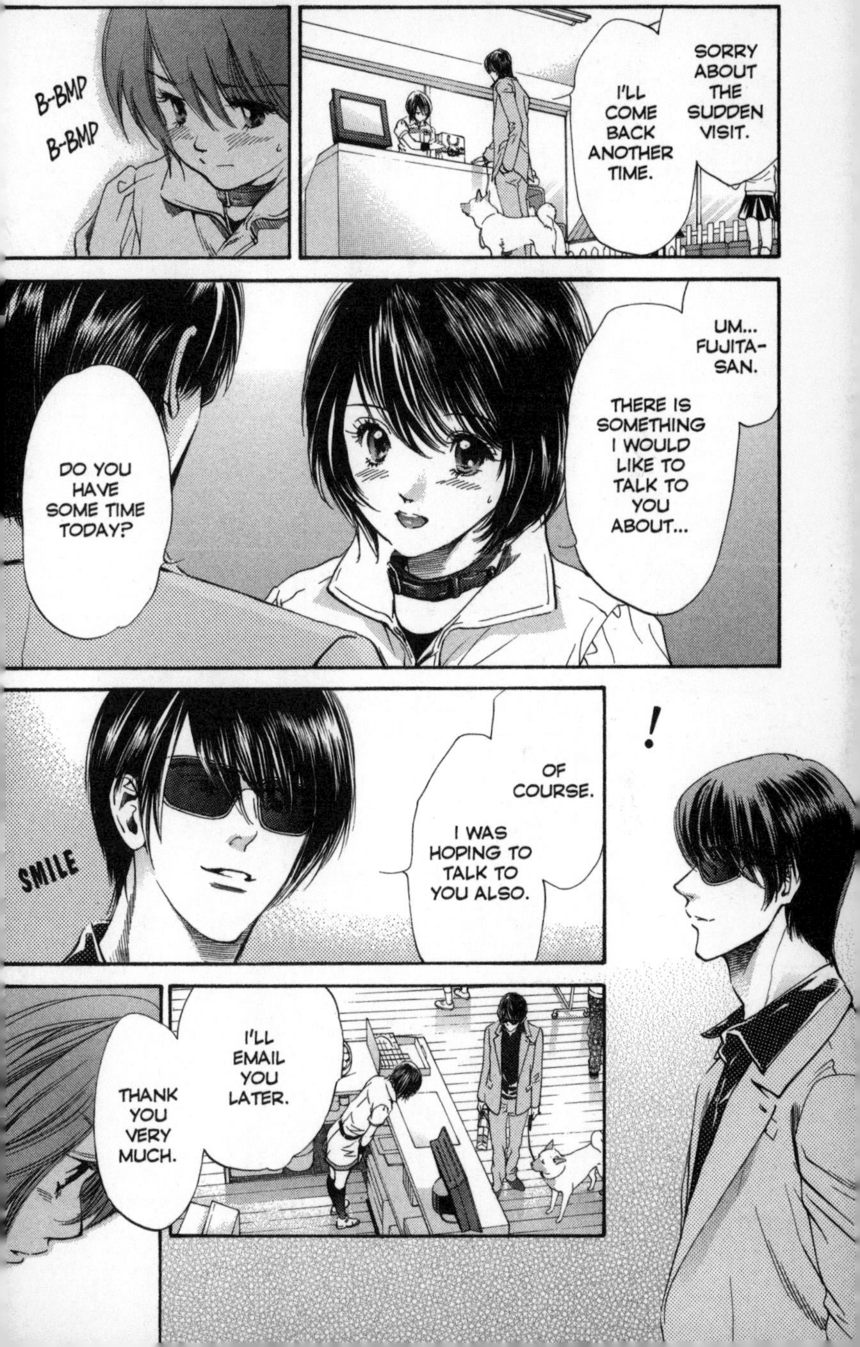
SORRY ABOUT THE SUDDEN VISIT.
I'LL COME BACK ANOTHER TIME.
B-BMP
B-BMP
UM... FUJITA-SAN.
THERE IS SOMETHING I WOULD LIKE TO TALK TO YOU ABOUT...
DO YOU HAVE SOME TIME TODAY?
!
OF COURSE.
I WAS HOPING TO TALK TO YOU ALSO.
SMILE
I'LL EMAIL YOU LATER.
THANK YOU VERY MUCH.

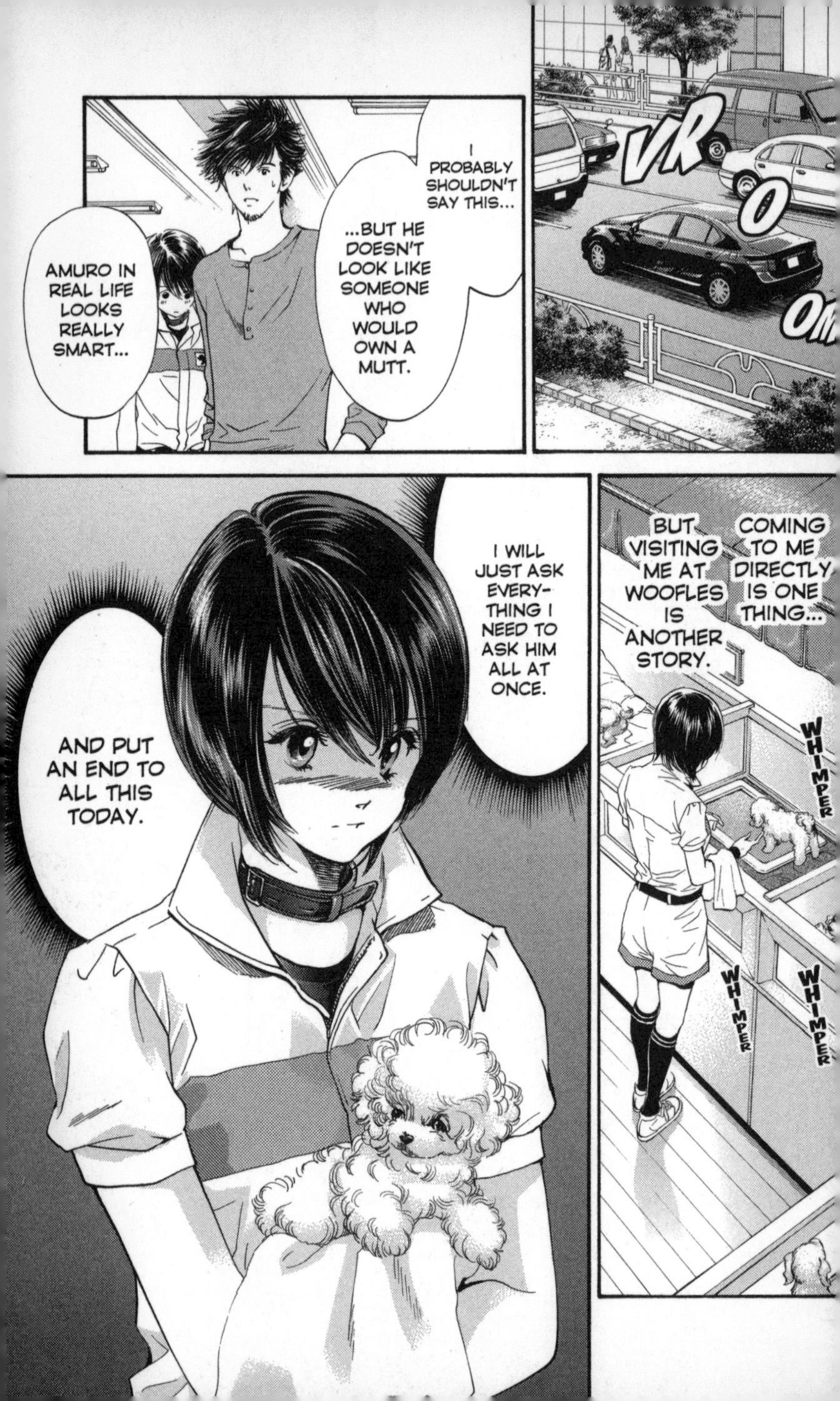
VROOOOM
I PROBABLY SHOULDN'T SAY THIS...
...BUT HE DOESN'T LOOK LIKE SOMEONE WHO WOULD OWN A MUTT.
AMURO IN REAL LIFE LOOKS REALLY SMART...
COMING TO ME DIRECTLY IS ONE THING...
BUT VISITING ME AT WOOFLES IS ANOTHER STORY.
WHIMPER
WHIMPER
WHIMPER
I WILL JUST ASK EVERY-THING I NEED TO ASK HIM ALL AT ONCE.
AND PUT AN END TO ALL THIS TODAY.

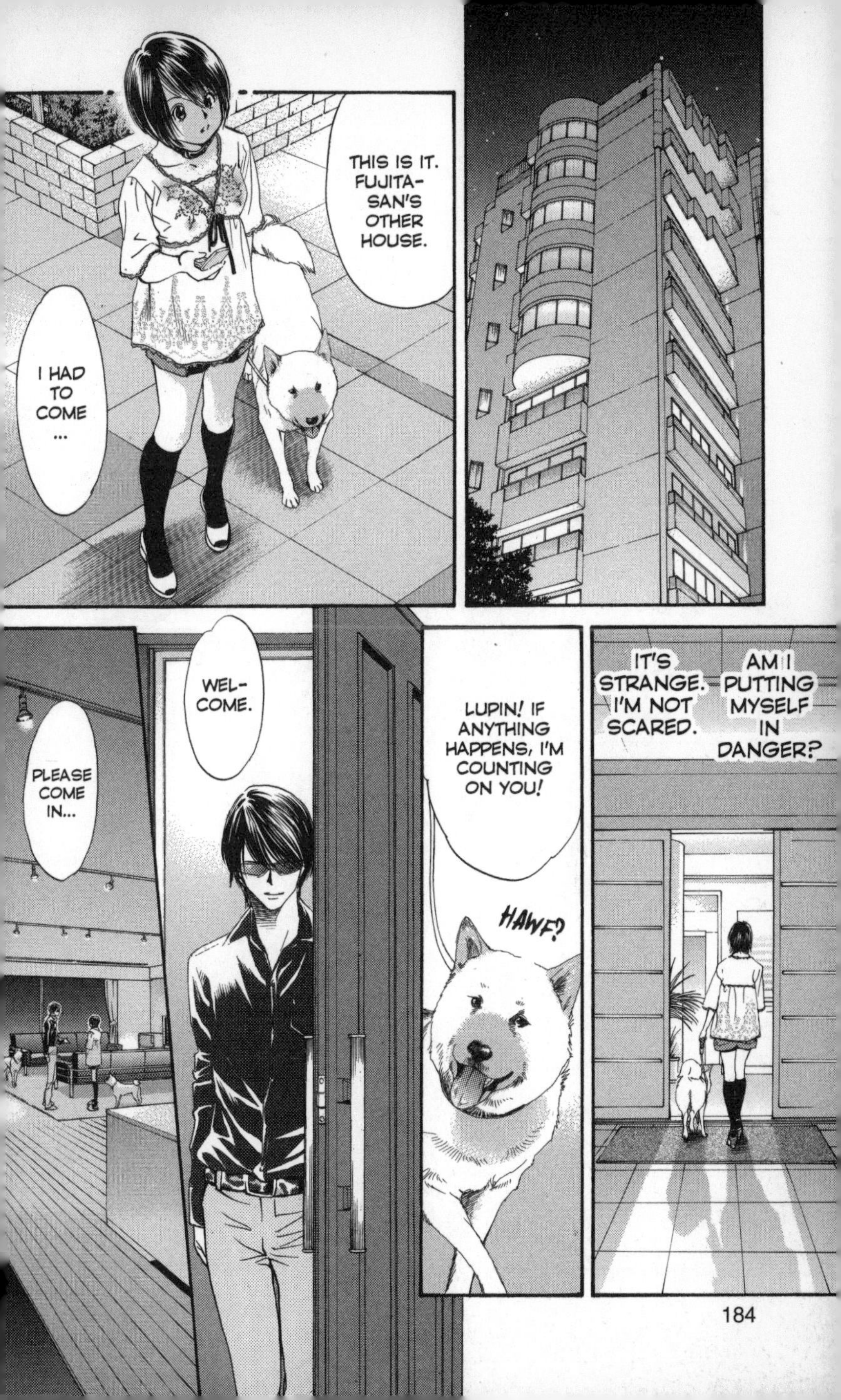
THIS IS IT. FUJITA-SAN'S OTHER HOUSE.
I HAD TO COME ...
AM I PUTTING MYSELF IN DANGER?
IT'S STRANGE. I'M NOT SCARED.
LUPIN! IF ANYTHING HAPPENS, I'M COUNTING ON YOU!
HAWF?
WEL-COME.
PLEASE COME IN...

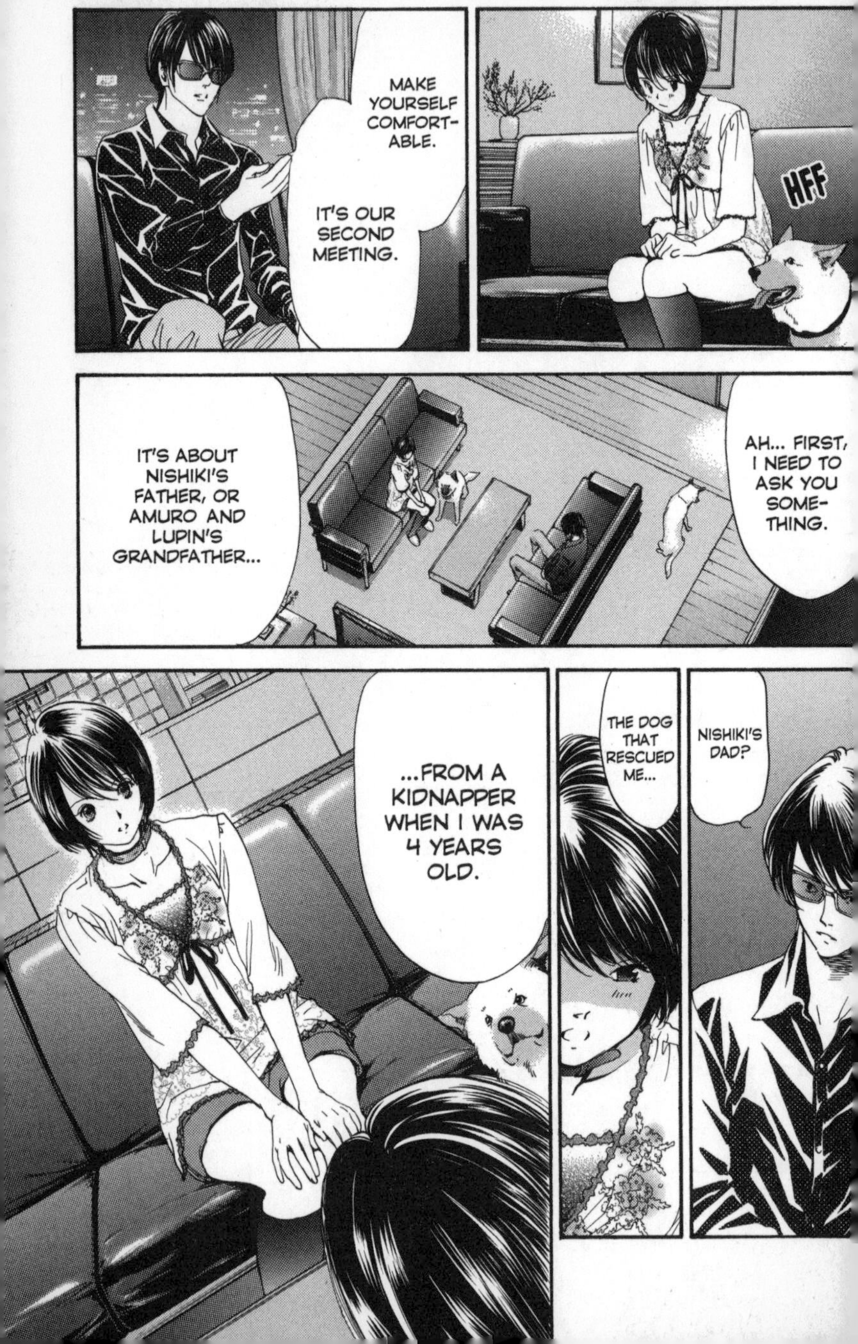
HFF
MAKE YOURSELF COMFORT-ABLE.
IT'S OUR SECOND MEETING.
AH... FIRST, I NEED TO ASK YOU SOME-THING.
IT'S ABOUT NISHIKI'S FATHER, OR AMURO AND LUPIN'S GRANDFATHER...
NISHIKI'S DAD?
THE DOG THAT RESCUED ME...
...FROM A KIDNAPPER WHEN I WAS 4 YEARS OLD.

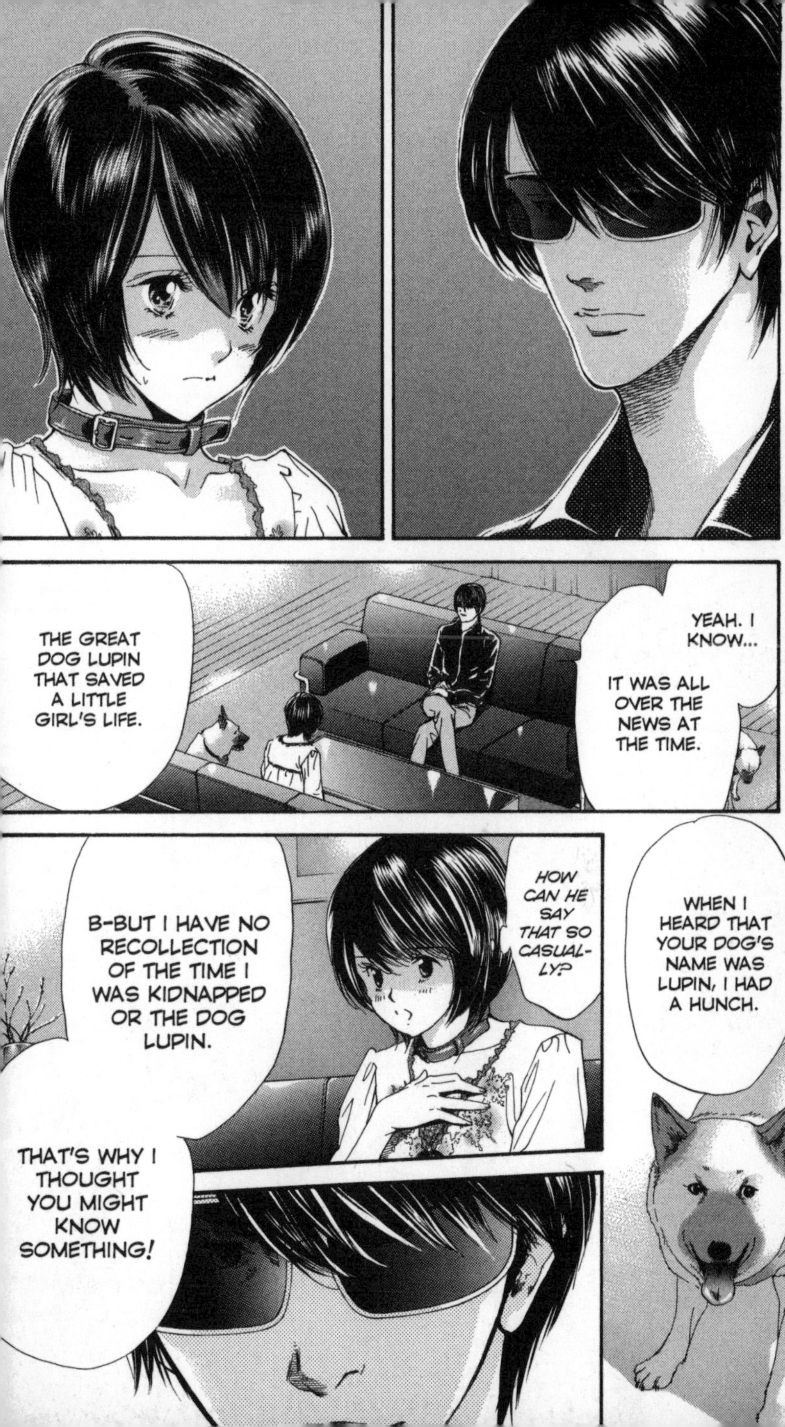
YEAH. I KNOW...
IT WAS ALL OVER THE NEWS AT THE TIME.
THE GREAT DOG LUPIN THAT SAVED A LITTLE GIRL'S LIFE.
WHEN I HEARD THAT YOUR DOG'S NAME WAS LUPIN, I HAD A HUNCH.
HOW CAN HE SAY THAT SO CASUAL-LY?
B-BUT I HAVE NO RECOLLECTION OF THE TIME I WAS KIDNAPPED OR THE DOG LUPIN.
THAT'S WHY I THOUGHT YOU MIGHT KNOW SOMETHING!

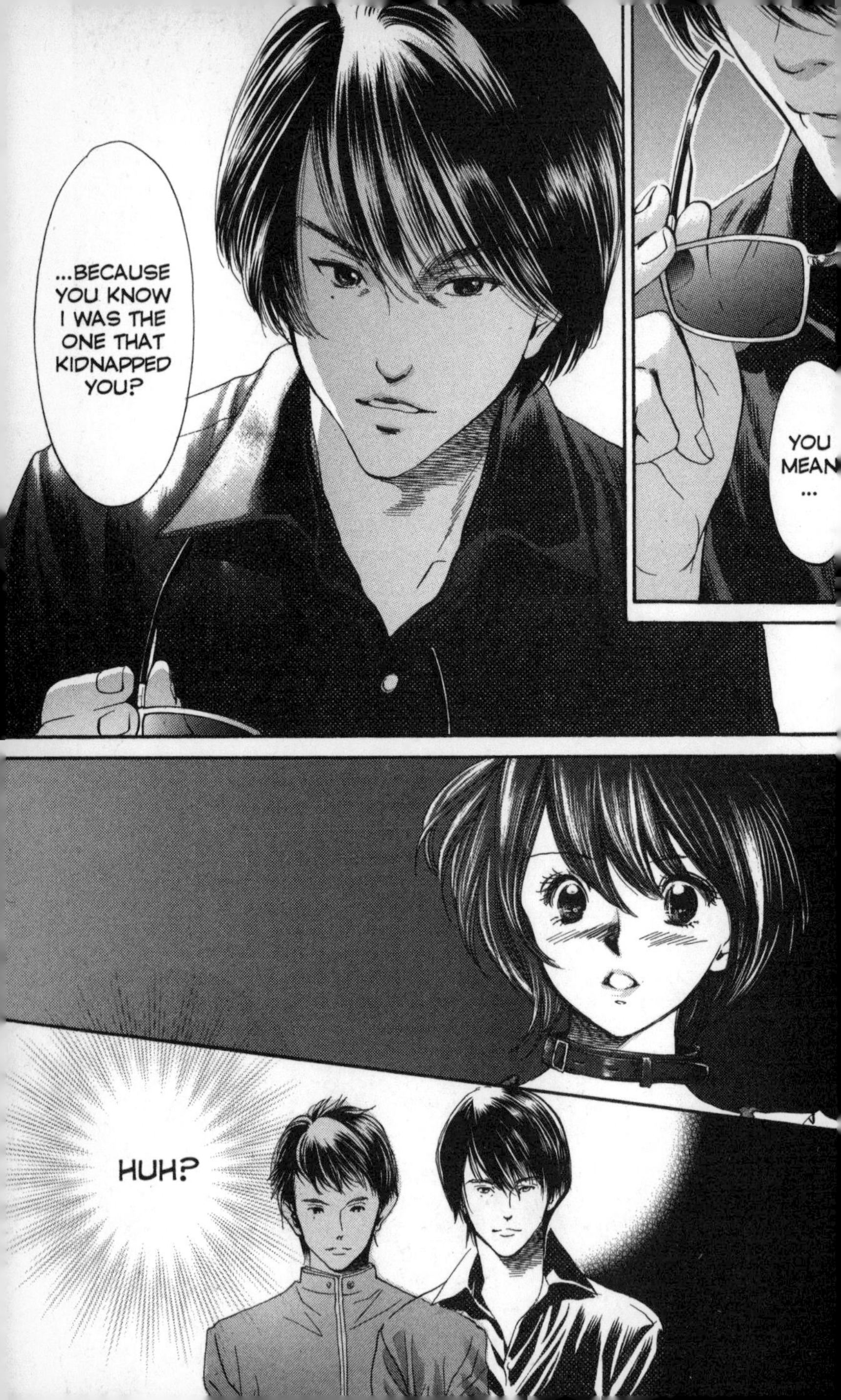
YOU MEAN ...
...BECAUSE YOU KNOW I WAS THE ONE THAT KIDNAPPED YOU?
HUH?

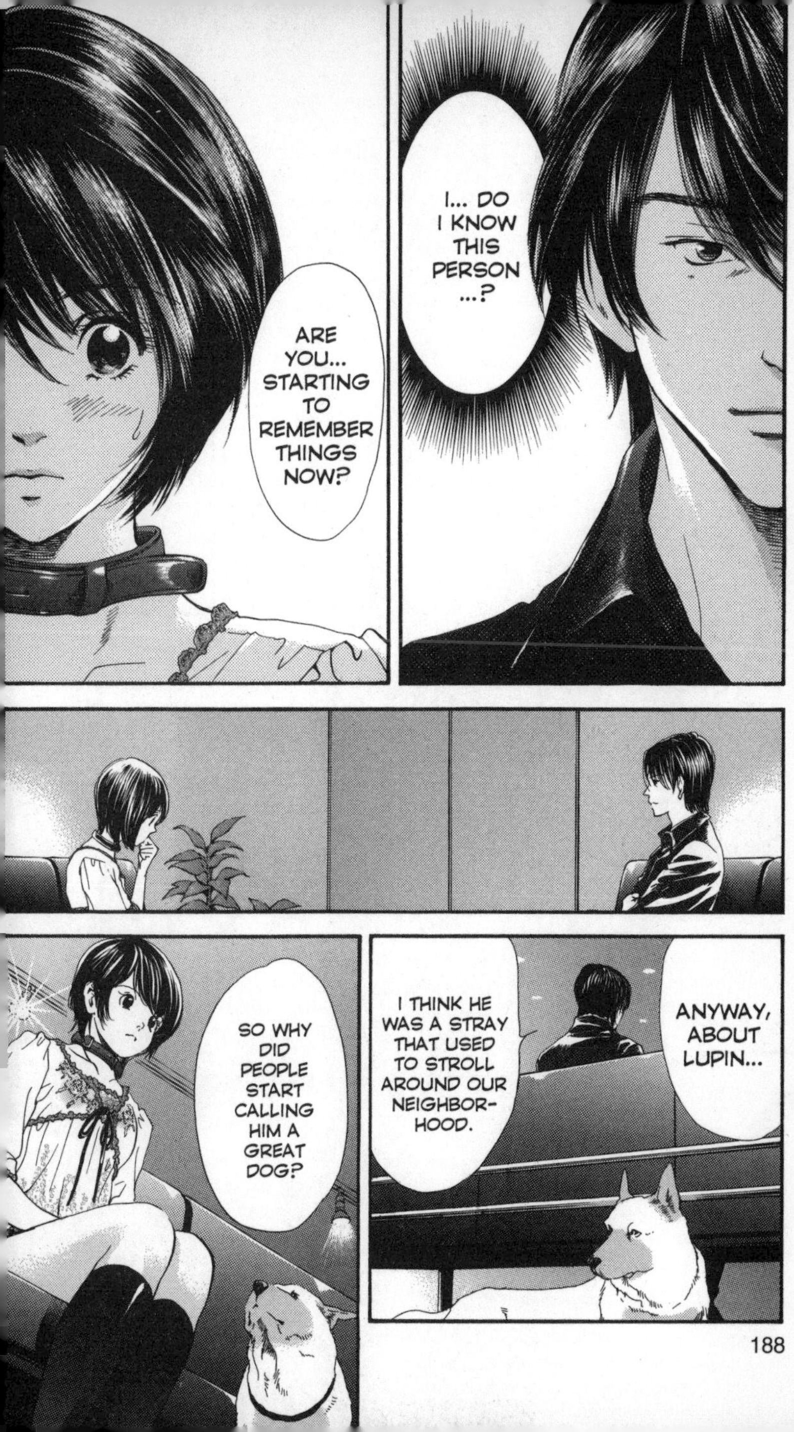
I... DO I KNOW THIS PERSON ...?
ARE YOU... STARTING TO REMEMBER THINGS NOW?
ANYWAY, ABOUT LUPIN...
I THINK HE WAS A STRAY THAT USED TO STROLL AROUND OUR NEIGHBOR-HOOD.
SO WHY DID PEOPLE START CALLING HIM A GREAT DOG?

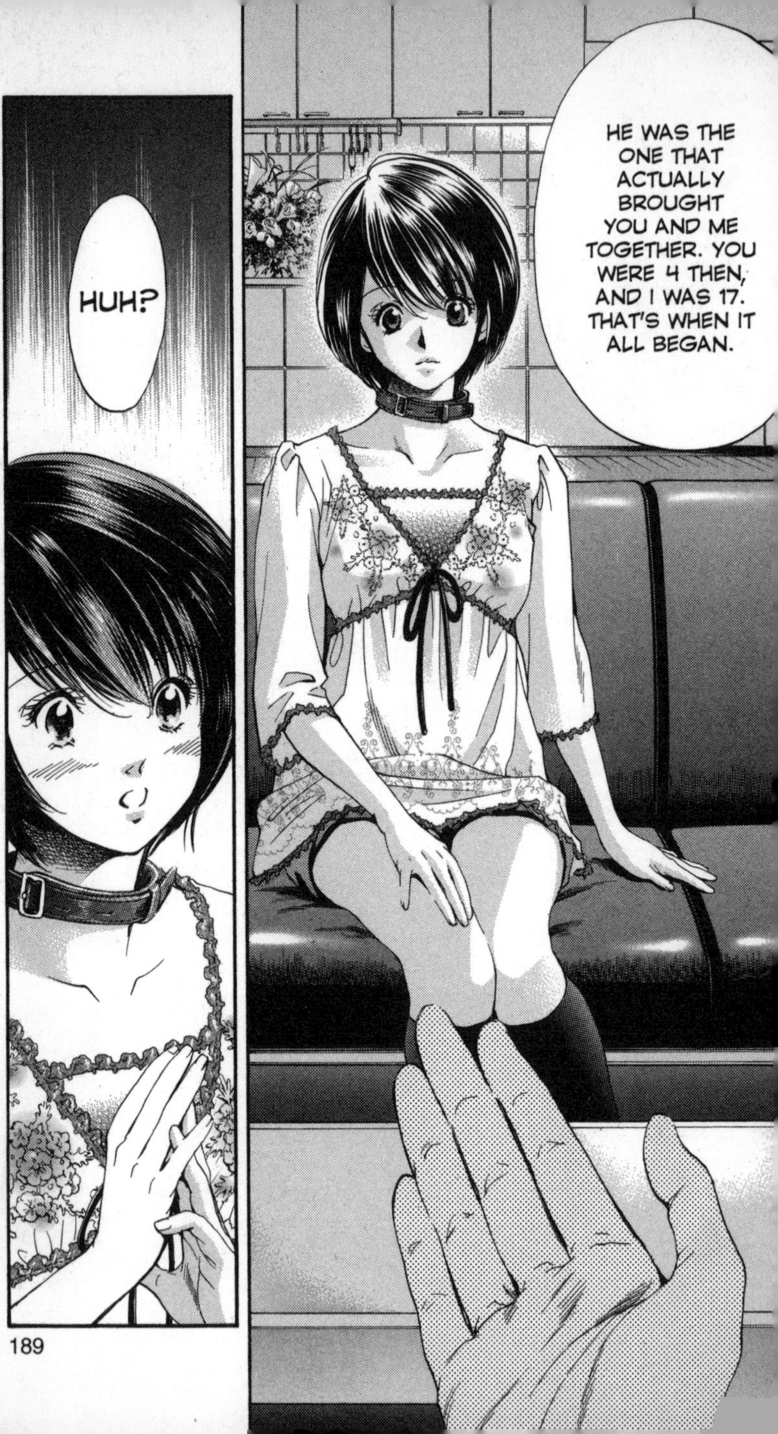
HE WAS THE ONE THAT ACTUALLY BROUGHT YOU AND ME TOGETHER. YOU WERE 4 THEN, AND I WAS 17. THAT'S WHEN IT ALL BEGAN.
HUH?

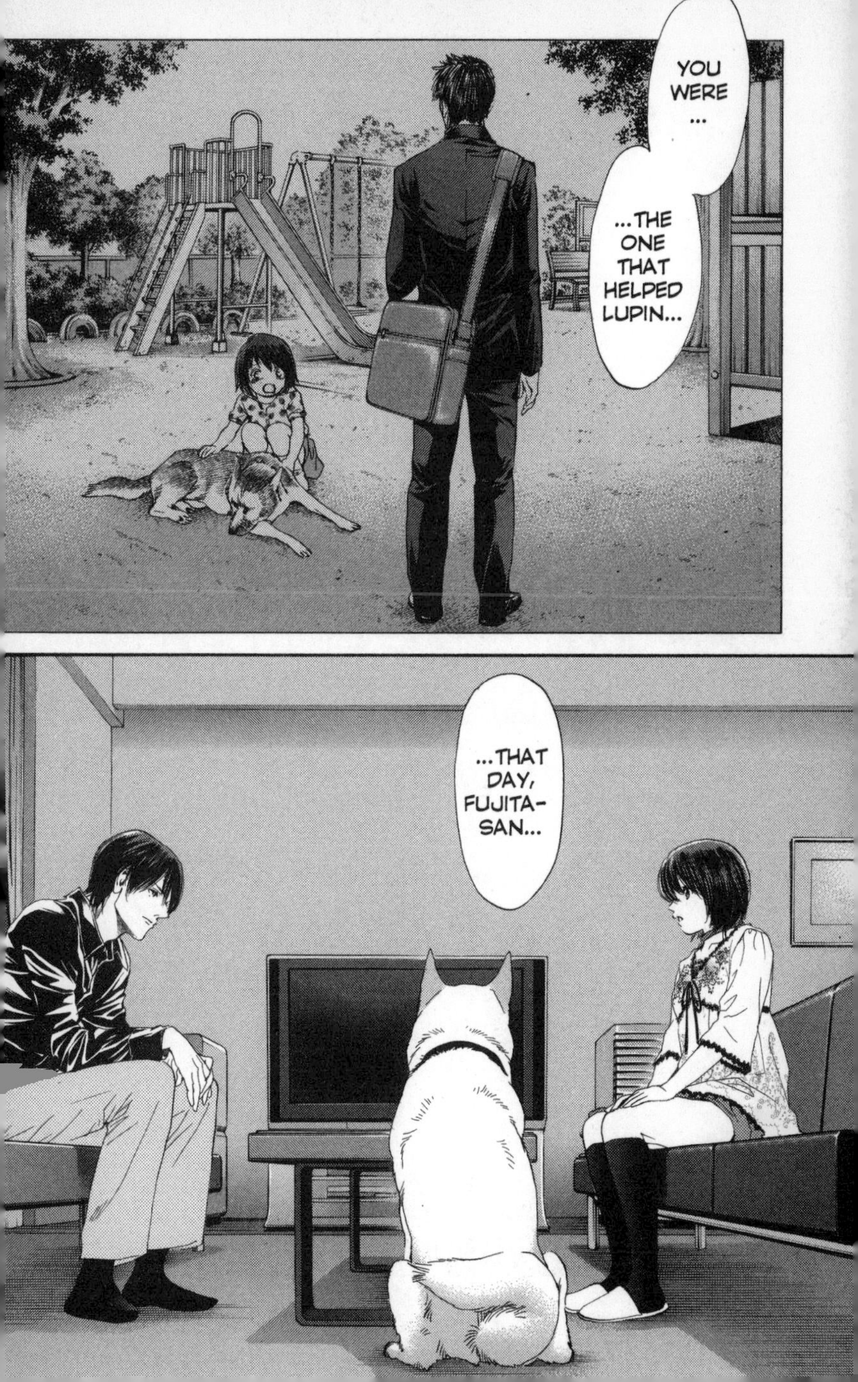
YOU WERE ...
...THE ONE THAT HELPED LUPIN...
...THAT DAY, FUJITA-SAN...

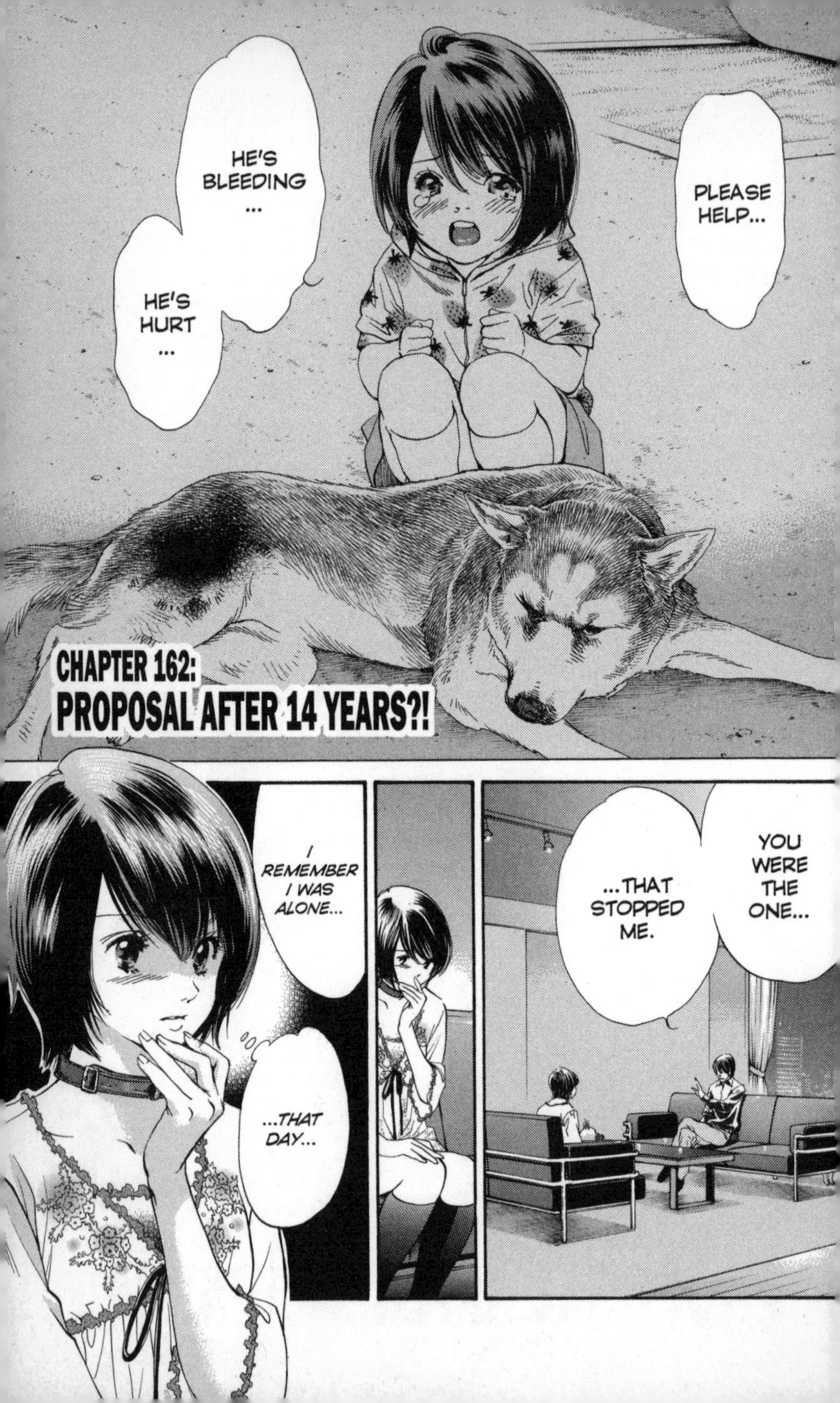
PLEASE HELP...
HE'S BLEEDING ...
HE'S HURT ...
CHAPTER 162:
PROPOSAL AFTER 14 YEARS?!
YOU WERE THE ONE...
...THAT STOPPED ME.
I REMEMBER I WAS ALONE...
...THAT DAY...

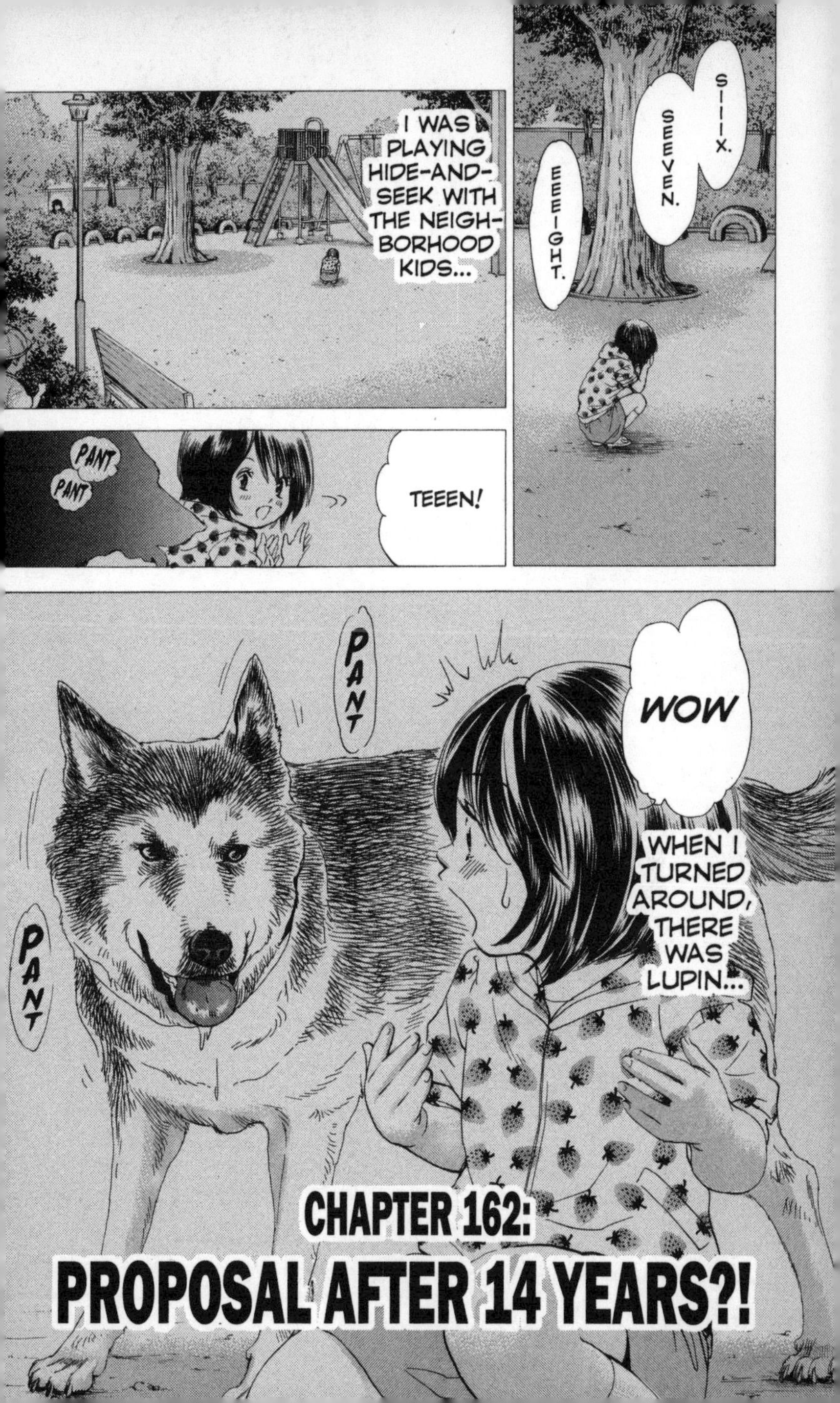
SIIIX.
SEEVEN.
EEEIGHT.
I WAS PLAYING HIDE-AND-SEEK WITH THE NEIGHBORHOOD KIDS...
TEEEN!
PANT PANT
WOW
PANT
WHEN I TURNED AROUND, THERE WAS LUPIN...
PANT
CHAPTER 162:
PROPOSAL AFTER 14 YEARS?!

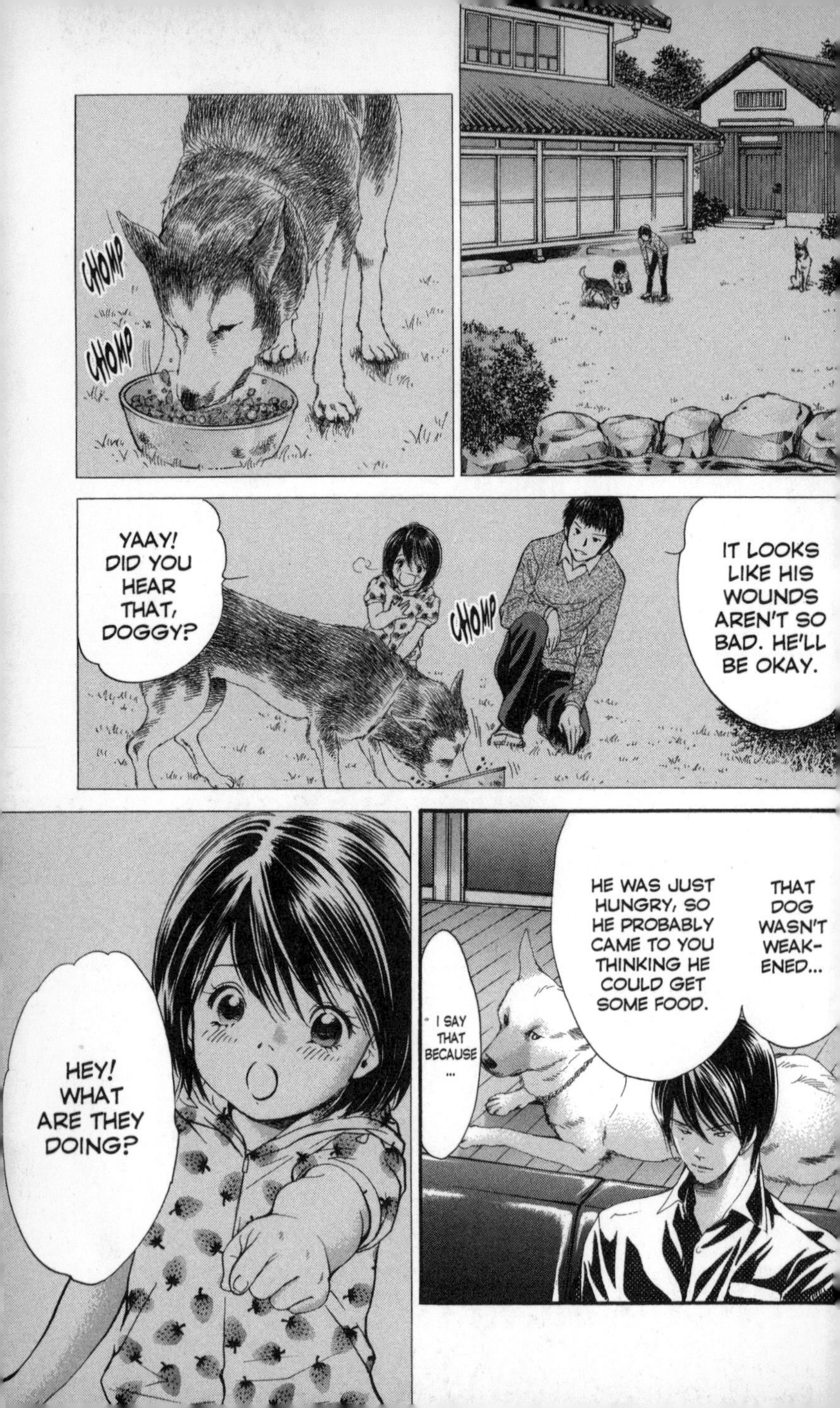
CHOMP
CHOMP
IT LOOKS LIKE HIS WOUNDS AREN'T SO BAD. HE'LL BE OKAY.
CHOMP
YAAY! DID YOU HEAR THAT, DOGGY?
THAT DOG WASN'T WEAK-ENED...
HE WAS JUST HUNGRY, SO HE PROBABLY CAME TO YOU THINKING HE COULD GET SOME FOOD.
I SAY THAT BECAUSE ...
HEY! WHAT ARE THEY DOING?

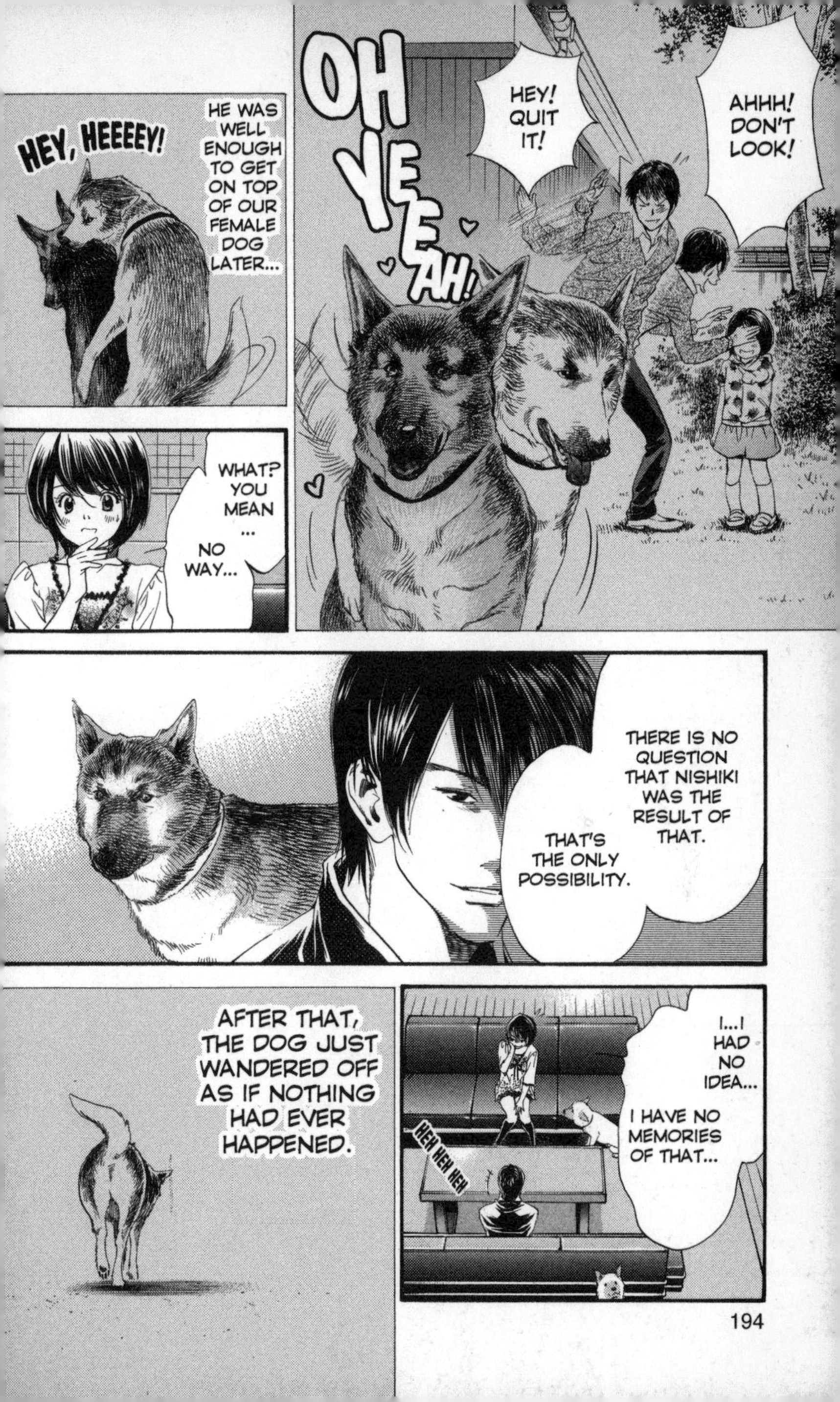
AHHH! DON'T LOOK!
HEY! QUIT IT!
OH YEEAH!
HE WAS WELL ENOUGH TO GET ON TOP OF OUR FEMALE DOG LATER...
HEY, HEEEEY!
WHAT? YOU MEAN ...
NO WAY...
THERE IS NO QUESTION THAT NISHIKI WAS THE RESULT OF THAT.
THAT'S THE ONLY POSSIBILITY.
I...I HAD NO IDEA...
I HAVE NO MEMORIES OF THAT...
HEH HEH HEH
AFTER THAT, THE DOG JUST WANDERED OFF AS IF NOTHING HAD EVER HAPPENED.

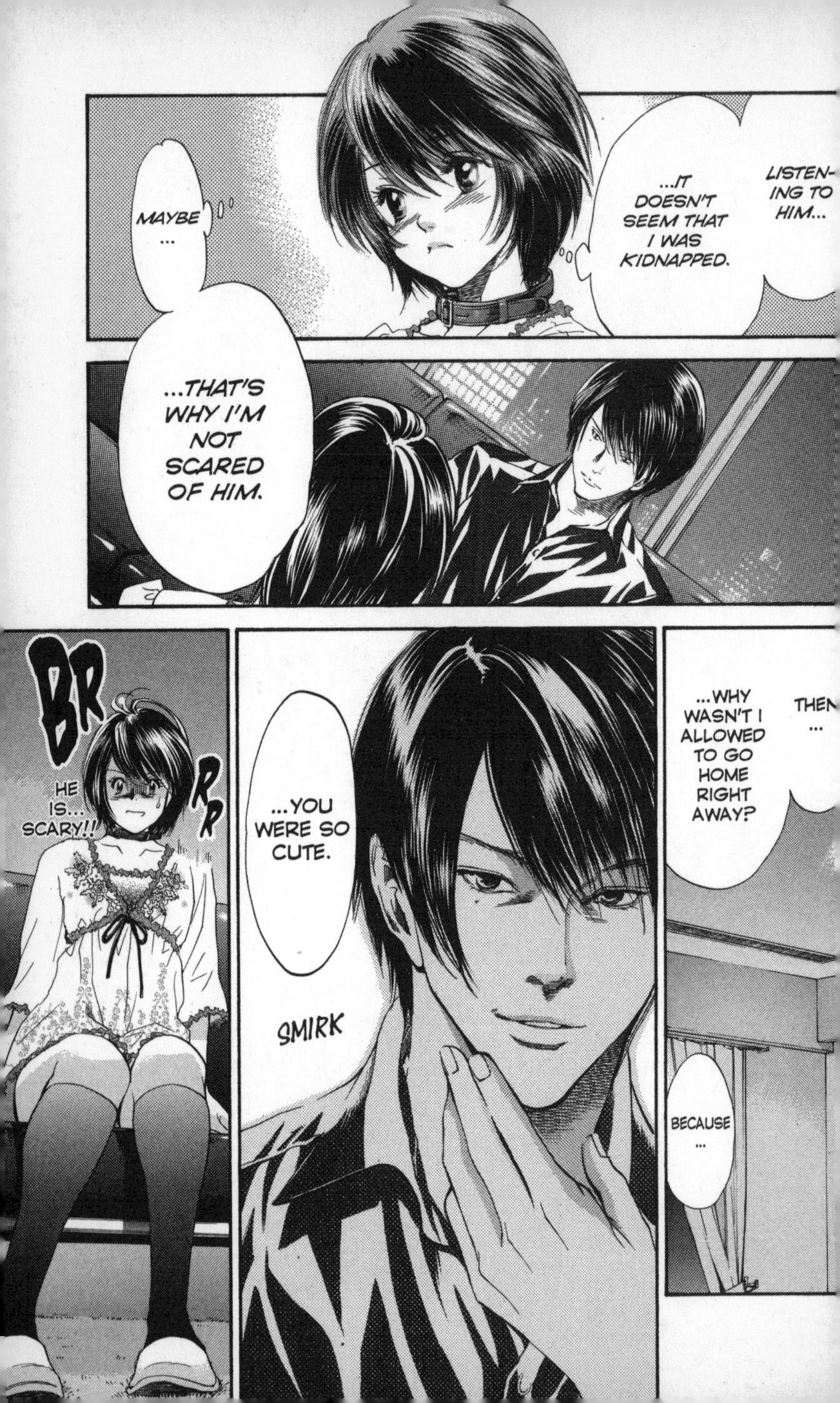
LISTEN-ING TO HIM...
...IT DOESN'T SEEM THAT I WAS KIDNAPPED.
MAYBE ...
...THAT'S WHY I'M NOT SCARED OF HIM.
THEN ...
...WHY WASN'T I ALLOWED TO GO HOME RIGHT AWAY?
BECAUSE ...
...YOU WERE SO CUTE.
SMIRK
BRRR
HE IS... SCARY!!

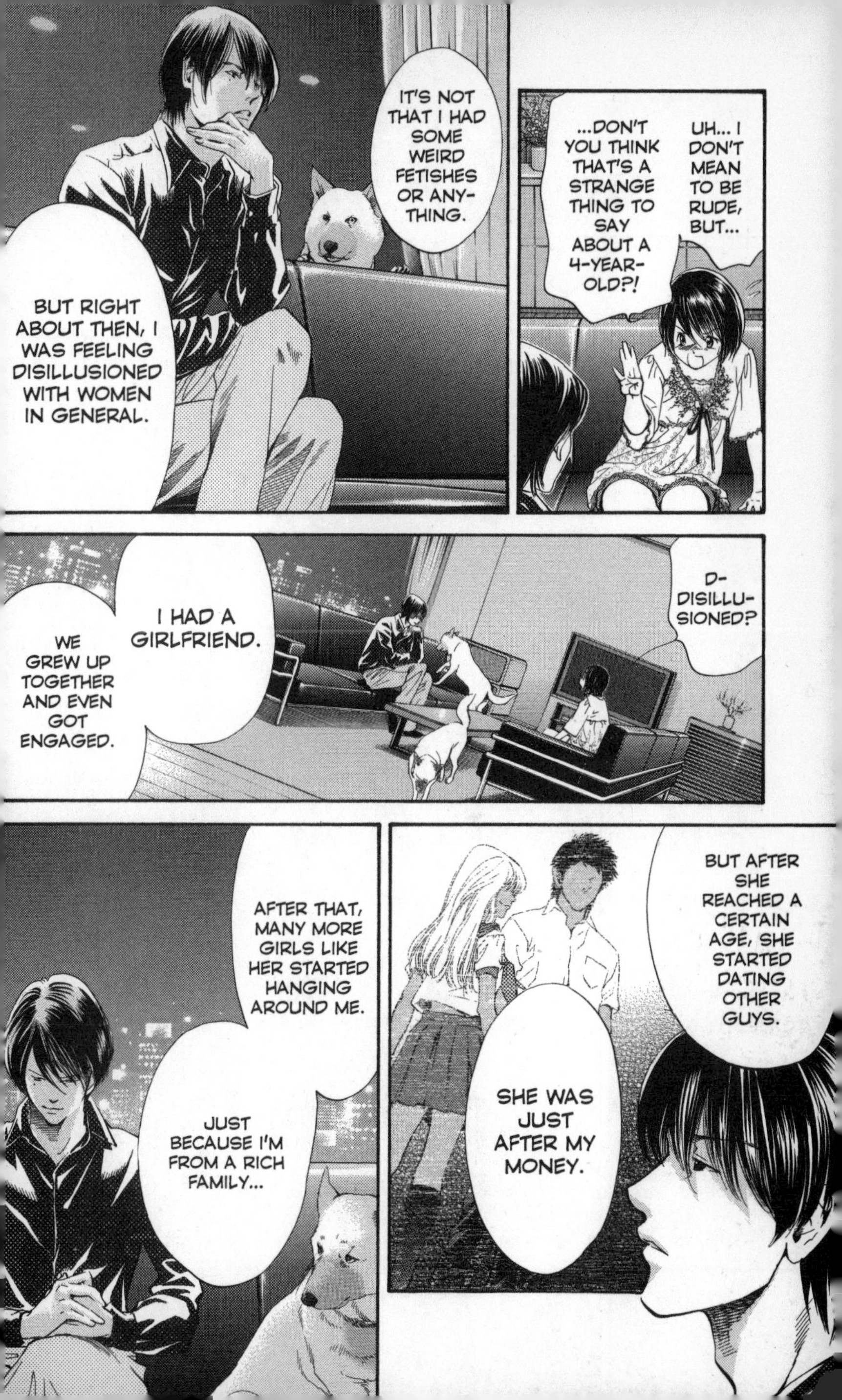
UH... I DON'T MEAN TO BE RUDE, BUT...
...DON'T YOU THINK THAT'S A STRANGE THING TO SAY ABOUT A 4-YEAR-OLD?!
IT'S NOT THAT I HAD SOME WEIRD FETISHES OR ANY-THING.
BUT RIGHT ABOUT THEN, I WAS FEELING DISILLUSIONED WITH WOMEN IN GENERAL.
D-DISILLU-SIONED?
I HAD A GIRLFRIEND.
WE GREW UP TOGETHER AND EVEN GOT ENGAGED.
BUT AFTER SHE REACHED A CERTAIN AGE, SHE STARTED DATING OTHER GUYS.
SHE WAS JUST AFTER MY MONEY.
AFTER THAT, MANY MORE GIRLS LIKE HER STARTED HANGING AROUND ME.
JUST BECAUSE I'M FROM A RICH FAMILY...

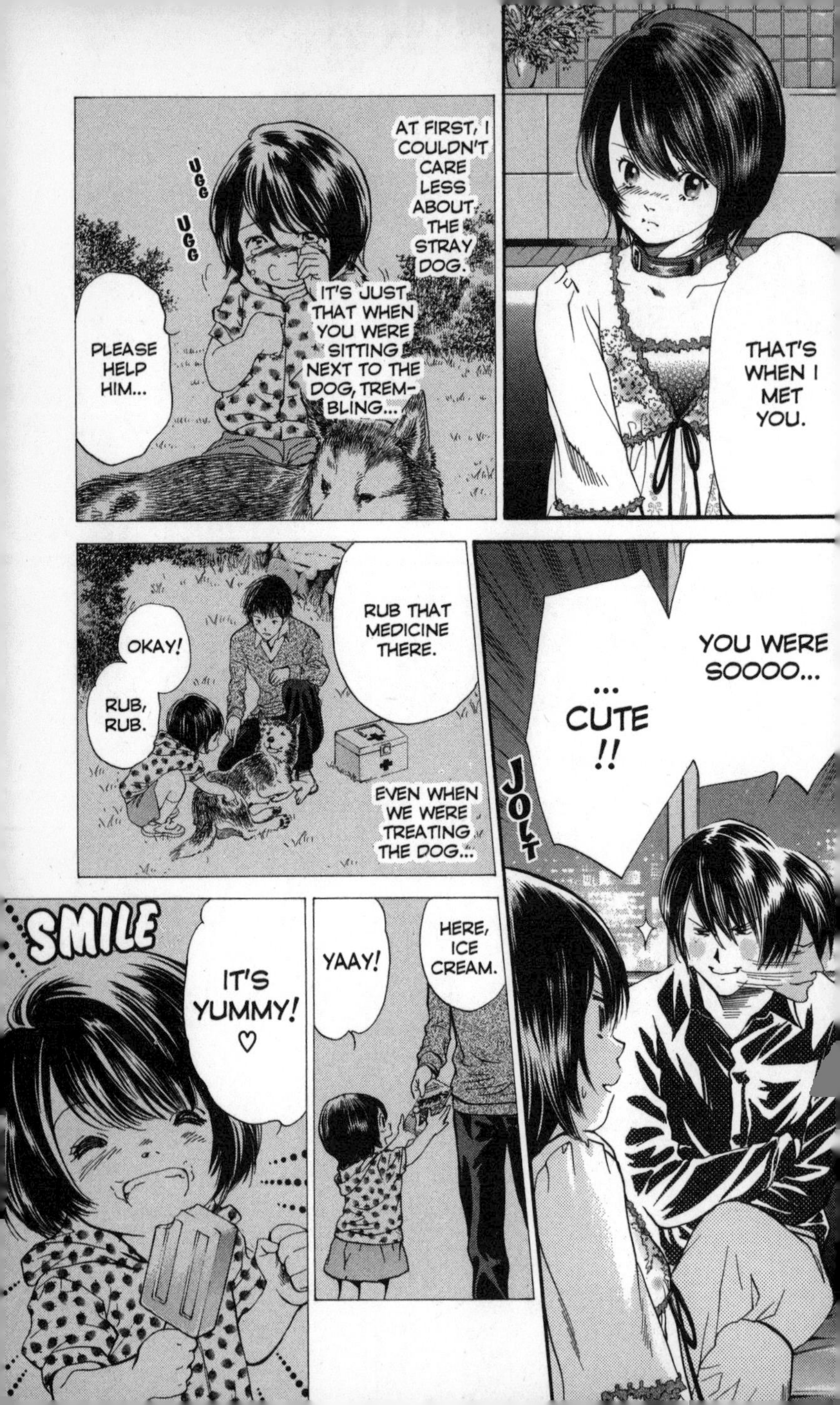
THAT'S WHEN I MET YOU.
AT FIRST, I COULDN'T CARE LESS ABOUT THE STRAY DOG.
IT'S JUST THAT WHEN YOU WERE SITTING NEXT TO THE DOG, TREMBLING...
UGG
UGG
PLEASE HELP HIM...
YOU WERE SOOOO...
... CUTE !!
JOLT
RUB THAT MEDICINE THERE.
EVEN WHEN WE WERE TREATING THE DOG...
OKAY!
RUB, RUB.
HERE, ICE CREAM.
YAAY!
IT'S YUMMY! ♡
SMILE

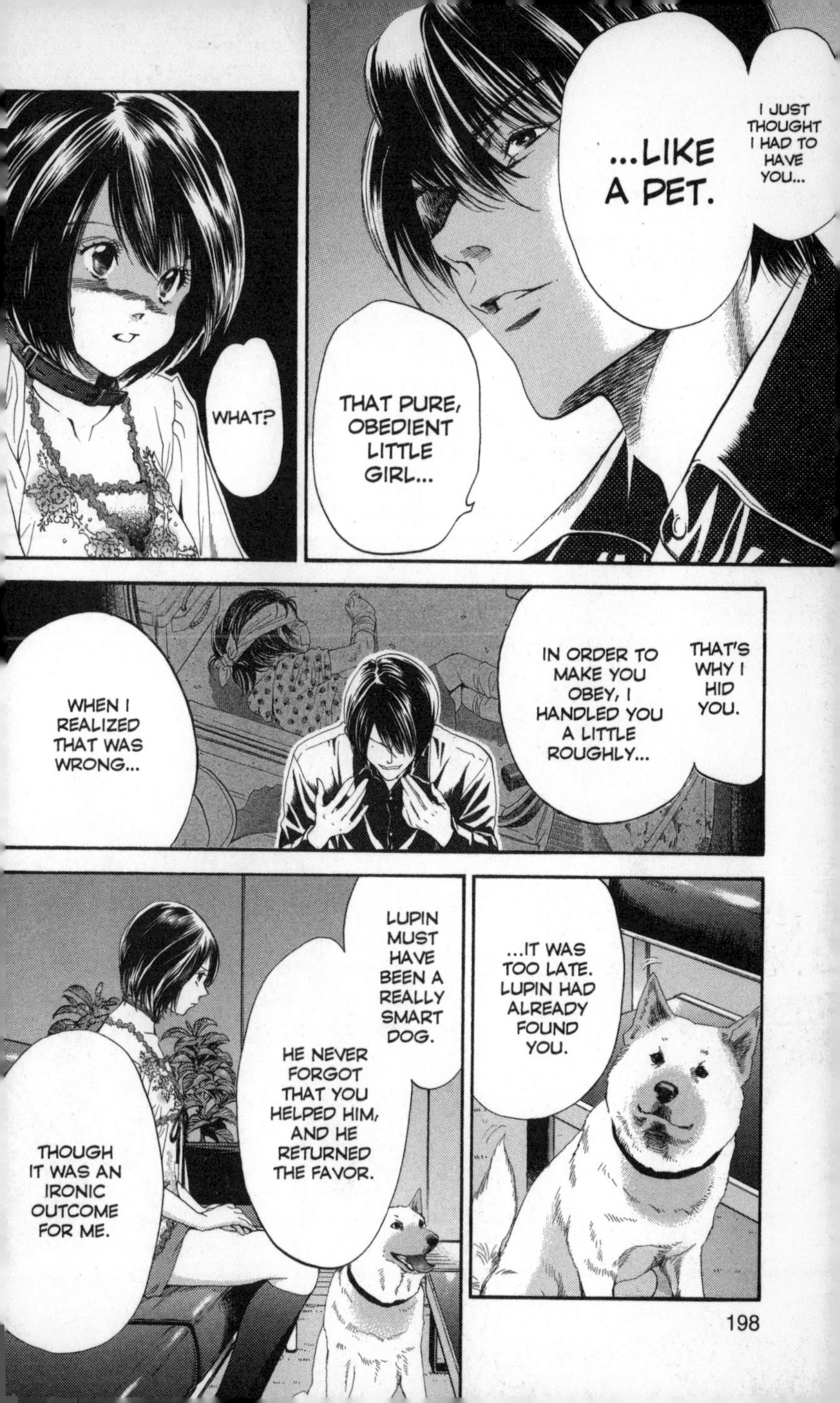

I JUST THOUGHT I HAD TO HAVE YOU...
...LIKE A PET.
THAT PURE, OBEDIENT LITTLE GIRL...
WHAT?
THAT'S WHY I HID YOU.
IN ORDER TO MAKE YOU OBEY, I HANDLED YOU A LITTLE ROUGHLY...
WHEN I REALIZED THAT WAS WRONG...
...IT WAS TOO LATE. LUPIN HAD ALREADY FOUND YOU.
LUPIN MUST HAVE BEEN A REALLY SMART DOG.
HE NEVER FORGOT THAT YOU HELPED HIM, AND HE RETURNED THE FAVOR.
THOUGH IT WAS AN IRONIC OUTCOME FOR ME.

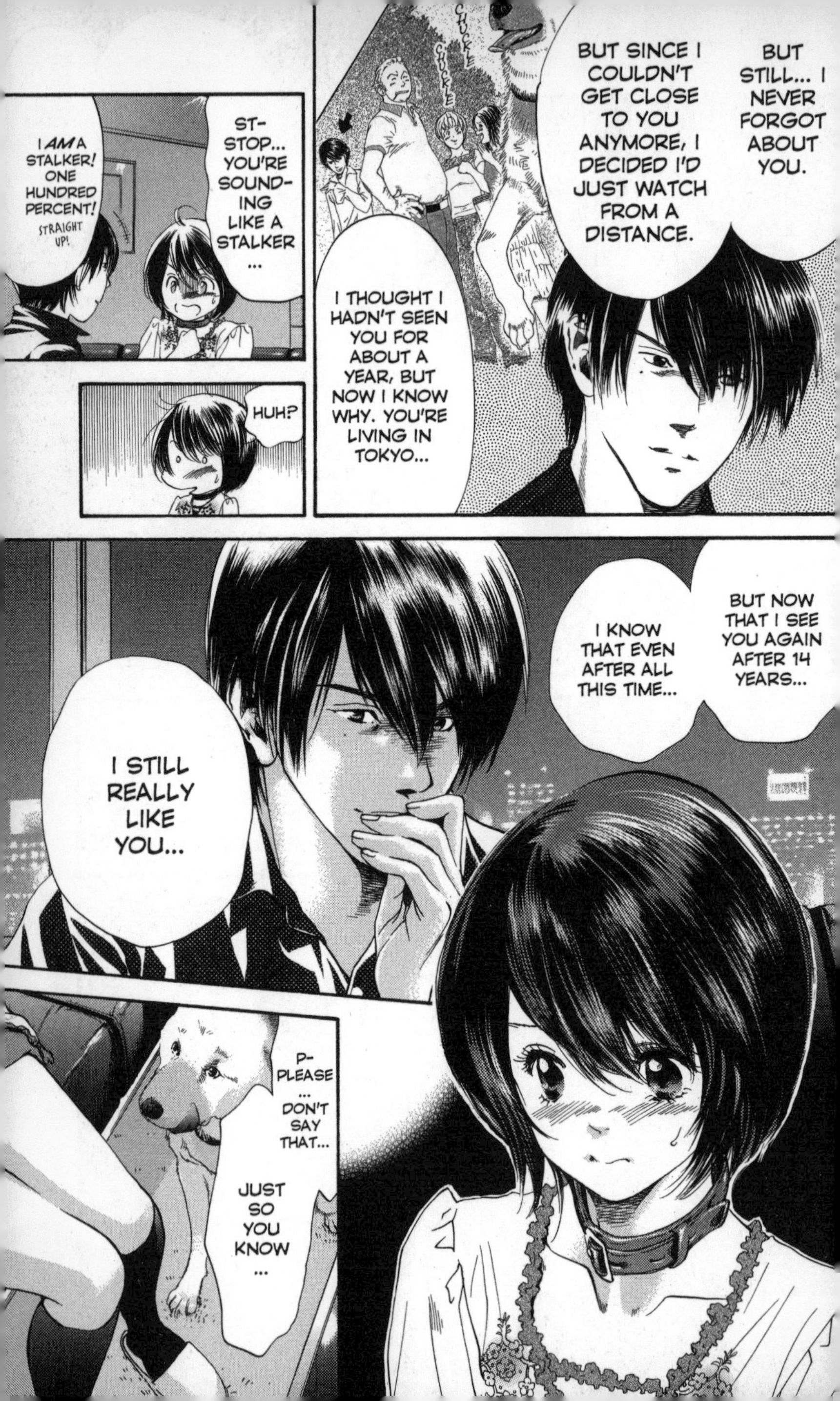
BUT STILL... I NEVER FORGOT ABOUT YOU.
BUT SINCE I COULDN'T GET CLOSE TO YOU ANYMORE, I DECIDED I'D JUST WATCH FROM A DISTANCE.
CHUCKLE
CHUCKLE
I THOUGHT I HADN'T SEEN YOU FOR ABOUT A YEAR, BUT NOW I KNOW WHY. YOU'RE LIVING IN TOKYO...
ST-STOP... YOU'RE SOUNDING LIKE A STALKER...
I AM A STALKER! ONE HUNDRED PERCENT!
STRAIGHT UP!
HUH?
BUT NOW THAT I SEE YOU AGAIN AFTER 14 YEARS...
I KNOW THAT EVEN AFTER ALL THIS TIME...
I STILL REALLY LIKE YOU...
P-PLEASE... DON'T SAY THAT...
JUST SO YOU KNOW...

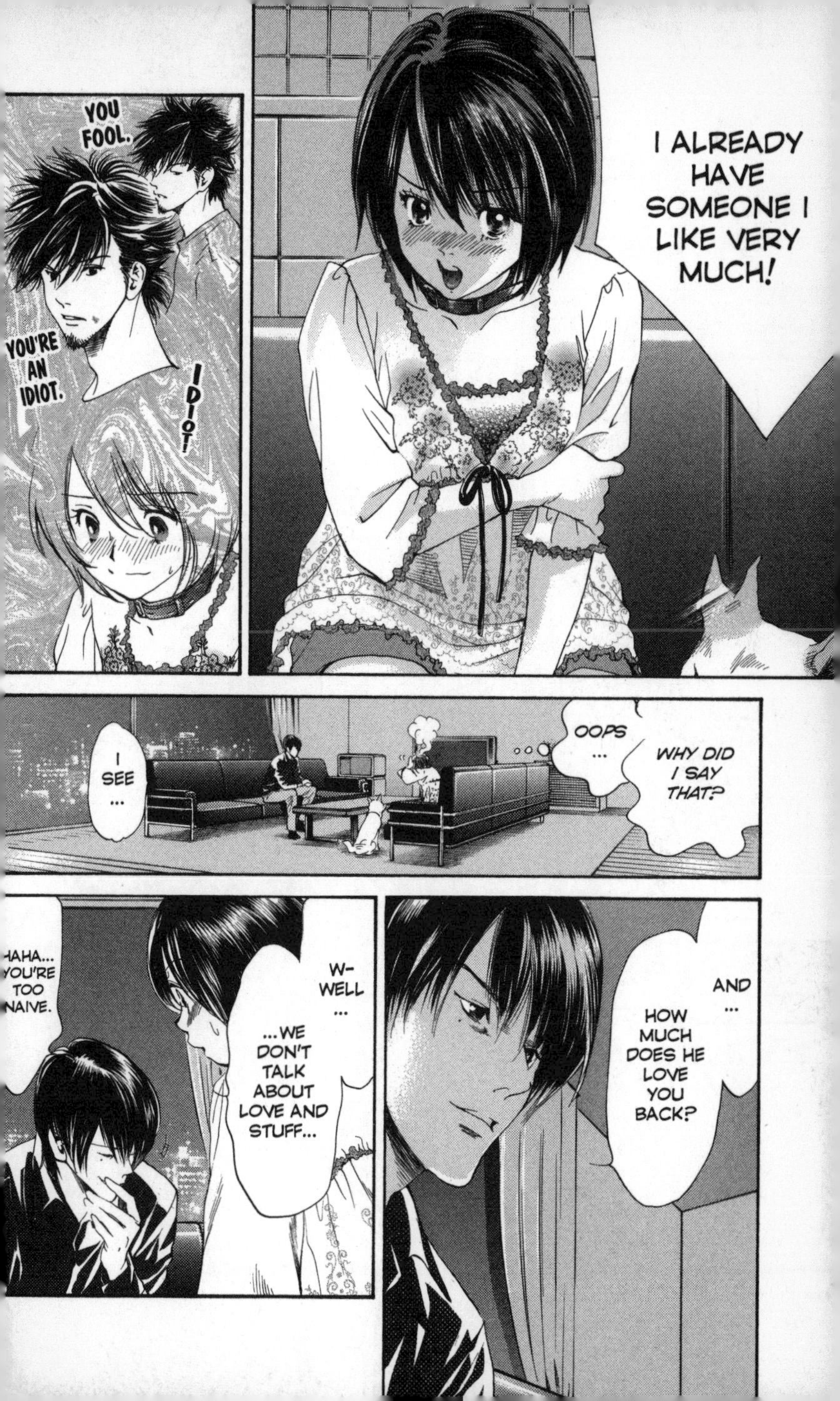
I ALREADY HAVE SOMEONE I LIKE VERY MUCH!
YOU FOOL.
IDIOT!
YOU'RE AN IDIOT.
OOPS...
WHY DID I SAY THAT?
I SEE...
AND...
HOW MUCH DOES HE LOVE YOU BACK?
W-WELL...
...WE DON'T TALK ABOUT LOVE AND STUFF...
HAHA... YOU'RE TOO NAIVE.

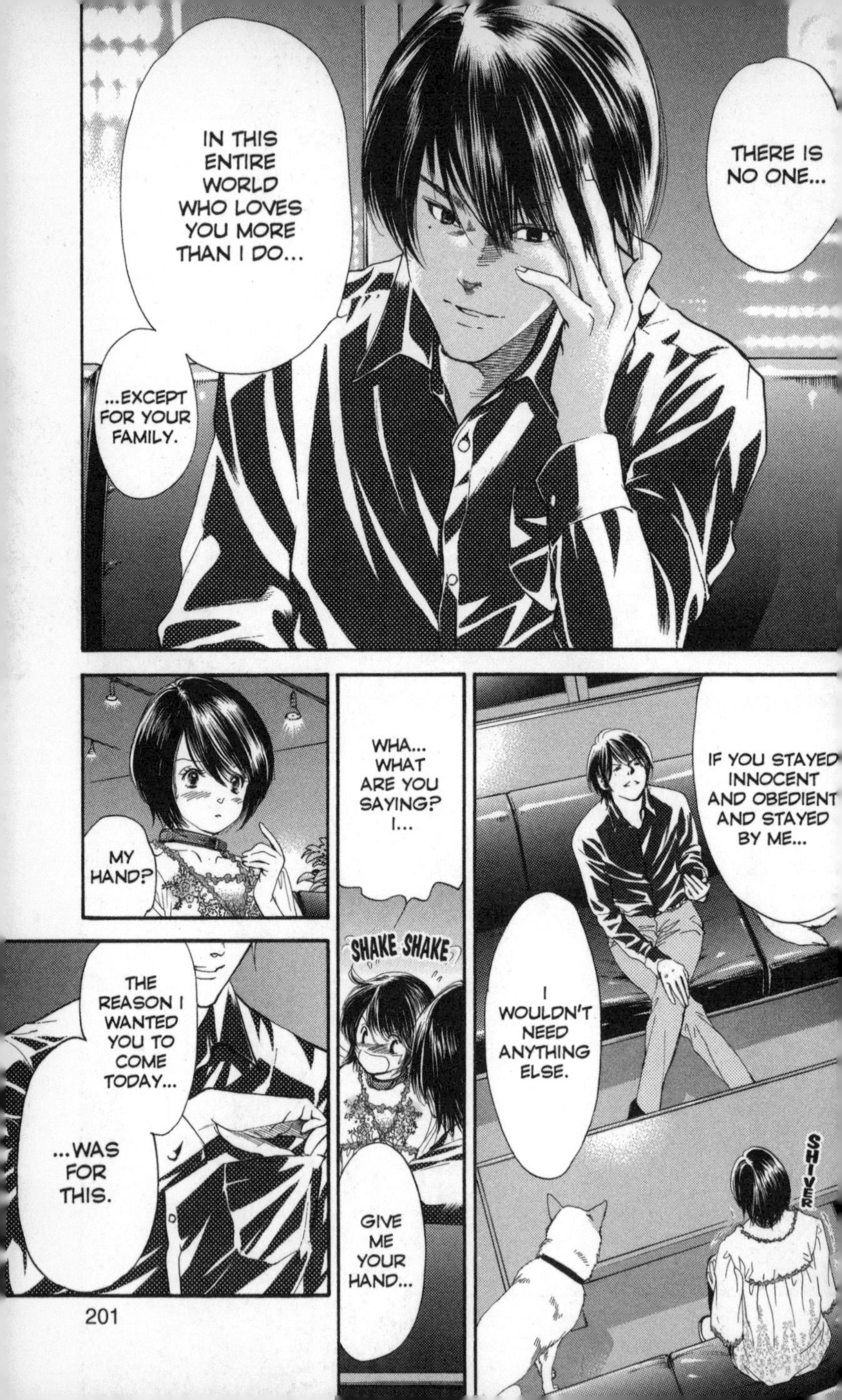
THERE IS NO ONE...
IN THIS ENTIRE WORLD WHO LOVES YOU MORE THAN I DO...
...EXCEPT FOR YOUR FAMILY.
IF YOU STAYED INNOCENT AND OBEDIENT AND STAYED BY ME...
I WOULDN'T NEED ANYTHING ELSE.
SHIVER
WHA... WHAT ARE YOU SAYING? I...
MY HAND?
SHAKE SHAKE
GIVE ME YOUR HAND...
THE REASON I WANTED YOU TO COME TODAY...
...WAS FOR THIS.

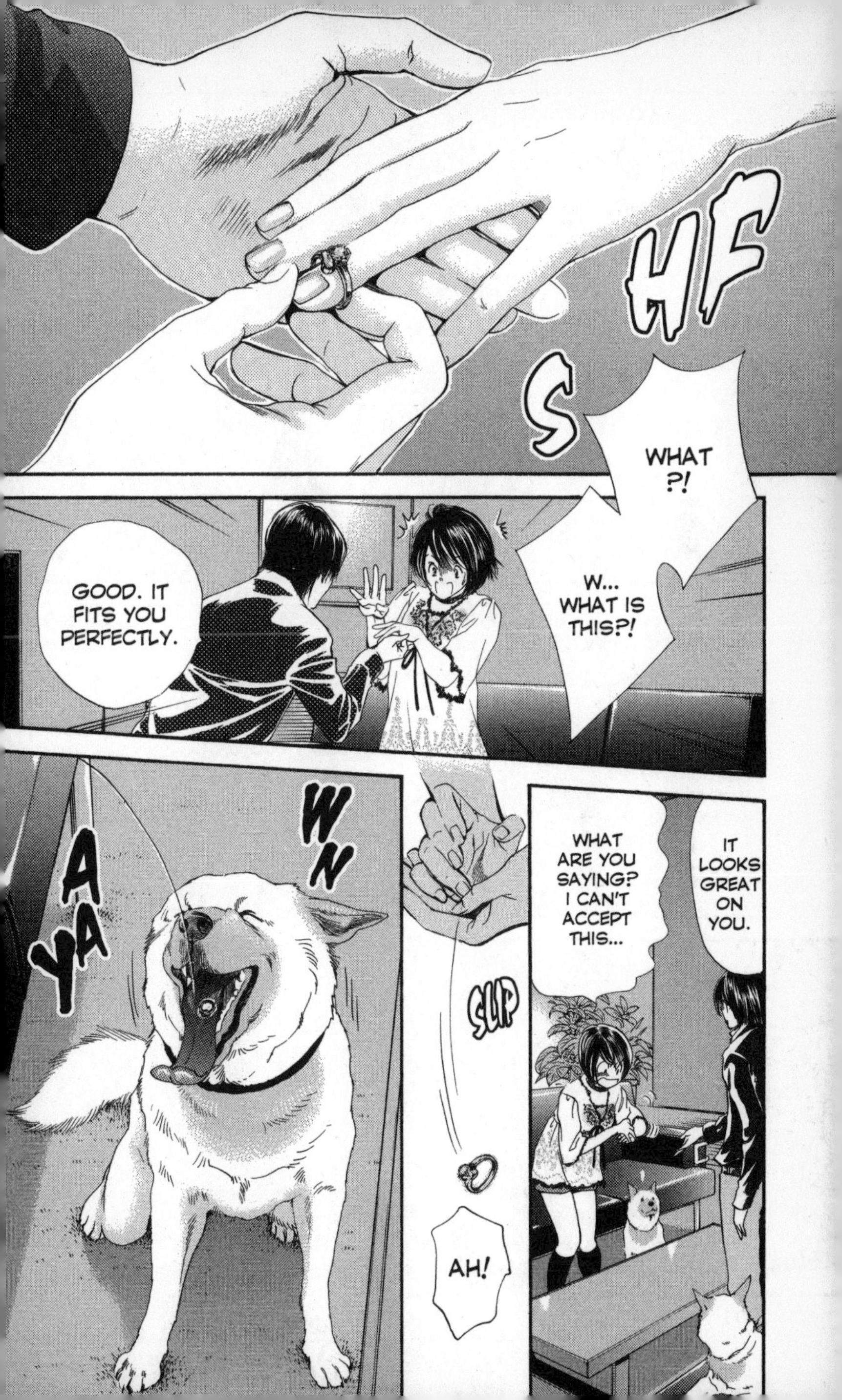
S HF
WHAT ?!
W... WHAT IS THIS?!
GOOD. IT FITS YOU PERFECTLY.
IT LOOKS GREAT ON YOU.
WHAT ARE YOU SAYING? I CAN'T ACCEPT THIS...
SLIP
AH!
WN
A YA

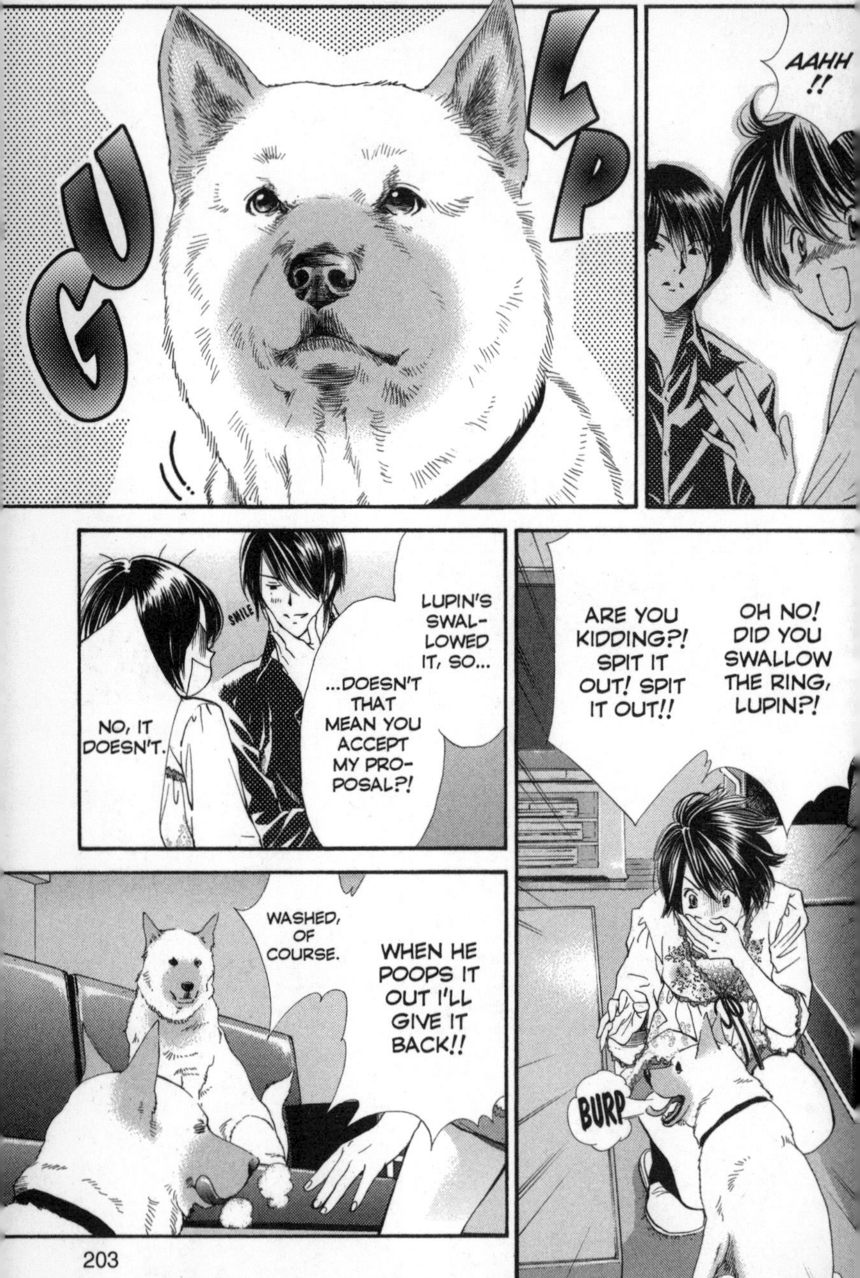
AAHH !!
GULP
OH NO! DID YOU SWALLOW THE RING, LUPIN?!
ARE YOU KIDDING?! SPIT IT OUT! SPIT IT OUT!!
BURP
LUPIN'S SWAL-LOWED IT, SO...
...DOESN'T THAT MEAN YOU ACCEPT MY PRO-POSAL?!
SMILE
NO, IT DOESN'T.
WHEN HE POOPS IT OUT I'LL GIVE IT BACK!!
WASHED, OF COURSE.

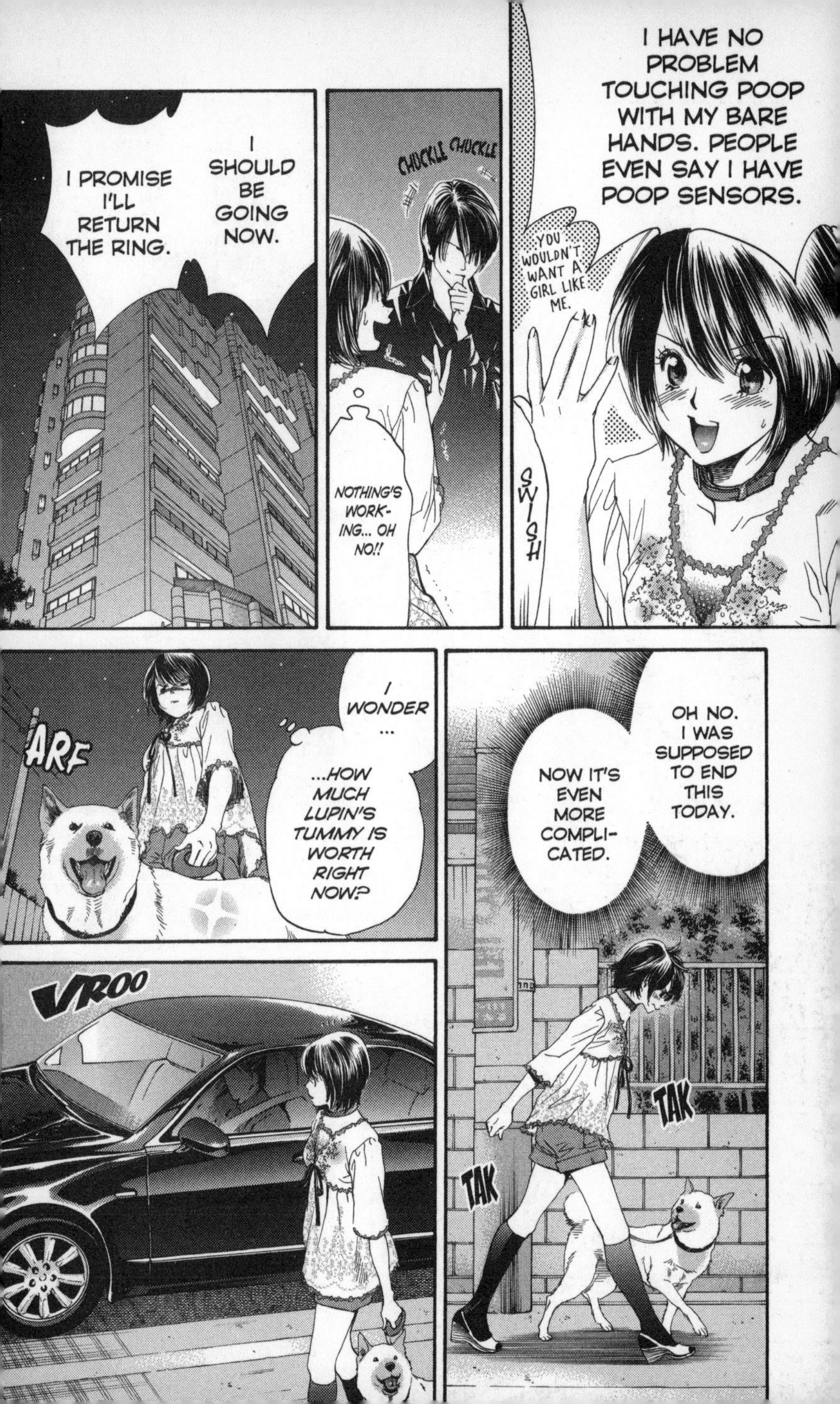
I HAVE NO PROBLEM TOUCHING POOP WITH MY BARE HANDS. PEOPLE EVEN SAY I HAVE POOP SENSORS.
YOU WOULDN'T WANT A GIRL LIKE ME.
SWISH
CHUCKLE CHUCKLE
NOTHING'S WORKING... OH NO!!
I SHOULD BE GOING NOW.
I PROMISE I'LL RETURN THE RING.
OH NO. I WAS SUPPOSED TO END THIS TODAY.
NOW IT'S EVEN MORE COMPLICATED.
TAK
TAK
I WONDER...
...HOW MUCH LUPIN'S TUMMY IS WORTH RIGHT NOW?
ARF
VROO

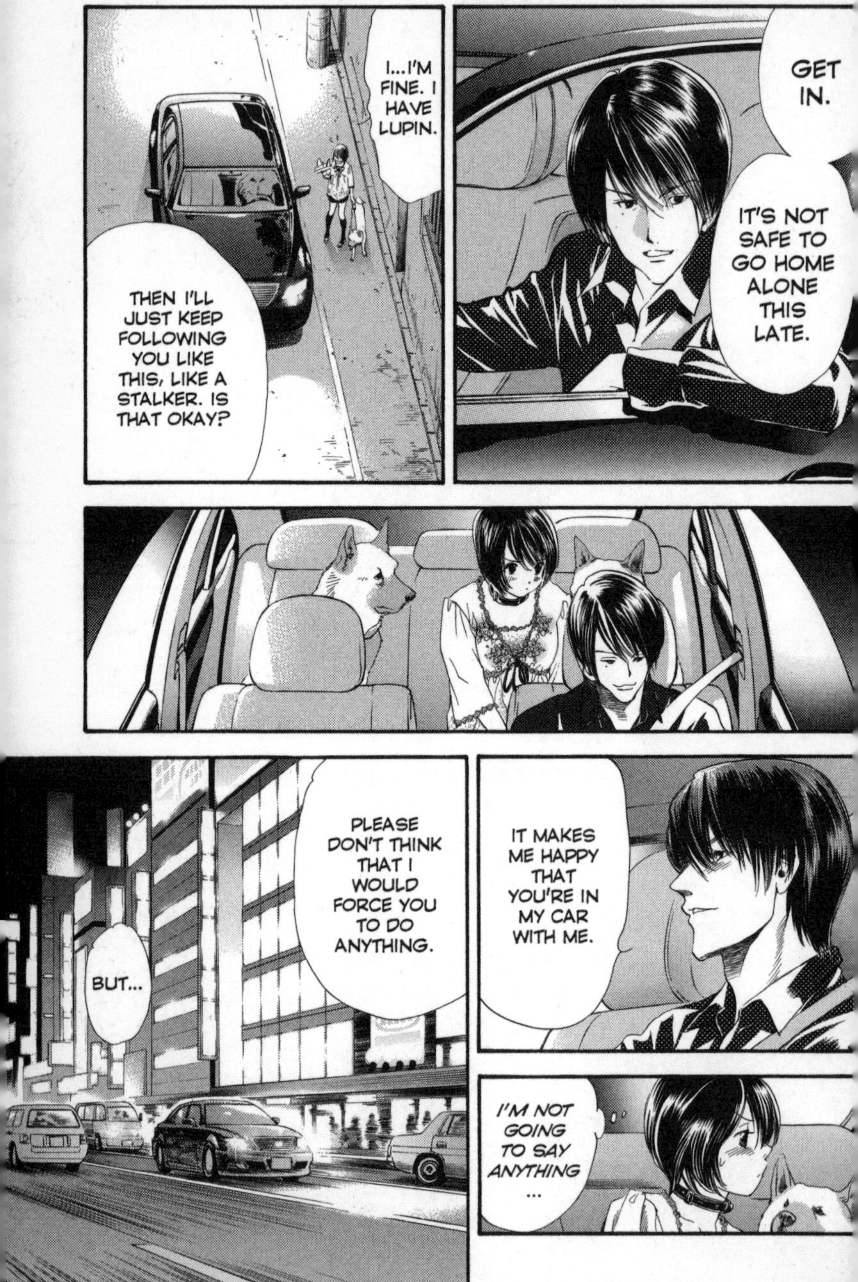
GET IN.
IT'S NOT SAFE TO GO HOME ALONE THIS LATE.
I...I'M FINE. I HAVE LUPIN.
THEN I'LL JUST KEEP FOLLOWING YOU LIKE THIS, LIKE A STALKER. IS THAT OKAY?
IT MAKES ME HAPPY THAT YOU'RE IN MY CAR WITH ME.
I'M NOT GOING TO SAY ANYTHING ...
PLEASE DON'T THINK THAT I WOULD FORCE YOU TO DO ANYTHING.
BUT...

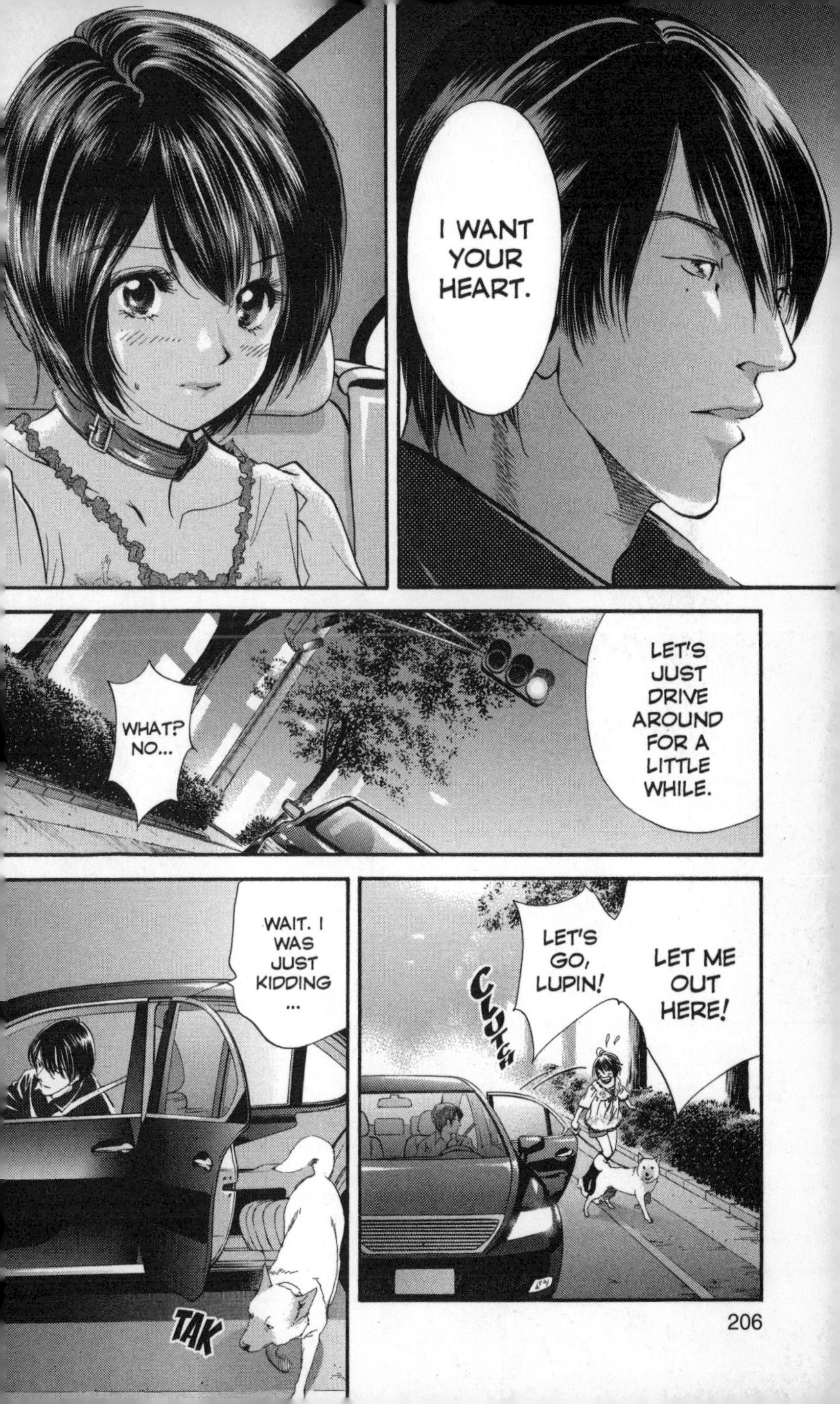
I WANT YOUR HEART.
LET'S JUST DRIVE AROUND FOR A LITTLE WHILE.
WHAT? NO...
LET ME OUT HERE!
LET'S GO, LUPIN!
CLUTCH
WAIT. I WAS JUST KIDDING ...
TAK

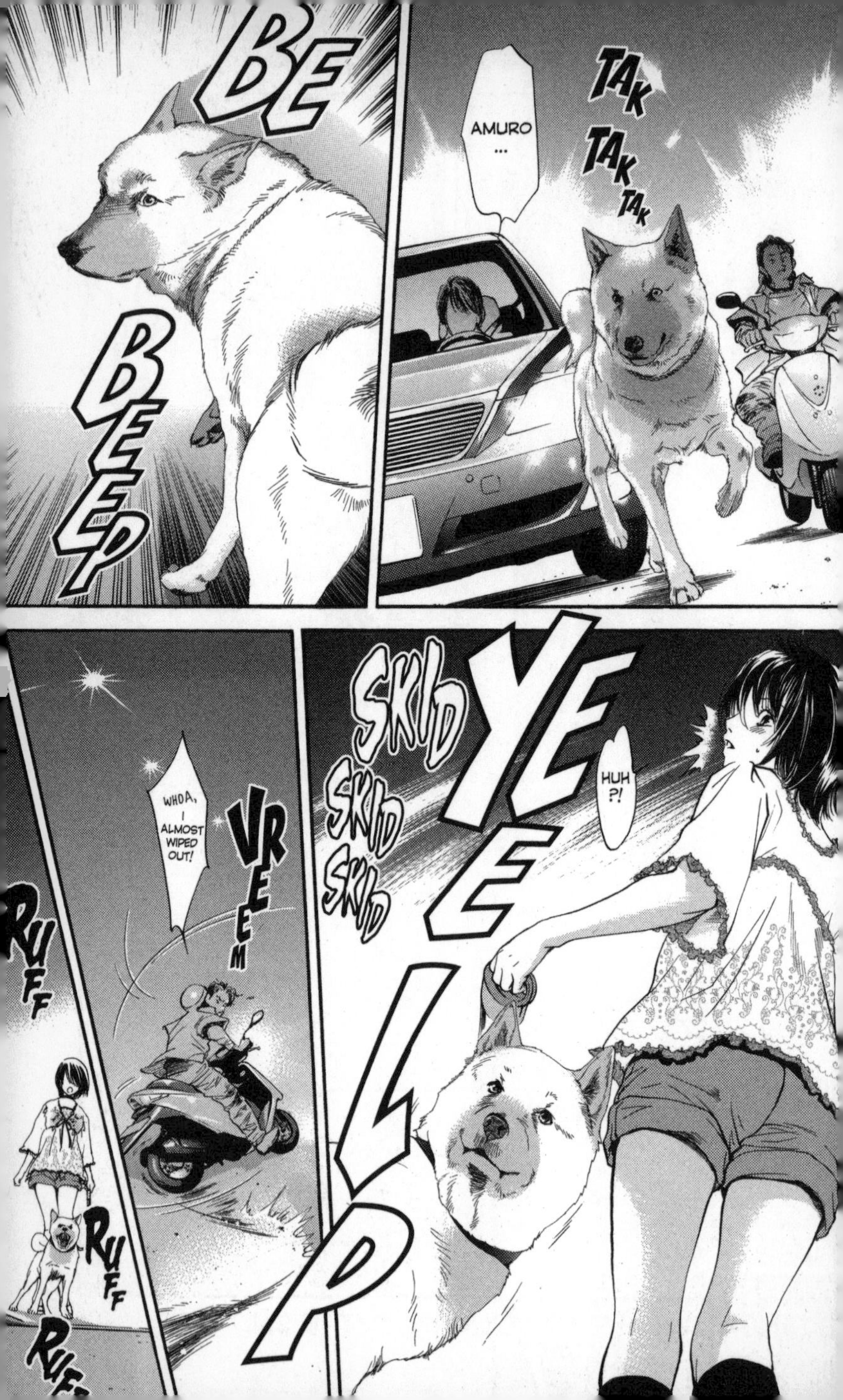
TAK TAK TAK
AMURO ...
BE BEEP
YEELP
HUH ?!
SKID SKID SKID
WHOA, I ALMOST WIPED OUT!
VREEEM
RUFF RUFF RUFF

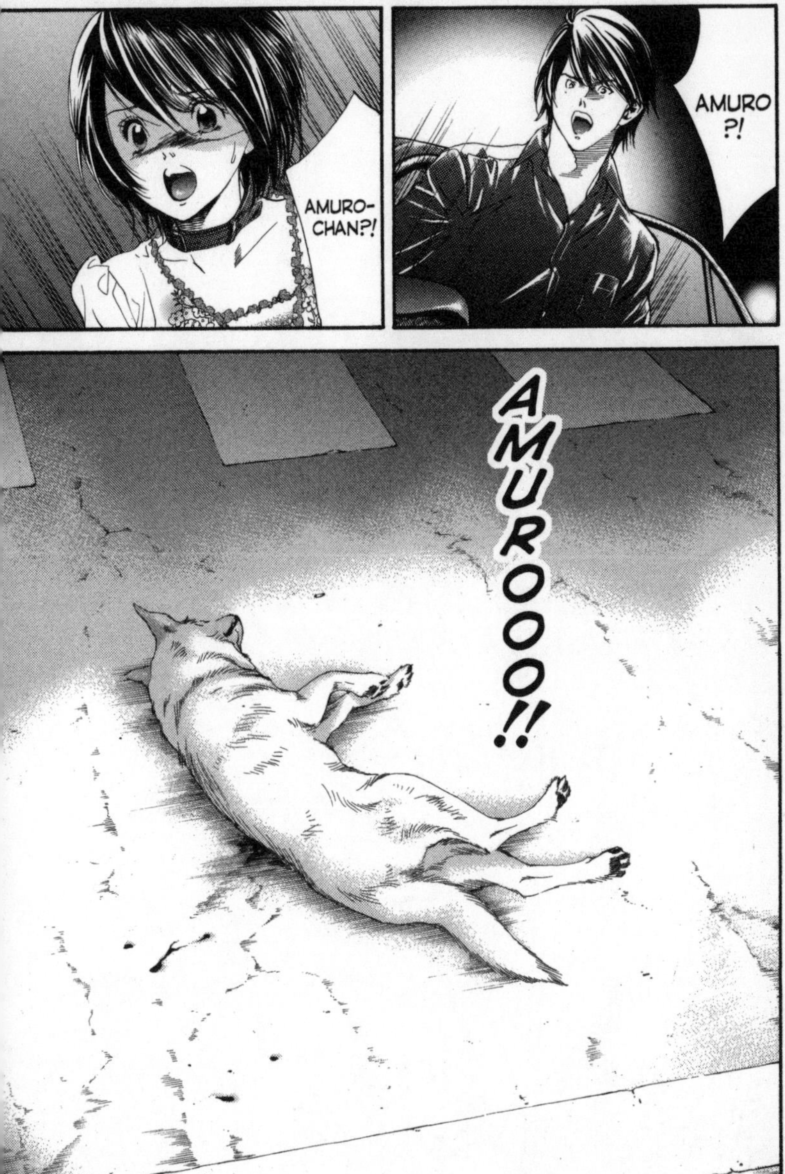
AMURO ?!
AMURO-CHAN?!
AMUROOOO!!

⑮ TEN PROMISES TO YOUR DOG/THE END

INUBA*KA

INUBAKA

Everybody's Crazy for Dogs!

From Erimon-san in Hokkaido

Karu-kun and Momo-chan (mix)
MONP-chan (Samoyed)

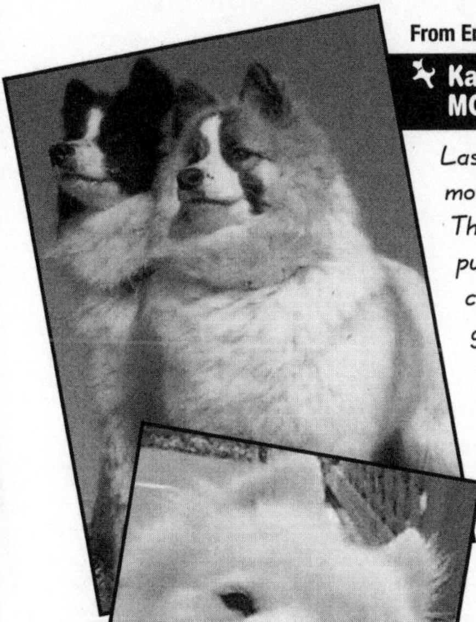

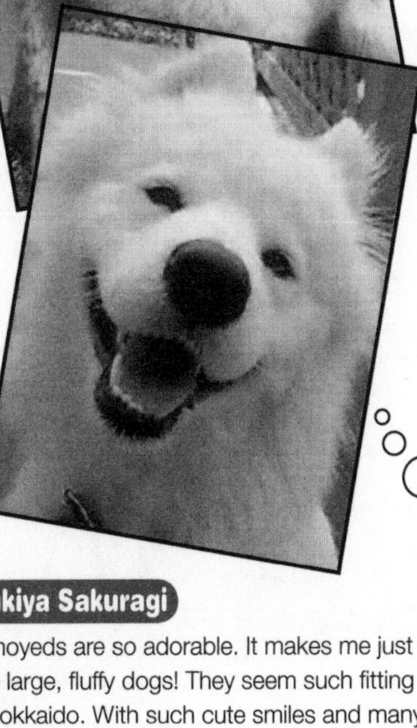

Last April, MONP-chan became a mother to her eight new puppies. The family lives with two of her puppies (Karu-kun and Momo-chan). Apparently, she's also a great goalkeeper when she plays soccer. She has many tricks, like bringing certain toys from her toy bin. Karu-kun and Momo-chan have a lot to learn from their mother.

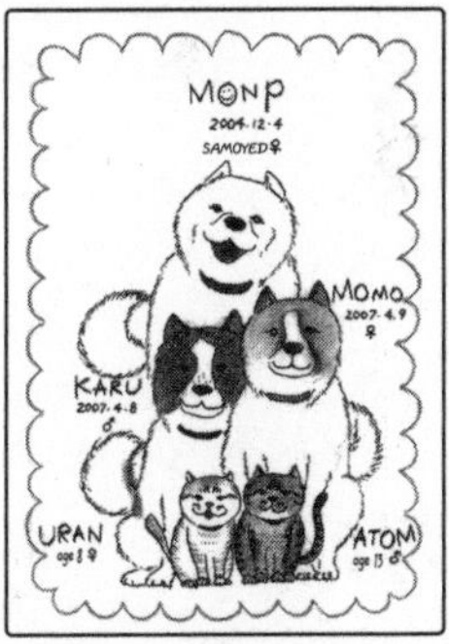
MONP
2004-12-4
SAMOYED♀
MOMO
2007-4-9
♀
KARU
2007-4-8
♂
URAN
ATOM

↑ And an illustration too!
You can tell they are one big happy family. How wonderful! ★

Yukiya Sakuragi

Samoyeds are so adorable. It makes me just want to give them a big hug!! I just love large, fluffy dogs! They seem such fitting dogs for the vast Kushiro landscape in Hokkaido. With such cute smiles and many tricks under their belts, they must make the family proud and happy.

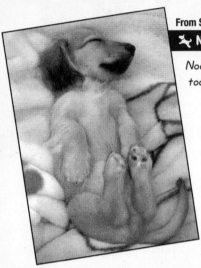

From Sano-san in Shizuoka Prefecture

🐾 Noa-chan (Kaninchen dachshund)

Noa-kun loves the futon... He is just too cute. I give up!! (>.<*)

Yukiya Sakuragi

So he likes to sleep in your arms too, huh? With this adorableness, you'd be crazy not to let him. He gets a 100 percent score for being so cute when he sleeps!

From Papipapa-san in Fukuoka Prefecture

🐾 Uran-chan (papillon)

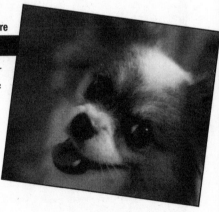

It's inevitable that some day our doggies will go to heaven before us parents. But until then, and even after, our doggies will always remain our children. Uran-chan, now's the time to get spoiled!

Yukiya Sakuragi

The story *Ten Promises to Your Dog* was written in hopes that all dog owners would keep those vows in mind. This was the theme when I was writing the Hinomaru story in particular. No matter how short a time it may be, dogs will always leave you with happiness. They really are irreplaceable companions.

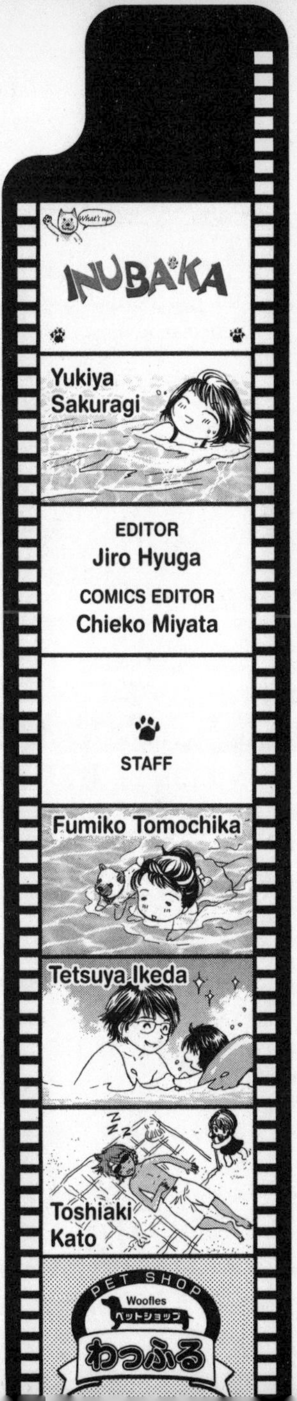
What's up!
INUBAKA
Yukiya Sakuragi
EDITOR
Jiro Hyuga
COMICS EDITOR
Chieko Miyata
STAFF
Fumiko Tomochika
Tetsuya Ikeda
Toshiaki Kato
PET SHOP
Woofles
ペットショップ
わっふる

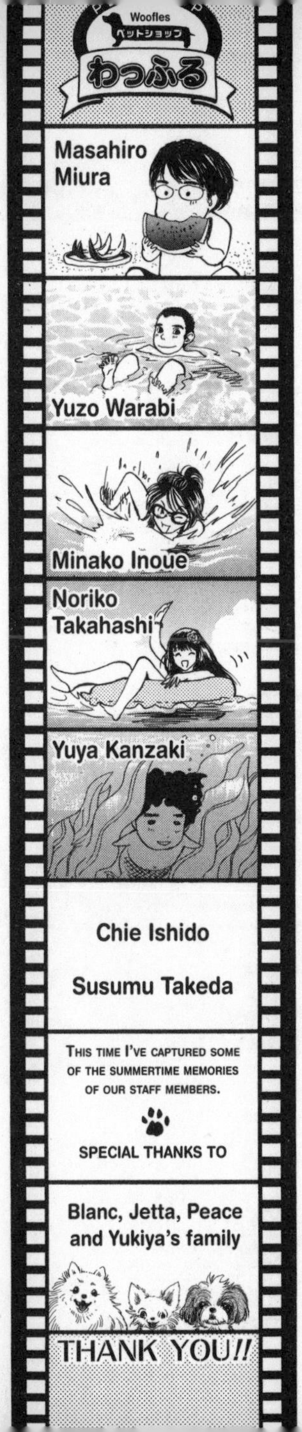
Woofles
ペットショップ
わっふる
Masahiro Miura
Yuzo Warabi
Minako Inoue
Noriko Takahashi
Yuya Kanzaki
Chie Ishido
Susumu Takeda
THIS TIME I'VE CAPTURED SOME OF THE SUMMERTIME MEMORIES OF OUR STAFF MEMBERS.
SPECIAL THANKS TO
Blanc, Jetta, Peace and Yukiya's family
THANK YOU!!

Inubaka
Crazy for Dogs
Vol. #15
VIZ Media Edition

Story and Art by
Yukiya Sakuragi

Translation/Maya Robinson, HC Language Solutions, Inc.
English Adaptation/Ian Reid, HC Language Solutions, Inc.
Touch-up Art & Lettering/Kelle Hahn
Cover & Interior Design/Hidemi Dunn
Editor/Carrie Shepherd

VP, Production/Alvin Lu
VP, Sales & Product Marketing/Gonzalo Ferreyra
VP, Creative/Linda Espinosa
Publisher/Hyoe Narita

Published by VIZ Media, LLC
P.O. Box 77010
San Francisco, CA 94107

10 9 8 7 6 5 4 3 2 1
First printing, March 2010

www.viz.com

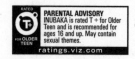

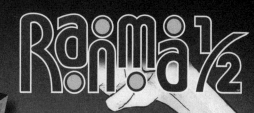
CHASE BRANCH LIBRARY
17731 W. SEVEN MILE RD.
DETROIT, MI 48235

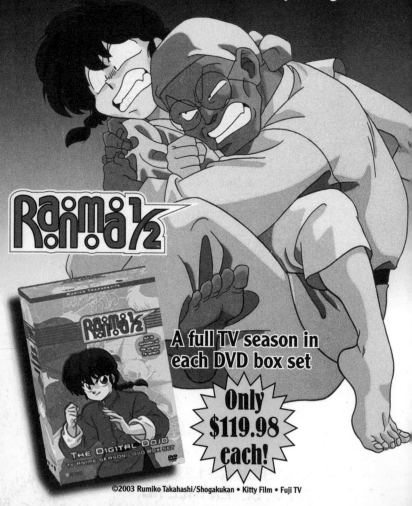

LOVE ♥ MANGA?

...what you think!

Our **MANGA SURVEY** is now available **ONLINE.**

Please visit: **VIZ.COM/MANGASURVEY**

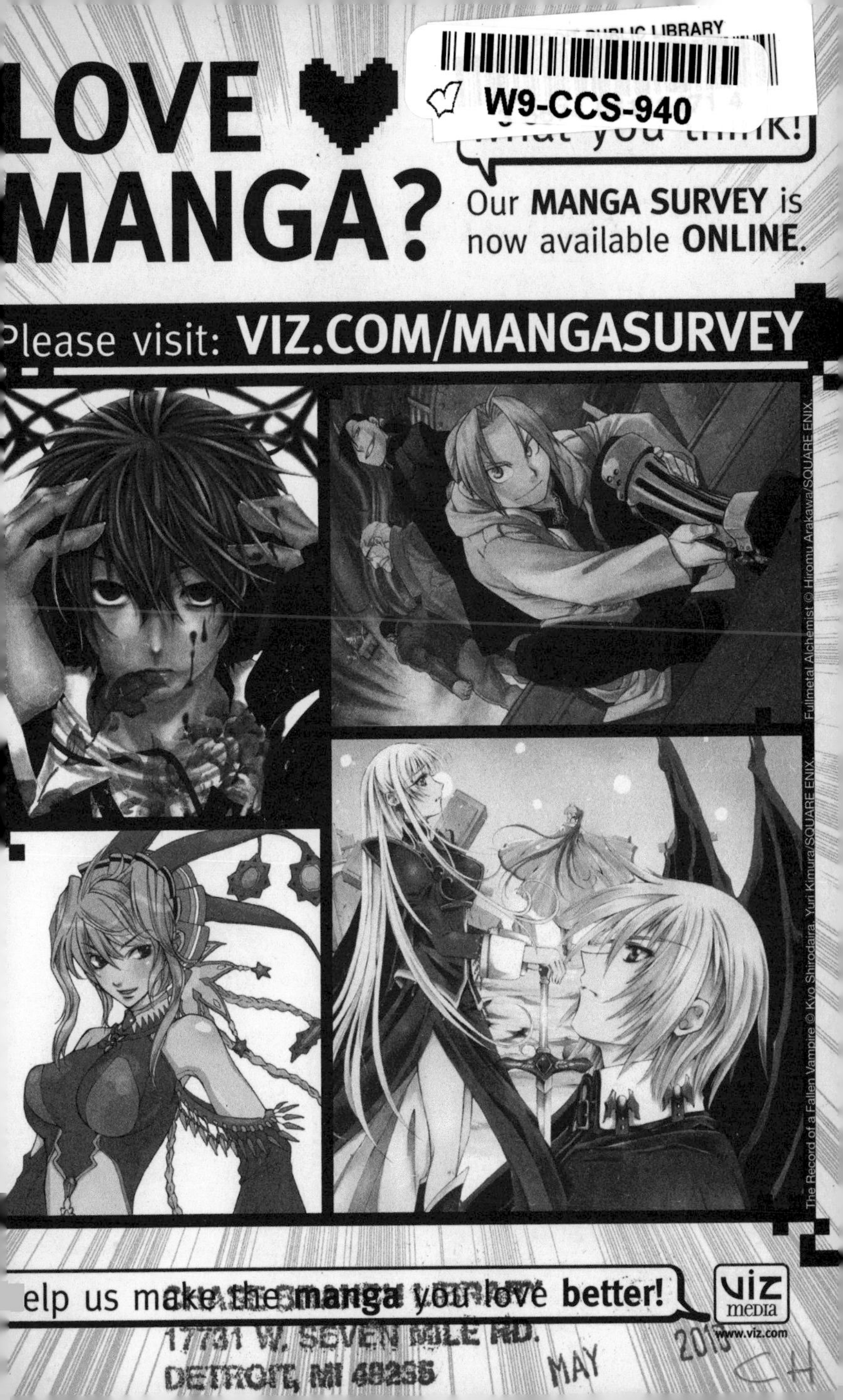

Fullmetal Alchemist © Hiromu Arakawa/SQUARE ENIX. The Record of a Fallen Vampire © Kyo Shirodaira, Yuri Kimura/SQUARE ENIX.

...elp us make the **manga** you love **better!**

VIZ media
www.viz.com